SHERABAD OASIS

Tracing Historical Landscape in Southern Uzbekistan

Editors
LADISLAV STANČO
PETRA TUŠLOVÁ

CHARLES UNIVERSITY
KAROLINUM PRESS 2019

Reviewed by Simone Mantellini and Sören Stark

Cataloging-in-Publication Data is available from the National Library of the Czech Republic

The work was supported by the European Regional Development Fund-Project
"Creativity and Adaptabilityas Conditions of the Success of Europe in an Interrelated World"
(No. CZ.02.1.01/0.0/0.0/16_019/0000734)

Cover illustrations:
1) Sardoba, vaulted structure protecting a water basin with a porch in a middle of Sherabad steppe as photographed in 1896 by L. Barscewski, from the archive of Igor Strojecki.
2) Terracotta head imported from Khotan, found at Baba Tepa, drawing by P. Kazakova.

ISBN 978-80-246-3902-4
ISBN 978-80-246-3923-9 (pdf)

Contents

Abbreviations

AIT	Archäologie in Iran und Turan
AMIT	Archäologische Mitteilungen aus Iran und Turan
AO	Arkheologicheskie otkrytiya
BAI	Bulletin of Asia Institute
CAKE	Central Asia in Kushan Period, proceedings of the international conference of the history, archaeology and culture of Central Asia in the Kushan Period, Dushanbe 27th September – 6th October 1968, Moskva, 1975.
IMKU	Arkheologicheskiye issledovaniya v Uzbekistane
KSIA	Kratkie soobshcheniya Instituta Arkheologii
MDAFA	Mémoires de la Délégation Archéologique Francaise en Afghanistan
MTE	Materialy tokharistanskoy ekspeditsii. Arkheologicheskie issledovaniya Kampyrtepa
PIFK	Problemy istorii, filologii, kul'tury
ONU	Obshchestvennyye nauky v Uzbekistane
RA	Rossiyskaya arkheologiya
SA	Sovetskaya arkheologiya
SH	Studia Hercynia
SRAA	Silk Road Art and Archaeology
TKhAEE	Trudy khorezmskoy arkheologichesko-ethnpgraphicheskoy ekspeditsii
USA	Uspekhy sredneaziatskoy arkheologii

Acknowledgements

The field part of the project took place in the course of four seasons 2008–2011. During this period, numerous people and organizations supported our efforts in various ways. We would like to thank all those who have helped us, both in the Czech Republic and Uzbekistan, and contributed to the completion of the work and appearance of this publication, and who have also permitted the research project itself to take place – in particular, those institutions that provided finance. The main part of the funds came from the Faculty of Arts of Charles University, Prague, which contributed by awarding several grants both to principal researcher and students. In 2009, it was the project "*The archaeological map of the watershed of the Sherabad Darya: development of settlement pattern in Ancient Bactria,*" in 2010 "*Systematic surface survey in the Sherabad Darya valley, southern Uzbekistan, using non-destructive methods and ArcGIS software;*" and the "*Systematic field survey in Sherabad District, south Uzbekistan.*" Lastly, in 2011, the field work run under the project "*Systematic field survey in south Uzbekistan.*" The Faculty of Arts has also financed the preparatory work for this publication in 2015 (Post-Doc grant of L. Stančo entitled) and throughout the project funded the travel costs of students. The Faculty, more precisely the Institute of Classical Archaeology, also provided institutional support, including most of the needed technical equipment. About 500 sq. km of archive IKONOS images were granted to our project by the GeoEye Foundation.

The work itself could not be completed without a great help of students of the Institute of Classical Archaeology in Prague, namely: Petra Belaňová, Věra Doležálková, Viktoria Čisťakova, Adéla Minaříková (Dorňáková), Martin Odler, and Tereza Včelicová (Machačíková), which all participated on the data collecting in the field as well as on the data post-documentation.

We are also very much indebted to the Termez State University in Termez for their support and aid, above all to the former rector of the University, late prof. M. Haydarov.

We should also like to convey our thanks to the representatives of the Czech Embassy in Tashkent for their availability, frequent help and significant contribution to the success of the expedition. We would also like to thank those who helped us with the final work on the publication, including Judd Burden, who proofread the texts, and Polina Kazakova, who has carefully redrawn old topographic plans of various archaeological sites. We are also very appreciative of the help and kindness of our hosts and friends in the village of Akkurgan.

Finally, the principal authors and editors from their part would like to thank our closest colleagues and friends (and co-authors of this volume) Shapulat Shaydullaev for all the care he lavished on us, and Alisher Shaydullaev, for all his dedication and hard work in the field.

Introduction

Ladislav Stančo

An oasis, a peculiar word with a seemingly clear meaning: "an area in a desert where there is water and plants" or broadly perceived as a general idea: "a pleasant place that is surrounded by something unpleasant".[1] The very first idea that usually comes to our mind hearing that word is a palm-tree island lost in the middle of sand dunes of a great desert of northern Africa or Inner Asia being approached by a slowly moving camel caravan. A well in the centre and men smoking a water pipe are an inevitable component of this rather romantic picture.

For us, however, oasis simply means a more or less well-defined area of land with limited water sources allowing for agricultural activities almost exclusively based on local water management, more precisely on artificial irrigation. It implies firstly that the oasis does not have firm and stable delimitations; its extent is bound to the ability of the human population – and its leadership – to build, and not least to maintain, the irrigation systems, to keep the water canals clean and working. Thus, the extent could vary considerably in individual historical periods as the techniques of water management improves or diminish. Secondly, it means that the water source has not necessarily to be found inside the oasis territory, it could be brought from elsewhere by means of sophisticated water canals. The specific environment in Central Asia with mixed zones of semi-deserts, deserts, steppe, dry piedmonts and high bare mountains, offers here and there fertile soil frequently lacking sufficient precipitation, which would enable agricultural production.

Our research area is such an example of a micro-region with changing boundaries depending on human activities. It is situated in the lowland steppe area of the southern Surkhandarya province of Uzbekistan (see map on p. 12). The landscape here is far from being anhydrous. The main problem seems to be that the waters of the local river – Sherabad Darya are difficult to exploit for the irrigation of the surrounding plains.

The Czech-Uzbek archaeological mission started cooperation in 2002 already, excavating for five years an important site of Jandavlattepa,[2] a tell-type walled multicultural settlement situated near the town of Sherabad in southern Uzbekistan. A new joint project was started in the same region in 2008, with the aim of the research focused on a detailed examination of the settlement pattern based on the mapping of all archaeological sites in the given area. The main reasons for this decision were particularly the need for putting the history of the settlement in the particular research area into the context of the dynamics of the whole region, including sorting and completing already known data and their further processing, but also an increasingly urgent need for a complete mapping of archaeological sites for the sake of heritage preservation and protection. A rapid increase of population in recent decades, expanding irrigation systems,[3] mending areas of cultivated fields and a related growth of villages (they are several times larger than even fifty years ago) in the area, brought a serious threat to a significant number of these monuments. Heritage protection unfortunately did not manage to keep pace with the drastic change of the economic system, and many sites have been irreversibly – and without documentation – destroyed. Since the archaeological research and mapping of the piedmont steppe and mountains of the north-west part of Sherabad District is by no means complete, we limited ourselves in this first volume to the publication of the data concerning the lowlands of the Sherabad District or the so-called Sherabad Oasis.[4]

---

[1] These two definitions are given by Merriem-Webster dictionary, see http://www.merriam-webster.com/dictionary/oasis.
[2] Most recently see esp. Abdullaev – Stančo eds. 2011; preliminary excavation reports are available online at http://arcis.ff.cuni.cz/.
[3] This is for example the expansion of the area of cultivated land into the previously unused steppe.
[4] The original definition of research area should reflect very clearly defined territorial boundaries, which was in the past nicknamed by researchers as Sherabad Oasis (see Masson 1974, 5–6; Pidaev 1978, 16–17; Rtveladze 1973), a region around Shearabad with fertile-soil plains that has been in the historical periods irrigated and cultivated and which for a long time (probably since the Achaemenid period to Late Antiquity) has its centre at the site of Jandavlattepa, which was centrally located even in

Our research has been henceforth directed towards the collecting of both spatial and chronological data and also to mapping of the preservation and current state of archaeological sites and historic buildings as such. Although in Uzbekistan there exists legislation on monuments protection, its observance is, in practice, almost never enforced. Recently, however, the government has declared efforts to change this state of affairs, which includes the education of local authorities (*hakimiyat*) and the police (*militsija*) and the creation of a new inventory of sites across the country.

The project was conducted within the framework of collaboration between Charles University and Termez State University.[5] The cooperation with the Archaeological Institute of the Academy of Sciences of Uzbekistan in Samarkand was established to coordinate work within the region.

Preliminary background research of the relevant previous scientific literature had indicated clearly that one of the major difficulties of the survey will be inadequate way of description of the locations of the already known archaeological sites. Frequently, it was based on the mere statement that the settlement is situated – for instance – "on the territory of

the kolkhoz named after V. I. Lenin, 15 km southeast of Sherabad." It was clear from the publications that there is substantial amount of insufficient spatial data or errors in the determination in cardinal points, and also confusions in present names, locations, etc. Therefore, it was decided in the early stages of the project to detect newly all topographically and morphologically distinct anomalies of the Sherabad plain, enter them into the GIS-based map, to verify their anthropogenic origin, names, and to obtain other necessary information (see further subheading 2.1 about the applied methods). Only then we have compared the data with previously published information, including comparison of chronological indicators (i.e., published information versus datable material collected during our team's survey). All maps, photographs and drawings are by the authors of the chapters unless otherwise stated.

To sum up, this book aims to contribute to the knowledge of the history of settlement in the southern part of Central Asia through a detailed analysis of the development of a specific, clearly defined area: Sherabad Oasis. How have we succeeded in fulfilment of this intention, let the kind reader assess after reading of this work.

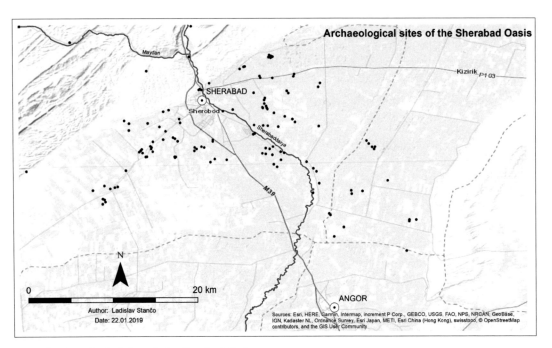

Map of archaeological sites of the Sherabad Oasis.

---

geographic terms. Circumstances eventually forced us to reconsider that definition and expand the area of interest into the piedmont and mountain belt in the north and north-west part of the Sherabad District so as to correspond with the current administrative boundaries of the Sherabad District. The main reason for this shift was the initiative of the Government of Uzbekistan, encouraging the compilation of the archaeological map of the entire state, which was logically based on the territorial-administrative division. In doing so, we realized that our data for the lowlands are almost complete, while the information for the piedmonts are fragmented even after several years of survey, and thus we have decided to return to the original extent of the research area, at least for the first volume.

[5]　In this project participated following archaeologists: L. Stančo (2008–2011), A. Danielisová (2009, 2010), Sh. Shaydullaev (2008–2010), T. Annaev (2010, 2011), and students of archaeology: A. Shaydullaev (2008–2011), M. Odler (2009), P. Belaňová (2009), P. Tušlová (2010, 2011), T. Machačíková (Včelicová; 2010, 2011), V. Doležálková (2010, 2011), V. Čisťakova (2010) and A. Dorňáková (Minaříková; 2011). The main part of the ceramic assemblage processing was entrusted to M. Kobierská.

1. Research area

Ladislav Stančo

1.1 Natural conditions

1.1.1 Geography and geomorphology

The Surkhandarya province forms the southern-most region of present-day Uzbekistan and as a whole is clearly defined by natural conditions. It is bordered on the three sides by high mountain ranges: by Babatag in the east, Hissar and Baysun in the north, and Kugitang in the west. The southern border on the other hand is formed by the course of the great Amu Darya. The main river in the western half of the Surkhan Darya province is Sherabad Darya, the real north-south axis of the Sherabad District. Its lower reaches, starting form Sherabad itself, bear, however, the name of Kara Su (Black water) and under this name almost disappears being distributed into uncountable water channels and cotton fields. This heavy exploitation prevents the waters of the Sherabad Darya from reaching the Amu Darya.[6]

The proper research area is situated in the present day Sherabad District of the Surkhandarya province, but some parts exceed the district border into the Kyzyrik District[7] and elsewhere. The Sherabad District is the third largest among 14 districts of Surkhandarya province, reaching officially 2730 sq. km (source: *O'zbekiston milliy ensiklopediyasi*). The north-south axis measures 60 km, the west-east one 64 km. The western border of the district matches with the national Uzbekistan – Turkmenistan border, while the southern part of the district is separated by the Zang Canal from a narrow strip of land on the right bank of the Amu Darya that forms the present-day Muzrabad District (former Gagarin D.). The eastern district border runs along the other huge canal called Bol'shoy Zaur that collects waste waters from the fields of the left-bank Sherabad Darya and becomes its tributary. The flat lowlands to the east of it as far as Haudag hills, which actually belong to the historic Sherabad Oasis form the above mentioned present-day Kizirik District. The northern border with Baysun District lies partly in the steppe, partly follows the road leading from the Sherabad river valley to the village of Khatak at the foot of the main Kugitang range.

Fig. 1.1 Kugitang mountains, view from the east, photo by A. Augustinová.

---

[6]   The river reaches the maximum flow rate in May (20.6 m³/s), in August on the other hand it drops to 4 m³/s (Stride 2005, vol. I, 235). Fluctuations in water flow of the river, or water shortages in the summer months, are compensated by the water of the Sukhan Dayra that is brought by a channel built in 1970s and called the Big Sherabad Canal. Even this source seems not to have a steady flow and the water level in the channel varies widely.

[7]   In 2010, the two small districts bordering Sherabad in the east: Bandykhan and Kyzyrik have been merged into a new administrative unit.

The main centre of both the oasis and the modern district is the town of Sherabad located at the place where the river leaves the mountain valleys and flows into the lowlands. In recent years, the town has grown rapidly, since adjoining villages have gradually been joining it. Despite the substantial area covered by the town, our knowledge of the historic settlement here is rather sketchy. We noticeably lack archaeological supervision of earthworks at the numerous new constructions. Most information is thus provided only by the marginally situated site of Kafirkala, a former stronghold of the local Sherabad Beg, where we can, however, prove much earlier phases of settlements as well.

In terms of natural conditions, we can divide the Sherabad District into two very different areas: lowlands in the south and south-east of the region with an elevation of about 340 to 400 m.a.s.l., which are intensively artificially irrigated, and the north and north-western parts, consisting of arid and semi-arid piedmont steppes (ca. 400–1200 m.a.s.l.) with considerably steep mountain ranges, including the main ridge of Kugitang Tau reaching an altitude of 3000 m.a.s.l., which forms the border with Turkmenistan (**Fig. 1.1**). Between the Sherabad plains and the piedmont steppe, there is another series of steep, although basically not that high, mountain ranges, stretching from the southwest to the northeast. Just a few of these ridges exceeds an altitude of 1000 m.a.s.l.; in the south-western part there are three such ridges: Khojambesh (1134 m.a.s.l.), Pyshtykara (1011 m.a.s.l.) and Karachagyl (1116 m.a.s.l.), and to the north of the plains lies only Takasakyrt (1058 m.a.s.l.) (**Fig. 1.2**). All these form impenetrable natural barriers due to their steepness. The only relatively passable ways are the natural deep valleys

of mountain streams. The plains around Sherabad are separated from the river valley of the Surkhan Darya lying to the east by a low, but very dry ridge of Haudag (max. 554 m.a.s.l.), which runs north to south, while south of Sherabad, the plain of the irrigated and agriculturally exploited lands extends down to the Amu Darya.

The choice of a route for long-distance travels in the lowland areas seems to be radically different from that of the trails in the mountains and piedmont steppes. The landscape here – especially in non-irrigated areas – was freely and easily penetrable, and the primary criterion evidently remained in the distance: the way should have been as short as possible, a direct route between points of interest was ideal. Overland communication with the southern part of Bactria / Tokharistan could therefore have several branches, leading from the area of Sherabad to a few ferries crossing the Amu Darya. The main stations of this kind were undoubtedly located at Old Termez and Kampyrtepa. On the contrary, the main communication link with the regions north of Sherabad (mainly Sogdiana) was clearly determined by the Sherabad Darya river valley that runs up to the cultural border between the two areas, which had been called Iron Gate. Its guard- and perhaps also customs function is attested in written sources.

1.1.2 Waters

The waters of the Sherabad Darya / Karasu are salty from the upper course of the stream, which has always represented a limiting factor for long-term irrigation systems and even for settlement sustainability. Among the main tributaries of the Sherabad

Fig. 1.2 Cotton fields with the mountain ridge of Takasakyrt in the background, photo by L. Stančo

Fig. 1.3 Wide riverbed of the Karasu River in the neighbourhood of sites no. 002 and 003, photo by L. Stančo.

Darya belong mostly the seasonal mountain streams the Loylagan Say, the Jidabulaq Say and the Maydan Say. All of them are right bank tributaries. The river bed of Sherabad Darya itself is cut deeply into piedmont steppe areas, and even into the Sherabad alluvial plains after leaving the mountain ranges (**Fig. 1.3**). Here, it would be very difficult to irrigate the surrounding – considerably higher lying – fields. It was therefore necessary to divert some of the water from the river upstream in places, where the difference in the altitude between the canal and the surrounding terrain was more favourable. Among the smaller streams that flow out of the southwest foothills of the Kugitang Tau directly to the Amu Darya, belong the Talkhab and the Muzrabad.

The extent of the arable lands differs nowadays from the extent of agriculturally used lands in historic periods, since the modern irrigation systems are more sophisticated and bring water from the valley of the Surkhan Darya by two channels – the Zang Canal and the Sherabad Canal. As is clearly seen from the CORONA satellite imagery, large parts of the Sherabad plains were not irrigated even in the quite recent past. One can speak rather of a Sherabad steppe. The main source of water for agriculture in the lowlands is nowadays, as said above, a huge backbone canal bringing fresh water from the adjacent river valley of the Surkhan Darya, more precisely from Kumkurgan dam on that river. The main channel, built in 1971, runs through the Sherabad District from northeast to southwest just by the edge of the mountains, and crosses the Sherabad Darya in the town of Sherabad itself (**Fig. 1.4**). This modern construction has changed dramatically the possibility of irrigating the entire lowland steppe and affects the spatial distribution of today's villages. The scope of the original irrigated areas in Antiquity and the Middle Ages is therefore one of the main issues on which the project sought an answer. Old maps of the region – as well as Google Earth – show in the southern part of the Sherabad Oasis close to the site no. 22 (Taushkantepa) an important geographic feature that no longer exists: it is Kul' Maygyr lake which was rather salty swamp with some shallow water area.

Fig. 1.4 Shearabad Canal to west of the town, photo by A. Danielisová.

1.1.3 Climatic conditions

The climatic conditions[8] of this area are very specific: the whole region is well protected from northern winds by mountain range and opened to the flow of warm winds from the southern Afghan deserts, which results in very high average temperatures in the summer and relatively mild winters. The average temperature here reaches 17–18 degrees Celsius, while in the summer the temperature can reach up to 50 degrees Celsius. The southern part of the Sherabad District is also affected by the strong wind that brings heavy dust from deserts in the north of Afghanistan, and is therefore locally called "Afghan". It is most strongly felt in the town of Termez and its surroundings that are not protected by natural barriers. Precipitation occur mainly in winter and early spring. The summer

season from May to September is dry, with no rain. Rainfall amounts in the annual aggregate of 154 mm (Stride 2004, vol. I, 234), with precipitation increasing in the direction from southwest to northeast (Pidaev 1978, 15).

A typical soil cover is represented by luvisoil and salinated takir soil.[9] Aside from irrigated fields, on which mostly cotton is grown these days (**Fig. 1.5**), there is a typical spring vegetation cover consisting of low grass and herbs, and thorny bushes. In the summer, the vegetation largely disappears, and the landscape looks very dry. Only in the high mountains, there appears sparse coniferous forest zone. The lowlands of the region belong to the Badkhiz-Karabil semi-desert ecosystem (PA1306), while the piedmont steppes are part of the Alai-Western Tian Shan Steppe (PA0801).[10]

Fig. 1.5 Sherabad oasis nowadays – hand harvesting of cotton still predominates in this area, photo by A. Danielisová.

---

[8] This part of Uzbekistan belongs to group BSk (meaning Arid – Steppe – Cold, where MAT<18) after the Köppen-Geiger climate classification (Peel et al. 2007).

[9] After "Pochvennaya karta Uzbekskoy SSR" made in 1960 (1:1,500,000), available online at URL http://gpsvsem.ru. This map distinguishes in the Sherabad plain between three soil types: 10 – irrigated takir soil (salinated clay), 18 – solonchaks on the alluvial or proluvial sediments, 23 – light solonchak luvisoil, and in a small area in the southwest of the region also 4 – grey-brown soil; see also Stride 2005, vol. I, 235–236, who follows the map of Sh. Ergashev.

[10] Description of this ecosystem in detail is accessible here: http://www.worldwildlife.org/science/wildfinder/profiles//pa1306.html; In the clmap part of the application this type seems to cover almost entire Surkhan Darya province. In the text part, however, the eastern border of the given ecosystem seems to be marked by the Kugitang Mountains.

1.2 Previous research

Archaeological mapping and analysing settlement patterns is far from being a new phenomenon in the archaeology of the Soviet and post-Soviet Central Asia. On the contrary, we should say that former Soviet scholarship put an emphasis on this branch of archaeological research and studied it systematically, and the data gained by our predecessors are of great value for the current work. A weak point of all previous mapping projects was the spatial component: in publications, coordinates are missing, maps are inaccurate or absent, descriptions of the locations are often confusing or completely wrong, the use of the local place names varies, etc. If we omit mentions of the individual sites in Surkhandarya province including the Sherabad District by older travellers, Tsarist military officers and local antiquarians, then the first relevant source of a more general description of landscapes and archaeological sites seems to be the work of Parfyonov, primarily devoted to the Stone Age / Lithics, and providing data from the thirties and forties of the 20th century (Parfyonov, s.d.).[11] In the 1950s and 1960s many scholars started to pay attention to the Surkhandarya province, but mostly to other subregions, predominantly to the area around Termez and the upper reaches of the Surkhan Darya, eventually reaching sites around Angor.[12] At the beginning of the 1970s a new wave of interest arose and there were initiated not only new excavation projects, but also survey activities leading to the compilation of the first inventories and maps of all known archaeological sites. A leading figure in this regard has become E. V. Rtveladze of the Institute of Art History in Tashkent, whose publications have introduced a site coding system that is still in use today (Rtveladze – Khakimov 1973; Rtveladze 1974; Rtveladze 1976). Rtveladze walked the landscape of Surkhan Darya Province – including the region of Sherabad – in a systematic way, and identified a number of archaeological sites and monuments, which were dated by him and his colleagues on the basis of surface material, additionally by material from trial trenches. At the same time Sh. Pidaev (1974; 1978)

also contributed to the detection and identification of the sites. The main attention was paid then to the monuments dated back to the Antique period, more precisely, mainly to Kushan sites. In the 1980s, there were attempts to map the sites of Early Medieval (Annaev 1988)[13] and generally Medieval sites (Arshavskaya et al. 1982; see also Rtveladze 1990, esp. 26–27, **Fig. 7**). At the same time, there were also excavated and studied in detail some of the major sites of the Bronze Age: Jarkutan and Bustan (Askarov 1977, 1980a, 1980b; Askarov – Abdullaev 1978, 1983), and Early Iron Age: Talashkan I (Rtveladze – Pidaev 1993; Shaydullaev 2000; Shaydullaev 2002). Survey activities in the piedmonts of Kugitang touched also the northern periphery of the Sherabad District (Bobokhadzhayev et al. 1990). After the collapse of the Soviet Union, these activities were temporarily reduced. Newly organized international expeditions started to organize mainly systematic excavation projects of the large or otherwise important sites. They have paid just little attention to a surface survey and mapping, focusing only on the neighbourhood of the given site.[14] The first scholar to concentrate on the archaeological geography of the Surkhan Darya province in a systematic way was quite recently Sebastian Stride, a member of the French mission "MAFOuz B". He has been collecting data during the second half of the nineties and his monumental dissertation covers the whole province including the Sherabad District (Stride 2004). Despite unquestionable benefits of this work, which necessarily became a fundamental reference overview, many questions and problems remained unresolved. The methodologically controversial approach of the author will be discussed below.

In the previous research the attention was paid not only to the detection of the new sites, but also to particular chronological as well as spatial analyses, and first of all to the typology of the settlements. In the 1960s and 1970s there was developed several typologies of the settlements of the Kushan period. Yurkevich divided Kushan settlements into two basic

---

[11]　His book was never published, but it is available as a typescript in the archive of the Termez Archaeological Museum.

[12]　For a brief overview of the research see Stančo 2005, 54–55; for more detail see Pidaev 1978, 6–14 or Masson 1985, 251–255.

[13]　The work of Annaev is of value primarily for his analysis of pottery shapes.

[14]　In the Sherabad District this goes especially for two projects in the vicinity of Pashkhurt, i.e., outside the oasis itself: a German-Uzbek expedition exploring initially under the leadership of D. Huff already mentioned the site of Jarkutan and later under the supervision of his former student K. Kaniuth another site of the Bronze Age called Tilla Bulak (see Kaniuth 2007; Kaniuth 2010; Kaniuth – Herles – Shejko 2009) and the Russian-Uzbek expedition working at the ancient site of Dabilkurgan see Solov'ev 2013. A different situation exists in other parts of ancient Bactria: the eastern margin of Bactria near Ai Khanum was mapped in the first half of the 70s by French archaeologists and their exemplary results were published gradually in three volumes (see Gentelle et al. 1989; Lyonnet 1997; Gardin 1998). The extent of the work of this expedition is hard to compare: during the years 1974–1978 an area of 1,700 sq. km was explored, 800 sites have been found and irrigation canals with a length of ca. 1,000 km were mapped.

groups: 1. towns and town-like settlements, 2. rural settlements. Both groups comprised subtypes based on the size, ground-plan shape, presence/absence of a citadel, character of the fortifications (Yurkevich 1965, 166–167), while Rtveladze divided the settlements into four types: 1. Big walled town-like settlements (with four sub-types), 2. Settlements with some characteristics of a town and others of a village, 3. Rural settlements (with 3 sub-types), and 4. Mountain settlements. The sub-types were specified according to the size, shape and fortification (Rtveladze 1974, 83–85). This typology was further adjusted by B. Staviskiy, whose typology consists of 1. Big towns (more than 100 ha), 2. Towns (15–80 ha), 3. Little towns (5–13 ha), 4. Big villages (1.5–4 ha), 5. Villages (less than 1 ha), and 6. Hamlets (less than 0.6 ha). He added as the 7th and 8th type to the latter group Oasis-type settlement and mountain settlement respectively (Staviskiy 1977, 43–44). In this typology, one is obviously at first glance surprised by the gaps in the reported ranges of sizes, which would ultimately result in the omission of certain settlements from typology. Staviskiy speaks generally of 25 sites of the Kushan period in Sherabad District, among them only two are situated beyond Sherabad plain itself, i.e., up in the piedmonts (Staviskiy 1977, 52–53). Sh. Pidaev had set an essential criterion for his simpler settlements division, which is exclusively their size; categories such as "city" or "village" he found not archaeological enough and thus established four types of settlements with surface up to 1 ha, 6 ha, 15 ha, and more than 15 ha respectively. For the Kushan period he finds in the "Sherabad Valley" 16 settlements of the first type, six of the second, one of the third and none of the fourth type (Pidaev 1978, 15–28, esp. 18–22). The difficulties of this approach, which one must necessarily encounter, are obvious: it is uncertainty of exact determining, but often of just a gross determining of the extent and,

thus of the real size of the settlements. Only rarely we get by with simple measuring of the site area of the tell-type settlement. On the contrary, it often exceeds the extent of its core, sometimes even considerably.[15] Besides, it is also very difficult to define precisely the extent of the given settlement in a particular time period of their inhabitation.

Stride, who was first engaged in the settlement pattern of Surkhandarya and its complex dynamics, divided the Sherabad Oasis into two parts: the right-bank and the left-bank area of the Sherabad Darya. According to him, the right-bank area covers 13,668 ha, of which about 10,000 ha were irrigated. To this part, he localizes two sites of the Bronze Age, four proto-historic sites, fourteen dated back to Antiquity, ten of the Early Middle Ages, nine pre-Mongol ones and six post-Mongol sites. On the left bank (16,189 ha / 12,000 ha irrigated), he lists 11 sites inhabited in Antiquity, 11 in the Early Middle Ages, one pre-Mongol and one post-Mongol settlement (Stride 2004, vol. I, 237–239). The following table summarizes the representation of individual sites and periods in the area of interest according to the knowledge prior to the start of our project. The distribution is based on Stride's division of the region.

Another product of the generally geographic approach to the analysis of settlement pattern was the definition of smaller cultural units based on access to natural water sources, eventually with regard to the expected (rarely clearly documented) artificial irrigation systems – called Oases. In accordance with the premise that every large accumulation of settlements linked to the (usually single) presumed source of drinking water is one separate unit, Masson distinguished within the area of Surkhandarya four basic units: 1. region Denau – Shurchi, 2. Jarkurgan area, 3. region of Angor, 4. region of Sherabad (Masson, 1974, 4–5). Staviskiy subsequently determined

Chronology – Period	Lowlands around Sherabad		Total
	Right bank	Left bank	
Bronze Age	2	0	2
Protohistory	4	0	4
Antiquity	14	11	25
Early Middle Ages	10	11	21
Pre-Mongol period/High Middle Ages	9	1	10
Post-Mongol period	6	1	7
General number of sites	25	16	41

---

[15] This applies particularly to the Middle Ages, but we have clear evidence that allows us to speak analogically of this phenomenon in Antiquity. Such evidence is given by complexes of monuments around Babatepa, Kulugshakhtepa, Jandavlattepa or Kattatepa, for instance. This issue will be discussed below in this book by P. Tušlová see Chapter 3.

six major irrigation regions: 1. Termez area, 2. Angor – Jarkurgan area, 3. Sherabad area, 4. Shurchi area, 5. Khalchayan area, and 6. Karatag area (Staviskiy 1977, 47–56). Pidaev then defined in the Surkhandarya five main oases: 1. Sherabad valley, 2. the upper reaches of the Surkhan Darya, 3. The lower reaches of the Surkhan Darya, 4. Zang area (belonging to the irrigation system of the Zang Canal), and 5. Right-bank area of the Amu Darya (Pidaev 1978, 16 and 18, tab. 1). The first four areas are *de facto* identical both in the Masson's and the Pidaev's division. For us and for the focus of this book it is essential that all researchers agree on the definition of a separate Sherabad Oasis, although Staviskiy functionally connects it with the valley of Surkhan (Staviskiy 1977, 47). It is noteworthy that in his more recent work on the subject E. V. Rtveladze (1990, 2–3) talks in general about "Surkhandarya Oasis" as of a unit. A summary of the longstanding debate about the proper identification of the Surkhandarya area with one of the larger cultural and political entities of the ancient and early Medieval period – to Bactria and Sogdiana – is clearly given by E. V. Rtveladze (1990, 4–6). The typology of the settlements of the Medieval period is so far missing, even though the available data would allow for at least basic classification.

2. Extensive archaeological survey

L. Stančo

2.1 Methods and pre-processing

The field survey was prepared in advance by using a systematic evaluation of newly available high-quality satellite images (GeoEye IKONOS, LANDSAT, CORONA and since 2008 especially the high-resolution data in Google Earth, see below in detail), where the sites were detected and consequently entered into the database. The resulting set of data was confronted with information given in publications and completed by them.

The field part of the project took place in the dormancy period, when the data gained from satellite imagery were verified on the spot. Chronologically sensitive archaeological material was collected and also in-detail documentation of the sites including precise geodetic measurements was conducted. Occasionally photogrammetric documentation was made as well as topographic plans.

In addition to gathering the largest possible amount of data, the aim of survey was also the methodological issues related both to the detection of anthropogenic features in the landscape, and to subsequent documentation of the sites, which due to various reasons (not least the limited funds) could only take place with basic equipment.

The gained data were processed and spatially analysed using geographical information systems. This part focused on the evaluation of site from the point of view of its relation to the surrounding landscape and particular features (topography, irrigation systems, settlement pattern), and chronology (settlement dynamics). The aim was in particular:
- Mapping the settlement structure
- Evaluation of the use of space in the prehistoric and Early Medieval period
- Reconstruction of resource use and economic strategies in relation to the natural environment and political systems in different periods

- Reconstruction of cultural and social interactions between centres and their agricultural hinterland

2.1.1 Base data layers for detection of the sites and digitizing

The basic prerequisite for the compilation of the archaeological map of the region was the obtaining of the appropriate raster documents necessary for 1) the detection of historical anthropogenic features and 2) the digitization of other important geographic features that shape environment for the archaeological record. To gain a picture as complete as possible, it was necessary to combine data from satellite images and topographic maps.

2.1.1.1 Satellite imagery and its usage

Shortly after the declassification of CORONA espionage satellite imagery in the 1990s archaeologists began to use it as a tool for sophisticated surface archaeological prospecting and the creation of archaeological maps and GIS-based models. Paradoxically, the satellite images were at our disposal before the appropriate topographic maps. Gradually we started to use the images from Google Earth, CORONA and IKONOS. Apart from these, we also worked with images of Landsat distributed free by the USGS.

Google Earth
The basic impulse for the use of remote sensing methods in our work was the launch of Google Earth (2005), which in 2007/2008 gradually made available new land surface images at high resolution. In individual parts, it is possible to achieve a high delineation of detail.[16] Exported raster can easily be

---

[16] In some parts of the planet the resolutions of up to 0.1 meter is achieved, in these cases, however, orthophotographs are used, while the original basic resolution of older LANDSAT images was 15 m. According to some sources these were gradually replaced by SPOT images with a basic resolution of 2.5 m. The main supplier of images to Google Earth, the company Digital-Globe, operates satellites of Early Bird 1 (resolution 3 m), Quickbird (0.6 m), WorldView 1 (0.5 m), and WorldView 2 (0.46 m). At the time of the project was not possible to download a particular area at a given resolution in a freely available version of

2. Extensive archaeological survey

georeferenced in any GIS software. An important advantage is represented by the integration of a digital elevation model (DEM), created by NASA and using SRTM (Shuttle Radar Topography Mission), in this application, which provided a 3D visualization of the environment. Other features that the Google Earth Pro version – that was not used by our team at the time of the project, but is distributed freely at the moment (since spring 2015) – has, is communication with a GPS receiver. It was possible to easily replace this function by a simple format conversion KML / KMZ to GPX using freely available software.

In archaeology and especially in the archaeological surface survey, Google Earth has been used since the very beginning. The first publications on the possibilities of the using of this environment appeared in 2006 (Madry 2006; Bousman 2006; Ur 2006) and Parcak consequently paid her attention to them in her monograph on remote sensing in archaeology (Parcak 2009). Google Earth is based on the World Geodetic System, 1984 (WGS 84). The resolution varies considerably from area to area, from the basic Landsat images (15 m), which are used globally for the whole planet, to the very detailed (0.5 m). Certain areas are even covered by orthophotography (aerial photographs) with high resolution (0.1 m). It should, however, be added that fast and comfortable work with Google Earth requires a fast computer if possible. A high-speed internet connection is also essential, since the pictures consist of large volumes of data that is continuously downloaded during work.

Actual work with the program is very easy, and its operation is intuitive. In addition to moving around over the selected section of the earth's surface, we can zoom in, and set the picture to horizontal. This means that with the setting on a reasonably pronounced relief, the impression of a 3D model of the landscape can be gained. For detecting anthropogenic features the best view is that from above, although an oblique view can also be used in certain specific cases. The picture may also be rotated at will. It is also possible to try out less detailed detection by "flying" slowly back and forth over the landscape. A very important tool is the ability to save places, with detailed data about them, and export current pictures in the form of JPG pictures. Our first testing of Google Earth took place in 2008 (Stančo 2009). We used Google Earth mainly for the detection of anthropogenic features.

The first step was to "walk over" the area in question using Google Earth, which happened as soon as the higher-definition picture was made available in March 2008. This work lasted a mere 7–8 days. During this short period, we looked at a segment meas-

uring 22 × 25 km, with its centre 2–3 km to the south of the town of Sherabad. We used the then-current Google Earth software version 4.3.7204 from March 2008. In the older versions, lower-resolution pictures had covered the region in question. Starting with version 4.3, the Sherabad District has been covered by high-resolution pictures allowing for our work. Later on (March 2009), we switched to Google Earth version 5.0.11337, but the quality of the imagery was identical to the previously-mentioned one. All the features in the landscape of a potentially historical or anthropogenic character were marked and exported. The first catalogue of archaeological sites in the Sherabad District was then put together. We did not intend, at that time, to cover all archaeological sites that were already known to scholars or even excavated or otherwise explored, but only those that had been detected with the help of Google Earth. Data from scholarly literature was included alongside them, however. The aim of this was merely to permit the identification of sites detected with those that were already known in order to ascertain more precisely the position of the latter and to compare the dating.

For comparison with the final results it would be interesting to discuss briefly the summary of data gained in the first preparatory season (2008). A total number of 47 presumed settlements in the lowlands were included in the catalogue, as well as several dozen features that were – as we believed – highly likely to have originated in connection with human activity. In all, almost a hundred features that may be considered archaeological sites were ascertained in the Sherabad Oasis and the adjoining northern foothills, plus a further 40 unclear features. For each site, two pictures were downloaded from Google Earth: one detailed one (the modelled height from the surface was ca. 500–600 m) and the second also including part of the surrounding area for easier orientation (modelled height from the surface was 1–1.5 km). In addition to the pictures, the catalogue also contained precise data on position, the approximate height above sea level, the dimensions of the site (all these data gained from Google Earth) and, where relevant, references to literature, topographic maps etc. As well as the grid references of the features detected, the routes of presumed optimum access to them were also indicated, with an emphasis on logistical economy. As a test sample of the detected sites, we preferred clusters rather than spatially isolated features. Data from Google Earth in KML format was transferred into GPX format and saved to a hand held GPS receiver. For our purpose, we used a standard walker's instrument, the GARMIN eTrex Vista C.

---

this application, a single output as raster images remained within the scope of the current screen, which was missing georeferencing. Since 2014, however, Google has made the Pro version, which allows the user to download high reslotion images of selected area, free for all users. Georeferencing of the exported images is still missing.

GeoEye IKONOS

Images of IKONOS, distributed by the GeoEye company,[17] reach the highest resolution among raster datasets used in our work. The reported resolution of the panchromatic images is 0.82 m, while the multispectral images reach only 3.2 m. The cost of acquiring these images is generally very high, but for the purposes of the project, archive images were granted, in limited extent, free of charge.[18] The given sequence was taken on August 18, 2001. The advantage over Google Earth's imagery was the integrity of the images when working off-line, an important drawback on the other hand was the fact that it did not cover the area of interest completely. GeoEye supplies images with accurate spatial data, which do not need be further georeferenced.

CORONA

Images, conventionally referred to as CORONA, were originally produced as a military espionage imagery in the 1960s and 1970s and represent the oldest complex spatial record of this area except for topographic maps. Their "declassifying" after the fall of the Iron Curtain (22/2/1992) placed into the hands of archaeologists a valuable source of spatial data on the areas that are often already irretrievably altered or destroyed, and also offered the possibility of creating a digital terrain model (DEM). This option is currently used in such areas, where archaeologists lack high-quality map data (see e.g., Gheyle et al. 2003; Goossens et al. 2006; Casana – Cothern 2008, here also detailed bibliography). Wide use offers the University of Arkansas project *CORONA Atlas of the Middle East*, in the frame of which georeferenced bands of these images are placed online.[19] Our research area, however, is unfortunately not included yet into this project.[20]

For our project, digital scans of photographic negative strips were acquired, belonging to series KH-4B, captured in the frame of the mission number 1112 that took place on November 21, 1970 with a very high resolution of 1.8 m.[21] The CORONA image ID DS1110-1137DF028 was acquired on 1970/05/29, for instance.[22] Additionally, we also got strips of Mission 1110 (20/5/1970)[23] and lower quality older

imagery of Mission 9038 (taken on June 28, 1962, a series of KH-4 with a resolution of 7.5 m)[24] and 1210 (June 12, 1975, a series of KH-9 Hexagon or so-called "Big Bird"), which was not captured in long and narrow horizontal bands, but wide rectangles.[25] CORONA imagery is supplied without geo-referenced data by standard. For setting it correctly into the map project it is necessary to use ground control points. In this case, we utilized precisely localized archaeological sites (their GPS coordinates) and in remote places we used positions of the crossing of canals or roads, whose position could have been verified in IKONOS and Google Earth imagery. Georeference error in this case is relatively insignificant.

Overview of satellite imagery used in the framework of the project:

Satellite	Provider	Resolution	Date
CORONA KH-4	USGS	7.5 m	1962
CORONA KH-4B	USGS	1.8 m	1970
CORONA KH-9	USGS		1975
Early Bird 1 Quickbird WorldView 1 WorldView 2	Google Earth	3 m 0.6 m 0.5 m 0.46 m and less	After 2000
IKONOS	GeoEye	0.82 m	2001

Comparison of the state of the sites as shown in CORONA and more recent satellite imagery attests to rapid changes of the landscape in general and archaeological record in particular (**Fig. 2.1**).

2.1.1.2 Topographic maps as base maps

One of the major difficulties in the implementation of this project has been the restrictive measures of the Uzbekistan government with regard to the distribution and use of detailed topographic maps. In the early 1950s, maps of the area at a scale of 1:10,000 were compiled, which would have provided an entirely sufficient basis for survey work. They record not only all the morphological anomalies on the surface, but we find in them incredible details such as individual yurts.[26] Unfortunately, these, and even less detailed

---

[17] GeoEye operates not only IKONOS satellite, but also GeoEye 1 (0.41 m), and has been preparing GeoEye 2 with the highest resolution among commercial space-imagery providers (0.34 m). The company has merged recently with DigitalGlobe.

[18] The GeoEye Foundaiton provided us with 500 sq. km of archived images covering the core area of the Sherabad Oasis.

[19] http://corona.cast.uark.edu/index.html.

[20] Valid for 13/5/2015.

[21] For the basic information about the mission see the web pages of NASA: http://nssdc.gsfc.nasa.gov/nmc/spacecraftOrbit.do?id =1970-098A.

[22] http://earthexplorer.usgs.gov/metadata/1051/DS1110-1137DF028/.

[23] http://nssdc.gsfc.nasa.gov/nmc/spacecraftOrbit.do?id=1970-040A.

[24] http://nssdc.gsfc.nasa.gov/nmc/spacecraftOrbit.do?id=1962-027A.

[25] KH-9 Hexagon actually took picture in a very high quality (up to 0.6 m), and the available data was declassified only in late 2011 and 2012. The images that we acquired in 2009 have a very low quality, and there is no doubt about the deliberately reduced resolution. For demonstration of the full resolution of this mission, see: http://www.nro.gov/history/csnr/gambhex/docs/hexagon _kh-9_imagery_web.pdf.

[26] See e.g., a sample of the map sheet J-42-64-Bb-3 (city of Denau) published in: Stride 2005, Vol. V, fig. 09.

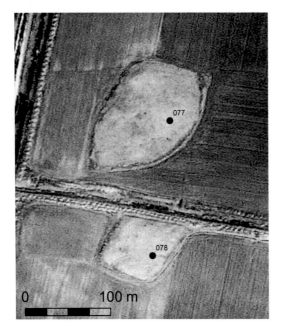 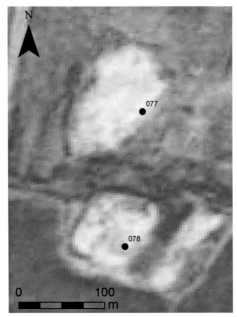

Fig. 2.1 Comparison of Corona (right) and Ikonos (left) images content.

maps at a scale of 1: 25,000 (made around 1970) are classified, and could not be legally obtained. Only in the final phase of the project we did manage to get at least map sheets at scales of 1:100,000, drawn mainly during the 1980s. These are available online for free.[27] In these sets of maps we can also find some sheets at the scale of 1:50,000, but even though they are available for the whole Afghanistan, half of Tajikistan and many other countries, the sheets of southern Uzbekistan are absent in the open sources.

Among the maps, the sheet of 100k--j42-086 has to be highlighted, since the data for its compilation had been collected early in the 1970s, about ten years before the other parts of the district. Thus it offers great comparison with the sheet of 200k--j42-19 of the same area showing many substantial changes in the landscape.

Overview of the used map sheets:[28]

Map sheet	Data collected	Date of issue	Scale
Map 100k--j42-074	1983	1986	1:100,000
Map 100k--j42-075	1983	1986	1:100,000
Map 100k--j42-086	1974	1980	1:100,000
Map 100k--j42-087	1975–1985	1988	1:100,000
Map 200k--j42-19	1983	1986	1:200,000
Map 200k--j42-20	1983	1986	1:200,000
U.S. Army map txu--oclc-6559336-nj42-9	1952[29]	1955	1:250,000

2.1.1.3 Vector data

Unlike raster data, the availability of digital vector data is even worse, particularly as regards the non-commercial sphere. For the southern region of Uzbekistan, there are actually available only very basic data sets,[30] which are moreover relatively inaccurate and outdated. These sets contain vector data on roads, waterways, railroads, location of settlements and administrative units and surface waters. Paradoxically, much more carefully prepared are, as in the case of topographic maps, freely available data for neighbouring Afghanistan. In this situation, almost all vector data for the project maps were gained mainly by digitalization of raster documents and spatial data collection in the field.

2.1.2 Digitization

The above mentioned raster documents were used to build comprehensive maps, out of those we got by way of digitization (vectorization) the following data: CORONA mainly provided us with information on the extent and course of irrigation canals as they existed in the early seventies prior to the beginning of agricultural intensification and expansion of sown areas. IKONOS was a good source of information on modern irrigation canals of the early 21st century (the comparison between the two situations is very

---

27 Cf. http://loadmap.net/en for instance.
28 For easier reading of the Soviet topographic maps the U.S. Army prepared their own manual „Soviet Topographic map symbols", issued in 1958. The manual is available online as well, see http://cluster3.lib.berkeley.edu/EART/pdf/soviet.pdf for instance.
29 Compilation based on the General Staff of the Red Army maps of 1931–1937 at the scale of 1:200,000 and of 1939 at the scale of 1:500,000.
30 The data are freely accessible from the following URL: http://www.diva-gis.org/datadown for instance; beyond basic vector data here, thrree are not very accurate raster datasets representing altimetry, population and climate.

interesting) as well as on areas / surfaces of particular archaeological sites as known today. In parts of the territory not covered by IKONOS, Google Earth was used in order to determine the surface area of the sites. Basic information about the location of sites (points with coordinates) were also exported from Google Earth. that were already set at the primary detection and later rarely corrected.

From the topographic maps (mostly at a scale of 1:100,000), information of water sources/springs, rivers and other waterways, wells and artificial and natural water reservoirs, distinguished tombs, caves and especially small mounds in the lowlands, mostly representing archaeological sites of the tell type were taken position. For monitoring the dynamics of the development of rural areas, villages have also been mapped, allowing a comparison with the current situation reflected on the recent satellite images (cf. chapter 5.10).

Finally, the U.S. Army map seemingly offering few details on the region, turn to be of high value to us, since it was the only source showing the system of water canals before the beginning of Soviet collectivisation and fundamental change of the landscape in the second half of the 20th c. Thus, again the canals, wells, springs and ruins has been digitized from this map.

2.1.3 Detection of anthropogenic features from the satellite imagery

The detection of features, which could be assumed as being of anthropogenic historical origin was conducted as systematic visual browsing of the selected part of the satellite image. No automatic detection method was tested, which would in any case require feedback control. In the first year of the survey (2008), attention was paid to several groups of features. The first – and most important – group were settlements, represented as the characteristic mounds (tell, *tepa*) situated in irrigated lowlands. These are easily identifiable and there is little chance of errors. Thus only a fraction of these characteristic morphological features proved negative during field verification. The other groups of features were detected in the piedmonts and thus their verification and further study is not included in this volume.[31]

Satellite images were also used to search for modern Islamic cemeteries (sometimes missing on the older maps), which, as it turned out, were a good source of archaeologically relevant information (see below chapter 2.2.4).

The limits of the sites detection from the satellite imagery were revealed during the field survey, especially by the systematic survey of agricultural areas (Tušlová 2011a; 2011b; 2012a; 2012b and below in this volume), but also during surveys of modern cemeteries, where the presence of settlements outside of the *tepas* themselves was documented. Similarly, while traveling to the locations of targets detected on the imagery and maps, we succeeded more than once in accidentally discovering a new archaeological site (or simply a place with a high density of pottery fragments). This happened mainly in the fields where images or topographic maps did not show any morphological anomalies.

2.1.4 Detection of anthropogenic features from the topographic maps

As in the case of satellite imagery, we did not develop any automatic system of detection of the significant morphological features drawn in the topographic maps.[32] The time period of the data acquisition for the Soviet topographic maps (see table above) correlated roughly with the time of capturing the satellite imagery in the framework of the project CORONA. These maps thus offered opportunity to find more sites, which, since the turn of the seventies and eighties, have completely disappeared or were seriously damaged. This was the case mainly for small mounds in the irrigated lowlands, which – except for absolute exceptions – are not visible today on the satellite images or in the field. All other small mounds, detected from the Soviet map at a scale of 1:100,000, whose largest clusters are found in the south-western part of the district (near the site and village of Talashkan), are lost forever.[33] The scale did not offer too much precision, so that verification of these phenomena in the field required walking a large area (partly randomly, partly systematically), until at least a minor accumulation of ceramics was found, allowing us to assume that there was once a settlement. In many cases, however, it was found negative (Tušlová 2012b, 75).

[31] For the preliminary discussion see Stančo 2009.
[32] A French-Italian team working in Samarqand region states the same (Mantellini et al. 2011, 389).
[33] An Uzbek-Italian team working in Samarkand Oasis published statistics of ratio between the preserved and destroyed (known only from old maps) sites. The proportion varies in the individual districts of the Samarkand province, but the average rate is 40% (Mantellini 2014, 43). For the Sherabad District similar figures cannot be obtained, since we did not have analogically accurate maps of the region at our disposal.

2.2 Survey process: field data collection

The procedures applied in the field phase of the research can be subdivided into methods related to the acquisition of spatial data on the observed sites and methods of dating.

2.2.1 Spatial data

For each explored site we measured coordinates in the global coordinate system by a GPS receiver; as the measurement point was defined a central place (or centre points of multiple components). In selected cases, the measured circumference of the *tepa* (if, for example, the centre was not accessible). The circumference was measured also in cases, where the exact extent of the site was not obvious in the satellite imagery. The other features of selected – usually more complex – archaeological sites, such as water canals and similar features, were also spatially measured. As a rule, we documented water sources which are not detectable on satellite images, but this was the case usually of the piedmont steppe areas.

For the collection of spatial data hand held GPS receiver (Garmin e-Trex) and a precise geodetic GPS with external antenna TRIMBLE and TOPCON GM 2 were combined.[34] The GPS instruments were used to navigate to pre-selected targets, to record routes, save waypoints and ground control points.

2.2.2 Topographic documentation of the sites

For the already known sites the topographical characteristics, size and shape of the sites, were in the first phase derived from the published information. Given that many of the data were inaccurate or erroneous, it was necessary to revise these topographical characteristics of sites using satellite images and a field survey. The newly detected sites have been dealt with similarly, although the field survey became primary source of information. In addition to standard photographic documentation, the creation of detailed topographic plans and 3D models using photogrammetry has been tested as well as making topographic plans using GPS receivers. The making of detailed topographic plans of the individual sites was, however, not our primary goal.

The geodetic GPS was used to collect data primarily for new topographical plans, because in addition to fewer errors in the x and y axes, it mainly provides more accurate elevation data. We got a very good picture of more complex or composite sites whose shape was either not obvious in the satellite imagery or was not fully published see (**Ch. 4 cat. nos. 23, 26, 54, pp. 139, 141, 147, 195**). Originally we considred making of topographic plans of all the sites. We, however, gave up this plan, since it was too time-consuming and/or technically too difficult to do.[35]

2.2.3 Dating the sites

One of the major preconditions for the success of the project was to obtain sufficient chronologically sensitive material, mainly ceramics, from the surface of the surveyed sites. The amount of such archaeological material on the surface varies at the individual sites considerably. The main role, besides the original extent and duration of the settlement, is being played by erosion, and also the current utilization of the settlement surface. At the surfaces of all sites, where it was possible, an unspecified amount of pottery shards was collected. The main criteria in the selection of the material laid in their informative value concerning duration and intensity of the given settlement. We concentrated on the characteristic fragments of a diagnostic nature: rims, bases, decorated fragments. Non-diagnostic fragments were, however, not entirely omitted. In individual cases, they were employed also, thus sometimes the field *Ceramics* of the site catalogue (chapter 4.2) admits pottery, even if the following catalogue of pottery (chapter 6) does not. In the preliminary dating of the material experts on the local ceramic production in various periods Sh. Shaydullaev and T. Annaev were involved. The dating of ceramic assemblages from various sites lead to determining of the dominant component in each assemblage that not always correspond to the expected final phase of the site occupation. Unique reference pottery assemblage has been gained by the excavations of the site of Jandavlattepa, especially in the Sector 02a, the so-called stratigraphic trench. This 14 m deep sounding covered periods from 2nd half of the 2nd millennium BC to 5th c. AD, i.e., almost 2000 years long! The

---

[34] TOPCON GM2 has the advantage that it combines the receiving signals from both the American GPS system and from the Russian GLONAS and thus leads to a significantly more accurate measurement (function nowadays common, but just several years ago not yet). As data analysis programs were used Garmin-MapSource, Topcon Tools v.7.5 and above all ESRI ArcGIS (ArcView license in Version 9.3 to 10.0), which served for setting up maps and creating and maintaining geodatabase.

[35] The other archaeological team experienced the same (cf. Mantellini et al. 2011).

proper publication of the material from this trench is, however, still in preparation. The sites that yielded no pottery or the pottery material is not sufficient for exact dating (usually a few insignificant fragments) are classified here as having no dating. This fact is indicated in the catalogue entries by empty fields of the respective periods.

2.2.4 Archaeology of modern cemeteries

While examining the satellite imagery of the research area it became clear that the surfaces of some of the local – and presumably modern – cemeteries are uneven and in some cases graves within these cemeteries even cover small mounds resembling *tepas*. Since our experience from Jandavlattepa (and from elsewhere in the region, including Talashkan II and Dal'verzintepa), where pre-modern graves were scattered across all the surface of the site, has confirmed this assumption, we decide to verify the presence or absence of the traces of historical settlement. Thus, as a very special part of the survey we conducted an

investigation on the surface of the modern cemeteries of the Sherabad lowlands. Since typical grave in the area is simply covered by a pile of earth excavated from beneath, one can come across archaeological material from as much as 2 m deep "soundings". Larger modern cemetery in this way offers set of regularly distributed test-trenches allowing for localization of the extent of an eventual archaeological site. An important advantage represents the fact that local people use to embellish the grave-covering earth pile with objects they had found in the grave pit itself. Typically, it is a larger fragment of pottery (frequently also decorated), or, in some cases, complete vessel (**Fig. 2.2**). Among other objects we should mention Medieval fired bricks, Arabic inscriptions in stone, and a clay water pipe. In this way, several cemeteries in the Sherabad District has been surveyed with positive results: the archaeological material was attested at Akkurgan village (085),[36] Gambir village (026 and 125), Kishlak Bozor village (102, 128), Yakhte Yul'/ Dekhkanabad (033, 159), cemetery close to the Chinobod village (100), Takiya (079) and Hurjok (162). Besides, modern cemeteries cover also the

Fig. 2.2 Medieval pottery decorating a modern grave-covering at the site no. 033. photo by L. Stančo.

---

[36] Numbers in brackets indicate serial number in the catalogue of the sites below.

surface of the sites mentioned in scholarly literature already, such as Chopan Ata (035), or above mentioned Jandavlattepa (001). Let us summarize that it has been conclusively demonstrated that at almost all modern cemeteries in the Sherabad plain, there are ancient and Medieval artefacts exhibited by local grave diggers on the modern graves attesting existence of an earlier settlement at the same places. The prevalent period of occupation of these sites is Medieval one. In some cases, but not exclusively, finds are concentrated on a small mound / *tepa* within the cemetery, although finds in the flat cemeteries are also common. It is noteworthy that at the cemetery of Chinobod (100), for instance, we were able to define precisely the formerly inhabited area, since the pottery fragments appeared on the surface of the limited south-eastern part of the large cemetery. This research showed clearly that our knowledge of settlement pattern based on the in-depth study of tell-like sites reveals only a fraction of relevant data and that substantial information are still available under the surface. The interpretation of individual situations depends on various circumstances. While some sites in frame of modern cemeteries seem to represent "lower towns" of a larger *tepa* in their neighbourhood (as in the case of Kulugshatepa 004 and the pottery finds in the modern cemetery No. 098 next

to it), other cemeteries cover complete settlement areal including its central architectural complex or citadel (as in the case of Yalangoyoqotatepa, nos. 026 and 125).

2.2.5 Intensive field survey

In 2009 we decided to employ also an intensive field survey in order to investigate special areas of the research region in detail. This concerned especially the neighbourhood of the *tepas* themselves. The skilled field archaeologist P. Tušlová was entrusted with this task. She with her team worked in two consecutive seasons (2010 and 2011). The intensive field survey was conducted in large polygons, while selected locations were subject to total pick-ups and additionally also to micro-trenches (in this case areas with the highest density of pottery were targeted). This sub-project, methodologically quite unique in this region, brought many interesting ideas and greatly enriched the whole mapping program of the Sherabad District. Its methodological basis, workflows, and results are described in detail in separate articles (Tušlová 2011a; 2011b; 2012a) and an MA-thesis (Tušlová 2012b). It is also presented as final report here in this volume (see chapter 3).

2.3 Evaluation of previous literature and confrontation with previous research

The collected data were continuously compared with the information provided by the work of Soviet researchers mainly from the 70s and 80s of the last century (see chapter 1.4 Previous research). The work of E. V. Rtveladze and his colleagues from the 70s remain the base (Rtveladze – Khakimov 1973; Rtveladze 1974; Rtveladze 1976; Arshavskaya et al. 1982). Besides the aforementioned shortcomings in the majority of these publications many problems arise by a strange convention, according to which some smaller monuments are not dealt with separately, but grouped together or included in the description of some of the nearby major sites. In some cases, clusters of various topographic features are grouped and described under the name of central *tepa*, as in the case of Kattatepa (Rtveladze – Khakimov 1973, 19; Rtveladze 1974, 77). Accordingly, we considered a feature detected in the field or in the satellite imagery to be a new site, but it turned out to

be a site already known to our predecessors, its description though was published only within the publication of the larger nearby site. The other "newly" detected sites were known to other scholars, but the information was not properly published, not to mention sites kept secret by fellow scholars. The greatest problems, however, were paradoxically caused by the most recent work and most ambitious publication on the settlement pattern in Surkhan Darya, which in its assumptions and objectives in many respects coincide with the objectives of the current volume (Stride 2004). The author – as it turned out – in the case of our research area worked (with exceptions) only with the aforementioned Soviet literature and has not verified the data in the field. This led to the situation that many sites are mistakenly identified by him as other features in the field, many are completely wrongly localised, since the coordinates are based on inaccurate and poorly understood descriptions in older literature, and especially the dating of the sites that demands revision is adopted without any corrections, although these data are then used for significant historical interpretations. It confirmed the legitimacy of the practical procedure we employed in the following order 1) detection in satellite imagery, 2) verification in the field, 3) verification in the literature.

2.4 General results: statistic overview of the gained data

After four seasons of fieldwork, the overall database consists of 126 individual archaeological sites, of which only 12 belong to a group of the sites which we ourselves have not visited, but the information about their existence and characteristics were taken from publications. Some sites were visited more than once, some of them had been reported even before the commencement of systematic mapping (2002–2006). Most of the 112 surveyed sites yielded pottery material and consequently 27 sites have been dated for the first time, while dating of many other sites has been refined or updated.

As for the typology of the sites, we divided the sites into the basic types consisted of settlements, forts, single architectures, burial sites, and their combinations, and also find spots of individual objects without topographical anomalies. A limiting factor for developing an in-depth typological study was state of preservation of individual sites. Besides many completely destroyed or ploughed *tepas* that are scarcely recorded in historical maps or CORONA imagery, many other sites were partially damaged or disturbed, at least in their lower parts especially in

the recent decades. Typically – as we assume – a well preserved main *tepa* represents only a central elevated part of an otherwise destroyed site, as in the case of Jandavlattepa, Kattatepa, Khosiyattepa and others. Nevertheless, following the basic typology given above, the prevailing type of sites in the research area, judging from surveyed sites only, is the tell-type multicultural settlement (tepa). We have documented 101 such sites (in 11 cases it was ploughed *tepa* that was with all probability originally settlement, too), two forts, eight single structures typically well-preserved architectures and eight burial sites. In one case the settlement is combined with mausoleum. Specific case is represented by a site interpreted as fire temple.

One site is marked as find spot, since it has yielded only one, but interesting find (clay figurine), without being otherwise morphologically distinct. This category may have been much more numerous, but we have not documented single finds in a systematic way (not to mention single highlight quoted in scholarly literature). Four sites are not typologically determined.

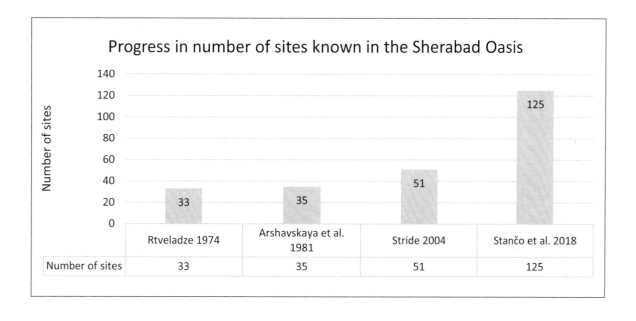

	Rtveladze 1974	Arshavskaya et al. 1981	Stride 2004	Stančo et al. 2018
Number of sites	33	35	51	125

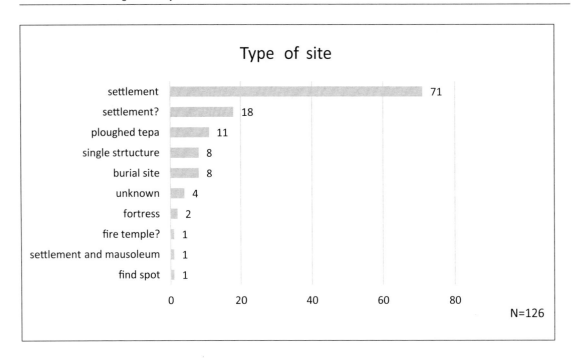

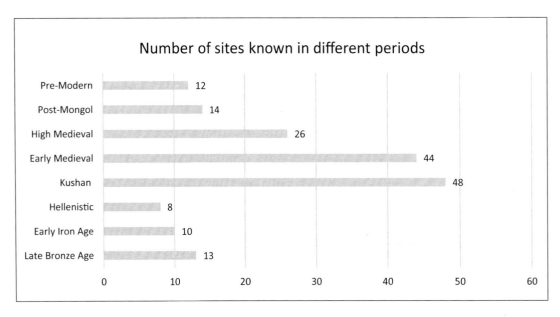

3. Intensive surface survey

P. Tušlová

3.1 Introduction

The following chapter summarizes the results of a two-year intensive surface survey conducted on the cultivated lowlands of the Sherabad District in 2010 and 2011. The project was initiated in the year 2010 as an extension of the ongoing research of Ladislav Stančo, during this time focusing on the ground control of archaeological sites detected in satellite imageries and topographic maps and their reconnaissance in the terrain (Stančo 2009; Danielisová et al. 2010).

The short term project had two main tasks to fulfil. The first aim was to complement the selected Czech–Uzbek investigation with the intensive surface survey;

the second task was to test the potential and suitability of the field survey methodology in the area of Sherabad District for future large-scale research.

The project, conducted all together in a period of seven weeks, was carried out in September 2010 and during October and November 2011. Selected fields were first intensively and systematically surveyed; later specific areas were chosen for total pickups and test pits. All the field work was carried out by students of the Institute of Classical Archaeology at Charles University. Aside from the author, four students participated in the data collecting in the field and their later post-processing.[37]

3.2 The agricultural conditions of the Sherabad Oasis

The favourable climatic conditions of the Sherabad Oasis are reflected in the intense agricultural activity. The main crop of the Sherabad Darya valley is cotton. Its cultivation was enhanced during the Soviet period when a dense network of irrigation channels was built to supply fields with a sufficient amount of water (Stride 2004, 61).

Other agricultural products in the area include spring and autumn vegetation common in Central Asia in general. In early spring, cereals, particularly wheat, barley and millet, are planted to be harvested at the end of May. Autumn plantation includes cotton, corn, sorghum and cucurbitaceous which are sown after the May crop is harvested (Stride 2004, 136). The cotton bushes remain on the field until November when they are cut and collected. In September, our team encountered also rice, sunflowers,

pomegranates and melons in the fields, all however covering only small fractions of them.

During the two-year investigation our team familiarized itself with the agricultural system in Uzbekistan which is based on a variation of the principal crops, cotton and cereals, which are annually rotated. This is very important knowledge for field survey planning as almost every extensively cultivated field has low vegetation cover period and is therefore possible to be properly investigated. While surveying in autumn, the fields covered by cereals are uncultivated. In such a case, every year only the harvested fields can be investigated with the possibility to cover a continual area with excellent surface visibility in a two-year period. During the first year season of our project, cotton fields, around the areas of our investigation, were drawn in the form of polygons into the GIS and the

[37] Great thanks belong to participating students: Věra Doležálková, Adéla Minaříková (Dorňáková), Viktoria Čisťakova and Tereza Včelicová (Machačíková) for their help and hard work.

31

next year compared with the current situation. While considering the cotton and cereal, the rotation worked in approximately 95%; only on one of the investigated fields the cotton persisted into the next year.

Diverse vegetation covering smaller areas such as rice, corn and sunflowers were not included into the previous statistics of rotation as they are not that clearly predictable. In some cases, sunflower fields of the first year turned into cotton fields the next year and therefore the visibility and passability did not distinctly change from year to year. Grasslands field cover either persisted to the next year with no changes or started to be cultivated (most frequently it was turned into a cotton field).

3.3 The field cover, factors of visibility and passability

During the course of the project the main characteristics of the investigated fields were recorded. An emphasis was placed on a detailed description of the field cover, land use, vegetation characteristics and its density. Furthermore, factors of passability and surface visibility, which proved to be very closely connected to each other, were marked.

The visibility of the surface of each field was recorded in a percentage in the range of 100–80% (excellent), 80–60% (very good), 60–40% (good), 40–20% (low), 20% > (very low). The passability (the walking conditions) was expressed as excellent, medium-hard and difficult. According to the two-year observations the surveyed fields were divided into the following classes with more or less consistent characteristics:

- **Ploughed fields** contained deep furrows reaching up to 50 cm underground. Their surface visibility was excellent and the passability ranged from medium-hard to difficult. In September these fields were very dry and hard. From October to November the soil was softer, sporadically moistened due to occasional rain (**Fig. 3, 1**).
- **Harrowed fields** featured excellent visibility in general. During September hard and dry lumps of clay of variable sizes accumulated on the field surface making the passability medium-hard. From October and November surface of those fields was softer, but muddy, keeping the passability on medium-hard (**Fig. 3, 2**).
- **Furrows** in the Uzbek context are freshly piled up parallel lines of earth separated by narrow and reg-

Fig. 3, 1 Ploughed field, captured in autumn, south of Gorintepa. Photo by Petra Tušlová.

Fig. 3, 2 Harrowed field with Gilyambobtepa in the background, captured in summer. Photo by Petra Tušlová.

Fig. 3, 3 Furrows in summer, captured without water, north of Shishtepa. Photo by Petra Tušlová.

Fig. 3, 4 HDS field in summer. Photo by Petra Tušlová.

Fig. 3, 5 Pasture during autumn (originally HDS field), area of Shishtepa. Photo by Petra Tušlová.

ularly irrigated channels approximately 30 cm deep. In general, the visibility and passability is excellent, although these good conditions might be negatively influenced by water flooding parts of the fields making them difficult for walking or simply inaccessible (**Fig. 3, 3**).

- **HDS** is a term artificially created by our team, which stands for harvested beaten furrows that are no longer irrigated; they are flattened and covered by varying amount of straw as a result of the past agricultural activity. HDS stands for <u>H</u>ard, <u>D</u>ry with <u>S</u>traw, indicating the basic characteristic of the field surface (**Fig. 3, 4**). These specific features however apply to the dry weather only. In October and November, although the straw cover did not change, the soil became softer due to the rain. The visibility on the surface worsened with the passing months (in some cases probably also years) after the harvest as weeds started growing on the uncultivated soil. In fact, in some places it was difficult to separate HDS from pasture. In the result the visibility varied between very good (100%) and

very low (up to 20%). Surface visibility below 20%, although in combination with formal shaped HDS, was automatically considered as pasture.

- **Pasture** – uncultivated fields – contain permanent amount of surface vegetation ranging from sparse to mature. This influences the visibility covering almost the entire spectrum, except the excellent one (consequently ranging from 80% > 0). The passability is in general excellent or medium-hard while waterlogged (**Fig. 3, 5**).
- **Harvested cotton fields** were investigated during the 2011 season only when they were partly or entirely harvested. There were either leafless cotton bushes standing in the field or cut shrubs piled up on the field surface. In both cases the visibility was on the average very good, although excellent or low visibility was also possible. The passability differed depending on the growth stage of the bushes (**Fig. 3, 6–7**).

The following table illustrates the extent of each land cover within the total amount of fields walked in September 2010 and October/November 2011:

Fig. 3, 6 Leafless cotton bushes. Area of Jandavlattepa. Photo by Petra Tušlová.

Fig. 3, 7 Harvested cotton bushes piled up on the fields. Area of Jandavlattepa. Photo by Petra Tušlová.

Year	HDS	Ploughed	Pasture	Harrowed	Furrows	Harvested Cotton
2010	47%	23%	20%	7%	3%	0
2011	49%	6%	3%	9%	9%	24%

There were also other aspects of the surface visibility and passability besides the density of the vegetation cover. For instance, the soil aridity or, by contrast, the soil moisture level influenced the clarity of sherd recognition in the terrain. Pottery fragments were easier to find on wet grounds as they were "disappearing" to the neaked eye when coated with dust. For sherd identification late autumn featured slightly better conditions as most fields were wet.

Another outstanding aspect influencing visibility around some of the investigated areas was salinization. The water of Sherabad Darya, which is used for the irrigation of the oasis, is partly salty. When the water evaporates a thin layer of white salt crust remains on the surface obscuring both the soil and any potential artefacts (**Fig. 3, 8**). Regarding the investigated area, this effect was particularly noticeable around Kulugshatepa.

Enclosures for domestic animals and mobile shelters for the shepherds were another significant impediment to the intensive field survey. They are simple wooden or metal fence structures standing in the middle of a field surrounded by straw, with domestic animals (mostly goats and sheep) covering the area with a layer of excrement (**Fig. 3, 9**). The enclosures were often accompanied by guard-dogs which also very effectively eliminated the passability in their surroundings.

The investigated areas are interlaced with an ingenious network of channels bringing water to irrigate the field (called *arik*, **Fig. 3, 10–11**) and diverting water to drain off the field (called *zeber*, **Fig. 3, 12**). The first channels are shallow, mostly of concrete, either recessed in the ground, placed directly on the

Fig. 3, 8 A field covered by a soil crust. Area of Jandavlattepa. Photo by Tereza Včelicová.

Fig. 3, 9 Domestic-animals enclosures with temporary dwelling placed on the fields. Area of Ayritepa. Photo by Tereza Včelicová.

Fig. 3, 10 A concrete *arik* placed on the ground, area of Gilyambobtepa. Photo by Tereza Včelicová.

Fig. 3, 11 An elevated *arik* made of concrete, area of Gorintepa. Photo by Tereza Včelicová.

field or slightly elevated. The latter channels are several meters wider and deeper. An appropriate example of a modern day *zeber* is the one east of Ayritepa which is approximately 12 m wide and seven meters deep (**Fig. 3, 48**). During the field walking the water channels represented the main boundaries between the fields, and in some cases they were very difficult to cross. Some of the *zebers* do not have a crossing for several kilometres, although in some places it is

possible to wade through if the water is low. *Ariks* are easy to climb over or crawl underneath, however for the agricultural machines both types of channels represent impassable boundaries. The cultivation of fields is thus undertaken in a delimited area which does not allow the movement of surface materials to great distances. This is an excellent premise for the field survey as artefacts in irrigated lowlands accumulate around the place of their original deposition.

Fig. 3, 12 Wide water channel – *zeber*, area of Gilyambobtepa. Photo by Tereza Včelicová.

3.4 Methodology

The project was based on the intensive field survey of selected areas chosen according to their proximity to *tepas*, their (easy) passability and (excellent to good) visibility. The survey was complemented by total pickups which were performed on all of the detected scatters, and by several test pits which were carried out in the areas with the highest pottery accumulation.

During the project, satellite images (CORONA, IKONOS, Google Earth) were combined with Soviet topographic maps (1:500,000, 1:200,000 and 1:100,000 scale), and processed in an application based on Geographic Information System (GIS). This technology was used to facilitate the data collecting, visualisation and evaluation. The digital data were dabbled by paper forms to collect maximum information and to prevent their loss.

In the landscape the topographic maps proved to be a much better tool for orientation than the satellite images. The majority of the depicted main roads and irrigation channels with the corssings did not change much from the current situation, which helped with navigation on roads as well as in terrain.

3.4.1 Data collecting

During the field walking data were collected on a PDA Trimble Juno SB equipped with a GPS and running ArcPAD, the mobile application of ESRI ArcGIS. IKONOS satellite imagery and the topographic maps served as base maps, while the integrated GPS showed to the field walking team its constant position in the terrain. Surveyed areas were drawn into the PDA in the shape of polygons and were numbered to facilitate the post-processing. For better orientation and additional back up, tracklog and navigation points were kept by a hand held GPS Garmin eTrex. Digital spatial records were accompanied by detailed paper forms containing information about each field (**Fig. 3, 13**). Both sources of data were daily processed and combined in the project geodatabase, back on the archaeological base.

Fig. 3, 13 PDA Trimble Juno SB, GPS Garmin eTrex and the paper documentation. Photo by Tereza Včelicová.

The paper forms recorded the agricultural and walking conditions, the visibility and the passability of fields, waterlogging or dryness of the soil, the slope of the investigated fields and the information about the stone amount accumulated on the field (**Fig. 3, 14**). The main information however comprised the count of artefacts (pottery, fragments of architectural ceramics and single finds).

3.4.1.1 Intensive field survey

The intensive field survey was applied in areas in the immediate vicinity of *tepas*, previously investigated by the team of Ladislav Stančo. An average amount of material located on the fields was deter-

mined, visualized in the GIS application and evaluated in accordance to its growing and falling tendencies in separated polygons which created a basic unit of the research.

The methodology of the project was based on the multidisciplinary Tundzha Regional Archaeological Project (TRAP) conducting field survey in the Yambol and Kazanlak Districts of Bulgaria between 2009 and 2011 (Ross et al. 2010; Ross – Sobotková 2010; Sobotková et al. 2010; Sobotková 2009).[38] As a permanent member of the research team in Bulgaria I learned the methodology and the documentation processes. Therefore, the project in Sherabad District was inspired by the TRAP procedures but the approaches were modified to suit the different environmental conditions and cultural-historical development of Central Asia.

In contrast to the TRAP, only the intensive field survey strategy was utilized. The visibility 100–50% used by the TRAP for the intensive survey was by our team extended to 100–40%. This approach enabled us to intensively cover a more extensive area. Furthermore, the spacing between field walkers was set at a permanent 15 m instead of the original TRAP range which varied between 10 m and 20 m (Sobotková et al. 2010, 58–61). The different agricultural and climatic conditions of the Central Asia had to be also taken into consideration in the field work preparation, undertaking and evaluation.

The investigated fields in the Sherabad District were walked in transects with participants spaced side by side at 15 m intervals. Artefact densities were also called out by walkers at 15 m intervals as they progressed. This formed "cells" of 15 × 15 m. After five rows were walked the polygon was closed and drawn in the portable electronic device. The dimensions of one polygon approximated a rectangle of 60 × 75 m (covering about 0.45 ha), i.e., four walkers by five rows (**Fig. 3, 15–16**). The polygons were prolonged by up to two more rows or shortened and narrowed when necessary, depending on the fields' dimensions or anomalies revealed during the field walking.

					Sherabad 2010 - 2011		Date:	
					Polygon:			
					Shard count type: Row count		Walk. Interval: 15 x 15m, 10 x 10m	
					Visibility: 100-80% x 80-60% x 60-40% x 40% > 0		Stones: 5 x 3 x none	
					Land use: Annual x PerAnnual x Pasture		Pottery Frag.: 5 x 4 x 3 x 2 x 1	
					Vegetation: Dense x Sparse x None		Worn: 5 x 3 x 1	
					AgrC: Plow x Harrow x Furrows x HDS x Cotton		WalkingC: Excellent x M.H. x Difficult	
					SurfaceC: Waterlogged x Optimal x Very Dry		Sample: Yes/No	
					Slope: Steep x Gentle x None		Same as below ☐	
					NOTE:			

Fig. 3, 14 Paper form for each polygon recording basic data about the fields and the material which was found there. The particular amount of finds (pottery/AC/other) was filled into the cells on the left, representing four lines/four people walking five rows. The form is inspired by TRAP, modified for the area of South Uzbekistan.

---

[38]   More about the project and its personnel might be found at: http://www.citiesindust.org/.

Fig. 3, 15 Intensive survey of HDS field with 15m spacing between individual members, area south of Ayritepa. Photo by Petra Tušlová.

Fig. 3, 16 Visualisation of the intensive field survey polygon by polygon. Created by Petra Tušlová.

The project aimed to obtain a representative field sample without any ambition to cover the entire Sherabad District. As already stated by Alcock et al. (1994, 137), intensive field survey is based on quantified observations and controlled artefact collection in the defined area. As a result, effort was made to proceed in more detailed intensive survey rather than aiming to cover an overwhelmingly extensive area. The spacing between participants defines the size of the smallest detectible scatter/site (Plog et al. 1978, 383–421). In this sense the approaches were chosen in accordance with the desire to examine smaller areas in detail rather than focus on covering an extensive region.

The approximate area observed by each participant was around a two meters wide corridor – one meter to each side of their walking line (e.g., Bevan – Conolly 2012; Sobotková et al. 2010, 58).[39] As a result the final numbers given in the following text represents only a fraction of the total amount of the surface material, counted in 600 sq. m out of 4,500 sq. m of one regular polygon, i.e., about 13% of all of the estimated artefacts prevalence in one polygon, scatter or site.

Information about the amount of pottery fragments, architectural features or other material detected on the field was written into the paper forms regarding each polygon. If possible, modern pottery was distinguished from ancient pottery to study patterns of modern debris deposition. Diagnostic fragments from each polygon, including bases, rims, handles, decorated or otherwise significant pieces were collected for further investigation, while insignificant fragments were only counted for comparative purposes and left in place.

3.4.1.2 Test pits

The test pits were placed on three out of four detected scatters (ShFS01, ShFS02 and ShFS03; **Fig. 3, 17**). The last scatter (ShFS04) was omitted due to its remoteness as well as to lack of a time. The test pits'

---

[39] Bintliff and Snodgrass (1988) consider a range of 2.5 m on either side of each field-walker, thus creating five-meter-wide corridors. As a result of my previous field survey experiences the number seems to be exaggerated. Therefore, the two-meter definition mentioned in other scientific works was preferred. Consequently, participants were instructed to count one meter to both side of themselves to gain a uniform average number from each of them.

dimensions were established at 100 × 80 cm[40] with an intention to reach 100 cm underground – to fully remove the topsoil and to understand the possible revealed stratigraphy underneath. Individual spits were approximately 20 cm thick. However, in several cases the excavation work was stopped either due to groundwater appearing approximately 80 cm underground or by the presence of a mud-brick wall covered by the topsoil. In such cases the test pits were not fully excavated to the desired depth. By contrast, two test pits at scatter ShFS02 were excavated to a depth of approximately two meters. This was due to the softness of the soil – irrigated by water channels – which enabled easy digging. The advantage of favourable conditions was utilized to dig up to the maximum possible depth in order to reach bedrock or sterile soil. However, neither one of them was reached in any of the test pits.

Pottery fragments gained from the test pits were divided according to the spits and counted for further analysis. Diagnostic fragments were retained and evaluated for comparisons with the collected surface material and also in order to trace remains of stratigraphy. However, the main aim of the test pits was to verify the field survey results – to reveal a continuity of the material under the topsoil whilst also excluding the secondary displacement of the surface material. The final evaluation of the scatter chronology was then based on a combination of data gained from the surface survey and also from the test pits.

3.4.1.3 Total pickups

The TRAP again inspired the project's total pickup methodology by way of re-sampling the investigated scatters (Sobotková et al. 2010, 61). On each surveyed area featuring a large amount of surface material a total pickup was placed in several different places. A square of 10 × 10 m was marked in the selected area and all the material concentrated within was collected (**Fig. 3, 18–19**). The artefacts gathered in the square were then divided into individual groups based on their main characteristics (see 3.5 "The surface material division"). The artefact groups were processed in the field: weighed, counted and photographed. The non-diagnostic fragments were left on the same place as found on the field whilst the diagnostic ones were retained for further study.

The method of total pickups provided the project with a representative and quantified sample of the material present on the fields, including classes of tiny artefacts which might be easily omitted during the field survey. The total pickups enable evaluations of the variability of surface artefacts within one investigated scatter and comparison among the other areas of interest. Different chronological or typological components can also be identified, changing the general idea of a scatter after the evaluation of the intensive field survey.

Fig. 3, 17 Test pit carried out in a corn field – area of Pachmaktepa. All of our field activities enjoyed a great attention among locals who often helped with the work. Photo by Petra Tušlová.

---

[40] As described further in the text the first test pits placed on SHFS03 had smaller dimensions (50 × 80 cm), which proved to be insufficient.

Fig. 3, 18 Total pick up (polygon 10 × 10 m) carried out next to a Khosyattepa (the first test pick up). Photo by Petra Tušlová.

Fig. 3, 19 Sorting and counting of the material collected during the total pick up. Photo by Petra Tušlová.

3.5 The surface material division

3.5.1 Classification of the material

The collected surface material was divided into several groups based on its characteristics. These groups were material-based classifications, not chronological divisions as the fragments were mostly non-diagnostic, i.e., not suitable for this approach. The main aspects of the characteristic classifications considered the material, the main function and the appearance of the artefacts.

Firstly, different materials were separated within the scatter assemblage. Pottery, various types of architectural ceramics, glass, metal, bones and wasters were grouped together. Rarely detected small finds sometimes represented a unique group as a single piece, for example special objects such as a terracotta bead or part of a stone pestle were found.

Fig. 3, 20 Illustrative example of a pottery group – yellow ware – collected within one pickup. The group is counted and weighted; the diagnostic fragments collected for further documentation (in this case the rim of pithos, see Tab. 3, 3:3). Photo by Petra Tušlová.

The pottery was further divided according to its function and appearance.[41] The subgroups are: kitchen ware (KW), grey ware (GW), fine ware (FW) and common ware (CW).[42] The maximum thickness for FW sherds was decided as 0.5 cm which created an appropriate division between FW and CW classifications as the clay of FW and CW sherds featured very similar characteristics otherwise. The CW was further divided into red ware (RW) and yellow ware (YW), reflecting the standard colour of the clay (for example see **Fig. 3, 20**).

The fabric colour of KW varied between ochre, brown and black. The surface was smoothed to cover the higher amount of inclusions, reaching up to 20%. Variable shapes of pots, generally burned from outside, were found. The pottery was in majority wheel made, with several handmade fragments.

The GW fragments have a solid grey color of the fabric. They are covered from both sides by a thin layer of slip of the same colour. The fabric is very well levigated, with a maximum of 5% of inclusions. This group is represented by five pieces only, connected solely with scatter ShFS03. These sherds were all, except one fragment, dated to the end of the 4th century BC (by Sh. Shaydullaev). The reminding GW sherd belongs to Timurides period and it will be discussed in connection to ShFS03.

The fabric colour of the FW category, and its charactristis in general, varied. In all cases, however, the fabric was very well levigated with a small amount (up to 5%) of tiny inclusions. The shapes included different types of table ware – predominantly bowls, plates and small jugs. This group, most of all, reflected the chronology of fragments regarding colour, slip / glaze and decoration.

The fabric of CW may be both fine and coarse, ranging from 5% to 20% of inclusions. Red and yellow colours for the sherd fabric completely dominate, however no relation between specific morphological types and colouring was detected. Most common in both categeories are bigger size jars, stands and storage vessels.

The Architectural Ceramic (AC) was placed into a single group with the intention to divide the collected material into sub-groups of bricks and daubs if possible. There were no roof-tile fragments on the fields which reflected the practice of rooves constructed from organic materials, a combination of wooden trusses, clay and straw which is still used nowadays.

---

[41] The material classification was inspired by the Czech-Uzbek team division whilst excavating Jandavlattepa.

[42] Since all coarse wares which had been found relate to kitchen/cooking ware, or to storage wares, the term coarse ware was not used, consequently the abbreviation CW stands for common ware.

Due to the late date of the field survey in 2011 and almost daily rain, not only the investigated fields, but also the collected pottery and architectural ceramics were all soaked and muddy. In order to obtain the real weight of the collected material to compare it with the extremely 'dry' data of the previous year, one kilogram of variable pottery types and of AC fragments was gathered from the wet field, washed, dried, and again weighed. After eight days the weight was established at 816g. Because the conditions of the total pickups were very similar for all of the scatters, the final pottery and AC weight of every detected category collected during the 2011 season was in the end reduced by 0.184 grams per gram to obtain comparable data for both years.

The collected material was processed at the archaeological base – drawn, photographed and analysed for fabric type, colour, manufacture etc. Preliminary classification and identification of the pottery was conducted by collaborators of the Czech team T. Annaev and Sh. Shaydullaev, respected authorities on the issue in Surkhan Darya province, who kindly assessed the fragments and helped with their dating. During preparation of the ceramic material for publication, pottery forms for comparision were seaked for in literature, as well as compered with exhibited material

in archeological museums in Sherabad, Termez and Tashkent. No convenient literature for the pottery of the 16th century AD further to the modern days was available (at least up to 2012 when the material was procesed). Consequently, all of the 'younger' material presented here, if not stated otherwise, was recognized by Tokhtash Annaev.

3.5.2 The size of the fragments

To determine the approximate fragmentation of pottery and AC material, a basic definition relating to the sherd dimensions was applied:
- coin size (a regular-size coin such as a quarter dollar or euro 50 cent)
- half palm size
- palm size
- hand size (the palm with fingers)

The different dimensions used in the text derive from those four basic ones or represents their variants. For example, descriptions such as "smaller than a coin size" and "dimension between palm and hand size" were used in the descriptions. The indicated dimensions are based on the covered surface, not on the shape resemblance.

3.6 Introduction to the Field Survey

The intensive field survey was undertaken only in the cultivated areas including both banks of the Sherabad Darya as far as 18 km from the centre of the town of Sherabad. During the seven-week investigation conducted over the two seasons of the duration of the project, 1567 polygons were set up, covering approximately 731 ha (**Fig. 3, 21**). Out of them 245 polygons with the overall surface area of 114 ha are connected to the scatters subsequently described in the text. On average, about 16% of all of the surveyed areas revealed enough surface material to be classified as an artificially created cluster connected with previous human activity. The clusters are predominantly represented by scatters marked as ShFS01, ShFS02, ShFS03 and ShFS04,[43] partly also by the material accumulations ascertained in several areas in the immediate vicinity of Jandavlattepa, particularly with the clusters numbered as 150, 154, 155 and 155.

The chronology of the surface material is based on determined diagnostic fragments which make up about 62% of all of the collected and documented pottery. The remaining amount was insufficiently significant to provide any further data. The pottery drawings in tables shown in the text regard each scatter, representing a selection of the most diagnostic examples, used here to illustrate the most characteristic types for each period. They are a mixture of material gained from the intensive survey, test pits as well as from the total pickups.

If not stated otherwise, the chronology of *tepas* mentioned in connection with the investigated scatters is based on the field walking and pottery studies of the Czech-Uzbek team. For more information regarding the *tepas* itself see chapter 3.8.6, which offers their detailed description.

---

[43] The abbreviation „ShFS" stands for Sherabad Field Survey. The subsequent number reflects the order in which the scatters were found.

Fig. 3, 21 Map of the Sharabad Oasis showing all of the areas surveyed in 2010 and 2011. High pottery concentrations are marked by the red colour. Map by Petra Tušlová.

3.7 The scatter and the site

3.7.1 The definition of the scatter and of the site

For better understanding of the following text it is now necessary to clarify in what sense the terms "scatter" (or cluster) and "site" are used in this chapter.

The term "scatter" is used for the surface material spread over the fields or accumulated in the vicinity of elevated tepas. The term "site" basically stands for the *tepa* – settlement – itself. It might be applied to the elevated mounds recorded by the field survey as well as to those newly detected in topographic maps or in satellite imagery (as in the area of Jandavlattepa).

3.7.2 The character of the scatter and of the site

The investigated fields in general revealed a small amount of the surface material which has been pre-

dominantly connected with the immediate vicinity of tepas. The accumulations may be divided into two groups.

The first one is connected with light pottery scatter concentrated in the immediate vicinity of *tepa* (in our case namely around Taushkantepa, Gilyambobtepa and the southern part of Khosyattepa). The pottery dispersion reaches up to a maximum distance of 350 m from the *tepa* and reveals the same pottery types and thus identical chronology with the closest site. Due to the small amount of pottery fragments and architectural ceramics whose quantity sharply decreases with growing distance from the *tepa* it seems that these scatters only result from the *tepa* fallouts. The distribution of the material over the closest fields was then caused by agricultural activity, but as well various human or natural factors might be involved.

The second group is created by several outstanding surface accumulations of pottery and architectural ceramics. In our investigated sample they are again

42

connected with tepa, but the raised amount of surface material reaches up to 800 m from the centre of the closest *tepa* (measured on ShFS03 – Shishtepa). The amount of the material concentrated around the *tepas* is usually constant for several tens of meters and dwindling gradually after a few polygons. Generally, it is possible to determine the core and the margin of the cluster; also the borders of the scatter are clear, very well differentiable from the surrounding fields. In this case we are either dealing with new sites or, more likely, with continuation of the nearby tepas.

It is impossible to distinguish precisely the original dimension of the site out of the dispersion of the surface material. The dimensions and number of the discovered material discussed in the following text therefore regards the core and the marginal areas

of surface scatters, without attempting to define the original extent of the settlement. In several places, the underground continuity of the surface material was attempted to be determined by means of the test pits which without exception confirmed the pottery presence down to the deepest excavated spits.

Different approaches were embraced in the area of Jandavlattepa where the presumable archaeological sites were detected on the basis of the topographical map and verified by the field survey. Since these sites were sought for in specific area, even a small amount of the surface material found in the vicinity of the predicted feature was considered as a site. The lowest number connected with a scatter was 45 fragments collected in an area of approximately 200 sq. m.

3.8 The areas of the field survey

The intensive survey – introduction

Before the beginning of the project, several areas suitable for prospecting had been chosen in advance from the IKONOS and Google Earth satellite images. The main criteria for the selection were the extensiveness of the area, the low habitation rate and presence of at least two known *tepa*. During the first days of the terrain work the chosen areas were visited and evaluated according to their surface vegetation cover and passability which set aside only a few of them as suitable for further research.

The main investigated fields were located next to the village of Hurjak, about 6.5 km south of Sherabad in the surroundings of Kulugshatepa (the area of the scatter ShFS01). The other surveyed areas started about 5.5 km to the east of Sherabad, right to the south of the village of Gorin, and continued for another four kilometres to the east covering the vicinity of the archaeological sites of Gorintepa (ShFS02); Gilyambobtepa and Shishtepa (ShFS03). Later the area was extended to the south into the immediate vicinity of Ayritepa (ShFS04), about two kilometres away from Shishtepa (**Fig. 3, 21**).

The topographic maps of 1:100,000 scale gained in 2010 showed six features (sites) no longer visible in the landscape located in the surroundings of Jandavlattepa. The area of the predicted features was intensively surveyed to determine their precise position and chronology (**Fig. 3, 51**).

Only a single day of prospecting focused on the area about 18 km to the south-west of Sherabad and

2.5 km to the west of Talashkantepa II, the closest well-known archaeological site. About 21 sites in total were marked on the topographical map in this area covering a strip of eight by four kilometres. However, due to the limited time only two of the features were surveyed (**Fig. 3, 57**).

3.8.1 The area of Kulugshatepa (scatter ShFS01)

Location

The first pottery scatter is located 6.5 km to the south of the town of Sherabad in the immediate vicinity of the village of Hurjak. The main site of the area called Kulugshatepa covers about 5.5 ha; three other smaller *tepas* are located up to one kilometre from the centre of the main tepa. At a distance of 550 m to the north-east is situated Tigrmantepa, 760 m to the east is Khosyattepa and 315 m to the south-west is situated another *tepa* whose name remains unknown (catalogue No 73 "No name tepa": Danielisová et al. 2010, 85).

The area directly adjacent to the Kulugshatepa from the north-west is occupied by a modern-time cemetery which covers 7 ha. The rest of the northern and north-eastern part is then covered by the Hurjak village which is slowly expanding southwards, closer to the tepa. Two lines of houses with gardens are not yet visible in the IKONOS imagery captured in 2001, although they are present on the Google Earth

Fig. 3, 22 Area of ShFS01: Kulugh-Shakhtepa showing recently inhabited areas and the modern-day cemetery covering part of the site. IKONOS satellite imagery. Map by Petra Tušlová.

imagery from which they are redrawn to the map in a shape of a polygon under the term "urban area" (**Fig. 3, 22**).

A general description

The extent of the area connected with the site is approximately delimited by 86 polygons covering 37 ha, which produced altogether a statistical amount of 5000 ancient pottery fragments, 110 modern sherds and 575 fragments of architectural ceramics. On average 154 various fragments were discovered per hectare. The highest amount of the pottery finds was concentrated further south and east from the *tepa* as far as 580 m away (**Fig. 3, 23**).

In connection with this site the highest amount of ancient pottery fragments detected in one single polygon was recorded, the number reaches up to 472 pieces. Furthermore, a high amount of modern pottery was detected in marginal areas of the field. The outstanding concentration of the modern pottery is connected to polygons directly situated along the village of Hurjak, where occasionally half or a quarter of a vessel was noted. The surprisingly low modern pottery fragmentation is due to a quite recent dispersion of the material, still accumulated around the place where it was disposed of. The most often recognizable types are dishes with a characteristic cot-

ton-boll pattern and white painted porcelain which are both still in use.

Stones of pebble-size were detected only in six polygons, east of the tepa, in an area of a north-south strip leading along the newly build houses. The ancient architectural ceramics were mainly represented by bricks, belonging according to their measurement (26 × 26 × 8 cm) to the Islamic Middle Ages (**Fig. 3, 32**). The biggest concentration was detected in the immediate vicinity of the tepa, with the biggest portion concentrated to the north, reaching up to 430 m from the centre of the tepa. A smaller amount of AC was spread all over the eastern field, with variable amounts in individual polygons. Another minor isolated group of the AC was identified about 300 m south of the tepa. The total dimensions of the architecture ceramics scatter measured 300 m in the north-south and 200 m in the east-west direction (**Fig. 3, 24**).

Season 2010 and 2011

During the project's first year a pottery scatter was discovered concentrated about 300 m to the northeast and to the east of Kulugshatepa (**Fig. 3, 23** and **25**). The area surrounding the *tepa* was covered by dense cotton fields, which did not allow a surface survey in its immediate vicinity. About 12 ha were as-

44

Fig. 3, 23 Area of ShFS01: Kulugh-Shakhtepa showing raised amount of pottery and the approximate location of the two accidental pottery finds made by locals. IKONOS satellite imagery. Map by Petra Tušlová.

Fig. 3, 24 Area of ShFS01: Kulugh-Shakhtepa showing raised amount of Architectural Ceramics (AC) concentrated around the tepa. IKONOS satellite imagery. Map by Petra Tušlová.

Fig. 3, 25 Area of ShFS01: Kulugh-Shakhtepa with marked fields surveyed in 2010 and 2011. IKONOS satellite imagery. Map by Petra Tušlová.

Fig. 3, 26 Area of ShFS01: Kulugh-Shakhtepa with marked Total pickups and Test pits conducted in specific polygons. IKONOS satellite imagery. Map by Petra Tušlová.

signed to the site with apparent continuity under the surrounding houses and gardens.

Local inhabitants testified several random finds in their properties. The first one was located about 150 m to the east of Tigrmantepa, accidentally unearthed during the excavation of an *arik*. It consisted of one vessel of approximate height 50 cm with a neck broken off (**Fig. 3, 27**) and of one terracotta whistle (**Fig. 3, 28**). According to the characteristic decoration of parallel wavy lines of the vessel we may date it to the High Middle Ages. The other notification of a single pottery find came from a spot about 650 m to the west of the first one, but no finds were available for consultation (**Fig. 3, 23**).

The area investigated in 2010 was covered by HDS field treatment which revealed overall 531 ancient pottery fragments, 86 modern ones, and a further 86 pieces of architectural ceramics. Overall it was possible to consider 38 polygons as a part of the concentration covering about 12 ha with the average number of 59 fragments in one polygon. The scatter revealed the smallest amount of all of the other investigated clusters which were detected during the first season; it was nevertheless interpreted as an individual site with continuity under the surrounding houses.

During the second year of the field survey the area adjacent to the *tepa* was harvested and covered by HDS field treatment. The remaining un-surveyed fields located directly to the south of Kulugshatepa

could also be examined; their surface was overgrown by seedlings with excellent and very good visibility. An additional 25 ha was investigated, disclosing the highest pottery concentrations. In total 4493 ancient pottery fragments, two modern ones and 486 pieces of architectural ceramics were uncovered in 48 polygons, i.e., 199 various fragments per hectare.

These results distinctively changed the general view of the pottery dispersion. The amount of the finds concentrated around Kulugshatepa revealed the continuity of the surface material away from the previously detected scatter. It turned out that during the 2010 season the margin of the eastern part of the scatter had been discovered. During the following year (2011) the core of the concentration, which accumulated around the tepa, had been surveyed. The area further to the south yielded an increased number of surface materials as well; especially the architectural ceramics fragments were represented in a high number.

Also the second year the local inhabitants were very helpful. A little girl, living in a house in the recently urbanized area half way between Kulugshatepa and the scatter discovered during the first year, brought us a small vessel with the neck broken off with the remains of a red slip resembling the Kushan pottery (**Fig. 3, 29**). She also gave us several fragments of big vessels decorated in a way characteristic of the High Middle Ages (**Fig. 3, 30; Tab. 3, 1:8**), all originating in the area of Kulugshatepa.

Fig. 3, 27 Area of ShFS01: Kulugh-Shakhtepa. Pottery vessel about 40 cm high, with characteristic decoration of High Middle Age, which was found together with a clay whistle while digging an *arik*. Photo by Tereza Včelicová.

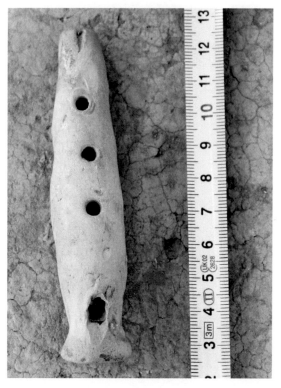

Fig. 3, 28 Area of ShFS01: Kulugh-Shakhtepa. The clay whistle found together with the vessel. Photo by Tereza Včelicová.

Fig. 3, 29 Area of ShFS01: Kulugh-Shakhtepa. Small vessel with remains of a red slip found by locals on their garden, we could only make a fast photograph before returning the vessel to the owners. Photo by Tereza Včelicová.

The test pits

Two test pits were placed in the area located east of Kulugshatepa, in the polygons with the highest concentration of the surface material. The first pit was placed in the polygon 10135; the other one in the polygon 10120 (**Fig. 3, 26**). The test pits (l.100 × w.80 × d.100 cm) were excavated in spits approximately 20 cm deep. Both pits featured the same character-

Fig. 3, 30 Area of ShFS01: Kulugh-Shakhtepa. A little local girl was supplying us by the pottery dug out on their garden (as she is living in the recently urbanised area north-east from Kulugh-Shakhtepa). On the photo she is holding High Middle Age pottery stand (Tab. 3, 1:8). Photo by Petra Tušlová.

istics. There were no visible stratigraphic layers, only the soil of the upper approximately 40 cm had a grey-brown colour while the deeper part was more dark-brown and soft. However, the transition was hard to determine. The profiles of the pits showed pottery, stones and charcoal in unchanged proportions all the way through, however the freshly uncovered soil more noticeably. In this case I would assume that those differences were due to the dryness of the newly un-covered soil and mean nothing more than different moisture (**Fig. 3, 31**).

The polygon and the test pit 10135

The surface material of the polygon 10135 contained 72 ancient pottery fragments, four modern ones, and another four architectural ceramics. In the test pit altogether 147 diverse fragments were recognized, from these there were 138 pottery fragments, eight architectural ceramics and three pieces of animal bones.

The amount of material obtained (in pcs.) in each spit is summarised in the following chart. The three upper grey rows represent the top soil (spit 1, 2 and 3), the lower white ones (spit 4 and 5) cover the remaining 60 to 100 centimetres underground.[44]

In the depth of about 50 cm (spit 3) an intact High Middle Ages brick was uncovered (**Fig. 3, 32**) as well as a fragment of a rim with characteristic turquoise glaze classed into the same period. A large fragment of a brick was also detected at the depth of 60–70 cm (spit 3–4) stuck in the western profile (**Fig. 3, 31**). At the depth of 90–100 cm (spit 5), a partly preserved vessel was found dated into the Early Middle Ages. Since the vessel had been broken in antiquity and the pieces remained together in one spot, it seems as if it had been preserved *in situ*. (**Tab. 3, 1:1**).

Polygon	AC	Pottery	Other	Total
10135	4	72	4	80

Test Pit			Polygon	10135
Layer	AC	Pottery	Other	Total
Surface		2		2
Spit 1	4	59	2	65
Spit 2	2	18		20
Spit 3	1	26	1	28
Spit 4	1	9		10
Spit 5		26		26
Total	8	140	3	151

---

[44] According to the observation of the ploughed fields the top soil reaches in average to 50 cm with maximum of 60 cm underground.

The polygon and the test pit 10120

In the polygon 10120, 73 ancient and 19 modern pottery fragments were discovered as well as ten sherds of AC. Much more material was detected on the other hand in the test pit: overall 435 pottery fragments, 19 AC and 16 bones. In the spit 2 a high amount of terracotta pieces smaller than a coin size appeared. From an overall 171 small fragments more than 130 were not bigger than one centimetre. In the lowest spit five fragments of very soft stone (sand stone?) of approximately a palm size were detected. These finds have no analogy among the other examined material.

The pottery of the High Middle Age is represented in each of the spits down to the lowest excavated layer. The rest of the material is not diagnostic enough, but an increased amount of architectural ceramic, especially daub, should be emphasized. Rather than a decrease in number of finds under the top soil there is, on the contrary, more material cumulated in the two lowermost layers (spit 1 + 2 + 3 = 263/3 = 88 fragments; spit 4 + 5 = 207/2 = 104 fragments).

Polygon	AC	Pottery	Other	Total
10120	10	73	19	102

Test Pit		Polygon	10120
Layer	AC	Pottery	Other	Total
Surface		2		2
Spit 1	3	22	1	26
Spit 2	4	171	6	181
Spit 3	2	54		56
Spit 4	9	150	6	165
Spit 5	1	38	3	42
Total	19	437	16	472

The total pickup sampling

Three total pickups were undertaken in the area of the site ShFS01. Two of them were performed in the same polygons where the test pits had been placed, i.e in the polygons with the highest pottery concentration – 10120 (TPU 02) and 10135 (TPU 03). One additional total pickup was conducted later about 140 m west of the centre of Kulugshatepa, in polygon 11149 (TPU 04).

TPU 02

The first pickup was carried out in the polygon 10120 on a recently harvested cotton field. The surface visibility was excellent with no vegetation cover. The FW was represented in the highest amount, comprising fragments from the coin to the half palm size. Four pieces, mainly body fragments, were glazed with the characteristic High Middle Ages decoration (green and white engobe with incised parallel lines incrusted by black colour, **Tab. 3, 1:3**).

Several tiny FW body fragments also featured red slip, indicating the human occupation of earlier periods (from the Greco-Bactrian period up to Kushano-Sasanian period).

Among the RW and the YW no diagnostic fragments were recognized. The AC combined coin size and half palm size fragments including daub and bricks.

TPU 02	Fine Ware	Yellow Ware	Red Ware	Architectural Ceramic	Total
Count (pcs.)	73	37	51	17	178
Weight (g)	229	265	223	591	1308
AvgWeight (g)	3.14	7.16	4.37	34.76	7.35

TPU 03

The second pickup was performed in the polygon 10135, in the field with the same surface and visibility characteristics as the previous one of TPU 02. The detected finds however covered a wider spectrum of material types including (besides those present in TPU 02) also KW and one base of non-contemporary corroded green glass. The fragmentation of all represented classes decreased, with YW and RW reflecting a very similar average size. Among the YW, one decorated stand from the High Middle Ages was found (**Tab. 3, 1:2**). The FW was represented by the biggest amount containing seven glazed fragments, five with the red slip (**Tab. 3, 1:4**) and two body fragments with a textile pattern (**Tab. 3, 1:5–6**). The latter decoration is characteristic for 15th century AD or even more recent periods (Gardin 1957, 47). The AC was composed of four palm size and six coin size fragments, with the rest varying between those two dimensions. Detection of the KW was very important. Although only body fragments were detected, those were the first examples of cooking pots found during the field survey.

TPU 03	Fine Ware	Yellow Ware	Red Ware	Architectural Ceramic	Kitchen Ware	Glass	Total
Count (pcs.)	89	72	44	13	2	1	221
Weight (g)	717	3778	2278	2208	14	<1	8995
AvgWeight (g)	8.06	52.47	51.77	169.85	7	<1	40.7

Fig. 3, 31 Area of ShFS01: Kulugh-Shakhtepa. Photo of the test pit conducted in the polygon 10135. The two different colours visible on the profile are most likely caused by different dryness of the soil, as otherwise the soil characteristics are the same. Photo by Petra Tušlová.

Fig. 3, 32 Area of ShFS01: Kulugh-Shakhtepa. High Middle Age brick found in the Test pit of polygon 10135. Photo by Petra Tušlová.

TPU 04

The third and last total pickup of the ShFS01 was performed in the polygon 11149. The field was waterlogged but harvested, with traces of straw placed on the topsoil, reminiscent of the HDS surface treatment. The visibility varied between excellent and very good. In the polygon itself 171 ancient pottery fragments and pieces of 14 architectural ceramics were detected during the field survey.

In the pickup assemblage once again the FW dominated. It featured a very regular size of fragments ranging between coin and half palm size, among them only three glazed fragments and one red-slipped handle were detected. The YW contained one rim from the High Middle Ages (**Tab. 3, 1:7**) while the RW featured only non-diagnostic pieces. The KW consisted in body fragments of a coin and half palm size.

The number of collected AC – both bricks and daub – is outstanding in the amount regarding the scatter of ShFS01. Two AC fragments were of a palm size, the others varied between half palm size and coin sizes. One waster of 160g was found within the to-

tal pickup, but quite certainly it is all connected with a disused modern brick-kiln, located about 500 m to the west of the Kulugshatepa. The area surrounding the kiln revealed a high amount of greenish waster spread on the adjacent fields, often attached to a piece of a brick.

The scatter chronology and interpretation

The scatter spread around Kulugshatepa is basically constituted of the pottery and architectural ceramics from the High Middle Ages (**Tab. 3, 1:8–11**). In comparison with the other represented epochs, this period is characterized by far the greatest amount of fragments. One sherd of a base and another upper part of a decorated stand were found (**Tab. 3, 1:8–9**), as well as the characteristic appliqué decoration (**Tab. 3, 1:10–11; Tab. 3, 2:1**). One handle of a lamp of light-green glaze decorated by plant tendrils was also detected among the assemblage (**Tab. 3, 2:2**).[45] A similar lamp handle with a more complicated figural decoration was found in scatter

TPU 04	Fine Ware	Yellow Ware	Red Ware	Architectural Ceramic	Kitchen Ware	Total
Count (pcs.)	77	37	18	43	12	**187**
Weight (g)	655	1012	672	1839	236	**4575**
AvgWeight (g)	8.50	27.35	37.33	42.77	19.66	**24.34**

Fig. 3, 33 Area of ShFS01: Kulugh-Shakhtepa with marked features possibly relating to tepas described by Arshavskaya, Rtveladze and Khakimov (1982, 134). CORONA satellite imagery. Map by Petra Tušlová.

ShFS03 (**Tab. 3, 7:6**). Among the other fragments was further found a container for mercury (**Tab. 3, 2:3**), examples of which are known from the 10th–12th centuries AD (e.g., in the exposition of the Archaeological Museum in Termez) and also from the 12th–14th centuries AD in Khorezm (Tol'stov – Vorobeva 1959, 326–327).

The High Middle Ages material is mixed with a much lower amount of Kushan and Kushano-Sasanian pottery represented basically by small FW pottery fragments (**Tab. 3, 2:6**) and exceptionally by storage vessels (**Tab. 3, 2:4**). The Early Middle Ages pottery is present in even lower number than the Kushano-Sasanian pottery. Four pieces including a fragment of a pithos (**Tab. 3, 2:5**) and others of table ware (**Tab. 3, 2:7**) were identified. Except one (the pithos) they were all concentrated in a single polygon (10112) about 60 m distance from Tigrmantepa. Since the chronology of Tigrmantepa includes the Early Middle Ages, those fragments belong with a high probability to the tepa's fallouts.

Another three diagnostic pottery fragments dated to the 16th–18th centuries AD were concentrated in three different polygons – one fragment in each (an example **Tab. 3, 2:8**). Those polygons are located approximately 350 m to the north-east of the centre of Kulugshatepa one next to each other. No other

fragments of the same chronology were identified in the scatter. From the neighbouring tepas, only Kulugshatepa reveals pottery dated from the 16th–18th centuries AD. Due to the low amount of this material found on the fields I would again tend to explain it as fallouts, this time of Kulugshatepa.

During the intensive field survey, the majority of the Kushan and the Kushano-Sasanian pottery was concentrated around the Kulugshatepa itself, while the High Middle Ages pottery was spread all around the fields with a raised amount of the surface material. However, the TPU 03 in polygon 10135, as well as the test pit in the same polygon (over an *arik*, further east of the tepa) also revealed Kushano-Sasanian material.

Except the no-name tepa 73 (Danielisová et al. 2010, 85) which is not dated, the chronology of all of the others surrounding *tepas* feature very similar characteristics. Tigrmantepa covers the Early and the High Middle Ages, Khosyattepa and its immediate vicinity is dated into the Kushan, Kushano-Sasanian and High Middle Ages periods. Kulugshatepa itself might be dated to the Kushan period, the Kushano-Sasanian period, the Early Middle Ages, the High Middle Ages and to the 17th–18th centuries AD.

If we combine the results of the intensive field survey and the total pickups, the pottery scatter located

among those *tepas* is fully contemporary with Kulugshatepa and in the early period also with Khosyatepa (Kushan and the Kushano-Sasanian) and in
a later period with Tigrmantepa (the Early and the
High Middle Age). However, only the Kulugshatepa
was reoccupied during the 16th–18th centuries AD. The
burial-ground located to the north-west of the Kulugshatepa also produced pottery covering the same
time span as that from the scatter (from the Kushan
up to the High Middle Ages). Further, I would not
exclude the possibility of detecting earlier material
also in the case of Tigrmantepa as it is still preserved
into a height of approximately eight meters. The earlier pottery may simply not yet have been disclosed.

The test pits confirmed the chronology of the scatter and pointed to the stratigraphy indicated in the
polygon 10135. There, as mentioned above, the High
Middle Ages brick was placed about 60 to 70 cm
underground, while the Early Middle Ages vessel
(**Tab. 3, 1:1**) was detected between 90 to 100 cm
underground.

According to Arshavskaya et al. (1982, 134) another three *tepas* were visible in the area of Kulugshatepa
in the 80s of the 20th century. First, known as Shortantepa (dimensions 30 × 10 × 0.5 m), dated into the
High Middle Ages, it was located about 150 m to the
north-east of Kulugshatepa. The other two *tepas* are
said to have been located about 250 m and 300 m to
the south-east. First, Nagaratepa (30 × 20 × 3 m) was
dated into the Early Middle Ages. The latter one was
called Kultepa (20 × 10 × 0.5 m) with no closer chronological data.

If we compare the northern area of Kulugshatepa
with the archive CORONA satellite imagery, several
different places might be attributed to the Shortantepa, although none of them very clearly (**Fig. 3, 33**).
On the other hand, the south-eastern area does not
feature any anomaly at all, only ploughed fields. However, if we change the given direction from the south-
east to the south-west, two possible features appear.
Consequently, we could attribute the Nagaratepa to
No-name tepa 73 located about 190 m from the edge
of Kulugshatepa. No-name tepa 73 is still preserved
up to the three meters, which is also the height of
Nagaratepa given by Arshavskaya et al. (1982, 134).
Another feature in the map located about 320 m from
the edge of Kulugshatepa might then be associated
with Kultepa (**Fig. 3, 33**). On the current satellite image there is no such feature visible anymore which
might be easily explained by the height of the Kultepa
in the 80s, when it already measured 0.5 m only. To
undertake such an explanation, we have to presume
a confusion of cardinal directions mentioned in the
publication of Arshavskaya et al. (1982), then we

might quite easily attribute individual *tepas* to particular features.

Arshavskaya et al. (1982, 134) also suggest, that
all of the *tepas* they discuss, are remnants of one single site which used to be a part of Kulugshatepa.
I agree with this statement, and additionally, based
on the results of the survey, total pickups and test pits,
I would also suggest the area of the moder-day cemetery, No-name tepa 73 (Nagaratepa?), Tigrmantepa
and Khosyattepa be included into the one integrated
settlement, whose remnants are represented by all of
these surrounded mounds, but from the biggest part
by Kulugshatepa, which might be the elevated citadel
of the settlement.

3.8.2 The area of Gorintepa (scatter ShFS02)

3.8.2.1 Location

The pottery accumulation connected with the second scatter started about 5.5 km to the east of the
centre of Sherabad along the road heading for Kizirik
and Kumkurgan. The pottery finds were detected
largely south of the road, since the area to the north
of it was largely covered by the houses of the contemporary village of Gorin. Only one small field of an
area 0.51 ha could be surveyed in the agglomeration
north of the road (**Fig. 3, 21** and **34**).

About 110 m north of the road lies the four to
five meters high mound of Gorintepa. Another preserved *tepa* located nearby is called Gilyambobtepa,
located about 1200 m away from the eastern edge
of Gorintepa. According to the topographical map
(1:100,000 scale), another *tepa* was supposed to lie
about 1300 m to the west of the western boundaries
of Gorintepa (**Fig. 3, 35**). Despite its quite sizeable
dimensions (320 × 100 × 4 m) neither *tepa* nor surface
material was detected in the defined area. The feature
was investigated without setting up polygons as it was
located in the grounds of a factory which might have
caused its complete destruction.

3.8.2.2 A general description

The scatter is represented in total by 25 polygons
stretched along the road. They cover 13 ha spreading
over 746 m in the west-east and 300 m in the north-
south direction (**Fig. 3, 34**). Overall 727 pottery
fragments might be attributed to the site, on average
consisting of 56 fragments per hectare. There were
no stones or modern pottery fragments on the field.
Architectural ceramics were represented by ten fragments only which were concentrated in the marginal

---

[45] Very similar lamp fragment was found in Asanas dated into the 13th century AD (Bakturskaya 1979, 127–133).

Fig. 3, 34 Area of ShFS02: Gorintepa showing raised amount of pottery. IKONOS satellite imagery. Map by Petra Tušlová.

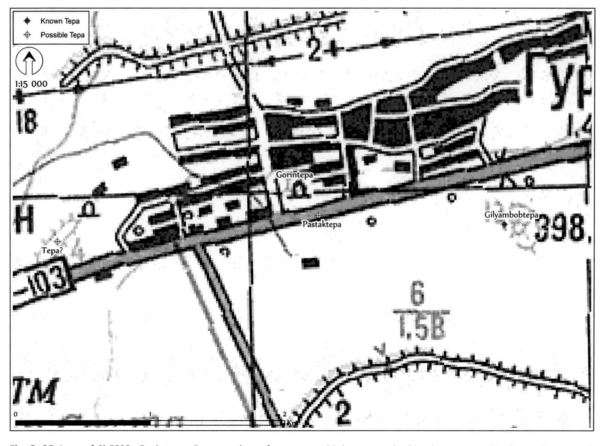

Fig. 3, 35 Area of ShFS02: Gorintepa. Feature about four meters high was marked in the topographical map (1:100,000) on the west from Gorintepa, while following the road to Sherabad. Currently neither the elevated hill, nor pottery scatter was found in there. Map by Petra Tušlová.

western part of the site next to the road leading to the south.

During the first year of prospecting we learned from the local inhabitants that a *tepa* called "Pastak-tepa" (in Uzbek meaning "wide and low tepa") was located in the area directly south of the road. According to the statement of residents, the *tepa* was visible in the time of their fathers and grandfathers. The *tepa* was presumably destroyed during the road construction, which seems to lead directly through the mound.

No other features except Gorintepa are visible in the CORONA satellite imagery (**Fig. 3, 36**). However, the area of the presumable location of Pastaktepa seems to have been already cultivated by the time the imagery was captured. Due to the basic characteristic of the Pastaktepa expressed by its name, "low and wide", it was susceptible to early destruction caused by agricultural activity.

Seasons 2010 and 2011

During the first year of prospecting the eastern part of the scatter was examined (**Fig. 3, 37**). An area of nine hectares revealed 508 pottery fragments concentrated in 18 polygons, i.e., 56 pottery pieces per hectare. The surface treatment combined transects of ploughed field of excellent visibility with pasture of very good or good visibility. The surveyed area also covered a small field placed in between a road (to the north) and an elevated *arik* (to the south) running parallel with the road at a distance of 30 m. In this small strip of private corn field, featuring very good to low visibility, two small polygons were placed. One of them, of dimensions 75 × 30 m covering 0.2 ha, produced a high amount of surface material: 45 ancient pottery fragments. No clear AC ancient fragments were found there. Several thick sherds of hand size were detected on the westernmost part of the surveyed field along the dirt road leading to the south, separating the ploughed field from the un-surveyed eastern part overgrown by cotton (which was examined the following year). The fragments lacking any diagnostic features might have been those of big vessels as well as of architectural ceramics. Ten hand and palm size fragments of a terracotta cauldron stand were also collected in four polygons. The fragments have a uniform dark red colour and about three centimetres thick walls. It seems they all belonged to a single vessel dated to the 17th–18th centuries AD (**Tab. 3, 3:1**).

The remaining area below the road was surveyed in the west-east direction from a distance of 720 m from the previously detected scatter. However, the area of increased pottery amount continued only in another three transects directly adjacent to the previously surveyed fields. In eight polygons covering four hectares, 219 pottery fragments and ten fragments of architectural ceramics were counted, with the average amount of 57 pieces per hectare.

The surface of the investigated area was a mixture of ploughed fields with excellent visibility and HDS surface treatments with good visibility. The other investigated area located further west did not reveal any surface material. It was covered by a combination of sparse cotton bushes, ploughed fields and HDS treatment.

One additional polygon located to the north of the road was surveyed. It represents the only connecting link between the Gorintepa and the scatter spread to the south of the road. The investigated field had HDS surface treatment with excellent visibility. In total 193 ancient pottery fragments and 11 pieces of AC were detected in the area of 0.51 ha, revealing a much higher amount of surface material than the rest of the polygons connected to the ShFS02.

3.8.2.3 The test pits

Four test pits were placed in the area of the presumable location of Pastaktepa. One of them was placed in polygon 10534, another one in polygon 10533. The remaining two were performed in the polygon 10610, located in a corn field. All of them were situated in the probable central part of the tepa, which was indicated by the locals. The dimensions of the test pits remained unchanged, the depth, however, varied according to the different conditions of every pit. Considering the polygon 10534 and 10533, the test pits were placed in the westernmost part of the investigated field, in the close vicinity of a dirt road leading in the north-south direction between the fields (**Fig. 3, 38**).

The polygon and the test pit 10534

During the intensive field survey in the polygon 10534 only 68 ancient pottery fragments were detected. No AC or modern pottery were registered at all. The surface of the examined field was ploughed, the soil was very dry and hard, which made the following excavation difficult. The upper 55 cm were uncovered, revealing about 26 pottery fragments. Most of the pottery was obtained, however, in the first 30 cm and the amount of the material sharply declined in the lower layer. The pottery was in general very fragmentary except the only diagnostic sherd dated to the 17th–18th centuries AD (**Tab. 3, 3:2**).

The excavation work was stopped at 55 cm because of the hardness of the soil. Since the test pit 10533 revealed a very similar characteristic it was decided to continue only in one place and to open two other trenches in the polygon 10610 with more favourable excavation conditions.

In the case of the test pit 10534, the top soil was probably fully uncovered, but the judgment is made only on the basis of the excavated depth. The soil kept a grey to grey-brown colour through all the mechanical layers with no apparent transition.

54

Fig. 3, 36 Area of ShFS02: Gorintepa. The Pastaktepa, known from the local oral tradition, is not even visible on the archive CORONA satellite imagery. Map by Petra Tušlová.

Fig. 3, 37 Area of ShFS02: Gorintepa with marked fields surveyed in 2010 and 2011. IKONOS satellite imagery. Map by Petra Tušlová.

Fig. 3, 38 Area of ShFS02: Gorintepa with marked areas of Total pickups and Test pits conducted in specific polygons. IKONOS satellite imagery. Map by Petra Tušlová.

The polygon and the test pit 10533

The test pit in the polygon 10533 was placed about 90 m to the north of the previous pit, in a field with the same characteristics. The intensive field survey revealed 79 ancient pottery fragments concentrated in the polygon, but no other material was detected.

The first 50 cm of the test pit revealed features very similar to the previous trench. Also the decreasing tendency of the material quantity was noted. However, below the depth of 50 to 60 cm the pottery amount started to increase again.

The soil was grey and grey-brown down to a depth of approximately 70 cm, where an orange and grey clay coloration with a low amount of charcoal appeared. After another 30 cm was excavated the soil became harder, resembling the characteristics of a mud-brick wall. Two palm size fragments of a big vessel divided the upper orange and grey soil from the harder, clayish one, placed beneath it. At about the same depth (ca. 100 cm) tiny white stripes appeared on the profiles accompanied by grey-green clayish layers and an increased amount of charcoal. The same characteristics continued down to 120 cm, the maximum excavated depth.

A few tiny fragments with a red slip resembling Kushan and Kushano-Sasanian pottery were detected in the top soil. One rim fragment of a pithos was dated

by T. Annaev to the turn of the Kushano-Sasanian period and the Early Middle Ages (**Tab. 3, 3:3**).

Polygon	AC	Pottery	Other	Total
10533		79		79

Test Pit			Polygon	10533
Layer	AC	Pottery	Other	Total
Surface		1		1
Spit 1	2	49	1	52
Spit 2	1	20		21
Spit 3		32		32
Spit 4	1	57	1	59
Spit 5	9	60	4	73
Spit 6	1	2	1	4
Total	14	220	7	241

The polygon and the test pit 10610_01

Two test pits were additionally opened in the corn field situated along the road heading for Kizirik and Kumkurgan (**Fig. 3, 38**). The field was regularly watered which made the soil softer and better suited for the excavation. During the field survey, 45 ancient pottery fragments were detected in this small-sized polygon with dimensions 75 × 30 m.

The first trench, numbered 10610_01, was placed to the north, at about 20 m distance from the test pit 10533. The trench was dug to the depth of 200 cm. In the profiles (but not on the excavated soil) two layers were distinguishable, not without difficulties. The first one, of light brown/grey clayish soil, covered approximately the upper 60 cm. It contained pottery, coin size pebbles and charcoal.

The second layer was basically grey, but coloured by the alternating dark grey and orange clayish lenses. In comparison with the previous layer, the amount of charcoal increased while the number of pebbles diminished. Not far from the bottom, at the depth of 185 cm, the charcoal and pottery disappeared. There were, however, no significant changes in the soil structure. The bedrock was not reached and the test pit was abandoned because of the threat of its potential collapse (**Fig. 3, 39**).

Fig. 3, 39 Area of ShFS02: Gorintepa. Test pit 10610_01. Photo by Petra Tušlová.

Fig. 3, 40 Area of ShFS02: Gorintepa. Test pit 10610_02. Photo by Petra Tušlová.

In the upper 50 cm (the top soil) a few small pottery fragments from the 17th–18th centuries AD were detected. In the lower layers, however, Kushan and Kushano-Sasanian pottery appeared in a bigger amount than was detected during the field survey. In the spit 7 (from 120 to 140 cm) Kushano-Sasanian pottery (**Tab. 3, 3:4**),[46] Kushan pottery (**Tab. 3, 3:5**) and Early Middle Ages fragments were detected. The material further included several fragments of a strainer, three different necks of jars, one spindle and a terracotta token (**Tab. 3, 4:1–4**). Diagnostic pottery, covering the periods mentioned above, was recognized down to the end of the spit 8, deeper spits revealed only non-diagnostic small FW sherds and body fragments of big jars.

The AC is represented by daub only. The "other" material includes solely bones. The number of the pottery fragments contained in the individual spits alternated with no evident pattern. The lowest number was detected in the top soil, while majority of the pottery is connected with a layer from 120 to 140 cm, which was rich on finds in general.

This test pit was the deepest one excavated during the project. Quite surprisingly sterile soil or bedrock was not reached. The depth of two meters and more of cultural layers might have been caused by alluvial deposits of a river as well as by long term artificial irrigation of the fields.

Polygon	AC	Pottery	Other	Total
10610		45		**45**

Test Pit			Polygon	10610_01
Layer	AC	Pottery	Other	Total
Surface				
Spit 1		11		11
Spit 2	1	15		16
Spit 3		13	3	16
Spit 4	2	35	2	39
Spit 5	19	34	2	55
Spit 6	2	16		18
Spit 7	1	63		64
Spit 8	2	22		24
Spit 9		27	1	28
Total	**27**	**236**	**8**	**271**

The polygon and the test pit 10610_02

The second pit placed in the same corn field was located about 11 m to the north of the first trench and about 12 m to the south of the road. It was excavated

---

[46] Determined according to similarity to the pottery found in Dalverzitepa (Nekrasova – Pugachenkova 1978, 157).

to the depth of 140 cm, to the surface of the spit 8, where the work was stopped due to groundwater flooding the trench.

The soil structure revealed very similar characteristics to the previous test pit in the area, only the upper layer reached 30 cm underground. The second layer was cut by a three centimeters thick grey-green sandy deposit, varying in depth from of 80 to 120 cm. The grey and orange clayish lenses were mixed with burned spots up to the bottom of the trench (**Fig. 3, 40**).

This test pit was not rich in diagnostic pieces. The detected material mainly contained small body fragments or non-significant sherds of big jars. Only the Kushan or Kushano-Sasanian red-slipped FW was recognized to the deepest layer, while body fragments of big vessels were present only down to the bottom of the spit 4. The architectural ceramics was again composed of daub only while the "other" group of bones only, see below table:

Test Pit			Polygon	10610_02
Layer	AC	Pottery	Other	Total
Surface		1		1
Spit 1	3	36		39
Spit 2	2	35		37
Spit 3	3	24	1	28
Spit 4	3	44	6	53
Spit 5	1	27	4	32
Spit 6	2	13	1	16
Spit 7	2	19	2	23
Total	16	198	14	228

Polygon	AC	Pottery	Other	Total
10610		45		45

3.8.2.4 The total pickup sampling

Two total pickups were realized in the area of ShFS02. The first one (TPU 05) was placed in the questionable area (polygon 11189) located to the north of the road, between the Gorintepa and the newly located Pastaktepa. The second one was performed in the central part of the polygon 10533 (TPU 6), in the probable original place of the Pastaktepa.

TPU 05

The first pickup was placed in the HDS field with very good visibility. During the field survey an outstanding amount of pottery fragments was detected in the polygon 11189 (193 pcs. of pottery and 11 pcs. of AC), but none of them was diagnostic. Consequently, the main aim of the total pickup was to detect some significant fragments that could help to assign the area either to Gorintepa or to Pastaktepa.

Overall 169 fragments were detected in the total pickup, with the highest portion of YW, which was unfortunately non-diagnostic. A similar situation was also in case of RW and KW, which were both represented by body fragments only. One third of the FW fragments is covered with red slip, but only three of them are significant enough, revealing one Kushan fragment[47] (**Tab. 3, 4:5**) and two Kushano-Sasanian sherds[48] (**Tab. 3, 4:6–7**). The rest of the FW material is quite fragmentary, ranging between the coin and the half palm size, reflecting the highest fragmentation of all of the material from the pickup. On the other hand, the lowest fragmentation is among YW and AC fragments, ranging around palm size.

The total pickup confirmed the presence of Kushan and Kushano-Sasanian periods, but as most of the collected material is non-diagnostic and quite fragmented, sherds of different periods possibly present in the remaining material cannot be excluded from the final consideration.

TPU 06

The TPU 06 took place in a harvested cotton field with the cotton bushes still left in place. The visibility on the surface was thus lowered from excellent to very good. The pottery and the AC fragments from the pickup were more fragmentary than in the previous case, but at the same time they were represented by a higher number – 221 fragments. The YW was again predominant in the assemblage, even though it was composed of smaller pieces. Most of the fragments might be parts of a big pithoi, such as the one with impressed finger decoration on the rim dated to the final

TPU 05	Fine Ware	Yellow Ware	Red Ware	Architectural Ceramic	Cooking Pots	Waster	Total
Count (pcs.)	47	73	24	19	5	1	169
Weight (g)	413	4940	1017	1085	92	54	7601
AvgWeight (g)	8.78	67.67	42.37	57.10	18.4	54	44.97

[47] Similar fragments are known from Ai-Khanum (Lyonnet 1997, 394).
[48] Both fragments have parallels in the material detected in Dalverzintepa (Nekrasova – Pugachenkova 1978, 157).

TPU 06	Fine Ware	Yellow Ware	Red Ware	Architectural Ceramic	Cooking Pots	Total
Count (pcs.)	50	110	49	9	3	221
Weight (g)	642	4135	1816	512	29	7134
AvgWeight (g)	12.84	37.59	37.06	56.88	9.66	32.28

stage of the Early Middle Ages (**Tab. 3, 4:8**). Another pithos dated to the turn of the Kushano-Sasanian period and the Early Middle Ages, was classed due to its dark red colour in the RW category (**Tab. 3, 4:9**). In the FW material, several red slipped pottery fragments were detected. One FW Kushan rim (**Tab. 3, 4:10**) has parallels in the settlement of Toprak-kala in Khorezm (Nerazik – Rapoport 1981, 15). Another fragment of a base of a small goblet might be dated to the end of Kushano-Sasanian period (**Tab. 3, 4:11**).

Three bricks and six pieces of daub belong to the AC material. The fragments range between absolutely tiny pieces and one palm-size sample, covering all size-categories in between them.

3.8.2.5 The scatter chronology and interpretation

First, I would like to mention the chronology of the *tepas* in the surrounding of the surveyed area. Gorintepa, as well as Gilyambobtepa were both occupied constantly from the Kushan through the Kushano-Sasanian period to the Early Middle Ages. The settlement chronology of the newly discovered Pastaktepa is, however, much longer. The surface material detected during the field survey consisted of several random fragments of the Greco-Bactrian period (**Tab. 3, 5:1–2**), and numerous fragments of Kushan (**Tab. 3, 5:3**) and Kushano-Sasanian pottery (**Tab. 3, 5:4**). The Early Middle Ages fragments were not detected during the field survey at all. A few of them were, however, concentrated in the TPU 06 (**Tab. 3, 4:8**). Only one fragment is decorated in a seemingly High Middle Ages manner (**Tab. 3, 5:5**). No other such fragments were found on the field or in the test pits. An unusual pottery class, not known from the surrounding tepas, is represented by the 17th–18th centuries AD material, recognized only to the south of the road to Kizirik. Several fragments of a cauldron stand have already been mentioned (**Tab. 3, 3:1**), besides these, a bowl with green/light-blue glaze and a rim of a pithos of pink fabric were found (**Tab. 3, 5:6–7** and **Tab. 3, 3:2**).

During the 2010 investigation, the 17th–18th centuries AD material was detected in the greatest amount. Only a few body fragments of Kushan and Kushano-Sasanian pottery were found. The 2011 season, however, disclosed much more numerous remains of both Kushan and Kushano-Sasanian pottery, although highly fragmented. The main classes of both periods encountered on the fields were FW together with pithoi.

Moreover, four Greco-Bactrian fragments (**Tab. 3, 5:1–2**) were detected during the field survey. This is the only scatter where this period is attested. The settlement might have already begun in the Greco-Bactrian period, but the revision of the material from the test pits did not produce any other proof to support this suggestion. Two hypotheses might come to consideration. Firstly: The Greco-Bactrian layers were not reached in the trenches as we did not excavate on the right spot, but they might have been brought to the surface from the lower layers by chance. Secondly: the pottery might have been brought here secondarily, having no connectivity with this area. In any case, the discovery of the Greco-Bactrian material on the surface is very rare in the Sherabad District, and so far, only several sites yield material from this period (see **Chapter 5.4.** in this book). The scatter ShFS02 might be interpreted as an individual site, and without hesitation associated with the Pastaktepa, a low mound destroyed in the past. However, the polygon 11189, located halfway between the Gorintepa and the probable site of Pastaktepa (**Fig. 3, 34**) might represent a connecting line between those two features. Both Gorintepa and Pastaktepa reveal Kushan, Kushano-Sasanian and Early Middle Ages pottery, which testifies to their belonging to the period from the 1st to the beginning of the 8th century AD.

The road to Kizirik seems to be built through the ancient settlement (the *tepa*), as the surface material dispersion continues on both sites into the immediate vicinity of the road. In such a case Gorintepa and Pastaktepa can also be seen as a single site, which was gradually destroyed by the road construction and by the agricultural activity ploughing away the remaining parts of the tepa. The pottery of the 17th–18th centuries AD may reflect a short-term settlement concentrated only in a limited part of the site – its southern area. The material dispersion reaching up to the road may be, of course, also caused by the road building activity, which brought the pottery closer to the road or simply mingled the material from one side of the road to the other. In any case, the existence and chronology of Pastaktepa was proven and approximately determined, while its possible connection to Gorintepa remains open.

3.8.3 The area of Shishtepa (scatter ShFS03)

3.8.3.1 Location

The third area with an increased number of surface pottery finds starts about two kilometres to the east of the second site, while following the road to Kizirik and Kumkurgan (**Fig. 3, 21**). The main *tepa* connected with the scatter is called Shishtepa and it is located about 540 m to the south of the road. The increased amount of pottery covers the immediate surroundings of the Shishtepa in all cardinal directions, but to the greatest extent in the northern area up to the road. Only one strip of ground, 360 m wide and 313 m long, leading directly from the Shishtepa to the road is built-on by houses and remained un-surveyed (**Fig. 3, 41**). The buildings have been constructed in the last 40 years as on the CORONA satellite imagery there are no visible structures (**Fig. 3, 42**).

There are no other *tepas* in the close vicinity of the scatter, except one questionable feature of dimensions 20 × 20 m noticeable on the CORONA satellite imagery. On the imagery it is located about 50 m to the south of the road (**Fig. 3, 42**). Nowadays, there are no remains of any elevation in the terrain, as well as no pottery scatter recognized on the field. The most recent Google Earth imagery does not capture any distinguishable anomaly in that area and, unfortunately, the IKONOS imagery does not cover this part; consequently, the phenomena cannot be compared with a recent picture.

A general description

The pottery scatter concentrated around Shishtepa covers 830 m in the west-east and 998 m in the north-south directions (**Fig. 3, 41**). The total area of 35 ha is represented by 69 polygons in which 4149 ancient pottery fragments, 11 modern ones and 183 architectural ceramics were detected. A high number of stones was marked only in the polygon 10784 with the highest pottery amount (392 pcs, see below). Modern pottery and AC were detected only in marginal areas of the scatter. The houses north of Shishtepa are most likely to be placed on the top of the site as they are surrounded by a dense pottery scatter. Further, a decreasing pottery amount correlating to a growing distance from the un-surveyed area might be noticed. From this phenomenon we can assume that the core of the ancient settlement lies under the houses.

During the field survey in 2010 our team learned from a local man living in the area adjacent to the scatter, that about three years ago a human skeleton, with earrings in the shape of a half-moon, was found during an excavation of a water channel. The find was supposed to have been made in a pit about 1.5 m deep. He localized the approximate place of the burial

Fig. 3, 41 Area of ShFS03: Shishtepa showing raised amount of pottery and the two special finds we have learned about from the locals. IKONOS satellite imagery. Map by Petra Tušlová.

Fig. 3, 42 Area of ShFS03: Shishtepa. North-west from Shishtepa a small feature (20 x 20m) might be detected in the CORONA satellite imagery. Currently, there is no elevated feature visible *in situ*, as well as the area did not revealed any particular amount of pottery. Map by Petra Tušlová.

Fig. 3, 43 Area of ShFS03: Shishtepa with marked fields surveyed in 2010 and 2011. IKONOS satellite imagery. Map by Petra Tušlová.

about 200 m to the east of Shishtepa. Another local man was supposed to have made a similar discovery. According to his words, he found a human skull in a big jar while he walked on a freshly ploughed field (**Fig. 3, 41–42**). Both of the human remains were allegedly reburied in a different place in the surroundings of the Shishtepa. During the prospecting of the field featuring the characteristics of a burial ground, no special finds were detected. The spot, where the skeleton was supposed to have been discovered, was localised by its finder into an irrigation channel creating a border between two fields. From this spot, the western field features an increased pottery amount which is considered as a part of the scatter. The eastern field, on the other hand, reveals almost no pottery finds. However, if the burials were placed at such a depth – 1.5 m – a possibility of material getting out to the surface is very small. In this case, only well positioned trenches may clarify this open question of a presence of a burial place in the vicinity of Shishtepa.

Seasons 2010 and 2011

During the project's first year, most of the area of the increased amount of surface material was investigated (**Fig. 3, 43**). The north-west and the north-east of Shishtepa with a small part to the south of the *tepa* were surveyed. In 42 polygons connected to the scatter 2123 ancient pottery fragments and 16 modern ones were counted. No ancient architectural ceramics were detected, only 11 fragments of modern bricks. In the overall 21 ha a high number of pottery finds was recorded: on average 102 various fragments per hectare. The surface of the field had been harrowed shortly before the survey and offered excellent visibility.

Irrigation channels created the borders of the scatter in the north-eastern and north-western part of the pottery dispersion (**Fig. 3, 41**). This is an excellent example of their secondary function – keeping the surface material in the approximate place of its origin. We can clearly see that the irrigation system was built at the same time the fields started to be regularly cultivated as there are no modern-time built water structures (*ariks* or *zebers*) visible at the CORONA imagery yet (**Fig. 3, 42**).

The few remaining areas of the scatter were investigated in the second year of the project. The western and the south-eastern parts in the close vicinity of Shishtepa were surveyed, with one additional area of four polygons, located to the north of Shishtepa, right next to the road. In a total of 24 polygons, 2026 ancient pottery fragments and 164 architectural ceramics fragments were detected. There was no modern pottery or modern fragments of architectural ceramics. The visibility of the field varied. It was partly composed of ploughed fields with very good visibility, by HDS fields, also with very good visibility, and by

partly harvested cotton field with changing conditions between very good and good visibility. Overall 13 ha were covered, making thus 169 fragments of variable material in one hectare.

The ancient AC fragments make up a strip about 160 m wide leading from Shishtepa to the east. It reaches a maximum distance of 550 m to the west of the tepa. Several other fragments were detected in the single polygon up to 200 m from Shishtepa (**Fig. 3, 44**).

The test pits

Two test pits were placed in the polygons 10783 and 10784, one in each. It was these two polygons which yielded the greatest amount of surface pottery found during the 2010 season. Both polygons lay to the north-east of Shishtepa at an approximate distance of 150 to 160 m (**Fig. 3, 45**).

The dimensions of the pits, the very first ones excavated, were smaller than of the later ones since we experimented with their size, trying to find the smallest possible, but still comfortable, dimensions. They measured 50 × 80 cm which however proved to be insufficient. It was difficult to excavate into the lower spits and also to evaluate the profiles. For these reasons it was decided to enlarge the area of the pit to 80 × 100 cm, which was much more suitable for digging (**Fig. 3, 17**).

The surface of the whole field was furrowed, however during the intensive field survey, which took place several days before the test pit, it was harrowed. The visibility was excellent in both cases, no matter which different field condition there was.

Both pits again revealed very similar characteristics. The soil was composed of a light-grey coloured soil with clayish lentils of a dark grey colour, small pebbles, charcoal and pottery fragments.

The polygon and the test pit 10783

The first test pit was placed in the polygon 10783 in which 320 ancient pottery fragments and one architectural ceramic sherd were detected during the field survey. The pit was dug down to the depth of 60 cm where a mud brick wall stopped the excavation. Three spits revealed 170 ancient pottery fragments, three shards of AC, two pieces of glass and 41 of bones.

Coin size glazed body fragments with a decoration characteristic of the High Middle Ages were detected in all three spits. The other material found in the test pit was non-diagnostic, with very high fragmentation. Not even body fragments of red-slipped sherds were detected in the whole assemblage. Among the AC only three bricks and one daub were found, which confirms the low rate of architecture ceramics fragments in this area in general.

Even though the test pit was smaller than those described above, it revealed a very similar amount of pottery. The pottery fragmentation was, however, very high in comparison to the other scatters.

Fig. 3, 44 Area of ShFS03: Shishtepa, showing raised amount of Architectural Ceramics (AC) concentrated around the tepa. IKONOS satellite imagery. Map by Petra Tušlová.

Fig. 3, 45 Area of ShFS03: Shishtepa with marked areas of Total pickups and Test pits conducted in specific polygons. IKONOS satellite imagery. Map by Petra Tušlová.

Polygon	AC	Pottery	Other	Total
10783	1	320		321

Test Pit			Polygon	10783
Layer	AC	Pottery	Other	Total
Surface		7		7
Spit 1	1	27	3	31
Spit 2	2	38	9	49
Spit 3	1	59	31	91
Total	4	124	43	171

The polygon and the test pit 10784

The polygon 10784 placed to the north-east of Shishtepa is adjacent to the polygon 10783 on its eastern side. The intensive field survey revealed 392 ancient pottery fragments accumulated on the surface of the polygon, while no modern sherds or architectural ceramics were detected.

The test pit was carried out to a depth of 90 cm, where groundwater appeared and stopped the excavation. Therefore, the last spit 5 remained unfinished and had to be reduced to the depth of ten centimetres only.

In total 142 ancient pottery fragments were revealed. The excavated material was very fragmentary, mostly represented by non-diagnostic body fragments. The AC was represented by seven daubs only. The same situation as in the previous pit repeated itself: the High Middle Ages sherds of small dimen-

Polygon	AC	Pottery	Other	Total
10784		392		392

Test Pit			Polygon	10784
Layer	AC	Pottery	Other	Total
Surface		3		3
Spit 1	1	29	1	31
Spit 2	1	30	2	33
Spit 3		20	1	21
Spit 4	4	45	4	53
Spit 5 ½	1	18	2	21
Total	7	142	10	159

sions were detected down to the lowest spit, while red-slipped ware was not found at all.

The amount of the pottery in the first three spits was 79 fragments, while it was 124 fragments in the case of the test pit in the polygon 10783. These results are contrary to the amount of the material found during the field survey, in which the polygon 10784 yielded 392 fragments, while in the polygon 10783 only 320 sherds were noted.

The total pickup sampling

Three total pickups were undertaken in the site ShFS03, each in a different direction from the Shishtepa. The TPU 07 was placed in the same square as the previous test pit – in the polygon 10783. The second one, TPU 08, was situated about 140 m from the *tepa* in the south-eastern direction, in the area in which the skeleton was allegedly discovered (polygon 11193). The last pickup TPU 09 (polygon 10899) was situated to the north-west, 330 m from Shishtepa (**Fig. 3, 45**).

TPU 07

The material assemblage of the TPU 07 was very heterogeneous. A large amount of FW fragments was detected. The two largest sherds were of a palm size, the other 21 pieces varied between palm size and a coin size and the remaining amount was even smaller than a coin. A vast majority of the diagnostic FW pottery fragments belonged to the High Middle Ages (**Tab. 3, 6:1–3**), most of them were, however, only body fragments with incised or glazed decoration (**Tab. 3, 6:2**). Only one FW fragment with a bright blue glaze and incised stripes in a black colour dated to the 16th–17th centuries AD was detected within the assemblage.

The YW was also highly represented; its fragmentation was more or less uniform, basically around the coin or half palm size. The RW featured similar fragmentation, although it consisted of a smaller sherd number. The AC was present as both bricks (7 pcs.) and daubs (18 pcs.). Out of them three sherds were hand size, five were bigger than a coin and the rest was about a coin size. The three fragments of glass were very tiny, all together not weighting even a gram.

TPU 08

The field in which the polygon 11193 was set up and where the eighth pickup was conducted, had been ploughed and therefore offered excellent visibility.

TPU 07	Fine Ware	Yellow Ware	Red Ware	Architectural Ceramic	Kitchen Ware	Glass	Total
Count (pcs.)	144	149	41	25	11	3	373
Weight (g)	840	3270	810	2982	197	<1	8099
AvgWeight (g)	5.8	21.9	19.8	119	17.9	<1	21.7

TPU 08	Fine Ware	Yellow Ware	Red Ware	Architectural Ceramic	Kitchen Ware	Total
Count (pcs.)	65	85	39	14	1	204
Weight (g)	264	1306	541	304	1	2416
AvgWeight (g)	4	15.4	13.9	21.7	1	11.8

During the intensive field survey 159 ancient pottery fragments were detected; no modern pottery, architectural ceramics or stones were noticed.

The field survey in the area around the TPU 08 revealed pottery of the Kushano-Sasanian period (**Tab. 3, 6:4**[49]**–5**[50]), which did not appear in the rest of the scatter. Consequently, its occurrence was the reason for placing the TPU 08 right here.

The FW pottery detected in the test pit was even more fragmentary than in the TPU 07, with about eight fragments ranging from half palm size to a coin size. The remaining number consisted of fragments smaller than a coin size, from which about seven pieces were red-slipped. The AC was represented by small fragments of daub, the biggest example of which measured only 5 × 4 cm. One sherd of a KW pot with a burned surface was counted. The YW and the RW was represented by body fragments only.

Compared to the previous total pickup (TPU 07), no glazed or otherwise decorated pottery characteristic of the High Middle Ages was found. On the contrary the red-slipped fragments reflect an earlier occupation concentrated in this south-eastern area.

TPU 09

The last total pickup of the scatter ShFS03 was placed in the polygon 10899, which had been surveyed during the first year of the project. The surface survey revealed 93 ancient pottery fragments, no other material was detected. During the total pickups the field was harrowed with excellent visibility.

The material found during the total pickup contained a surprisingly high amount of AC. The category was represented by 14 fragments of bricks and 51 lumps of daub. The size of the AC ranged from tiny pieces to palm size fragments with maximum dimensions 10 × 8 cm. The YW was again prevalent in number. Among the other fragments it included part of a decorated stand dated to the High Middle Ages (**Tab. 3, 6:6**), and several body fragments with incised decoration of the same date. Another High Middle Ages fragment, a rim of a bowl, was detected in the RW (**Tab. 3, 6:7**).

Among the FW pottery, pieces of the High Middle Ages and also of the 16th–17th centuries AD were represented. The latter two are both decorated by glaze, but with a different colour and pattern (**Tab. 3, 6:8–9**). An unusual find is a body fragment of an Arab GW, with impressed decoration and a letter, dated between the 12th–14th centuries AD (Vakturskaya 1959, 312; **Tab. 3, 6:10**).

An exceptional find was made by detecting several GW pottery fragments from the end of the 4th century AD (identified and classed by Sh. Shaydullaev; **Tab. 3, 6:11–12**). Similar fragments with the same characteristic were found during the field survey in polygon 10899, i.e., where the total pickup was placed. One more polygon 10900, attached to 10899 directly to the north, revealed several very similar pottery pieces.

The scatter chronology and interpretation

The area investigated during the first year of the prospecting revealed almost exclusively High Middle Ages pottery (**Tab. 3, 6:13; 7:1–6**). Two parts of different stands and a body fragment with imprinted floral decoration were detected (**Tab. 3, 7:1–3**). Also one handle of a green-glazed lamp again with an imprinted decoration, this time depicting two doves surrounded by plant tendrils, was found (**Tab. 3, 7:6**). Almost the same representation on the lamp is known from town of Bactra, where it is dated to the 14th–15th centuries AD (Gardin 1957, 66–68, Type 2).

In contrast, the areas surveyed in 2011 yielded a high amount of Kushano-Sasanian pottery (**Tab. 3,**

TPU 09	Fine Ware	Yellow Ware	Red Ware	Architectural Ceramic	Kitchen Ware	Grey Ware	Total
Count (pcs.)	67	75	27	65	16	10	260
Weight (g)	611	1501	760	3639	152	108	6771
AvgWeight (g)	9.1	20	28.1	56	9.5	10.8	26

---

[49] This morphological shape might be as well dated into the Kushano-Sasanian period (Nerazik – Rapoport 1981, 87) or into the Early Middle Ages (Suleymanov 2000, 181). The Kushano-Sasanian period is however preferred, as the red slip is thicker and very well done which refers to earlier production.

[50] The form is well known from Aktepa (Sedov 1987, Tab. XVI/3).

6:4–5; Tab. 7:7[51]). Also the architectural ceramics of this period were recorded in a higher amount, covering continually a strip of land directly to the west of Shishtepa. It seems probable, that the architectural fragments correspond to the earlier settlement. The area adjacent to the Shishtepa immediately to the west, south and east, features AC fragments and Kushano-Sasanian material, neither of which was detected in the northern parts of the scatter. The northernmost situated area with the earliest dated material is in the polygon 10899 (TPU 09), where the GW from the end of the 4th century AD was found (**Tab. 3, 6:11–12**).

The settlement chronology of Shishtepa itself is limited to the Kushano-Sasanian and to the Early Middle Ages period. According to the results of the prospecting and of the total pickups, it is probable that the habitation in the Kushano-Sasanian period concentrated directly on the Shishtepa and its immediate vicinity. The pottery scatter of the Kushano-Sasanian period reaches 200–300 m to the east and south of Shishtepa, while to the west it reaches as far as 500 m. This scatter might be either a result of *tepa* fallouts, or a remnant of the destroyed marginal areas of Shishtepa. However, none of the two test pits placed north-east of Shishtepa revealed earlier pottery than the High Middle Ages fragments.

The situation changed in the High Middle Ages, when the north-western and the north-eastern parts of Shishtepa were resettled (probably also the central part, now covered by modern houses). For some reason, the newly arrived inhabitants did not settle down on Shishtepa itself, but preferred its vicinity.

The presence of the graveyard remains a mystery, as well as the determination of the period to which it might belong. The rudimentary description of the finds and of the burial type did not allow its chronological classification.

The sporadic finds of the 16th–18th centuries AD pottery do not constitute any dispersion pattern. Altogether ten fragments were detected in the area of the scatter ShFS03, most of them located around the modern houses, in the probable centre of the High Middle Ages settlement. The central place covered with houses could also have been inhabited on a small scale during the period of the 16th–18th centuries AD, as it appears to be a case of the southern part of Pastaktepa (ShFS02). This assumption is difficult to prove without closer investigation of the area, which is disturbed by the buildings. This specific place, however, might have been resettled in modern times in a hypothetical continuity of the 18th century AD occupation.

3.8.4 The area of Ayritepa (scatter ShFS04)

3.8.4.1 Location

The fourth detected scatter is situated in the surroundings of Ayritepa, a mound of the same name as the village built on the western border of the dispersion. The other closest known archaeological site is Shishtepa, which is located about two kilometres to the north (**Fig. 3, 21**).

It is visible in the CORONA satellite imagery that the area enclosing the *tepa* was not cultivated by the time the picture was captured (**Fig. 3, 47**). Also the village did not yet exist. The imagery shows, however, another interesting feature. It is an irrigation channel about 25–30 m wide leading in the north-south direction next to the western part of the tepa. There are no visible remains of the channel in the most recently satellite imagery and the current irrigation network runs in different directions (**Fig. 3, 48**).

A general description

The area around the site was walked in 50 polygons, containing 2,218 ancient pottery fragments, 58 modern ones and 179 fragments of AC. Overall 21.5 ha were covered by the scatter, i.e., there was on average 104 pottery and architectural fragments altogether detected in one hectare. The scatter is in its greater part concentrated to the north-west and south-east of the *tepa* with the biggest pottery amount accumulated in the north-western part, in an area surveyed in 2010. The vast majority of the modern pottery was also found in this part, not surprisingly, as it is surrounded on both sides by recently built houses.

The test pits were not performed on this site because of a lack of time during the 2010 season. The second year of the investigation also proved unsuitable for the excavations due to rainy weather which also caused the flooding of the dusty driveway and complicated the access to the site in general.

Seasons 2010 and 2011

During the first year of the investigation only a small part of the site was surveyed because most of the area was overgrown by dense cotton bushes (**Fig. 3, 49**). The accessible fields were covered by HDS field treatment with good visibility. Only 15 polygons featured increased pottery amounts totalling 831 ancient fragments, 55 modern ones and 55 sherds of architectural ceramics. The scatter covered an area of 6.5 ha with an average number of 145 fragments per hectare.

---

[51] This rim of pithos resembles fragments found in Khan-Gaza (Sedov 1987, Tab. XXXII).

Fig. 3, 46 Area of ShFS04: Ayritepa showing raised amount of pottery. IKONOS satellite imagery. Map by Petra Tušlová.

Fig. 3, 47 Area of ShFS04: Ayritepa. CORONA satellite imagery showing almost uncultivated hinterland of the tepa. Remarkable is the wide *zeber* running next to Ayritepa. Map by Petra Tušlová.

Fig. 3, 48 Area of ShFS04: Ayritepa. Recent imagery capturing the very same area as previously the CORONA imagery (Fig. 3, 47). During past 40–50 years the adjacent area of Ayritepa started to be fully cultivated and small habitations on the west of the tepa appeared. Map by Petra Tušlová.

Fig. 3, 49 Area of ShFS04: Ayritepa with marked fields surveyed in 2010 and 2011. IKONOS satellite imagery. Map by Petra Tušlová.

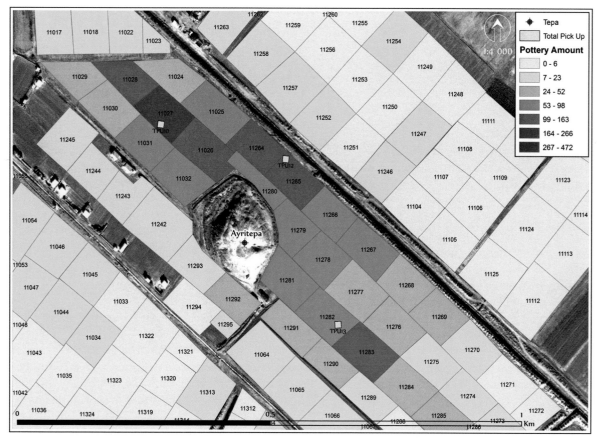

Fig. 3, 50 Area of ShFS04: Ayritepa with marked Total pickups in specific polygons. IKONOS satellite imagery. Map by Petra Tušlová.

Only a few sherds detected during the first year were diagnostic. There were several fragments bearing incised or glazed decoration characteristic of the High Middle Ages (**Tab. 3, 8:1–2**[52]). Only one pithos from the Kushan period was detected (**Tab. 3, 8:3**[53]).

During the 2011 season all the directly adjacent fields to Ayritepa were walked. They had in general very good visibility and HDS surface treatment, except for the part located directly to the east of the tepa, which featured a mixture of HDS and pasture. It turned out that the pottery accumulation found to the north/north-west of Ayritepa during the 2010 season was just the tip of the iceberg. The scatter continued in the south-eastern direction, about 450 m further from the tepa. 35 polygons in total revealed increased pottery number in the amount of 1,387 ancient pottery fragments, three modern ones and 122 pieces of architecture ceramics. In total 15 ha were walked, yielding on average 101 variable fragments each.

Although a few body fragments of High Middle Ages pottery were detected on the surface, earlier dated material appeared in much higher quantity. Several fragments of Kushan (**Tab. 3, 8:4**; **Tab. 3, 8:5–6**), Kushano-Sasanian (**Tab. 3, 8:7**) and the Early Middle Ages pottery (**Tab. 3, 8:8–9**) were found.

The total pickup sampling

Three total pickups ware carried out over the scatter ShFS04. The first one (TPU 10) was placed in the area investigated during 2010, located about 155 m north-west of the foot of Ayritepa. Another one (TPU 12) was situated about 110 m to the east of Ayritepa. The last one (TPU 13) was located approximately 135 m in the south-east direction of the same *tepa* (**Fig. 3, 50**).

TPU 10

This was the only total pickup in the area surveyed during the first year of the project. According to the

TPU10	Fine Ware	Yellow Ware	Red Ware	Architectural Ceramic	Kitchen Ware	Terracotta Bead	Total
Count (pcs.)	36	49	48	10	2	1	**146**
Weight (g)	393	2481	2848	2540	44	<1	**8306**
AvgWeight (g)	10.9	50.6	59.3	254	22	<1	**56.9**

[52] Similar fragments of such a lid are known from Khorezm (Vakturskaya 1959, 282, ris. 5:7).
[53] Determined in accordance to Lyonnet 1997, 395, fig. 56/10.

69

TPU12	Fine Ware	Yellow Ware	Red Ware	Architectural Ceramic	Kitchen Ware	Grey Ware	Waster	Bone	Total
Count (pcs.)	45	61	62	2	10	3	3	1	187
Weight (g)	285	3399	1920	88	180	28	124	<0	6024
AvgWeight (g)	6.3	55.7	31	44	18	9.3	41.3	<0	32.2

well-functioning rotation system of local agriculture, the sampled field was covered by a cotton field in the second year of the survey. The cotton bushes were mostly harvested; however, the leafless torsos of the plants were left on the field. This slightly reduced the surface visibility which, however, still remained very good.

The pickup was carried out in the polygon 11027 which contained the highest pottery amount of the entire scatter. 178 ancient pottery fragments, 26 modern pottery fragments and another 26 pieces of architectural ceramics were detected during the field survey.

In the pickup itself a total number of 146 fragments were detected without any other additional material. The category of architecture ceramic consisted of four brick fragments and six daub pieces. One of them was a quarter of a brick, one in the palm size and the others varied, with the smallest in the dimensions of a coin. The YW and the RW were represented by very similar amount of material, but the fragmentation of the YW was slightly higher. In both groups, there were few bigger pieces of approximately 5 × 5 cm; the rest was smaller, featuring quite uniform dimensions. The FW was composed of fragments of a uniform size in the dimensions of a coin. One rounded terracotta bead of 2.5 cm in diameter and a hole of 0.8 cm in the middle was also found within the pickup (**Tab. 3, 9:6**).

Several Kushano-Sasanian fragments were identified, mainly represented by fragments of storage vessels. Among them, one YW rim of a pithos (**Tab. 3, 9:1**)[54] and two RW rims of pithoi (**Tab. 3, 9:2**[55]–**3**[56]) were found. The FW was represented by two slipped rims, which could not be dated more exactly, however according to their surface treatment they might be assigned to the periods starting with the Greco-Bactrian epoch and ending with the Early Middle Ages (**Tab. 3, 9:4–5**).

TPU 12

The second pickup was placed in the polygon 11265 situated about 15 m to the west of a *zeber*. During the field survey, 121 ancient pottery fragments were found. Architectural ceramic and modern pottery were not detected at all. The area was partly covered by scrubs; therefore, it featured only good visibility.

All the material detected in this total pickup is more fragmentary than it was in the previous case, except for the YW, which together with the RW holds the first position in the sherd amounts. Groups of the KW and the GW were constituted by body fragments only. The majority of the KW was burned from both sides, which could be caused secondarily.

The FW pottery is very fragmentary without any diagnostic pieces. About ten sherds are of a coin size or slightly bigger, but the rest has much smaller dimensions. The preserved body fragments feature either a white or yellow surface, decorated with parallel incised lines (High Middle Ages?),[57] or a red slip (which can be dated from the Greco-Bactrian period up to the Early Middle Ages).

Although no AC material was detected on the surface, two pieces of brick of the dimensions 5 × 5 cm were found in the pickup. Furthermore, three pieces of grey/light green waster of similar dimensions as bricks were counted.

TPU 13

The last southernmost pickup of the site was located in the polygon 11282. Ninety-eight ancient pottery fragments and seven pieces of architectural ceramics were found during the field survey, no modern pottery was detected. The surface treatment featured HDS conditions with very good visibility.

The surface material was less diverse than in the previous pickups applied on the site. The FW consisted

TPU13	Fine Ware	Yellow Ware	Red Ware	Architectural Ceramic	Waster	Total
Count (pcs.)	19	25	23	16	2	85
Weight (g)	83	1119	313	1899	383	3797
AvgWeight (g)	4.4	44.8	13.6	118.7	191.5	44.7

---

[54] It was identified according to the material known from Dalverzintepa (Nekrasova – Pugachenkova 1978, 157).
[55] This shape is also known from Dalverzintepa (Nekrasova – Pugachenkova 1978, 157).
[56] A similar fragment was found in Darakhshatepa (Sedov 1987, Tab. XXXI/6).
[57] The fragment is dark red and roughly made, which makes it different from the typical YW High Middle Ages pottery decorated by this pattern. Also the High Middle Ages pottery is usually very well levigated. A very similar fragment to this red one was detected in the TPU 13, it is mentioned on the following page.

of very tiny pieces barely reaching a coin size. In the YW and the RW only one body fragment decorated by incised parallel lines was identified (High Middle Ages?). Otherwise, no red-slipped, glazed, or in any other way decorated (i.e., significant) pottery fragment was discovered.

Once again the YW and the RW yield a very similar amount of sherds, with a higher fragmentation of the RW composed from 50% of tiny pieces while the other half was composed of coin size and 5 × 5 cm fragments. The biggest dimensions of the YW sherds were in four cases around the palm size while the smallest had the size of a coin.

One of the two wasters detected in this square was rounded, in the size of a tennis ball; the other one was smaller of approximate dimensions 5 × 5 cm. The AC fragments consisted of daub only. Four fragments were of a palm size; six were smaller than a coin and the rest varied between these sizes.

The scatter chronology and interpretation

During the first year of the investigation, the scatter revealed only a few diagnostic fragments dated to the High Middle Ages (**Tab. 3, 8:1–2**) which preliminarily assigned the scatter into the same period. However, new pottery finds detected during the 2011 season extended the chronology. Kushan, Kushano-Sasanian, the Early Middle Ages and the High Middle Ages fragments were cumulated not only in the area adjacent to Ayritepa, but several fragments were also detected to the east behind the *zeber*, as well as to the west of Ayritepa, behind a dust road.

Despite the high amount of pottery finds connected with the site, still only a few of the fragments are diagnostic enough to permit us to state their date. A significant group of finds is however constituted mostly by large-size vessels and pithoi from the Kushan period (**Tab. 3, 8:3–4**), Kushano-Sasanian period (**Tab. 3, 9:1–3**) and from the Early Middle Ages (**Tab. 3, 8:8–9**).

The chronology of the scatter, however, does not follow any development pattern. The material from all the mentioned periods is spread around the *tepa* in all cardinal directions and, considering the sum of the 2010 and 2011 seasons, the amount of finds from the single epochs is equal.

Ayritepa itself reveals pottery material from the Kushan period – with the 3rd century AD fragments, which might then also include the Kushano-Sasanian period; and the Early Middle Ages. No High Middle Ages pottery is known from the tepa.

Although the pottery scatter reaches up to 500 m north-west and up to 450 m to the south-east of Ayritepa, the core of the scatter covers only 260–270 m in both directions. The dispersion apparently copies the ploughing direction which distributed the mate-rial from the foot of Ayritepa further away. Unfortunately, unlike the previous cases, we do not possess of any material from test pits placed in the area of this scatter and therefore we cannot follow the finds into the "depth". Nevertheless, when we consider that the dispersion of the pottery reaches as far as 80 m to the east and 50 m to the west, the original surrounded inhabitation was apparently not that large. The scatter is in those directions limited by *zeber* (to the east) and the dust road (to the west) and we may suppose that all fragments found across those man-made boundaries were brought to their finding place secondarily. There are more fragments behind the dust road (maximum 27 in one polygon) than behind the *zeber* (maximum nine) which reflects the difficulty of crossing these individual obstacles. For the secondary displacement it is more convenient to shift the material over a slightly elevated road than over a several meters-deep channel. This is another example of the recent irrigation channel network enclosing the pottery scatters nearby their original location.

It cannot be excluded, however, that the inhabited area was shaped into an oval which is currently marked by the increased pottery amount in the northern and the southern part of Ayritepa. This might be ascertained by test pits placed in the vicinity of the *tepa* in all cardinal directions.

The finds revealed another interesting phenomenon. On the *tepa* and also all over the scatter, an increased amount of pottery wasters was detected. This material was also sporadically found before in the other scatters, but always in small amounts. Its occurrence might be connected with clay processing or manufacture taking place on the site. However, there is also high possibility it comes form a recent human activity although we do not know about any workshop located in this area so far.

3.8.5 The area of Jandavlattepa

3.8.5.1 Location

Jandavlattepa is an archaeological site situated about ten kilometres to the south-east of Sherabad. It is placed along the western part of the village Saidabad and located about 800 m from the right bank of the Sherabad Darya (**Fig. 3, 21**).

A general description

The site which had been settled from the Early Iron Age to the Kushano-Sasanian period has a unique value for the Czech expedition. It was investigated from 2002 to 2006 by the Institute of Classical Archaeology (Abdullaev – Stančo 2003; Abdullaev – Stančo 2004a; Abdullaev – Stančo 2005; Stančo et al. 2006c; Abdullaev – Stančo 2007; Abdullaev – Stančo eds. 2011). During the excavation period several observations of cropmarks were noted in the immediate area of Jandavlattepa. The field survey was supposed to reveal the exact location and character of those features. Their cognition was very important for the understanding of the development of the settlement structures in the area adjacent to one of the biggest archaeological sites in the Sherabad District. Consequently, the prospecting of the surroundings of Jandavlattepa was one of the main reasons to start the intensive field survey project.

Two elevated features in Jandavlattepa's hinterland were observed and excavated in the past. One of them was investigated by the Czech expedition in 2005 (Urbanová 2011), the other one by the Soviet expedition during 1972 (Pidaev 1974). The first one was located about 700 m to the north-east of Jandavlattepa, while the exact location of the second one remained unknown, thus the discovery of its precise location became one of the main aims of the field survey in this area.

All of the measurements referring to the distance of newly identified sites or scatters used in the following text are measured from the citadel of Jandavlattepa. The elevation point (376.9 m.a.s.l.) is located on the western part of the tepa, as it is also marked on the topographical map at the scale 1:100,000 (**Fig. 3, 51**).

Seasons 2010 and 2011

Already in the first year of the field survey, the surroundings of Jandavlattepa had become the object of our interest. The adjacent area of the *tepa* was, however, covered by cotton and pasture and was therefore not suitable for investigation. Only several areas with good surface visibility were surveyed (**Fig. 3, 52**). Due to their limited extent, they could be walked in a single day of prospecting. On the north and on the north-west sides of Jandavlattepa, 69 polygons covering 2.7 ha were walked in the pasture, featuring very variable surface visibility. The results of the survey were 20 ancient and two modern pottery fragments and two pieces of architectural ceramics. All finds were body fragments with no diagnostic features to be determined.

Before the beginning of the 2011 season, topographic maps of Sherabad Oasis were obtained. These maps at the scale of 1:100,000 were compiled during the 1970s and 1980s. The investigated area is divided in these maps into four separate sheets, each covering 44 × 37 km (latitude×longitude). Jandavlattepa and the surrounding area are placed in the part of the overall map created between 1975 and 1985.

The *tepas* were marked in the maps in a form of different signs, however, most of them have a form of

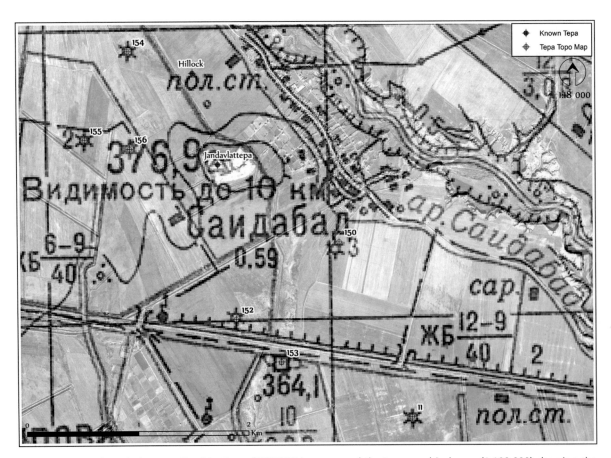

Fig. 3, 51 Area of Jandavlattepa. Combination of IKONOS imagery and the topographical map (1:100,000) showing the seven features (tepas) marked in the map. Map by Petra Tušlová.

72

Fig. 3, 52 Area of Jandavlattepa with marked fields surveyed in 2010 and 2011. IKONOS satellite imagery. Map by Petra Tušlová.

radiating circles (resembling a sun-symbol). Some of the bigger mounds are very clear on the map, revealing approximate dimensions and shape. Others are simple, delineated by a single contour line or marked by a number indicating their height in meters.

Seven features on the right bank of the Sherabad Darya, in the close vicinity of Jandavlattepa, were marked as *tepas* in the maps. All of them are situated within the range of two kilometres from the site. Four of them, the closest ones to Jandavlattepa, were intensively surveyed in the same way as the previously discussed scatters; on the map they are marked by numbers 150, 154, 155 and 156.[58] Two features (152 and 153), located more than a kilometre to the south of Jandavlattepa, were surveyed extensively without placing polygons. The last feature, more than two kilometers away to the south-east, was not surveyed at all due to the lack of time. It is labelled by a temporary field code 11, which does not belong among the examined sites. The so called hillock, excavated by the Czech team (Urbanová 2011) was not marked on the Russian topographic map at all (**Fig. 3, 51**).

From the literature we learned about a *tepa* located one kilometre to the south-east of the Jandavlattepa called Pachmaktepa which was excavated during the

year 1972 (Pidaev 1974, 32–42). By the time of the excavation it was reported to have 30 m in diameter and three meters in height.

In its present state, none of these features is elevated anymore. However, when we compare IKONOS and CORONA imagery we can clearly recognize one *tepa* marked on the CORONA imagery still preserved in the landscape. Its position roughly corresponds to one of the features from the topographic maps labelled with the number 150 (**Fig. 3, 53**).

The surface cover was diverse and it is discussed separately in each investigated area. If not stated otherwise, no unusual vegetation characteristic or soil mark was recognized.

Features 150, 154, 155 and 156

These four features were investigated through the field survey. The coordinates of each of them known from the maps were marked in a GIS application and downloaded to a PDA, which showed us the approximate location of the point on the map directly in the field. Considering the geographic deviation caused by the map georeference, each point was surveyed to 200 m distance from its predicted location in all cardinal direction (**Fig. 3, 54**).

---

[58] These are the respective numbers given by the Czech-Uzbek team to the sites of the Sherabad District as a whole.

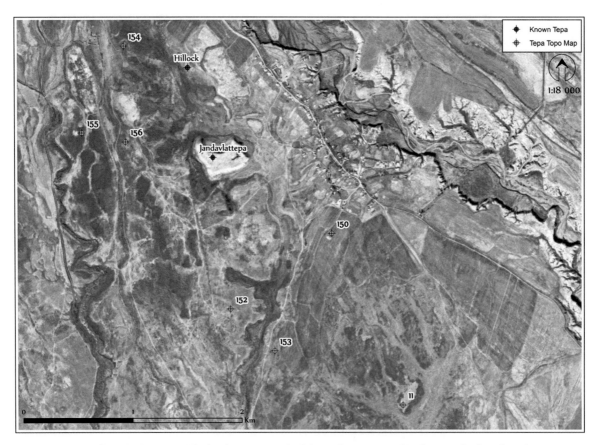

Fig. 3, 53 Area of Jandavlattepa with the features marked from the topographical maps displayed in the CORONA imagery. Special attention deserves no. 150 showing elevated feature. This is the area of predicted Pachmaktepa investigated by Pidaev (1974, 32–42). Map by Petra Tušlová.

Fig. 3, 54 Area of Jandavlattepa. Four of the features located around the tepa were intensively surveyed revealing raised amount of pottery – marked in the map by polygons. IKONOS satellite imagery. Map by Petra Tušlová.

Feature 150

Number 150 matches the best with the probable original position of the Pachmaktepa. Even though the pottery scatter was discovered about 150 m to the west of its location predicted from the maps, the material found on the field corresponds with the published assemblage from the excavation. The pottery is largely represented by cylindrical-conical vessels, typical for the area of North Bactria in the first half of the first millennium BC (Pidaev 1974, 35–37). The material is dated to Kuchuk III and Kuchuk IV (covering also the Achaemenid period; **Tab. 3, 10:1–7**). In South Uzbekistan, similar morphological forms are known from Talashkantepa I (Zapparov – Retvaladze 1976, 19–24) or Kuchuktepa (Askarov – Al'baum 1979).

The surveyed area is divided into two parts by an irrigation channel. The symbol pointing out a *tepa* detected on the topographical map was marked on the western side of the channel in HDS field with excellent to very good surface visibility. Around this feature three fragments were detected reflecting the main characteristics of the cylindrical-conical vessels and one small rim with red painting.

The area surveyed to the west of the channel brought to light a higher amount of pottery finds. The core of the accumulation is located in four polygons, containing altogether 128 pottery fragments. Modern pottery or fragments of architectural ceramics were not recognized at all. The surface was partly furrowed, partly pastured, with surface visibility varying between excellent, very good and good. The core of the scatter covered an area of 1.6 ha.

TPU 11

The only pickup made in the area around Jandavlattepa was placed in the polygon 11452, revealing the highest surface material of the site 150. During the field survey 55 ancient pottery fragments were detected in this polygon (**Fig. 3, 55**).

Almost twice as much material was found in the total pickup than in the polygon. The architectural ceramic, which was not detected during the field survey, was represented by two pieces of brick sized of approximately 5 × 5 cm. The quantity and the dimensions of the RW and the YW were almost equal, although the RW was represented by five big pieces of the palm size. The rest of the assemblage of both groups ranged between the palm and the coin size.

The characteristic cylindrical-conical vessels were detected in both mentioned groups (**Tab. 3, 10:1–7**). The FW was represented by body fragments, except for one very thin rim which belongs to a characteristic form of the Achaemenid period (**Tab. 3, 10:8**).

A unique find is a pestle made of a hard black stone according to Sh. Shaydullaev imported from an area of the present day Afghanistan. The lower grinding part is preserved while the handle part is broken. The height of the preserved piece is 4.1 cm, the diameter of the shaft 2.6 cm, and of the lower grinding part 3.1 cm (**Tab. 3, 10:9, Fig. 3, 47**).

Feature 154

Another point detected on the map is located about 1000 m to the north-west of Jandavlattepa. The scatter starts in the predicted area and continues for another 150 m further to the north. The four polygons set up in the area have yielded an increased pottery amount in the overall number of 57 ancient fragments and two pieces of architectural ceramics spread in 1.7 ha. The field was furrowed with increased soil moisture and the visibility varied between very good and low.

Three diagnostic fragments were found within the area: a rim, a base (**Tab. 3, 11:1–2**) and a piece of a body – transition between the conical and the cylindrical part of the vessel's walls. Chronologically they all belong to the same period, Kuchuk III and Kuchuk IV.

Feature 155

About 870 m to the west of the Jandavlattepa another small scatter corresponds to a feature known from the topographical maps. According to the information given by the map it should be two meters high at the time of the map creation (**Fig. 3, 51**). Five polygons create the scatter, covering 2.6 ha and containing 45 ancient pottery fragments and seven architectural ceramics. The surface was a combination of HDS and harvested cotton field covered with leafless bushes; all with excellent visibility.

The detected material revealed the same chronology as the previous assemblage, i.e., the periods of Kuchuk III and Kuchuk IV (**Tab. 3, 12:1**), but also one fragment of a cauldron stands very similar to the one found in ShFS02 (**Tab. 3, 3:1**). The stand is supposed to be dated to the 17th–18th centuries AD (according to T. Annaev). A further two rims of pithoi from the

TPU 11	Fine Ware	Yellow Ware	Red Ware	Architectural Ceramic	Pestle	Total
Count (pcs.)	19	34	38	2	1	94
Weight (g)	68	873	1064	116	57	2178
AvgWeight (g)	3.6	25.7	28	58	57	23.2

Fig. 3, 55 Area of Jandavlattepa focused on the site of Pachmaktepa. No. 150 possibly represents the tepa, which was marked from the topographical maps and CORONA imagery. The red colour encircled by the black contour line points to the raised pottery amount which is located about 150 m west from the predicted feature. IKONOS satellite imagery. Map by Petra Tušlová.

turn of the Kushano-Sasanian period and the Early Middle Ages were recognized (**Tab. 3, 12:2–3**).[59]

Feature 156

The last feature from the group of the closest scatters is located about 550 m to the west of Jandavlattepa. It is connected only with two polygons containing together 34 ancient pottery fragments and ten pieces of architectural ceramics. The surface was covered by HDS field surface cover with excellent visibility. Both polygons together covered one hectare.

The material once again points to the Achaemenid period (Kuchuk III); the assemblage is represented by one rim, one base, and by several body fragments (**Tab. 3, 12:4–5**). One pithos rim, however, resembles, as in the case of scatter 155, pottery from the turn of the Kushano-Sasanian period and the Early Middle Ages (**Tab. 3, 12:6**).[60]

Features 152 and 153

Numbers 152 and 153 represents features known from the topographic maps which were investigated extensively without placing polygons. The area of the

predicted *tepa* localisation was surveyed in wider intervals of 20 m between individual team members. In both cases we managed to cover about 300 to 400 m in the vicinity of the predicted points. The aim was to quickly localize the scatter and to place polygons right on the top of it. This plan failed already in its initial phase as we did not find almost any pottery on the fields.

Feature 152

The feature 152 was predicted about 60 m to the north of a drainage channel, described in detail in connection with the feature 153. The IKONOS and the CORONA satellite imagery in the approximate area of this point shows an indistinct rounded hillock of about 20 m in diameter, located about 70 m far from the "tepa sign" detected on the topographical map (**Fig. 3, 56**). On the most recent Google Earth imagery the area of the direct predicted feature is overgrown with vegetation, which plays a significant role in the feature identification (i.e., no unusual phenomena are observed in the imagery, nor in situ).

In spite of the fact that the surrounding fields encircling the surveyed area were waterlogged furrows,

---

[59] Both fragments are very similar to the types found in Aktepa II (Sedov 1987, Tab. XXIV/1-3).
[60] As before, the shape resembles finds from Aktepa II (Sedov 1987, Tab. XXIV/1-3).

Fig. 3, 56 Area of Jandavlattepa. No. 152 as identified from the topographical maps and the feature (tepa?) detected in IKONOS and CORONA imagery located about 70 m east from the predicted site. No pottery was found around any of these two marks, only several random finds came from the area further north-west. IKONOS satellite imagery. Map by Petra Tušlová.

quite a wide strip of a ground was walked (430 × 140 m) around the predicted *tepa* (especially of the northern area). There was almost no material on the field, except for the upper surveyed part of the field, located about 300 m to the north-west of the predicted feature and approximately 100 m to the south-east from the closest road. Several random pieces of architectural ceramics were found and also a mixture of about 12 pottery fragments. Among them a part of a mercury container dated to the High Middle Ages, a red slipped handle (either Greco-Bactrian, Kushan or Kushano-Sasanian period), or a conical item made in a hand which might be a leg of an animal statue, or a foot of a small stand. I would not connect the material with the feature detected on the topographical map due to the general low amount of the surface concentration and its wide dispersion over a large area. It is rather connected with some secondary displacement.

Consequently, the feature itself cannot be chronologically classed or interpreted. It might be an ancient structure of a specific character as those featuring no material found near Talashkantepa II (see below), as

well as quite recent relics of crumbled mud brick wall of a small house which are to be found all over the Sherabad Oasis.

Feature 153

The area of the feature 153 was placed in a harvested cotton field with very good surface visibility. On the topographical map it is marked by a sign different from the rest of the investigated features, combining an elevation symbol (364.1 m.a.s.l.) with a contour line. This symbol is, however, generally used also for the *tepa* which is elevated.[61] The point resembling a *tepa* is placed on the map directly next to a wide and deep drainage channel (*zeber*). The channel must have been created during the 1970s since it is not visible in the CORONA satellite imagery (**Fig. 3, 53**), but it is already drawn in the topographical map (**Fig. 3, 51**). During the field investigation the position of the elevation point was not found at all. The whole area running along the *zeber* has been disturbed, flanked by piles of excavated earth from the ditch on both sides. A dust road was built along the southern bank of the *zeber*.

---

[61] A very similar sign is adopted also in the case of Jandavlattepa, in which, however, a triangle with a dot in the central part is used instead of a square with a dot in a central part.

Judging from the very few finds detected in the adjacent field (only three body fragments in an area 250 × 300 m) the elevation point/the *tepa* was destroyed leaving very little traces. Only a circle with a small amount of not fully-grown vegetation among the cotton bushes placed about 60 m to the south of the channel might be a consequence of previous human activity. A similar situation was observed by the team of Ladislav Stančo during the year 2005 while excavating Jandavlattepa. According to the information given by L. Stančo, two flat spherical features were noted from the citadel of the Jandavlattepa. They were both located to the east of the irrigation channel leading to the north of the Jandavlattepa (approximately in the northern area covered by the polygons). Those flat features were perceptible during the 2005 season only. They were characterised by a small amount of very bad quality cotton which was stunted and crooked (Urbanová 2011, 102). However, during the field survey of the surrounding areas in 2010, no unusual cropmarks or increased amount of surface material was detected there.

The chronology and interpretation of the detected features

The amount of the material found in connection with the features 150, 154, 155 and 156 was much lower than in the previous cases. Their identification was done, however, on the basis of the "tepa sign" drawn in the topographic map and of the ascertainment of pottery presence on the field in the vicinity of the point. As stated above, except for the investigated scatters, the number of the surface material was in the surveyed areas very low in general. Therefore, an identification of at least a slightly increased amount of ancient material accumulated in the middle of a field is likely to be associated with previous human activity.

The features 150 and 154 revealed only Kuchuk III and IV pottery; the features 155 and 156 both yielded – besides the Kuchuk III and IV material – also rims of pithoi from the turn of the Kushano-Sasanian period and the Early Middle Ages. However, the Kuchuk type pottery predominated in the assemblage of all four mentioned features. As a result, all these sites marked by the scatters seem to be contemporary with each other, and also with the earliest layers of Jandavlattepa, which presumably played the role of the principal settlement in the area from the Early Iron Age onwards.

The exact location of the features 152 and 153 has not been ascertained. Both of the presumable *tepas* are on the topographical map located in the close vicinity of a wide *zeber* and of frequented dirt road. Both of these elements could contribute to their early destruction. There might be as well very few of material associated with them, which worsens identification of their placement.

The topographical map, however, does not show another feature still visible in the landscape, located about 700 m north-west of the Jandavlattepa, investigated by the Czech expedition during the 2005 season (**Fig. 3, 51**).[62] At the time of the excavations it was a hillock oval in plan with dimensions 8 × 6.5 m. According to the local inhabitants the feature was preserved until the mid 20th century AD to the height of a one-storey building before it got disturbed by agricultural activity. By the excavation itself, a few pottery finds were revealed dated to the Greco-Bactrian and the Late Kushan periods (Urbanová 2011, 102–104).

In summary, there are five verified features located within a distance of one kilometre from Jandavlattepa. The lower amount of surface material may perhaps reflect their function. They all seem to be small sized dwellings occupied only during a short-term period. The hillock investigated by the Czech expedition was interpreted as a funerary or cult structure of the Greco-Bactrian or Kushan period (Urbanová 2011, 12–14). According to the pottery types discovered during the field survey, the majority of the Iron Age pottery included table ware while the Kushano-Sasanian finds comprised storage vessels only. Those finds may very well refer to the residential character of the structures, although such vessels might have been used in shrines as well as containers for offerings.

While comparing the chronological data gained from the Czech-Uzbek investigations, it seems, that the hillock excavated in 2005, fills a gap between the occupations of the features known from the topographical maps (see the following table). We may only assume that all of the mounds played the same role, even though they were used in different periods.

The 17th–18th centuries AD cauldron was probably secondarily brought to the field and since we have only one fragment of such a data, I would not give it any weight. It is included in the following table only for illustration of all of the chronologically sensitive material detected on the field.

---

[62] It remains unclear for what reason some of the features were omitted from the topographical maps by the Soviet cartographers. The hillock must have been visible in the landscape when the maps were being compiled.

Feature	Kuchuk	Greco-Bactrian	Kushan	Kushano-Sasanian	17th–18th c. AD
No. 150	X				
No. 154	X				
No. 155	X			X	X
No. 156	X			X	
Hillock		X	X		

3.8.6 The area of Talashkantepa II

The area of Talashkantepa II, situated about 18 km to the south-west of Sherabad, was investigated by a one-day prospecting only. Two features out of 21 detected in the 1:100,000 scale topographic maps were surveyed (**Fig. 3, 57**). Only eight fragments were found in 71 polygons, covering about 40 ha. Among them four ancient, two modern pottery and two (none precisely identified) architectural ceramics fragments.

These structures might have been small dwellings for whose operation a large amount of pottery was not needed. They had to have been destroyed in past 40 years, however there are no modern structures in their vicinity which could cause their destruction. Probably they were of small dimensions and destroyed simply by agricultural activity.

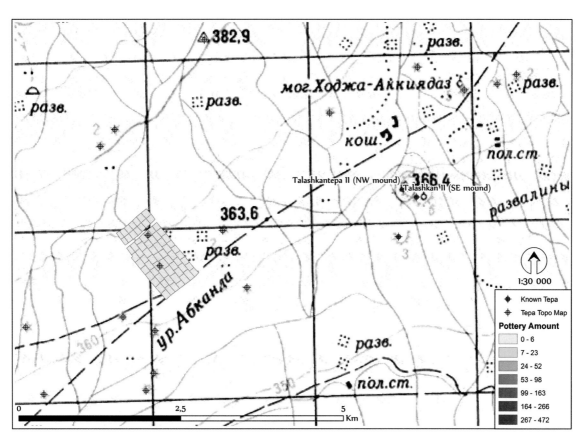

Fig. 3, 57 Area of Talashkantepa covered densely by tepa-signs marked from the topographical maps. Two of them were intensively surveyed by our team with no results (1:100,000). Map by Petra Tušlová.

3.9 Conclusion

The investigated fields covered approximately seven square kilometres, which represents only one percent of the whole cultivated lowlands of the Sherabad District. Consequently, the discussed results of the project are based on this representative sample only and might change while applied to a more extensive area.

All the numbers of pottery and architectural ceramics fragments recorded during the intensive field survey express a statistical sample, as do the amounts of material gained from the test pits and the total pickups. The resulting numbers gained through different approaches are compared in the tables shown in the text, which helps to build their interpretation and comparison among different scatters and approaches. The main aim of the pottery collecting was to gain enough material by various ways to determine the time-span of the surface dispersions.

Although the lowlands of Surkhan Darya province have been inhabited since the Bronze Age period (Abdullaev 2011b, 15) the earliest surface material detected during the field survey belonged to the Early Iron Age. The youngest assemblages encountered on the fields, which might be still considered as ancient, dates into the 18th century with modern day dishes spread only around the current habitations.

The systematic field survey proved to be an effective method for data collecting. The flat scatters concentrated around the settlement mounds were enormous while compared to the elevated (visible) part of the *tepa* itself – e.g., the scatter ShFS03 around Shishtepa covers 35 ha, while the Shishtepa mound itself occupies an area of 1.1 ha. Of course, not the whole area of the scatter might be attributed to the original dimensions of the settlement, but as we know from the field survey, some of the other *tepas* do not have a pottery accumulation in their vicinity at all (even though the adjectect fields are cultivated). If we consider the possibility of surveying the adjacent areas of all of the detected *tepas* in the Sherabad District, we would get a much better idea of their original size and shape. Also, we would better understand relation between individual features which quite often might be, in fact, one *tepa* cut into several parts leaving torsos of the original structures meters apart. These torsos might be in previous studies considered as individual habitations, not as a single site. In this point we may, again, question the division of the settlements based on their visible shape and size (Yurkevich 1965, 166–167; Rtveladze 1974, 83–85; Staviskiy 1977, 43–44).

There is although probability of the settlement size connected with their function. Small dispersions, such as those around Jandavlattepa, might reflect short-term settlements or small size construction of various purposes ranging from shrines to animal-pastoral shelters. The bigger *tepa* could reflect long-lasting settlements of greater importance. The question of the relationship between the small-size dwellings and the big settlement mounds in their vicinity was only opened by this study and deserves much greater attention in the future.

An exceptional situation was noted in the vicinity of Talashkantepa II, where no surface material was detected in the predicted area of the tepas. The amount of the material connected to these settlements/structures must have been very low, even in ancient times. Surveying of the remaining 19 *tepas* located in the area might perhaps better answer their character and function, which for now seems to be different from the other investigated sites.

The chronology of most of the investigated scatters was closely determined after the second year of the project, when the pottery dispersions were fully surveyed. The interpretation of the scatters drawn on the basis of a partial prospecting would have been different than it is now, when the concrete areas were covered. For this reason, the essential information of all of the investigated areas are described in the text according to the different seasons, in 2010 and 2011, to illustrate the differences between the possible results of the two years of investigation. Some examples revealed during the 2011 season follow: the scatter ShFS01 and ShFS04 disclosed much larger quantities of surface material than the first year; the survey in the area of ShFS02 indicated to the possible connection of Pastaktepa with Gorintepa; and the scatter ShFS03 revealed Kushano-Sasanian pottery which was not found during the first year investigation at all.

Several general conclusions involving the settlement practices can be drawn on the basis of the four investigated scatters. Settlements of the High Middle Ages seem to be spread over a more extensive area than those of the earlier periods. In the case of ShFS01, the majority of the discussed *tepas* (considering also those known only from literature) featured the High Middle Ages pottery, which was also predominantly represented in the flat scatter around. A similar situation appeared in the case of ShFS03, when the most extensive north-eastern and north-western area of the scatter yielded the High Middle Ages pottery only.

Another pattern results from the finds of the 16th–18th centuries AD pottery. Fragments of these periods were recognized in the ShFS02 accumulated in the limited southern part of the scatter. A similar cluster also revealing this chronology was the ShFS03, where there was 16th–17th centuries AD pottery concentrated around the modern settlement located in the centre of the High Middle Ages settlement. Another three fragments were found in the ShFS01. In contrast to the vast cover of the High Middle Ages, the pottery of the 16th–18th centuries AD seems to be concentrated in limited areas only.

All the above mentioned information might result in the better understanding of the settlement practises and of population growth or decline. Preliminary we may expect the growth of population in the High Middle Ages and its decline during the 16th–18th centuries AD.

The test pits performed in three out of four scatters proved to be an effective method for data sharpening. Their significance was proven the most while evaluating data from the ShFS04, the only scatter in which the test pits were omitted. The information usually given by the trenches was greatly missing while interpreting the scatter.

The tables regarding the test pits placed in the main text show variability of the results gained from the number of the material detected in each individual spit. Some of the basic observations based on the table's evaluation follow. The upper three spits (the topsoil) of the test pit in the polygon 10120 (ShFS01) contain less pottery than the two lower (culture) layers. In ShFS02, while considering the two pits performed in the same corn field, each of them revealed different results while comparing the upper three spits with the first three located under the topsoil. The 10610_01 revealed a much lower pottery amount accumulated in the topsoil, while in the case of 10610_02, the contrary proved true. Both spits however reveal almost the same pottery amount while counting all layers together down to the spit 7 (only nine sherds difference). The area of the scatter ShFS03 points to another phenomenon. While comparing the three upper layers with the average amount of the material detected during the field survey in each polygon, we obtain different results. The polygon 10783 revealed 321 pottery fragments, while the topsoil contained 171 fragments. In the polygon 10784, 392 fragments were detected, while in the topsoil only 85 pottery fragments were counted.

The cultural layers, rich in material, were found in the test pits right down to the deepest layers (maximum 200 cm). The topsoil was always very difficult to distinguish. It is represented by ca. 50 to 60 cm (three spits) which generally correspond to the depth of ploughing. The deep deposits of the cultural layers are perhaps caused by the location in the alluvial plains and by centuries of soil accumulation slowly burying the ancient landscape. This phenomenon

proved the best in the site of Pastaktepa (ShFS02), a mound which is no longer elevated and its existence is based on the testimony of the local inhabitants. It was a unique possibility to excavate beneath this *tepa* and to uncover 200 cm of cultural deposits concentrated underground, all without reaching the sterile soil or the bed rock. Such an experience brings up the question of the original height of *tepas* before their surroundings were covered by the alluvial soil.

The other complementary method used during the project was the total pickup sampling. As expected, it added more detailed information to the scatters. The efficiency of the total pickups was proven particularly in the TPU 08 by revealing Kushano-Sasanian pottery in the scatter ShFS03, which was during the first year observation attributed to the High Middle Ages only. In general, a higher amount of material types was found, including fragments of glass, beads, tokens, or a rare stone pestle (**Tab. 10:9**). In the case of ShFS04, a high amount of ceramic waste was found in the pickups located to the east (pol. 11265) and to the south (pol. 11282) of the tepa.

Regarding the field cover conditions, the best period for the field survey is autumn, late October and November, as the fields are mostly free of all vegetation. During our investigation in early November the work was stopped for three days by a snow storm. However, this was supposed to be a unique weather condition unusual for this time of the year. For the test pits I would recommend an earlier period, August and September, the soil is hard, but still it is better for excavations than the waterlogged fields in autumn. The total pickups might be applied in any of these periods, I would say, with the same results. In summer, the sherds are covered by dust, in autumn by wet clay. In both cases it is difficult to recognize its original colour and the type of decoration (except for the glazed ware) without further cleaning.

The crop rotation system, mentioned already many times, enables the investigation of most of the areas with good visibility. If there is a possibility for a two-year investigation, I would recommend to survey in August and September, different areas every year. The total pickups, however, have to be performed in the same year the intensive field survey is undertaken.

In conclusion, the intensive field survey (with its supplementary methods) proved to be an effective tool for the investigation of the lowlands of Sherabad District. The small scale project verified the presence of flat scatters in the immediate vicinity of *tepas* and brought a new perspective to the approach of field surveys in south Uzbekistan. A combination of data gained from the investigation of *tepas* and from the immediate areas adjacent to them is needed to achieve a comprehensive picture of the size and of the chronology of the investigated sites.

TABLE 01

SCALE 1:2

Tab. 3, 1 Pottery examples, area of ShFS01: Kulugh-Shakhtepa. 1: Early Middle Ages; 2–3: High Middle Ages; 4: red slipped fragment – Kushan or Kushano-Sasanian; 5–6: basket pattern, 15th century AD or younger; 7–11: High Middle Ages.

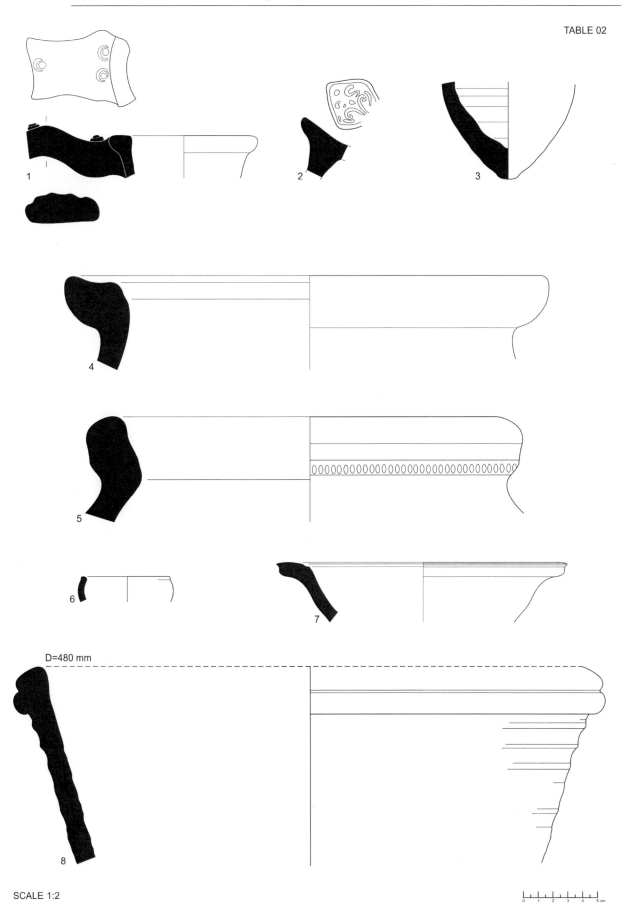

SCALE 1:2

D=480 mm

Tab. 3, 2 Pottery examples, area of ShFS01: Kulugh-Shakhtepa. 1: High Middle Ages handle with appliqué decoration; 2: handle of a lamp of light-green glaze, ca. 13th century; 3: container for mercury, ca. 10th–14th century; 4: Kushan or Kushano-Sasanian period; 5: Early Middle Age; 6: Kushan or Kushano-Sasanian; 7: Early Middle Age; 8: 16th–18th century.

TABLE 03

SCALE 1:2

Tab. 3, 3 Pottery examples, area of ShFS02: Gorintepa. 1: terracotta cauldron stand, ca. 17th–18th century; 2: 17th–18th century; 3: turn of the Kushano-Sasanian period and the Early Middle Ages; 4: Kushano-Sasanian; 5: Kushan.

TABLE 04

SCALE 1:2

Tab. 3, 4 Pottery examples, area of ShFS02: Gorintepa. 1–4: No chronological data; 5: Kushan; 6–7: Kushano-Sasanian; 8: Early Middle Ages; 9: turn of Kushano-Sasanian and the Early Middle Ages; 10: Kushan; 11: Kushano-Sasanian.

TABLE 05

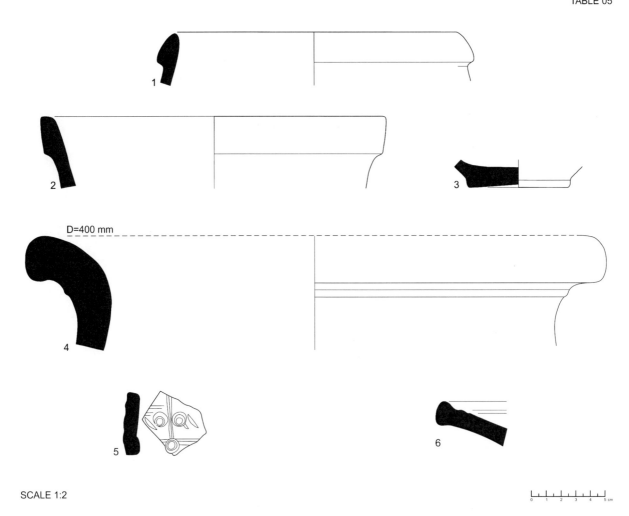

D=400 mm

SCALE 1:2

0 1 2 3 4 5 cm

Tab. 3, 5 Pottery examples, area of ShFS02: Gorintepa. 1–2: Greco-Bactrian; 3: Kushan; 4: Kushano-Sasanian; 5: High Middle Ages; 6: 17th–18th century.

TABLE 06

D=190 mm

SCALE 1:2

0 1 2 3 4 5 cm

Tab. 3, 6 Pottery examples, area of ShFS03: Shishtepa. 1–3: High Middle Ages; 4–5: Kushano-Sasanian; 6–7: High Middle Ages; 8–9: 16th–17th century; 10: Arab grey ware with impressed decoration, 12th–14th century; 11–12: grey ware pottery, end of the 4th century AD; 13: High Middle Ages.

TABLE 07

SCALE 1:2

Tab. 3, 7 Potter examples, area of ShFS03: Shishtepa. 1–5: High Middle Ages; 6: handle of a green-glazed lamp with an imprinted decoration depicting two doves surrounded by plant tendrils, High Middle Ages ca. 14th–15thcentury; 7: Kushano-Sasanian.

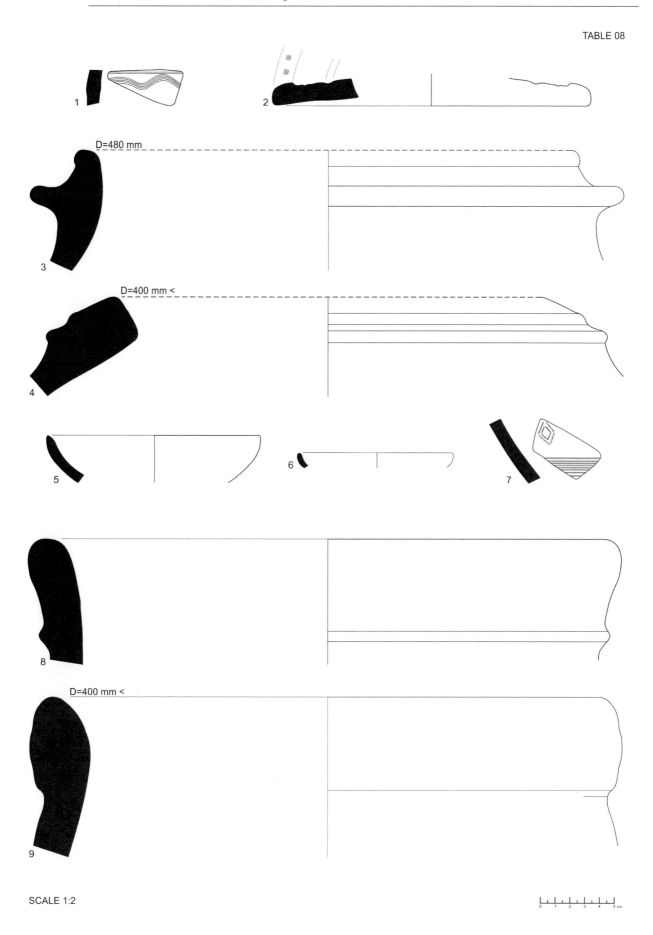

D=480 mm

D=400 mm <

D=400 mm <

SCALE 1:2

Tab. 3, 8 Pottery examples, area of ShFS04: Ayritepa. 1–2: High Middle Ages; 3–6: Kushan; 7: Kushano-Sasanian; 8–9: Early Middle Ages.

TABLE 09

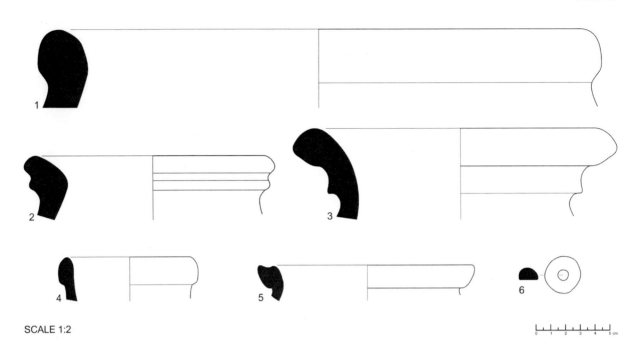

SCALE 1:2

Tab. 3, 9 Pottery examples, area of ShFS04: Ayritepa. 1–3: Kushano-Sasanian; 4–5: from Greco-Bactrian epoch to the Early Middle Ages; 6: terracotta bead of 2.5 cm in diameter, found within the pickup, no chronological data.

TABLE 10

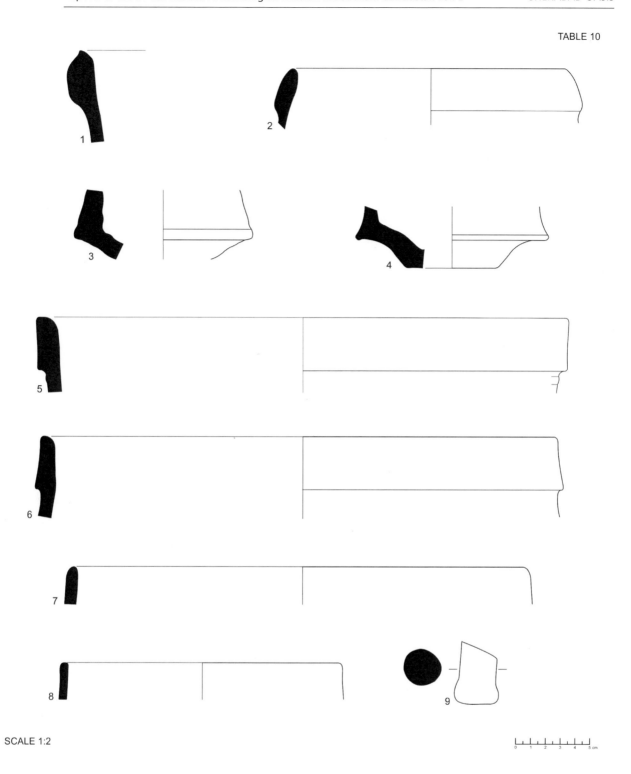

SCALE 1:2

Tab. 3, 10 Pottery examples, area of Jandavlattepa, feature no. 150. 1–8: pottery of type Kuchuk III and IV (the first half of the first millennium BC); 9: pestle made of a hard black stone, perhaps from Afghanistan, the same chronology.

TABLE 11

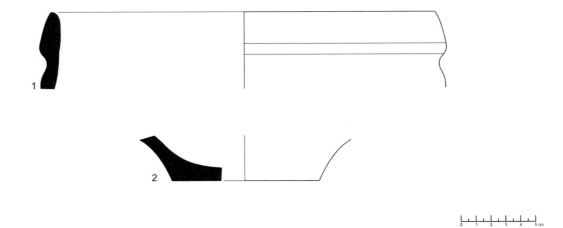

SCALE 1:2

Tab. 3, 11 Pottery examples, area of Jandavlattepa, feature no. 154. 1–2: pottery of type Kuchuk III and IV.

TABLE 12

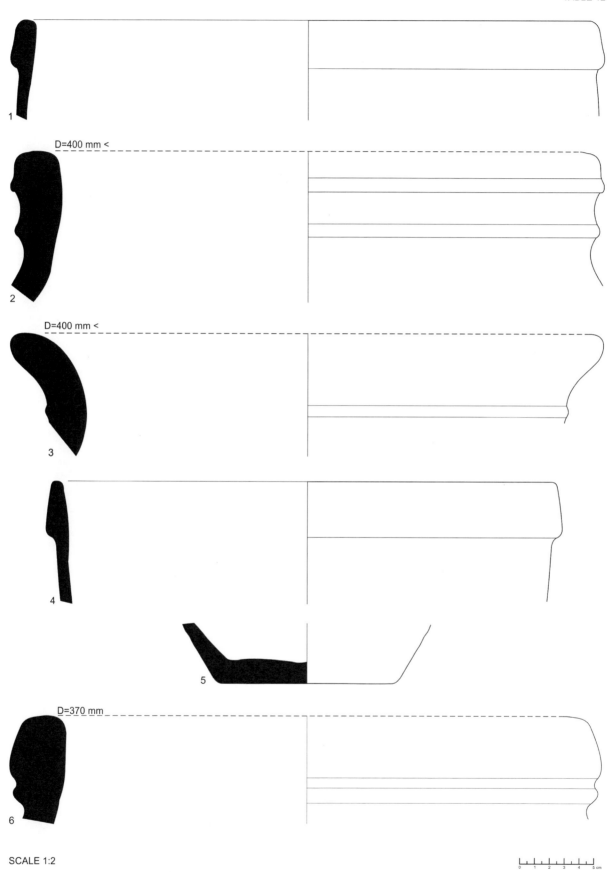

SCALE 1:2

Tab. 3, 12 Pottery examples, area of Jandavlattepa. Feature no. 155. 1: pottery of type Kuchuk III and IV; 2–3: turn of Kushano-Sasanian and the Early Middle Ages. Feature no. 156. 4–5: pottery of type Kuchuk III and IV; 6: *turn* of the Kushano-Sasanian period and the Early Middle Ages.

93

4. Archaeological sites in the Sherabad Oasis

L. Stančo, Sh. Shaydullaev, A. Shaydullaev, A. Danielisová, T. Annaev

4.1 Structure of the catalogue

The following chapter is intended as an overview of rough archaeological and geographic data we gained during the four seasons of field work in Sherabad Oasis (2008–2011). It is organized as a catalogue with each entry representing individual archaeological site as a geographically defined, i.e., spatial unit. This approach brings certain difficulties in those cases, where two or several morphological features or pottery scatters are situated close to each other and thus may be perceived either as an individual site, or as several parts (components) of one larger and complex site. In most cases, we decided to follow the conventions given by scholarly literature, which is the case of both Jarkutan and Bustan with long established enumeration of various parts of settlements and necropolises. There are several cases, however, where we have given an individual code to a separate part of a probably larger settlement. Typically, there was a *tepa* already known to archaeologists, to that we added a spot with high density pottery scatter in its neighbourhood as probable other site or a component of the previously known one. Such pottery scatter has received a new code.

Each catalogue entry has a simple structure emphasising several basic characteristics of the archaeological site in the given area. It is divided into three general sections. First gives general information about name and location of the site. Short characteristic of the local topography, which was originally meant to be a part of each entry, appears to be, however, very similar in all listed sites, since we deal with irrigated lowlands only, where just a few topographical anomalies occur. It provides also enumeration (codes) in various systems. Typically, there is a number given by E. Rtveladze and his colleagues in 1970s, a code given by S. Stride (2004), and our own site code, which is highlighted. Note, that the *elevation* given here is information about elevation above the sea level taken from GoogleEarth, since the other sources – such as maps of Gen. shtab – does not provide this for each and every spot we need. Our measurement using various GPS devices differed to such a degree that we found the results not consistent enough to use them.

The second section, *Description*, provides sum of metric and descriptive attributes, such as length, width, area, shape, etc. The field *Shape* refers to the ground plan of the given site. Note that the *length* and *width* entries were measured exactly in axes x (width) and y (length), i.e., in west-east and north-south direction respectively. Figures in description, on the other hand, provide the sizes of the site in its own axes varying according its real orientation. *Height* is missing in many cases, since our measurement using GPS gave not sufficient data, and other sources did not provide such information at all. *Pottery* indicates whether we have collected pottery material from the surface of the site or not. In most cases we did, if possible, with exception of the sites that had been excavated and their material properly published giving a clear dating. In these cases, we also indicate the period in the *Dating* section below, even if not based on our own survey results. *Pottery* thus features number of diagnostic pottery fragments in case we have them, while number in brackets means number of non-diagnostic pottery that was taken in account considering dating of the given sites. The field *Other finds* shows occasional non-pottery small finds collected during the survey, or more important small finds from the site published elsewhere, especially coins, which are indicative for dating.

Third section starts with *dating* based upon our field survey supplemented by dating published earlier that is based either on material of the archaeological excavations, or on the field survey of our predecessors. Quotations of literature follow below (if available), these, however, are not complete in the cases of the sites that received much attention in the scholarly literature, such as Jarkutan or Bustan. For the full bibliography we recommend to consult Stride (2004, vol. 3 and 4). The additional fields here provide the *date(s) of our field survey*, person responsible for the data, eventually some *notes* that does not belong to any other field, but bear some importance for the characterization of the site. We included in this field occasional knowledge of local people concerning the site, for instance.

Most of the sites was visited by our team members and surveyed, some of them, however, were not for various reasons. Firstly, we excluded the sites that were apparently subject of serious archaeological excavations recently and well described in scholarly literature. This concerns especially the sites of Jarkutan and Bustan, but along the same lines the description of Jandavlattepa – even if excavated by our team in recent past – was accordingly shortened being dealt with elsewhere in detail.

4.2 Catalogue of the archaeological sites of the Sherabad Oasis

IDENTITY

Site Code
1

Stride 2004
Uz-SD-155

Rtveladze 1974
B-033

Arshavskaya et al. 1982
155

Name of the site
Jandavlattepa

Translation
no

District
Sherabad

Type of site
settlement

Alternative name of the site
no

Latitude
37.61905

Longitude
67.088536

Elevation (m.a.s.l.)
367

Location
the site is located in an intensely irrigated and cultivated plains close to deep riverbed of the Sherabad River, 7.67 km from the town of Sherabad, the District headquarters

Topography
most of the surrounding fields are used for the cultivation of cotton, and the whole area is interwoven with irrigation ditches

DESCRIPTION

Basic description
large compact mound with a polygonal shape; separate citadel in the NW part; the height of the Citadel above the surrounding cotton fields is about 20 m, while the height of the Shakhristan varies between 12 and 18 m

Shape
the site has a polygonal shape, which resembles a deformed rectangle

Length
412

Width
290

Height
17

Surface area (sq m)
122797

Found
in publications

Preservation
high

Distortions
Modern times graveyard: recent grave pits all over the surface

Excavated
1993 trial excavations of D. Huff; 2002–2006 Czech-Uzbek excavations

Pottery
>3000 frg

Other finds
all kinds

DATING

Late Bronze Age	X	Early Iron Age	X	Hellenistic	X	Kushan and Kushan-Sasanian	X
Early Medieval	X	High Medieval		Post-Mongol		Pre-modern	

Dating published elsewhere: Achaemenid – Early Medieval (Rtveladze 1974); Achaemenid, Kushan, 5th–6th c. (Arshavskaya et al. 1982)

Bibliography
Abdullaev – Stančo 2004b; 2004c; 2005; 2006; 2007; 2009; Huff et al. 2001; 1974; Rtveladze 1974; 1982; Rtveladze – Khakimov 1973; Schachner 1995; 2004; Stančo 2005; 2006a; 2006b; Stride 2004, vol. 3, Uz-SD-155; Full bib.: Abdullaev – Stančo eds. 2011, 23

Notes

Date of survey
2002–2006

Entered by
Stančo

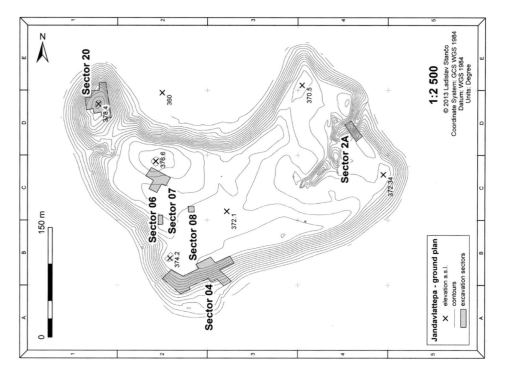

IDENTITY

Site Code
2

Stride 2004
no

Rtveladze 1974
no

Arshavskaya et al. 1982
no

Name of the site
Boshtepa

Translation
Main mound

District
Sherabad

Type of site
settlement and mausoleum

Alternative name of the site
no

Latitude
37.611844

Longitude
67.124819

Elevation (m.a.s.l.)
357

Location
3.2 km SEE form the site of Jandavlattepa across the Sherabad river; 3.2 km south of the village of Mekhnatabad

Topography
flat lowlands, close to the Sherabaddarya river bed, irrigated fields around

DESCRIPTION

Basic description
compact circular, shrine with a tomb of a holy man on the top

Shape
circular

Length
82

Width
77

Height
8

Surface area (sq m)
7607

Found
seen from Jandavlattepa, detected in GoogleEarth

Preservation
high

Distortions
concrete staircase from SE to the top, concrete platform and shrine on the top

Excavated
no

Pottery
34

Other finds
no

DATING

Late Bronze Age		Early Iron Age		Hellenistic		Kushan and Kushan-Sasanian	X
Early Medieval	X	High Medieval		Post-Mongol		Pre-modern	X

Dating published elsewhere   no

Bibliography
no

Notes
local knowledge: since the 13th century it has a been sacred place for local Muslim population

Date of survey
02.09.2009

Entered by
Stančo

IDENTITY

Site Code	Stride 2004		Rtveladze 1974	Arshavskaya et al. 1982
3	no		no	no

Name of the site	Translation	District	Type of site
Koshtepa I	Double mound	Sherabad	settlement

Alternative name of the site	Latitude	Longitude	Elevation (m.a.s.l.)
no	37.605092	67.132003	356

Location

4 km southeast of Jandavlattepa across the Sherabad River

Topography

two small mounds around within 100 m, maybe part of a larger settlement

DESCRIPTION

Basic description

compact circular mound

Shape	Length	Width	Height	Surface area (sq m)
circular	48	48		1148

Found	Preservation	Distortions
detected in GoogleEarth	high	no

Excavated

no

Pottery	Other finds
6	no

DATING

Late Bronze Age		Early Iron Age		Hellenistic		Kushan and Kushan-Sasanian	
Early Medieval	X	High Medieval		Post-Mongol		Pre-modern	

Dating published elsewhere	no

Bibliography

no

Notes

Date of survey	Entered by
02.09.2009	Stančo

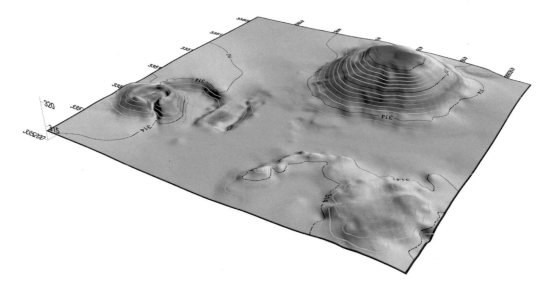

IDENTITY

Site Code	Stride 2004		Rtveladze 1974	Arshavskaya et al. 1982
4	Uz-SD-162		B-015	162

Name of the site	Translation	District	Type of site
Kulugshatepa	Bow-before-the-king mound	Sherabad	settlement

Alternative name of the site	Latitude	Longitude	Elevation (m.a.s.l.)
Kulug-Shakh-Tepe (Rtveladze 1974), Kulug-tepe (Arshavskaya et al. 1982)	37.625378	67.006622	378

Location

300 m south of the village of Hurjak south of a modern cemetery

Topography

the site is situated in flat irrigated lowlands with cotton fields to the south, several water canals in every direction, and modern village with cemetery to the north

DESCRIPTION

Basic description

compact mound, square in its groundplan; elevated citadel in the NW part with tower-like structure in the central part

Shape	Length	Width	Height	Surface area (sq m)
rectangular	175	186	17	42735

Found	Preservation	Distortions
detected in GoogleEarth	high	no

Excavated

no

Pottery	Other finds
22	Hephtalite coin reported

DATING

Late Bronze Age		Early Iron Age		Hellenistic		Kushan and Kushan-Sasanian	X
Early Medieval	X	High Medieval	X	Post-Mongol	X	Pre-modern	X

Dating published elsewhere

Bibliography

Kushan, 5th–15/16th c. AD (Rtveladze – Khakimov 1973; Arshavskaya et al. 1982); Anique, Early and Late Medieval (Rtveladze 1974)

Rtveladze – Khakimov 1973, 16; 12, ris. 2.8 – simple ground plan, here also a half of a Hephtalite coin reported; Rtveladze 1974, 76; Annaev 1988, 13; Arshavskaya et al. 1982, 134; Stride 2004, vol. 3, 133; Annaev 1988, 13; Stride 2004, vol. 3, Uz-SD-162

Notes

there are two more sites mentioned by Arshavskaya et al. 1982 besides Shortantepa, it is Nagaratepa (30×20×3 m) 250 m SE of Kulugsha (EM period) and Kul´tepe (20×10×0.5 m) 300 m SE? (see ch. 3.8.1)

Date of survey	Entered by
17-09.2009	Stančo

IDENTITY

Site Code **5**	Stride 2004 Uz-SD-145	Rtveladze 1974 B-023	Arshavskaya et al. 1982 145

Name of the site	Translation	District	Type of site
Aktepa	White mound	Sherabad	settlement

Alternative name of the site	Latitude	Longitude	Elevation (m.a.s.l.)
Chunayata (100k map)	37.617364	66.983342	370

Location

2.5 km south of the village of Navbog

Topography

the site is situated in flat irrigated lowlands

DESCRIPTION

Basic description

rectangular compact mound, max. NW–SE 56 m; max. SW–NE 74 m; upper surface indistinct

Shape	Length	Width	Height	Surface area (sq m)
eroded rectangular	75	81	18	7699

Found	Preservation	Distortions
detected in GoogleEarth	high	moderately eroded; two geodetic measurement points placed upon the summit

Excavated

no

Pottery	Other finds
58	no

DATING

Late Bronze Age		Early Iron Age		Hellenistic		Kushan and Kushan-Sasanian	X
Early Medieval	X	High Medieval	X	Post-Mongol		Pre-modern	

Dating published elsewhere: Kushan, parts 10th–12th c. (Rtveladze 1974); Kushan; parts 9th–12th c. (Arshavskaya et al. 1982)

Bibliography

Rtveladze – Khakimov 1973, 18; Rtveladze 1974, 76; Arshavskaya et al. 1982, 132, no. 145; Stride 2004, vol. 3, Uz-SD-145

Notes

Stride 2004 locates it to the place of the site of Akkurgan – 045 by mistake

Date of survey	Entered by
30.08.2009	Danielisová

IDENTITY

Site Code	Stride 2004	Rtveladze 1974	Arshavskaya et al. 1982
6	no	no	145

Name of the site

No name 1

Translation: no

District: Sherabad

Type of site: settlement

Alternative name of the site: no

Latitude: 37.616561

Longitude: 66.983733

Elevation (m.a.s.l.): 370

Location

30 m south of the site no. 005, 2.5 km south of the village of Navbog

Topography

the site is situated in flat irrigated lowlands

DESCRIPTION

Basic description

low flat elevated tepa, upper layer made of recent gravel, max. NW–SE 77 m; max. SW–NE 80 m; upper surface indistinct; originally parhaps part of the no. 005

Shape	Length	Width	Height	Surface area (sq m)
rectangular, low	79	87	3	8331

Found: detected in GoogleEarth

Preservation: poor

Distortions: used as a cantine during the road building

Excavated

no

Pottery: 9

Other finds: no

DATING

Late Bronze Age	X	Early Iron Age		Hellenistic		Kushan and Kushan-Sasanian	
Early Medieval	X	High Medieval	X	Post-Mongol		Pre-modern	

Dating published elsewhere: no

Bibliography

Arshavskaya et al. 1982, 132, no. 145

Notes

drawing together with 005

Date of survey: 30.08.2009

Entered by: Danielisová

IDENTITY

Site Code	Stride 2004	Rtveladze 1974	Arshavskaya et al. 1982
7	no	no	no

Name of the site	Translation	District	Type of site
Koshtepa II	Double mound	Sherabad	settlement

Alternative name of the site	Latitude	Longitude	Elevation (m.a.s.l.)
no	37.602058	67.135425	355

Location

4.4 km SEE of the site of Jandavlattepa across the Sherabad River, close to the site no. 003 (Koshtepa I)

Topography

the site is situated in flat irrigated lowlands

DESCRIPTION

Basic description

compact mound, dusty surface, surrounded by irregular lower settlement (a rabat ?) in the east

Shape	Length	Width	Height	Surface area (sq m)
oval, lower part irregular	63	72		21312

Found	Preservation	Distortions
detected in GoogleEarth	high	upper part with no distortions, lower part partly destroyed by ploughing; partly covered with vegetation

Excavated

no

Pottery	Other finds
5	no

DATING

Late Bronze Age	Early Iron Age	Hellenistic	Kushan and Kushan-Sasanian X
Early Medieval	High Medieval	Post-Mongol	Pre-modern

Dating published elsewhere   no

Bibliography

no

Notes

Date of survey	Entered by
02.09.2009	Stančo

IDENTITY

Site Code **8**	Stride 2004 Uz-SD-150	Rtveladze 1974 B-032	Arshavskaya et al. 1982 150

Name of the site

Batyrabadtepa

Translation	District	Type of site
Comfortable place	Sherabad	settlement

Alternative name of the site	Latitude	Longitude	Elevation (m.a.s.l.)
Chuyanchi ("Kvartal keramistov", Annaev personal communication)	37.665756	67.046342	399

Location

1.2 km west of the village of Chukurkul

Topography

the site is situated in flat irrigated lowlands

DESCRIPTION

Basic description

upper part made of gravel (water) – pebbles material, whole gravel layer seen in the section

Shape	Length	Width	Height	Surface area (sq m)
circular/upper part rectangular	78	76		6552

Found	Preservation	Distortions
detected in GoogleEarth	high	min. 3 old trenches, traces of heavy water erosion

Excavated

excavated by Pugachenkova and Rtveladze before 1973

Pottery	Other finds
17	coin of Soter Megas reported

DATING

Late Bronze Age		Early Iron Age		Hellenistic		Kushan and Kushan-Sasanian	X
Early Medieval	X	High Medieval		Post-Mongol		Pre-modern	

Dating published elsewhere   1st–3rd c.and 5th–6th c. AD (Rtveladze – Khakimov 1973; Rtveladze 1974; Arshavskaya et al. 1982)

Bibliography

Rtveladze – Khakimov 1973, 20–21 (in detail including excavations, p. 19 ris. 5.1 groundplan); Rtveladze 1974, 77; Arshavskaya et al. 1982, 133, no. 150; Stride 2004, vol. 3, Uz-SD-150

Notes

Stride 2004 placed this site to the place of the site of Kattatepa by mistake

Date of survey	Entered by
30.08.2009	Danielisová

IDENTITY

Site Code
9

Stride 2004
no

Rtveladze 1974
no

Arshavskaya et al. 1982
no

Name of the site
Khoja Qaptol Bobo?

Translation
no

District
Sherabad

Type of site
settlement

Alternative name of the site
no

Latitude
37.667314

Longitude
67.078386

Elevation (m.a.s.l.)
378

Location
northeast of the village of Chukurkul, south of Dehkhanabad village

Topography
the site is situated in flat irrigated lowlands, covered mostly with cotton fields

DESCRIPTION

Basic description
very low, barely elevated terrain feature

Shape
circular

Length
27

Width
25

Height
1

Surface area (sq m)
58

Found
detected in GoogleEarth

Preservation
poor

Distortions
the site is going to disappear due to the ploughing

Excavated
no

Pottery
1

Other finds
no

DATING

Late Bronze Age	Early Iron Age	Hellenistic	Kushan and Kushan-Sasanian
Early Medieval	High Medieval	Post-Mongol	Pre-modern

Dating published elsewhere   no

Bibliography
Tušlová 2012

Notes
it is probably only a tomb of a holy man

Date of survey
20.09.2010

Entered by
Stančo

IDENTITY

Site Code	Stride 2004	Rtveladze 1974	Arshavskaya et al. 1982
10	Uz-SD-159	B-035	159

Name of the site	Translation	District	Type of site
Kattatepa, the main mound	Big mound	Sherabad	settlement

Alternative name of the site	Latitude	Longitude	Elevation (m.a.s.l.)
no	37.667483	67.082472	379

Location

northeast of the village of Chukurkul, south of Dehkhanabad village

Topography

the site is situated in flat irrigated lowlands

DESCRIPTION

Basic description

compact mound, highest point at SW

Shape	Length	Width	Height	Surface area (sq m)
irregular	113	157		23237

Found	Preservation	Distortions
B-35	high	ravine in the eastern part (E-W) caused by seasonal rain water

Excavated

no

Pottery	Other finds
28	bronze (2 pieces)

DATING

Late Bronze Age		Early Iron Age		Hellenistic		Kushan and Kushan-Sasanian	X
Early Medieval	X	High Medieval		Post-Mongol		Pre-modern	

Dating published elsewhere   Kushan, Early Medieval (Rtveladze 1974; Arshavskaya et al. 1982)

Bibliography

Rtveladze – Khakimov 1973, 14–16; 12, ris. 2.7 – simple ground plan; Rveladze 1974, 78; Arshavskaya et al. 1982, 134; Stride 2004, vol. 3, Uz-SD-159

Notes

Stride 2004 placed this site to the place of the no name site no. 012 by mistake

Date of survey	Entered by
29.08.2009	Stančo

IDENTITY

Site Code
11

Stride 2004
no

Rtveladze 1974
no

Arshavskaya et al. 1982
159?

Name of the site
Kattatepa, the northern mound

Translation
Big Mound

District
Sherabad

Type of site
settlement

Alternative name of the site
no

Latitude
37.669306

Longitude
67.081889

Elevation (m.a.s.l.)
378

Location
northeast of the village of Chukurkul, south of Dehkhanabad village

Topography

DESCRIPTION

Basic description

Shape

Length
75

Width
79

Height

Surface area (sq m)
5598

Found
B-35

Preservation
not known

Distortions
no

Excavated
no

Pottery
7

Other finds
stone bead

DATING

Late Bronze Age		Early Iron Age		Hellenistic		Kushan and Kushan-Sasanian	X
Early Medieval	X	High Medieval		Post-Mongol		Pre-modern	

Dating published elsewhere Kushan, Early Medieval (Rtveladze 1974; Arshavskaya et al. 1982)

Bibliography
Rtveladze – Khakimov 1973, 14–16; 12, ris. 2.7 – simple ground plan; Rveladze 1974, 78; Arshavskaya et al. 1982, 134

Notes
identification with a site mentioned by Arshavskaya et al. 1982, 134, no. 159 is uncertain – the size differs, since there is stated 15×12×4 m

Date of survey
29.08.2009

Entered by
Stančo

IDENTITY

Site Code
12

Stride 2004
no

Rtveladze 1974
no

Arshavskaya et al. 1982
no

Name of the site
No name 2

Translation
no

District
Sherabad

Type of site
settlement

Alternative name of the site
Katta Tepe (Stride 2004)

Latitude
37.6587

Longitude
67.102111

Elevation (m.a.s.l.)
372

Location
2.8 km west of the village of Mekhnatabad

Topography
the site is situated in flat irrigated lowlands

DESCRIPTION

Basic description
round mound (originally rectangular?), relatively high in the centre

Shape
round

Length
87

Width
96

Height

Surface area (sq m)
10265

Found
detected in GoogleEarth

Preservation
high

Distortions
no

Excavated
no

Pottery
16

Other finds
no

DATING

| Late Bronze Age | Early Iron Age | Hellenistic | Kushan and Kushan-Sasanian | X |
| Early Medieval | High Medieval | Post-Mongol | Pre-modern | |

Dating published elsewhere   no

Bibliography
no

Notes
Stride 2004 placed Kattatepa to this place by mistake

Date of survey
03.09.2010

Entered by
Danielisová

IDENTITY

Site Code
13

Stride 2004
no

Rtveladze 1974
no

Arshavskaya et al. 1982
no

Name of the site
No name 3

Translation
no

District
Sherabad

Type of site
settlement

Alternative name of the site
no

Latitude
37.649019

Longitude
67.083669

Elevation (m.a.s.l.)
372

Location
1 km southeast of the village of Chukurkul

Topography
the site is situated in flat irrigated lowlands

DESCRIPTION

Basic description
low circular mound

Shape	Length	Width	Height	Surface area (sq m)
circular	69	72	1	400

Found
detected in GoogleEarth

Preservation
poor

Distortions
devastated by long term ploughing; the trace of ploughing visible even on the satellite image

Excavated
no

Pottery
no

Other finds
no

DATING

Late Bronze Age		Early Iron Age		Hellenistic		Kushan and Kushan-Sasanian	
Early Medieval		High Medieval		Post-Mongol		Pre-modern	

Dating published elsewhere   no

Bibliography
no

Notes

Date of survey
18.09.2008

Entered by
Stančo

IDENTITY

Site Code
14

Stride 2004
no

Rtveladze 1974
no

Arshavskaya et al. 1982
no

Name of the site
Qashqalambesh

Translation
no

District
Sherabad

Type of site
unknown

Alternative name of the site
no

Latitude
37.649431

Longitude
67.078697

Elevation (m.a.s.l.)
373

Location
750 m southeast of the village of Chukurkul

Topography
the site is situated in flat irrigated lowlands

DESCRIPTION

Basic description
compact low mound, covered with a dense vegetation

Shape
oval

Length
40

Width
19

Height

Surface area (sq m)
79

Found
detected in GoogleEarth

Preservation
moderate

Distortions
vegetation cover

Excavated
no

Pottery
no

Other finds
no

DATING

Late Bronze Age		Early Iron Age		Hellenistic		Kushan and Kushan-Sasanian	
Early Medieval		High Medieval		Post-Mongol		Pre-modern	X

Dating published elsewhere   Pre-Modern

Bibliography
no

Notes

Date of survey
18.09.2008

Entered by
Stančo

IDENTITY

Site Code
16

Stride 2004
Uz-SD-236 X

Rtveladze 1974
no

Arshavskaya et al. 1982
no

Name of the site
Shortepa (?)

Translation
Salty mound

District
Sherabad

Type of site
settlement

Alternative name of the site
Gilyambof Kurgan (100k map); Ikizak tepa (Stride 2004)

Latitude
37.688758

Longitude
67.137606

Elevation (m.a.s.l.)
384

Location
north margin of the village of Mekhnatabad, former "9th Sovkhoz"

Topography
the site is situated in flat irrigated lowlands

DESCRIPTION

Basic description
compact relatively high mound, water-made ravines

Shape
eroded oval

Length
38

Width
47

Height
19

Surface area (sq m)
30701

Found
detected in GoogleEarth

Preservation
high

Distortions
recent graves all over the surface

Excavated
no

Pottery
49

Other finds
no

DATING

Late Bronze Age		Early Iron Age		Hellenistic		Kushan and Kushan-Sasanian	X
Early Medieval	X	High Medieval		Post-Mongol		Pre-modern	

Dating published elsewhere no

Bibliography
Rtveladze – Khakimov 1973, 14–16; Rtveladze 1974, 78; Stride 2004, vol. 3, Uz-SD-236 X

Notes
In CORONA image a wall around the tepa is clearly visible, especially on the north side

Date of survey
04.09.2009

Entered by
Stančo

IDENTITY

Site Code
17

Stride 2004
no

Rtveladze 1974
no

Arshavskaya et al. 1982
no

Name of the site
Shishtepa (?)

Translation
Lump mound

District
Sherabad

Type of site
settlement

Alternative name of the site
no

Latitude
37.699667

Longitude
67.111175

Elevation (m.a.s.l.)
385

Location
in the Yange village, eastern – separate – part of the village of Gorin (Gurin)

Topography
the site is situated in flat irrigated lowlands

DESCRIPTION

Basic description
compact mound, NE part elevated

Shape
oval

Length
102

Width
108

Height
16

Surface area (sq m)
12599

Found
detected in GoogleEarth

Preservation
high

Distortions
no

Excavated
no

Pottery
11

Other finds
no

DATING

Late Bronze Age		Early Iron Age		Hellenistic		Kushan and Kushan-Sasanian	X
Early Medieval	X	High Medieval		Post-Mongol		Pre-modern	

Dating published elsewhere
no

Bibliography
Tušlová 2012, 17–18

Notes

Date of survey
31.08.2009

Entered by
Danielisová

IDENTITY

Site Code
18

Stride 2004
Uz-SD-151

Rtveladze 1974
no

Arshavskaya et al. 1982
151

Name of the site
Gilyambobtepa

Translation
Carpet-like mound

District
Sherabad

Type of site
settlement

Alternative name of the site
Gurintepa (Arshavskaya et al. 1982, 133)

Latitude
37.698153

Longitude
67.088758

Elevation (m.a.s.l.)
383

Location
350 m south of the village of Gorin (Gurin)

Topography
the site is situated in flat irrigated lowlands

DESCRIPTION

Basic description
compact circular mound with elevated central part

Shape
circular

Length
64

Width
65

Height
12

Surface area (sq m)
4945

Found
detected in GoogleEarth

Preservation
high

Distortions
no

Excavated
no

Pottery
24

Other finds
drilled stone object

DATING

Late Bronze Age		Early Iron Age		Hellenistic		Kushan and Kushan-Sasanian	X
Early Medieval	X	High Medieval		Post-Mongol		Pre-modern	

Dating published elsewhere   5th–8th c. AD – upper layers (Arshavskaya et al. 1982)

Bibliography
Arshavskaya et al. 1982, 133, no. 151 (description, size 12×10×3 m); Stride 2004, vol. 3, Uz-SD-151

Notes
Stride 2004 placed this site to the place of the site of Gorintepa by mistake

Date of survey
31.08.2009

Entered by
Danielisová

IDENTITY

Site Code	Stride 2004		Rtveladze 1974	Arshavskaya et al. 1982
19	Uz-SD-153		B-031	153

Name of the site		Translation	District	Type of site
Gorintepa		Dry apricot mound	Sherabad	settlement

Alternative name of the site	Latitude	Longitude	Elevation (m.a.s.l.)
Gilyambobtepa (Rtveladze – Khakimov 1973, 19; Rtveladze 1974, 77; Stride 2004)	37.700197	67.074833	390

Location

central part of the village of Gorin, close to the main Sherabad – Kumkurgan road

Topography

the site is situated in flat irrigated lowlands close to the mountains

DESCRIPTION

Basic description

compact high mound with concrete staircase on the southern slope

Shape	Length	Width	Height	Surface area (sq m)
eroded rectangular	80	68	10	7330

Found	Preservation	Distortions
detected in GoogleEarth	moderate	covered by layer of concrete/gravel

Excavated

no

Pottery	Other finds
8	no

DATING

Late Bronze Age		Early Iron Age		Hellenistic		Kushan and Kushan-Sasanian	X
Early Medieval	X	High Medieval		Post-Mongol		Pre-modern	

Dating published elsewhere: Kushan and Early Medieval (Rtveladze 1974)

Bibliography

Rtveladze – Khakimov 1973, 19 ("Gilyambob-tepe"); Rtveladze 1974, 77, B-31; Stride 2004, vol. 3, Uz-SD-153

Notes

once was a 2nd WW monument of the unknown soldier standing on the top (not preserved)

Date of survey	Entered by
31.08.2009	Danielisová

IDENTITY

Site Code
20

Stride 2004
Uz-SD-156

Rtveladze 1974
B-028

Arshavskaya et al. 1982
156

Name of the site
Dombratepa

Translation
no

District
Sherabad

Type of site
settlement

Alternative name of the site
no

Latitude
37.707503

Longitude
67.053775

Elevation (m.a.s.l.)
408

Location
central part of the village of Laylakan/Chigatay (Rtveladze: Chagatay village), 5 km east of the centre of Sherabad

Topography
flat irrigated lowlands close to piedmont steppe

DESCRIPTION

Basic description
high irregular compact mound with a depression in its central part

Shape
irregular

Length
61

Width
87

Height

Surface area (sq m)
6876

Found
detected in GoogleEarth

Preservation
high

Distortions
several living houses and farming buildings at the foot of the mound

Excavated
no

Pottery
no

Other finds
no

DATING

| Late Bronze Age | | Early Iron Age | | Hellenistic | | Kushan and Kushan-Sasanian | X |
| Early Medieval | X | High Medieval | | Post-Mongol | | Pre-modern | |

Dating published elsewhere
Kushan and Early Medieval (Rtveladze 1974); Kushan, 5th–6th c. (Arshavskaya et al. 1982)

Bibliography
Rtveladze – Khakimov 1973, 18, 19 ris. 5.2 – simple ground plan; Rtveladze 1974, 77, B-28; Stride 2004, vol. 3, Uz-SD-156

Notes

Date of survey
17.09.2008

Entered by
Stančo

IDENTITY

Site Code	Stride 2004		Rtveladze 1974	Arshavskaya et al. 1982
21	Uz-SD-234		B-029	no

Name of the site
Koshtepa 1

Translation	District	Type of site
Double mound	Sherabad	settlement

Alternative name of the site	Latitude	Longitude	Elevation (m.a.s.l.)
no	37.710047	67.059197	401

Location
eastern margin of the village of of Laylakan/Chigatay (Rtveladze: Chagatay village), 500 m from the site no. 020

Topography
the site is situated in flat irrigated lowlands close to the border of the piedmont steppe

DESCRIPTION

Basic description
low irregular / round mound

Shape	Length	Width	Height	Surface area (sq m)
round	59	57		4585

Found	Preservation	Distortions
detected in GoogleEarth	moderate	ploughing of the margins

Excavated
excavated by Pidaev in 1972

Pottery	Other finds
no	coin of Vima Kadphises reported by Pidaev (Pidaev 1978, 21)

DATING

Late Bronze Age		Early Iron Age		Hellenistic		Kushan and Kushan-Sasanian	X
Early Medieval		High Medieval		Post-Mongol		Pre-modern	

Dating published elsewhere   Kushan (Pidaev 1974; Rtveladze 1974)

Bibliography
Rtveladze – Khakimov 1973, 18–19; Rtveladze 1974, 77; Pidaev 1974, 40–41; Pidaev 1978, 21; Stride 2004, vol. 3, Uz-SD-234

Notes

Date of survey	Entered by
17.09.2008	Stančo

IDENTITY

Site Code
22

Stride 2004
no

Rtveladze 1974
no

Arshavskaya et al. 1982
no

Name of the site
Taushkantepa

Translation
Hare mound

District
Sherabad

Type of site
settlement

Alternative name of the site
no

Latitude
37.611803

Longitude
67.021731

Elevation (m.a.s.l.)
367

Location
2 km south of the village of Hurjak/Kulugsha, 1 km west of Seplon

Topography
the site is situated in flat irrigated lowlands

DESCRIPTION

Basic description
relatively low rectangular (slightly trapezoid) in ground plan, compact mound with a water canal in the midle of the west side

Shape
trapezoid

Length
132

Width
133

Height

Surface area (sq m)
27055

Found
detected in GoogleEarth

Preservation
high

Distortions
no

Excavated
no

Pottery
10

Other finds
no

DATING

Late Bronze Age		Early Iron Age		Hellenistic		Kushan and Kushan-Sasanian	X
Early Medieval		High Medieval		Post-Mongol	X	Pre-modern	

Dating published elsewhere   no

Bibliography
no

Notes

Date of survey
01.09.2009

Entered by
Danielisová

IDENTITY

Site Code
23

Stride 2004
Uz-SD-168

Rtveladze 1974
no

Arshavskaya et al. 1982
168

Name of the site
Tashlaktepa

Translation
Mound with little stones

District
Sherabad

Type of site
settlement

Alternative name of the site
no

Latitude
37.633331

Longitude
66.986594

Elevation (m.a.s.l.)
377

Location
0.6 km south of the village of Navbog, 1 km west of the village of Kulugsha

Topography
the site is situated in flat irrigated lowlands

DESCRIPTION

Basic description
high compact mound with elevated SE part

Shape
two squares

Length
87

Width
68

Height

Surface area (sq m)
5083

Found
detected in GoogleEarth

Preservation
high

Distortions
no

Excavated
no

Pottery
18

Other finds
no

DATING

Late Bronze Age		Early Iron Age		Hellenistic		Kushan and Kushan-Sasanian	X
Early Medieval	X	High Medieval	X	Post-Mongol	X	Pre-modern	

Dating published elsewhere   Early Medieval (Arshavskaya et al. 1982)

Bibliography
Arshavskaya et al. 1982, 135; Annaev 1988, 14; Stride 2004, vol. 3, Uz-SD-168

Notes
Stride 2004 locates it to the place of the site of Challkurgan – 063 by mistake.

Date of survey
16.09.2008,
04.09.2009

Entered by
Stančo

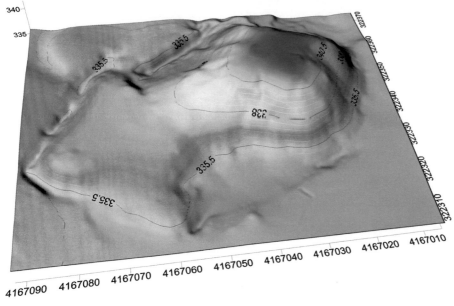

IDENTITY

Site Code	Stride 2004	Rtveladze 1974	Arshavskaya et al. 1982
24	Uz-SD-230	B-020	no

Name of the site	Translation	District	Type of site
Mozoroti baba tepa	Grave of "baba" mound	Sherabad	settlement

Alternative name of the site	Latitude	Longitude	Elevation (m.a.s.l.)
Mazarbaba-Tepe (Rtveladze 1974; Rtveladze – Khakimov 1973); Mazarbabatepa (Pidaev 1974)	37.651719	66.954864	386

Location

southern part of the Hojakiya village

Topography

the site is surrounded by flat irrigated lowlands, situated close to the mountains

DESCRIPTION

Basic description

irregular mound

Shape	Length	Width	Height	Surface area (sq m)
irregular	88	93	11	10623

Found	Preservation	Distortions
detected in GoogleEarth	moderate	recent cemetery all over the site (most recent are some children graves)

Excavated

surveyed by Pugachenkova in 1967, later one trench by Khakimov

Pottery	Other finds
30	coin of Vasudeva I and II reported

DATING

Late Bronze Age		Early Iron Age		Hellenistic		Kushan and Kushan-Sasanian	X
Early Medieval	X	High Medieval		Post-Mongol		Pre-modern	

Dating published elsewhere   Kushan and earlier (Rtveladze 1974), Early Kushan – Late Kushan (Pidaev 1978)

Bibliography

Rtveladze – Khakimov 1973, 19; Rtveladze 1974, 76; Pidaev 1978, 19; Stride 2004, vol. 3, Uz-SD-230

Notes

Date of survey	Entered by
01.09.2009	Stančo

IDENTITY

Site Code	Stride 2004	Rtveladze 1974	Arshavskaya et al. 1982
25	Uz-SD-167	B-024	167

Name of the site

Talagantepa

Translation	District	Type of site
Stolen mound	Sherabad	settlement

Alternative name of the site	Latitude	Longitude	Elevation (m.a.s.l.)
Tanlagan-tepe (Rtveladze – Khakimov 1973)	37.656069	66.988286	399

Location

southeastern part of the village of Akkurgan, close to the Sherabad road

Topography

the site is situated in flat irrigated lowlands

DESCRIPTION

Basic description

relatively high compact mound with several traces of heavy water erosion

Shape	Length	Width	Height	Surface area (sq m)
irregular	90	102	10	10572

Found	Preservation	Distortions
seen from the modern road from Sherabad to the former Akkurgan museum, detected in GoogleEarth	high	no

Excavated

no

Pottery	Other finds
27	no

DATING

Late Bronze Age		Early Iron Age		Hellenistic		Kushan and Kushan-Sasanian	X
Early Medieval	X	High Medieval		Post-Mongol		Pre-modern	

Dating published elsewhere   Kushan, Early Medieval (Rtveladze 1974; Arshavskaya et al. 1982)

Bibliography

Rtveladze – Khakimov1973, 18; Rtveladze 1974, 76; Arshavskaya et al. 1982, 135; Stride 2004, vol. 3, Uz-SD-167

Notes

Arshavskaya et al. 1982 speak of eastern direction instead of western direction from the town of Sherabad by mistake

Date of survey	Entered by
03.09.2009	Stančo

IDENTITY

Site Code **26**	Stride 2004 no	Rtveladze 1974 no	Arshavskaya et al. 1982 no

Name of the site
Yalangoyoq ota tepa

Translation
Mound of barefoot father

District
Sherabad

Type of site
settlement

Alternative name of the site
no

Latitude
37.634728

Longitude
67.024744

Elevation (m.a.s.l.)
376

Location
north of the village of Gambir, 100 m west of the main Tashkent – Termez road

Topography
the site is situated in flat irrigated lowlands

DESCRIPTION

Basic description
low compact mound (up to 5 m), surrounded by Muslim graveyard, southern part slightly elevated

Shape	Length	Width	Height	Surface area (sq m)
rectangular	39	38	4	2419

Found
detected in GoogleEarth

Preservation
high

Distortions
tomb of a mulla on the top

Excavated
no

Pottery
49

Other finds
no

DATING

Late Bronze Age	Early Iron Age X	Hellenistic X	Kushan and Kushan-Sasanian X
Early Medieval	High Medieval	Post-Mongol	Pre-modern

Dating published elsewhere   no

Bibliography
Annaev 1988, 13; Stančo 2018

Notes

Date of survey
01.09.2009

Entered by
Stančo

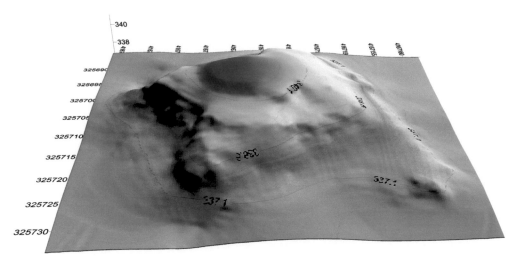

IDENTITY

Site Code	Stride 2004	Rtveladze 1974	Arshavskaya et al. 1982
27	Uz-SD-149	B-030	149

Name of the site

Babatepa (the main tepa)

Translation	District	Type of site
Mound of "baba" or "Ancient mound"	Sherabad	settlement

Alternative name of the site	Latitude	Longitude	Elevation (m.a.s.l.)
no	37.720108	67.089125	408

Location

in the southwestern part of the village of Babatepa (Istora?)

Topography

the site is situated in flat irrigated lowlands, surrounded by water canals and several small mounds

DESCRIPTION

Basic description

high elongated mound with a separate part, a "citadel" in the southern end and shakhristan in the northern part

Shape	Length	Width	Height	Surface area (sq m)
oval	152	73	13	30582

Found	Preservation	Distortions
in publications	high	tomb of a mullah on the top; recent cemetery all over the surface

Excavated

no

Pottery	Other finds
10	a platform made of unique burnt bricks of a size 60×60 cm (see picture); imitation of Heliocles and Kushan-Sasanian coin reported; terracotta head from imported from Khotan (Stančo 2015)

DATING

Late Bronze Age		Early Iron Age		Hellenistic		Kushan and Kushan-Sasanian	X
Early Medieval	X	High Medieval		Post-Mongol		Pre-modern	

Dating published elsewhere   Pre-Kushan and Kushan (Rtveladze – Khakimov 1973; Rtveladze 1974)

Bibliography

Parfyonov s.d., 168–169; Rtveladze – Khakimov; 1973, 19; Rtveladze 1974, 77; Nemtseva 1989; Stride 2004, vol. 3, Uz-SD-149

Notes

Date of survey	Entered by
17.09.2008, 06.09.2009	Stančo

IDENTITY

Site Code
28

Stride 2004
Uz-SD-149a

Rtveladze 1974
B-030

Arshavskaya et al. 1982
149

Name of the site
No name 4

Translation
no

District
Sherabad

Type of site
architecture

Alternative name of the site
no

Latitude
37.719992

Longitude
67.087144

Elevation (m.a.s.l.)
406

Location
130 m west of the site of Babatepa

Topography
flat irrigated lowlands, surrounded by water canals and several small mounds

DESCRIPTION

Basic description
high compact square mound (remains of a two-storey building?)

Shape
square

Length
25

Width
26

Height

Surface area (sq m)
47

Found
in publications

Preservation
moderate

Distortions
erosion after excavations

Excavated
fully excavated 1980–82, 1984 by Nemtseva

Pottery
no

Other finds
no

DATING

Late Bronze Age		Early Iron Age		Hellenistic		Kushan and Kushan-Sasanian	
Early Medieval	X	High Medieval		Post-Mongol		Pre-modern	

Dating published elsewhere   6th–7th c. AD (Nemtseva 1989, 62)

Bibliography
Arshavskaya et al. 1982, 132–133; Nemtseva 1989; Stride 2004, vol. 3, Uz-SD-317a

Notes

Date of survey
17.09.2008,
06.09.2009

Entered by
Stančo

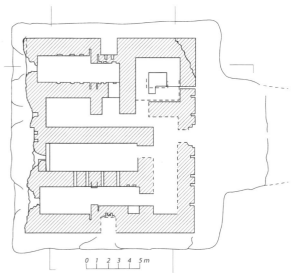

Ground plan of name 4, drawn by P. Kazakova after Nemtseva1989, 153.

IDENTITY

Site Code	Stride 2004	Rtveladze 1974	Arshavskaya et al. 1982
29	Uz-SD-149b	B-030	149

Name of the site

Chopantepa

Translation	District	Type of site
Shepherd´s mound	Sherabad	architecture

Alternative name of the site	Latitude	Longitude	Elevation (m.a.s.l.)
no	37.718903	67.087069	405

Location

150 m southwest of the site of Babatepa

Topography

the site is situated in flat irrigated lowlands

DESCRIPTION

Basic description

flat square mound, covered with vegetation

Shape	Length	Width	Height	Surface area (sq m)
square	55	55		198

Found	Preservation	Distortions
in publications	moderate	erosion after excavations

Excavated

fully excavated 1980–82, 1984 by Nemtseva

Pottery	Other finds
no	no

DATING

Late Bronze Age		Early Iron Age		Hellenistic		Kushan and Kushan-Sasanian	
Early Medieval	X	High Medieval		Post-Mongol		Pre-modern	

Dating published elsewhere   5th–6th c. AD (Nemtseva 1989, 162)

Bibliography

Arshavskaya et al. 1982, 132–133; Nemtseva 1989; Stride 2004, vol. 3, Uz-SD-149b

Notes

Date of survey	Entered by
17.09.2008	Stančo

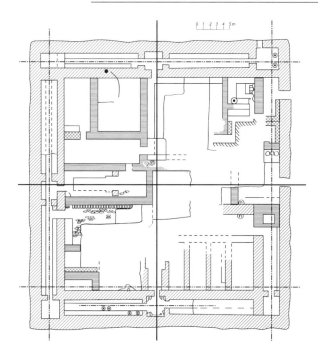

Ground plan of Chopantepa, drawn by P. Kazakova after Nemtseva1989, 135.

IDENTITY

Site Code
30

Stride 2004
no

Rtveladze 1974
no

Arshavskaya et al. 1982
no

Name of the site
No name 5

Translation
no

District
Sherabad

Type of site
settlement

Alternative name of the site
no

Latitude
37.719544

Longitude
67.084692

Elevation (m.a.s.l.)
407

Location
350 m SWW of the site of Babatepa

Topography
the site is situated in flat irrigated lowlands

DESCRIPTION

Basic description
high compact square mound (remains of a two-storey building?)

Shape
square

Length
27

Width
26

Height
3

Surface area (sq m)
64

Found
field walking

Preservation
high

Distortions
no

Excavated
no

Pottery
no

Other finds
no

DATING

Late Bronze Age	Early Iron Age	Hellenistic	Kushan and Kushan-Sasanian

Early Medieval	X	High Medieval	Post-Mongol	Pre-modern

Dating published elsewhere   no

Bibliography
Nemtseva 1989

Notes
dating to the 5th–7th c. is our estimate based on the analogy with 028

Date of survey
17.09.2008

Entered by
Stančo

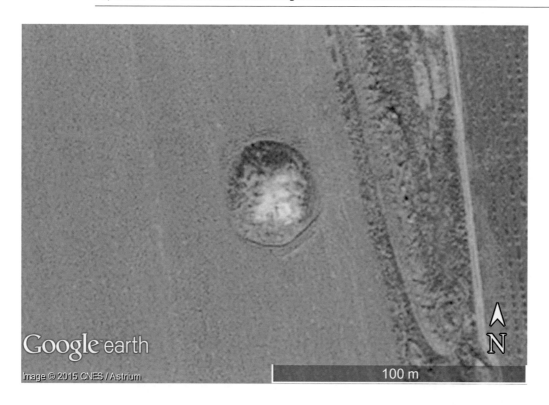

IDENTITY

Site Code
31

Stride 2004
no

Rtveladze 1974
no

Arshavskaya et al. 1982
no

Name of the site
No name 6

Translation
no

District
Sherabad

Type of site
settlement

Alternative name of the site
no

Latitude
37.721881

Longitude
67.085456

Elevation (m.a.s.l.)
409

Location
250 m west of the site of Babatepa

Topography
the site is situated in flat irrigated lowlands

DESCRIPTION

Basic description
low irregular mound

Shape
irregular

Length
167

Width
182

Height

Surface area (sq m)
149

Found
field walking

Preservation
poor

Distortions
several houses and other structures (a platform) built upon the site

Excavated
no

Pottery
no

Other finds
no

DATING

Late Bronze Age	Early Iron Age	Hellenistic	Kushan and Kushan-Sasanian
Early Medieval	High Medieval	Post-Mongol	Pre-modern

Dating published elsewhere   no

Bibliography
Nemtseva 1989

Notes

Date of survey
17.09.2008

Entered by
Stančo

IDENTITY

Site Code	Stride 2004	Rtveladze 1974	Arshavskaya et al. 1982
32	Uz-SD-228	B-013	no

Name of the site
Talashkantepa II (SE mound)

Translation	District	Type of site
High mound	Sherabad	settlement

Alternative name of the site	Latitude	Longitude	Elevation (m.a.s.l.)
no	37.573487	66.90858	361

Location
460 m east of the village of Talashkan

Topography
the site is situated in flat irrigated lowlands

DESCRIPTION

Basic description
compact mound with uneven surface; soft dusty soil on the surface

Shape	Length	Width	Height	Surface area (sq m)
pentagon	167	182	6	48238

Found	Preservation	Distortions
in publications	high	Pre-Modern graves all over the surface; small old cottage in the NE part

Excavated
yes – traces of a trench in the southern part

Pottery	Other finds
34	burnt bricks (th. 4 cm); slag in NW part; coins: imitation of Heliocles, Vima Kapdhises and Vasudeva II/Kanishka II reported by Rtveladze – Pidaev 1981

DATING

Late Bronze Age	Early Iron Age	Hellenistic	Kushan and Kushan-Sasanian
			X

Early Medieval	High Medieval	Post-Mongol	Pre-modern
X			

Dating published elsewhere: 1st c. BC, Kushan, Kushan-Sasanian (Rtveladze 1974)

Bibliography
Rtveladze 1974, 74–75; Rtveladze – Pidaev 1981, 51, 65; Stride 2004, vol. 4, 203

Notes

Date of survey	Entered by
16.10.2005, 05.09.2010	Stančo

IDENTITY

Site Code	Stride 2004	Rtveladze 1974	Arshavskaya et al. 1982
33	Uz-SD-148	no	148

Name of the site	Translation	District	Type of site
No name 7	no	Sherabad	settlement

Alternative name of the site	Latitude	Longitude	Elevation (m.a.s.l.)
no	37.677361	67.080556	378

Location

in the cemetery of the village of Yakhte Yul′ (or Dekhkanabad), so called Termez-ota

Topography

the site is situated in flat irrigated lowlands, with a large cemetery around

DESCRIPTION

Basic description

rectangular shape, covered by recent graves, NW part elevated, probably citadel

Shape	Length	Width	Height	Surface area (sq m)
rectangular	70	85	8	4700

Found	Preservation	Distortions
detected in GoogleEarth	moderate	Pre-Modern graves all over the site

Excavated

no

Pottery	Other finds
25	terracotta water pipe

DATING

Late Bronze Age	Early Iron Age	Hellenistic X	Kushan and X
			Kushan-Sasanian
Early Medieval X	High Medieval X	Post-Mongol	Pre-modern

Dating published elsewhere   Early Medieval (Arshavskaya et al. 1982)

Bibliography

Rtveladze – Khakimov1973, 16, described together with the site of Kattatepa; Arshavskaya et al. 1982, 132 (size 43×43m, height 4–5m; orientation NE–SW); Stride 2004, vol. 3, Uz-SD-148

Notes

Date of survey	Entered by
30.08.2009	Danielisová

IDENTITY

Site Code **35**	Stride 2004 Uz-SD-229	Rtveladze 1974 B-017	Arshavskaya et al. 1982 no

Name of the site
Chopan Ata

Translation	District	Type of site
no	Sherabad	settlement

Alternative name of the site
Chopon-Ata (Rtveladze 1974, 76; Stride 2004), Cholpon ota kabristoni (information boad on the spot)

Latitude	Longitude	Elevation (m.a.s.l.)
37.63715	66.981636	383

Location
500 m west of the southern end of the village of Navbog

Topography
the site is situated in flat irrigated lowlands, modern cemetery around

DESCRIPTION

Basic description
compact slightly elevated mound, square in ground plan

Shape	Length	Width	Height	Surface area (sq m)
square	116	118		19695

Found	Preservation	Distortions
detected in GoogleEarth	poor	all the surface covered with a modern cemetery and small chapel is situated on the top

Excavated
stratigraphic trench in spring 1973 – Baktriyskaya ekspeditsiya

Pottery	Other finds
6	no

DATING

Late Bronze Age		Early Iron Age		Hellenistic		Kushan and Kushan-Sasanian	X
Early Medieval	X	High Medieval		Post-Mongol		Pre-modern	

Dating published elsewhere Kushan and earlier (Rtveladze 1974)

Bibliography
Rtveladze – Khakimov1973, 17–18; Rtveladze 1974, 76; Nekrasova 1976, 76; Pidaev 1980, 20–21; Stride 2004, vol. 3, Uz-SD-229

Notes

Date of survey	Entered by
16.09.2008	Stančo

IDENTITY

Site Code
36

Stride 2004
Uz-SD-146

Rtveladze 1974
B-018

Arshavskaya et al. 1982
146

Name of the site
Anjirtepa

Translation
Fig mound

District
Sherabad

Type of site
settlement

Alternative name of the site
no

Latitude
37.636028

Longitude
66.983603

Elevation (m.a.s.l.)
382

Location
500 m southwest of the village of Navbog

Topography
the site is situated in flat irrigated lowlands

DESCRIPTION

Basic description
small irregular mound, diameter approx. 30 m

Shape
irregular

Length
38

Width
40

Height

Surface area (sq m)
99

Found
detected in GoogleEarth

Preservation
low

Distortions
eroded and probably intentionally disturbed; partly covered with a vegetation

Excavated
no

Pottery
3

Other finds
no

DATING

Late Bronze Age		Early Iron Age		Hellenistic		Kushan and Kushan-Sasanian	
Early Medieval	X	High Medieval		Post-Mongol		Pre-modern	

Dating published elsewhere   Early Medieval (Arshavskaya et al. 1982)

Bibliography
Rtveladze – Khakimov1973, 17; Rtveladze 1974, 76; Arshavskaya et al. 1982, 132; Stride 2004, vol. 3, Uz-SD-146

Notes

Date of survey
16.09.2008

Entered by
Stančo

IDENTITY

Site Code	Stride 2004		Rtveladze 1974	Arshavskaya et al. 1982
37	Uz-SD-143		B-036	143

Name of the site	Translation	District	Type of site
Ayritepa	Divided mound	Sherabad	settlement

Alternative name of the site	Latitude	Longitude	Elevation (m.a.s.l.)
Air Tepe (Rtveladze 1974; Stride 2004)	37.682567	67.105908	383

Location

2.5 km east of the village of Dekhkanabad

Topography

the site is situated in flat irrigated lowlands

DESCRIPTION

Basic description

high compact mound

Shape	Length	Width	Height	Surface area (sq m)
irregular	110	95	15	16502

Found	Preservation	Distortions
detected in GoogleEarth	high	no

Excavated

no

Pottery	Other finds
16	no

DATING

Late Bronze Age		Early Iron Age		Hellenistic		Kushan and Kushan-Sasanian	X
Early Medieval	X	High Medieval		Post-Mongol		Pre-modern	

Dating published elsewhere: Kushan and Early Medieval (Rtveladze – Khakimov 1973; Rtveladze 1974; Arshavskaya et al. 1982)

Bibliography

Rtveladze – Khakimov 1973, 21; Rtveladze 1974, 78; Arshavskaya et al. 1982, 132; Stride 2004, vol. 3, Uz-SD-143

Notes

Date of survey	Entered by
06.09.2010	Stančo

IDENTITY

Site Code
38

Stride 2004
no

Rtveladze 1974
no

Arshavskaya et al. 1982
no

Name of the site
No name 8

Translation
no

District
Sherabad

Type of site
settlement

Alternative name of the site
no

Latitude
37.655753

Longitude
67.110064

Elevation (m.a.s.l.)
370

Location
2 km west of the village of Mekhnatabad

Topography
the site is situated in flat irrigated lowlands

DESCRIPTION

Basic description
small rectangular site

Shape
rectangular

Length
38

Width
37

Height

Surface area (sq m)
139

Found
detected in GoogleEarth

Preservation
high

Distortions
completely covered with vegetation

Excavated
no

Pottery
1

Other finds
no

DATING

Late Bronze Age	Early Iron Age	Hellenistic	Kushan and Kushan-Sasanian

Early Medieval	High Medieval	Post-Mongol	Pre-modern

Dating published elsewhere   no

Bibliography
no

Notes
small amount of pottery

Date of survey
03.09.2010

Entered by
Danielisová

IDENTITY

Site Code	Stride 2004		Rtveladze 1974	Arshavskaya et al. 1982
39	no		no	no

Name of the site	Translation	District	Type of site
No name 9	no	Sherabad	settlement

Alternative name of the site	Latitude	Longitude	Elevation (m.a.s.l.)
no	37.652961	67.112778	367

Location

1.7 km west of the village of Mekhnatabad

Topography

the site is situated in flat irrigated lowlands

DESCRIPTION

Basic description

small rounded mound

Shape	Length	Width	Height	Surface area (sq m)
rectangular/rounded	43	37		1073

Found	Preservation	Distortions
detected in GoogleEarth	moderate	partially covered by vegetation

Excavated

no

Pottery	Other finds
no	no

DATING

Late Bronze Age		Early Iron Age	X	Hellenistic		Kushan and Kushan-Sasanian	
Early Medieval		High Medieval		Post-Mongol		Pre-modern	

Dating published elsewhere   no

Bibliography

no

Notes

large amounts of badly preserved pottery

Date of survey	Entered by
03.09.2010	Danielisová

IDENTITY

Site Code	Stride 2004		Rtveladze 1974	Arshavskaya et al. 1982
40	no		no	no

Name of the site	Translation	District	Type of site
Shortepa (?)	Salty mound	Sherabad	settlement

Alternative name of the site	Latitude	Longitude	Elevation (m.a.s.l.)
no	37.648508	67.138178	368

Location

northern part of the village of Mekhnatabad ("9th Sovkhoz")

Topography

the site is situated in flat irrigated lowlands

DESCRIPTION

Basic description

relatively high compact mound with elevated northern part

Shape	Length	Width	Height	Surface area (sq m)
circular/oval	105	100	9	15950

Found	Preservation	Distortions
detected in GoogleEarth	high	no

Excavated

no

Pottery	Other finds
26	Kushan-Sasanian coin

DATING

Late Bronze Age		Early Iron Age		Hellenistic		Kushan and Kushan-Sasanian	X
Early Medieval	X	High Medieval		Post-Mongol		Pre-modern	

Dating published elsewhere   no

Bibliography

no

Notes

Date of survey	Entered by
04.09.2009	Stančo

IDENTITY

Site Code	Stride 2004		Rtveladze 1974	Arshavskaya et al. 1982
41	no		no	no

Name of the site	Translation	District	Type of site
No name 10	no	Kizirik	settlement

Alternative name of the site	Latitude	Longitude	Elevation (m.a.s.l.)
Besh-tepe (Parfyonov s.d.)	37.579136	67.172264	351

Location

1.1 km west of the village of Takiya

Topography

the site is situated in flat irrigated lowlands

DESCRIPTION

Basic description

rectangular mound with "citadel" on the west, all NW part elevated

Shape	Length	Width	Height	Surface area (sq m)
rectangular	116	112	10	2002

Found	Preservation	Distortions
detected in GoogleEarth	moderate	traces of modern structures in the central part; minor digs here and there

Excavated

no

Pottery	Other finds
5	no

DATING

Late Bronze Age		Early Iron Age		Hellenistic		Kushan and Kushan-Sasanian	
Early Medieval		High Medieval		Post-Mongol	X	Pre-modern	

Dating published elsewhere   no

Bibliography

no

Notes

traces of a moat on the south

Date of survey	Entered by
10.09.2010	Danielisová

IDENTITY

Site Code	Stride 2004	Rtveladze 1974	Arshavskaya et al. 1982
42	Uz-SD-344 or Uz-SD-144	B-039	144

Name of the site	Translation	District	Type of site
Aysaritepa	(female name)	Kizirik	settlement

Alternative name of the site	Latitude	Longitude	Elevation (m.a.s.l.)
Maysaratepa (locals, 2nd variant)	37.557253	67.150033	347

Location

on the southeastern margin of the village of Hokimishanov (Center Progres)

Topography

the site is situated in flat irrigated lowlands; right bank of Kara Su River

DESCRIPTION

Basic description

middle size compact mound, slightly elevated in SW part

Shape	Length	Width	Height	Surface area (sq m)
rectangular	87	83	10	12411

Found	Preservation	Distortions
detected in GoogleEarth	high	no

Excavated

Pidaev (1972, two trenches in NE part)

Pottery	Other finds
11	glass

DATING

Late Bronze Age		Early Iron Age		Hellenistic	X	Kushan and Kushan-Sasanian	X
Early Medieval	X	High Medieval		Post-Mongol		Pre-modern	

Dating published elsewhere   2nd c. BC–2nd c. AD, 3rd–4th (Pidaev 1974); Antique (Rtveladze – Khakimov 1973; Rtveladze 1974)

Bibliography

Rtveladze – Khakimov 1973, 22; Rtveladze 1974, 78; Pidaev 1974, 38–40 (in detail, size – 55×60×9 m); Arshavskaya et al. 1982, 144; Stride 2004, vol. 3, Uz-SD-344 and 144

Notes

Stride 2004 placed this site to the place of the site of Shortepa II – 040 by mistake.

Date of survey	Entered by
08.09.2010	Stančo

IDENTITY

Site Code
43

Stride 2004
no

Rtveladze 1974
B-040?

Arshavskaya et al. 1982
no

Name of the site
No name 11

Translation
no

District
Kizirik

Type of site
settlement

Alternative name of the site
Some local people say "Karatepa"

Latitude
37.544747

Longitude
67.163917

Elevation (m.a.s.l.)
344

Location
2 km southeast of the village of Hokimishanov, 1 km north of Zang Canal

Topography
the site is situated in flat irrigated lowlands

DESCRIPTION

Basic description
two relatively flat mounds

Shape	Length	Width	Height	Surface area (sq m)
irregular	220	113	8	12463

Found
detected in GoogleEarth

Preservation
high

Distortions
partially covered with vegetation

Excavated
no

Pottery
15

Other finds
no

DATING

Late Bronze Age	Early Iron Age	Hellenistic	Kushan and Kushan-Sasanian
			X

Early Medieval	High Medieval	Post-Mongol	Pre-modern

Dating published elsewhere
1st–3rd c. AD (Rtveladze – Khakimov 1973); Antique (Rtveladze 1974)

Bibliography
Rtveladze – Khakimov 1973, 21–22; Rtveladze 1974, 78

Notes
soft and dusty soil, bad for the preservation of pottery; identification with no. B-040 is uncertain – according to the Rtveladze (1974, 78) it is located 300 m to the east of Aysaritepa (no. B-039, our no. 042), which is not true.

Date of survey
09.09.2010

Entered by
Danielisová

IDENTITY

Site Code	Stride 2004	Rtveladze 1974	Arshavskaya et al. 1982
44	Uz-SD-143	no	132

Name of the site	Translation	District	Type of site
Teshiktepa	no	Kizirik/Angor	settlement

Alternative name of the site	Latitude	Longitude	Elevation (m.a.s.l.)
no	37.535172	67.153828	343

Location

2.5 km south of the village of Hokimishanov on the "island" between two branches of the Zang Canal

Topography

the site is situated in flat irrigated lowlands

DESCRIPTION

Basic description

rectangular tepa with elevated southern part – a citadel ?; long axis SE–NW 133 m, SW–NE 100 m

Shape	Length	Width	Height	Surface area (sq m)
rectangular	140	144	12	23211

Found	Preservation	Distortions
detected in GoogleEarth	high	no

Excavated

no

Pottery	Other finds
no	no

DATING

Late Bronze Age	Early Iron Age	Hellenistic	Kushan and Kushan-Sasanian X
Early Medieval	High Medieval X	Post-Mongol	Pre-modern

Dating published elsewhere   Kushan and 11th–12th c. AD (Arshavskaya et al. 1982)

Bibliography

Pidaev 1974, 40; Arshavskaya et al. 1982, 132, no. 132 (belonging to Angor District); Stride 2004, vol. 3, Uz-SD-143

Notes

Date of survey	Entered by
not surveyed	no

IDENTITY

Site Code
45

Stride 2004
no

Rtveladze 1974
B-019

Arshavskaya et al. 1982
no

Name of the site
Akkurgan

Translation
no

District
Sherabad

Type of site
settlement

Alternative name of the site
no

Latitude
37.644528

Longitude
66.934803

Elevation (m.a.s.l.)
400

Location
500 m south of the western margin of the village of Khojakiya across the water canal

Topography
the site is situated in flat irrigated lowlands close to the mountains

DESCRIPTION

Basic description
compact site with apparent trenches on the surface

Shape
rectangular, oblong

Length
113

Width
103

Height
11

Surface area (sq m)
10010

Found
GoogleEarth/local knowledge

Preservation
moderate

Distortions
erosion after excavations

Excavated
stratigraphic trench in spring 1973 – Baktriyskaya ekspeditsiya; Pidaev 1975, whole surface excavated

Pottery
13

Other finds
no

DATING

Late Bronze Age		Early Iron Age		Hellenistic		Kushan and Kushan-Sasanian	X
Early Medieval	X	High Medieval		Post-Mongol		Pre-modern	

Dating published elsewhere   coins of 1st–3rd c. AD, upper strata: 1st half of 4th c. AD (Pidaev 1978)

Bibliography

Nekrasova 1976, 76; Pidaev 1978, 50–81

Notes

Date of survey
01.09.2009

Entered by
Danielisová

182

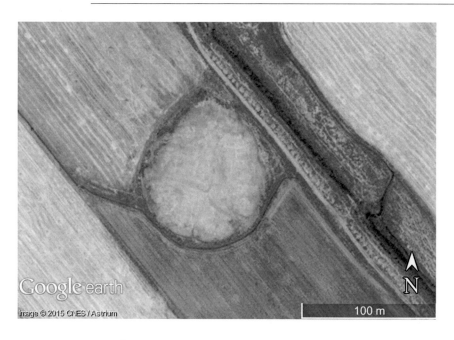

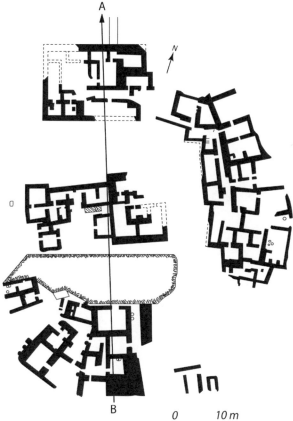

Ground plan of Akkurgan, drawn by P. Kazakova after Pidaev 1978, 51, ris. 16.

IDENTITY

Site Code
48

Stride 2004
no

Rtveladze 1974
no

Arshavskaya et al. 1982
no

Name of the site
Kattatepa (SE mound)

Translation
no

District
Sherabad

Type of site
settlement

Alternative name of the site
no

Latitude
37.666264

Longitude
67.083403

Elevation (m.a.s.l.)
377

Location
300 m north of the eastern margin of the village of Chukurkul

Topography
the site is situated in flat irrigated lowlands

DESCRIPTION

Basic description
flat oblong mound, divided diagonally into two parts

Shape
irregular

Length
69

Width
54

Height
3

Surface area (sq m)
345

Found
detected in GoogleEarth

Preservation
moderate

Distortions
margins of the site gradually destroyed by ploughing; partly covered by a vegetation

Excavated
no

Pottery
7

Other finds
no

DATING

Late Bronze Age	Early Iron Age	Hellenistic	Kushan and Kushan-Sasanian
Early Medieval	High Medieval	Post-Mongol	Pre-modern

Dating published elsewhere   no

Bibliography
Rtveladze – Khakimov 1973, 14–16; 12, ris. 2.7 – simple ground plan; Rveladze 1974, 78; Arshavskaya et al. 1982, 134

Notes

Date of survey
29.08.2009

Entered by
Stančo

IDENTITY

Site Code
49

Stride 2004
no

Rtveladze 1974
no

Arshavskaya et al. 1982
159

Name of the site
Olleiortepa

Translation
(male name: God with him forever)

District
Sherabad

Type of site
architecture

Alternative name of the site
no

Latitude
37.671756

Longitude
67.080044

Elevation (m.a.s.l.)
379

Location
southeastern part of the village of Dekhkanabad between houses

Topography
the site is situated in flat irrigated lowlands

DESCRIPTION

Basic description
remains of the small compact building preserved up to the 1st floor

Shape	Length	Width	Height	Surface area (sq m)
rectangular (square)	20	22	8	39

Found
seen from Kattatepa

Preservation
high

Distortions
no

Excavated
no

Pottery
1

Other finds
Hephtalite coin reported by Rtveladze – Khakimov 1973

DATING

Late Bronze Age		Early Iron Age		Hellenistic		Kushan and Kushan-Sasanian	
Early Medieval	X	High Medieval	X	Post-Mongol	X	Pre-modern	

Dating published elsewhere

Bibliography
Rtveladze – Khakimov 1973, 14–16; 12, ris. 2.7 – simple ground plan; Rveladze 1974, 78; Arshavskaya et al. 1982, 134

Notes

Date of survey
30.08.2009

Entered by
Danielisová

IDENTITY

Site Code
50

Stride 2004
no

Rtveladze 1974
no

Arshavskaya et al. 1982
145

Name of the site
No name 12 (Aktepa east)

Translation
no

District
Sherabad

Type of site
tepa (ploughed)

Alternative name of the site
no

Latitude
37.617232

Longitude
66.984493

Elevation (m.a.s.l.)
370

Location
just 50 m east of the site nos. 005 and 006 across the road, 2.5 km south of the village of Navbog

Topography
the site is situated in flat irrigated lowlands

DESCRIPTION

Basic description
flat, low, distorted remians of a tepa, covered by the vegetation

Shape
irregular

Length
40

Width
20

Height

Surface area (sq m)
39

Found
local knowledge

Preservation
poor

Distortions
ploughed ?, vegetation

Excavated
no

Pottery
4

Other finds
no

DATING

Late Bronze Age		Early Iron Age		Hellenistic		Kushan and Kushan-Sasanian	
Early Medieval		High Medieval	X	Post-Mongol		Pre-modern	

Dating published elsewhere   no

Bibliography
no

Notes
reportedly, this site had the form of a tepa once but had been ploughed or otherwise distorted

Date of survey
30.08.2009

Entered by
Danielisová

IDENTITY

Site Code	Stride 2004	Rtveladze 1974	Arshavskaya et al. 1982
52	Uz-SD-158	no	158

Name of the site

Khosyattepa

Translation: Peculiar mound

District: Sherabad

Type of site: settlement

Alternative name of the site

Katta-tepe or Khasilot-Tepe (Arshavskaya et al. 1982, 133, no. 158)

Latitude: 37.626814

Longitude: 67.014961

Elevation (m.a.s.l.): 374

Location

at the southern margin of the village of Kuluksha; ca. 600 m east of the site of Kulugshatepa
south of the village of Hurjak; east of the site of Kulugshatepa (ca. 600 m)

Topography

DESCRIPTION

Basic description

long rectangular mound consists of two parts: N smaller, S longer, relatively narrow; this tepa seems to be only part of a larger settlement spreading westwards and including most probably aslo the site of Tigrmantepa

Shape	Length	Width	Height	Surface area (sq m)
long rectangular	140	155	10	483

Found

detected in GoogleEarth and subsequently identified with a known site

Preservation: high

Distortions

erosion following a large scale excavations

Excavated

excavated in 1979–1984 by T. Annaev; and reportedly again by T. Annaev in 1992–1993

Pottery: 4

Other finds

Coins of Vima Kadphises, Hephtalite imitation of Peroz (2×) and early Abbasid coin reported by Annaev

DATING

Late Bronze Age		Early Iron Age		Hellenistic		Kushan and Kushan-Sasanian	
Early Medieval	X	High Medieval		Post-Mongol		Pre-modern	

Dating published elsewhere: Early and High Medieval (Annaev 1988, 46–48)

Bibliography

Arshavskaya et al. 1982, 133–134 (size of the town: NW–SE 510m, NE–SW 390 m, 19.9 ha); Annaev 1988, 13–14, 30–35; Stride 2004, vol. 3, Uz-SD-158

Notes

Date of survey: 01.09.2009

Entered by: Danielisová

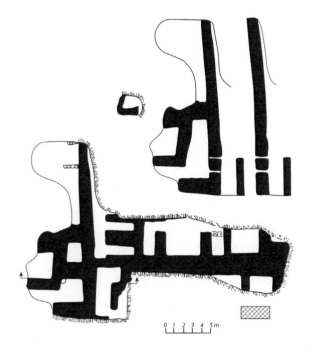

0 1 2 3 4 5 m

Ground plan of Khosyatepa, drawn by P. Kazakova after Annaev 1988, ris. 12.

IDENTITY

Site Code **53**	Stride 2004 no	Rtveladze 1974 no	Arshavskaya et al. 1982 158

Name of the site
Tigrmantepa

Translation
Millstone mound

District
Sherabad

Type of site
architecture

Alternative name of the site
Shamol-tegerman (Arshavskaya et al. 1982)

Latitude
37.627802

Longitude
67.011871

Elevation (m.a.s.l.)
374

Location
southern margin of the Kulugsha village

Topography
the site is situated in flat irrigated lowlands

DESCRIPTION

Basic description
ruins of a standing wall belonging to a massive building / fortification made of mud bricks preserved

Shape
rectangular

Length
26

Width
32

Height
7

Surface area (sq m)
84

Found
detected in GoogleEarth

Preservation
high

Distortions
eroded

Excavated
no

Pottery
2

Other finds
no

DATING

Late Bronze Age		Early Iron Age		Hellenistic		Kushan and Kushan-Sasanian	
Early Medieval	X	High Medieval	X	Post-Mongol		Pre-modern	

Dating published elsewhere   Early and High Medieval (Annaev 1988, 46–48)

Bibliography
Arshavskaya et al. 1982, 133 (52×26×10 cm bricks, allegedly part of city walls of the Khosyattepa)

Notes
Build of mud bricks 12×25×42(?) cm

Date of survey
01.09.2009

Entered by
Danielisová

IDENTITY

Site Code
54

Stride 2004
Uz-SD-170

Rtveladze 1974
B-021

Arshavskaya et al. 1982
170

Name of the site
Anjirtepa

Translation
Fig mound

District
Sherabad

Type of site
settlement

Alternative name of the site
Khojakiya (Arshavskaya et al. 1982; Stride 2004)

Latitude
37.651707

Longitude
66.934929

Elevation (m.a.s.l.)
405

Location
western part of the Khojakiya village

Topography
the site is situated in village, between gardens in flat irrigated lowlands, close to the border of the piedmont steppe

DESCRIPTION

Basic description
small, but relatively high compact mound

Shape	Length	Width	Height	Surface area (sq m)
rectangular	27	42	5	1320

Found
detected in GoogleEarth

Preservation
high

Distortions
eroded, walked frequently by local people

Excavated
stratigraphic trench in spring 1973 – Baktriyskaya ekspeditsiya

Pottery
3

Other finds
no

DATING

Late Bronze Age	Early Iron Age	Hellenistic	Kushan and Kushan-Sasanian	X
Early Medieval	High Medieval	Post-Mongol	Pre-modern	

Dating published elsewhere Early Medieval (Arshavskaya et al. 1982)

Bibliography
Rtveladze – Khakimov 1973, 19 (?); Rtveladze 1974, 76; Nekrasova 1976, 76; Pidaev 1978, 19–20; Arshavskaya et al. 1982, 135; Annaev 1988, 14; Stride 2004, vol. 3, Uz-SD-170

Notes
Trimble GPS plan

Date of survey
01.09.2009

Entered by
Stančo

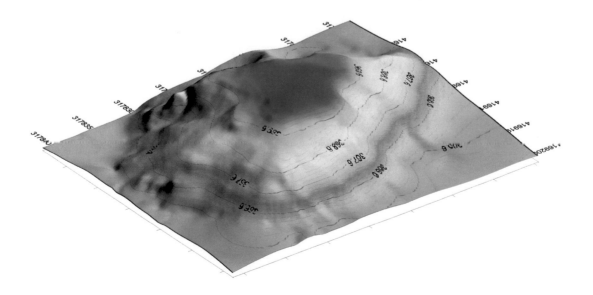

IDENTITY

Site Code	Stride 2004	Rtveladze 1974	Arshavskaya et al. 1982
55	Uz-SD-171	B-014	171

Name of the site

Khalinchaktepa

Translation	District	Type of site
Swing mound	Sherabad	settlement

Alternative name of the site

Khylynchak-Tepe (Rtveladze 1974; Arshavskaya et al. 1982; Stride 2004); Khalinchaktepa (Pidaev 1978); Tamynchaktepa (100k map)

Latitude	Longitude	Elevation (m.a.s.l.)
37.603187	66.931456	373

Location

eastern part of the village of Buston close to the main Sherabad – Muzrabad road

Topography

the site is situated in village amidst gardens next to the asphalt road, in flat irrigated lowlands

DESCRIPTION

Basic description

compact mound, elevated in corners, flat central part

Shape	Length	Width	Height	Surface area (sq m)
rectangular	105	145	6	14130

Found	Preservation	Distortions
detected in GoogleEarth	high	remains of a concrete building in the center, 18 pilasters left, it was restaurant in 1987–1989

Excavated

no

Pottery	Other finds
9	no

DATING

Late Bronze Age	Early Iron Age	Hellenistic	Kushan and Kushan-Sasanian
			X

Early Medieval	High Medieval	Post-Mongol	Pre-modern
	X	X	

Dating published elsewhere Kushan – 14/15th c., northern part 10th–14th c. (Rtveladze 1974, Arshavskaya et al. 1982)

Bibliography

Rtveladze – Khakimov 1973, 75–76; Pidaev 1978, 19; Stride 2004, vol. 3, Uz-SD-171

Notes

Date of survey	Entered by
02.09.2009	Stančo

IDENTITY

Site Code	Stride 2004	Rtveladze 1974	Arshavskaya et al. 1982
58	Uz-SD-232	B-022	no

Name of the site	Translation	District	Type of site
Anjirtepa	Fig mound	Sherabad	settlement

Alternative name of the site	Latitude	Longitude	Elevation (m.a.s.l.)
no	37.665236	66.977162	409

Location

center of the northern separate part of the village of Akkurgan; so-called Old Akkurgan (close to the 4th school)

Topography

the site is situated in village, between gardens and houses, in flat irrigated lowlands, close to the border of the piedmont steppe

DESCRIPTION

Basic description

compact small mound

Shape	Length	Width	Height	Surface area (sq m)
irregular	40	47		1876

Found	Preservation	Distortions
GoogleEarth / local knowledge	poor	digged of from on the sides / slopes

Excavated

no

Pottery	Other finds
7	no

DATING

Late Bronze Age		Early Iron Age		Hellenistic		Kushan and Kushan-Sasanian	X
Early Medieval	X	High Medieval		Post-Mongol		Pre-modern	X

Dating published elsewhere	no

Bibliography

Stride 2004, vol. 3, Uz-SD-232

Notes

Date of survey	Entered by
04.09.2009	Danielisová

IDENTITY

Site Code	Stride 2004	Rtveladze 1974	Arshavskaya et al. 1982
60	no	no	no

Name of the site	Translation	District	Type of site
No name 14 (part of Babatepa settlement area)	no	Sherabad	settlement

Alternative name of the site	Latitude	Longitude	Elevation (m.a.s.l.)
no	37.720925	67.087355	406

Location

100 m west of the site of Babatepa (no. 027)

Topography

the site is situated in village, between gardens, just behind one of houses, in flat irrigated lowlands

DESCRIPTION

Basic description

low irregular mound, barely noticable

Shape	Length	Width	Height	Surface area (sq m)
irregular	5	5	1	142

Found	Preservation	Distortions
field survey (shown by locals)	poor	recently disturbed by local people, new houses build on and around

Excavated

no

Pottery	Other finds
25	pottery lamp, 24 completely preserved vessels of the Kushan period

DATING

Late Bronze Age		Early Iron Age		Hellenistic		Kushan and Kushan-Sasanian	X
Early Medieval		High Medieval		Post-Mongol		Pre-modern	

Dating published elsewhere   no

Bibliography

Stančo 2015, 219

Notes

find spot definitely attests to a larger size of the settlement around Babatepa in the Kushan period

Date of survey	Entered by
06.09.2009	Stančo

IDENTITY

Site Code
61

Stride 2004
no

Rtveladze 1974
no

Arshavskaya et al. 1982
no

Name of the site
No name 15

Translation
no

District
Sherabad

Type of site
settlement

Alternative name of the site
no

Latitude
37.71966

Longitude
67.087769

Elevation (m.a.s.l.)
406

Location
65 m west of the site of Babatepa (no. 027) across the water chanel

Topography
the site is situated in flat irrigated lowlands near modern village, separated from Babatepa by a water canal, part of its larger suburb

DESCRIPTION

Basic description
low mound, partly covered with a vegeataion

Shape
irregular

Length
60

Width
70

Height

Surface area (sq m)
1758

Found
field survey

Preservation
poor

Distortions
recently disturbed by local people (buldozer work)

Excavated
no

Pottery
4

Other finds
no

DATING

Late Bronze Age		Early Iron Age		Hellenistic		Kushan and Kushan-Sasanian	X
Early Medieval	X	High Medieval		Post-Mongol		Pre-modern	

Dating published elsewhere   no

Bibliography

Notes

Date of survey
17.09.2008,
06.09.2009

Entered by
Stančo

IDENTITY

Site Code	Stride 2004	Rtveladze 1974	Arshavskaya et al. 1982
63	Uz-SD-172	B-016	172

Name of the site

Chalakurgan

Translation	District	Type of site
Undone mound (unfinished)	Sherabad	settlement

Alternative name of the site

Challa-Tepe (Rtveladze – Khakimov 1973; Rtveladze 1974, 76), Chala-tepe (Arshavskaya et al. 1982); Jelaktepa (100k map)

Latitude	Longitude	Elevation (m.a.s.l.)
37.643553	66.97371	384

Location

western margin of the New (southern) Akkurgan village, close to the Sherabad – Muzrabad road

Topography

the site is situated in flat irrigated lowlands

DESCRIPTION

Basic description

square compact mound slightly elevated in NW part (citadel ?)

Shape	Length	Width	Height	Surface area (sq m)
square	115	85	7	8165

Found	Preservation	Distortions
GoogleEarth / seen from the Sherabad road	moderate	recently disturbed by local people

Excavated

stratigraphic trench in spring 1973 – Baktriyskaya ekspeditsiya

Pottery	Other finds
10	no

DATING

Late Bronze Age		Early Iron Age		Hellenistic		Kushan and Kushan-Sasanian	X
Early Medieval	X	High Medieval	X	Post-Mongol		Pre-modern	

Dating published elsewhere   Kushan (Rtveladze 1974); Kushan, 5th–13th c. (Arshavskaya et al. 1982)

Bibliography

Rtveladze – Khakimov 1973, 17; Rtveladze 1974, 76; Nekrasova 1976, 80–82; Arshavskaya et al. 1982, 135; Stride 2004, vol. 3, Uz-SD-172

Notes

Stride locates it to the place of the site of Aktepa – 005 by mistake.

Date of survey	Entered by
06.09.2009	Danielisová

204

IDENTITY

Site Code	Stride 2004		Rtveladze 1974	Arshavskaya et al. 1982
65	Uz-SD-227		B-012	no

Name of the site		Translation	District	Type of site
Talashkantepa I		High mound	Sherabad	settlement

Alternative name of the site	Latitude	Longitude	Elevation (m.a.s.l.)
no	37.568976	66.906511	357

Location

150 m to the east of the village of Talashkan
200m E from the village of Talashkan

Topography

the site is situated in flat irrigated lowlands, in the fields

DESCRIPTION

Basic description

low, regularly rounded mound

Shape	Length	Width	Height	Surface area (sq m)
circular	140	140	3	19649

Found	Preservation	Distortions
in publications	moderate	erosion after excavatios

Excavated

fully excavated

Pottery	Other finds
no	no

DATING

Late Bronze Age		Early Iron Age	X	Hellenistic		Kushan and Kushan-Sasanian	
Early Medieval		High Medieval		Post-Mongol		Pre-modern	

Dating published elsewhere   Achaemenid (Rtveladze 1974)

Bibliography

Rtveladze 1974, 74; Sagdullaev – Khakimov 1976; Pidaev – Rtveladze 1978; Rtveladze – Pidaev 1983; Shaydullaev 1988; 1990; 2000 and 2002; Stride 2004, vol. 3, Uz-SD-227

Notes

Date of survey	Entered by
16.10.2005	Stančo

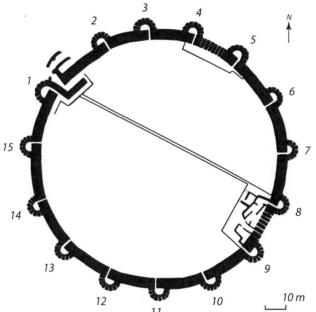

Ground plan of Talakhantepa I, drawn by P. Kazakova after Šajdullaev 2002, 288, Abb. 34.

IDENTITY

Site Code	Stride 2004	Rtveladze 1974	Arshavskaya et al. 1982
69	Uz-SD-366	no	no

Name of the site	Translation	District	Type of site
Jarkutan - citadel	no	Sherabad	settlement

Alternative name of the site	Latitude	Longitude	Elevation (m.a.s.l.)
Jarkutan 1 (Askarov 1983)	37.632908	66.960288	373

Location

4.8 km southwest of Sherabad on the left side of the road from Sherabad to Muzrabad; 1.7 km southwest of the village of Akkurgan

Topography

slightly raised elevation in the midst of flat irrigated lowlands; near the Bustan creek

DESCRIPTION

Basic description

ca. 100 ha large settlement and cemetery

Shape	Length	Width	Height	Surface area (sq m)
irregular	190	180		5770

Found	Preservation	Distortions
1973 (Pidaev and Pilipko?)	low	margins of the site gradually destroyed by ploughing

Excavated

1973–1990 excavations lead by Askarov, Ionesov, Shirinov, Baratov; 1994–2002 German-Uzbek excavations (Huff, Shaydullaev); 2007–2012 French-Uzbek excavations (Francfort, Bendezu-Sarmiento)

Pottery	Other finds
no	no

DATING

Late Bronze Age	X	Early Iron Age	X	Hellenistic		Kushan and Kushan-Sasanian	
Early Medieval		High Medieval		Post-Mongol		Pre-modern	

Dating published elsewhere Late Bronze Age (2nd half of 2nd millennium BC) (Askarov – Abdullaev 1983); Yaz I (Lhuillier et al. 2013)

Bibliography

Askarov – Abdullaev 1983, Askarov – Shirinov 1989; Huff 1997; Huff – Shaydullaev 1999; Huff et al. 2001; Görsdorf – Huff 2001; Stride 2004, vol. 3, Uz-SD-366; Luneau et al. 2014; Bendezu-Sarmiento – Mustafakulov 2007; 2013

Notes

Date of survey	Entered by
x.10.2002	Stančo

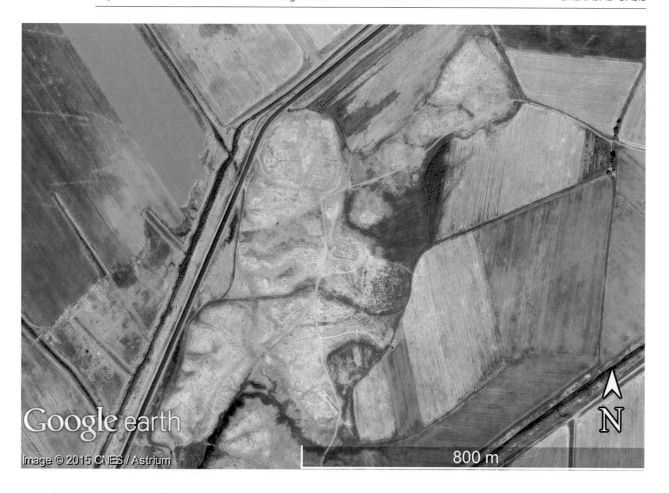

IDENTITY

Site Code	Stride 2004	Rtveladze 1974	Arshavskaya et al. 1982
70	Uz-SD-317	no	no

Name of the site	Translation	District	Type of site
Bustan 3	no	Sherabad	burial site

Alternative name of the site	Latitude	Longitude	Elevation (m.a.s.l.)
no	37.622022	66.945768	363

Location

6.5 km southwest of Sherabad on the left side of the road from Sherabad to Muzrabad; 400 m east of the village of Bustan

Topography

slightly raised elevation in the midst of flat irrigated lowlands, close to the riverbed of the Bustan creek

DESCRIPTION

Basic description

Large necropolis

Shape	Length	Width	Height	Surface area (sq m)
irregular	100	165		25221

Found	Preservation	Distortions
1973 (Askarov)	low	margins of the site gradually destroyed by ploughing

Excavated

Askarov excavated in 1974 38 gaves

Pottery	Other finds
no	no

DATING

Late Bronze Age	X	Early Iron Age		Hellenistic		Kushan and Kushan-Sasanian	
Early Medieval		High Medieval		Post-Mongol		Pre-modern	

Dating published elsewhere   Late Bronze Age

Bibliography

Askarov 1977, 58; Khalilov 1986; Askarov – Ruzanov 1990; Stride 2004, vol. 3, Uz-SD-317

Notes

Late Bronze Age

Date of survey	Entered by
24.09.2010	Stančo

IDENTITY

Site Code
71

Stride 2004
no

Rtveladze 1974
no

Arshavskaya et al. 1982
no

Name of the site
No name 16

Translation
no

District
Sherabad

Type of site
settlement

Alternative name of the site
no

Latitude
37.648166

Longitude
67.095029

Elevation (m.a.s.l.)
368

Location
2 km east of the village of Gegirdak

Topography
the site is situated in flat irrigated lowlands

DESCRIPTION

Basic description
small, relatively flat circular mound

Shape
circular

Length
22

Width
32

Height
3

Surface area (sq m)
106

Found
detected in GoogleEarth

Preservation
high

Distortions
no

Excavated
no

Pottery
1

Other finds
no

DATING

Late Bronze Age	Early Iron Age	Hellenistic	Kushan and Kushan-Sasanian
Early Medieval	High Medieval	Post-Mongol	Pre-modern

Dating published elsewhere
no

Bibliography

Notes
few ceramic on the surface

Date of survey
20.09.2010

Entered by
Stančo

IDENTITY

Site Code **72**	Stride 2004 Uz-SD-228	Rtveladze 1974 B-013	Arshavskaya et al. 1982 no

Name of the site
Talashkantepa II (NW mound)

Translation	District	Type of site
High mound	Sherabad	settlement

Alternative name of the site
no

Latitude	Longitude	Elevation (m.a.s.l.)
37.574294	66.906771	361

Location
360 m east of village of Talashkan

Topography
the site is situated in flat irrigated lowlands

DESCRIPTION

Basic description
high compact mound almost square in its ground plan, slightly elevated in several part; salty dry soil

Shape	Length	Width	Height	Surface area (sq m)
rectangular	150	140	6	2448

Found	Preservation	Distortions
in publications	high	several Modern time graves

Excavated
yes (visible traces of a big trench in E part)

Pottery	Other finds
8	no

DATING

Late Bronze Age	Early Iron Age	Hellenistic	Kushan and Kushan-Sasanian
Early Medieval	High Medieval	Post-Mongol X	Pre-modern

Dating published elsewhere Late Medieval (Rtveladze 1974)

Bibliography
Rtveladze 1974, 74; Stride 2004, vol. 3, Uz-SD-228

Notes
few ceramic on the surface compare to 032

Date of survey	Entered by
16.10.2005, 05.09.2010	Stančo

214

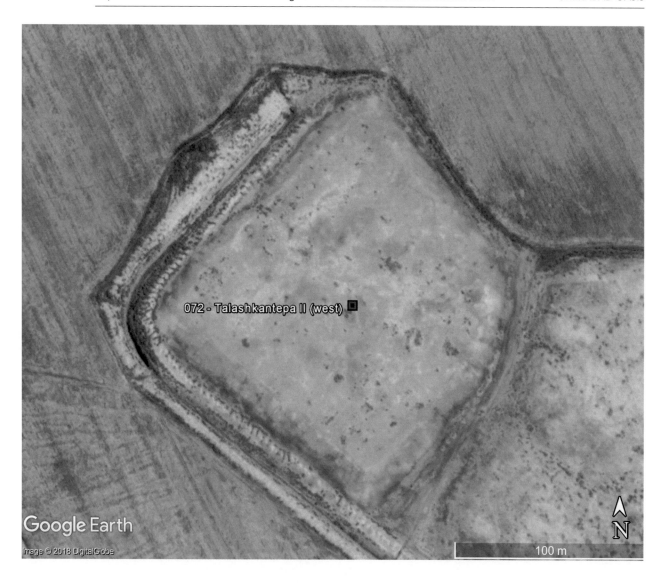

IDENTITY

Site Code	Stride 2004		Rtveladze 1974	Arshavskaya et al. 1982
73	no		no	no

Name of the site		Translation	District	Type of site
No name 17		no	Sherabad	settlement

Alternative name of the site	Latitude	Longitude	Elevation (m.a.s.l.)
Kul´Tepa (Rtveladze – Khakimov 1973, 12)	37.623448	67.004094	374

Location

500 m south of the village of Hurjak close to the modern cemetery and to the site no. 004

Topography

the site is situated in flat irrigated lowlands

DESCRIPTION

Basic description

Low square/round mound

Shape	Length	Width	Height	Surface area (sq m)
oval	35	35		89

Found	Preservation	Distortions
detected in GoogleEarth	moderate	no

Excavated

no

Pottery	Other finds
no	no

DATING

Late Bronze Age	Early Iron Age	Hellenistic	Kushan and Kushan-Sasanian
Early Medieval	High Medieval	Post-Mongol	Pre-modern

Dating published elsewhere   no

Bibliography

Rtveladze – Khakimov 1973, 12

Notes

identification with the site of Kul´Tepa (Rtveladze – Khakimov 1973, 12) is uncertain for the location on the drawing seems to be mirror-like reversed

Date of survey	Entered by
17.09.2008	Stančo

IDENTITY

Site Code
74

Stride 2004
Uz-SD-169

Rtveladze 1974
no

Arshavskaya et al. 1982
169

Name of the site
Talimarantepa

Translation
no

District
Angor

Type of site
settlement

Alternative name of the site
no

Latitude
37.520504

Longitude
67.230139

Elevation (m.a.s.l.)
342

Location
300 m south of the Zang Canal, 2.3 km west of the Khaudag range

Topography

DESCRIPTION

Basic description

Shape
rectangular

Length
248

Width
230

Height

Surface area (sq m)
1415

Found
detected in GoogleEarth

Preservation
not known

Distortions
no

Excavated
no

Pottery
no

Other finds
no

DATING

Late Bronze Age		Early Iron Age		Hellenistic		Kushan and Kushan-Sasanian	
Early Medieval	X	High Medieval	X	Post-Mongol		Pre-modern	

Dating published elsewhere   Early and High Medieval (Arshavskaya et al. 1982)

Bibliography
Arshavskaya et al. 1982, 125; Stride 2004, vol. 3, Uz-SD-169

Notes

Date of survey
not surveyed

Entered by
no

IDENTITY

Site Code **75**	Stride 2004 no	Rtveladze 1974 no	Arshavskaya et al. 1982 no

Name of the site
No name 18

Translation	District	Type of site
no	Kizirik	settlement

Alternative name of the site	Latitude	Longitude	Elevation (m.a.s.l.)
no	37.552205	67.240331	353

Location
3.3 km north of the Zang Canal, 1.5 km west of the Khaudag range; 4.24 km southeast of the village of Takiya

Topography
the site is situated in flat irrigated lowlands

DESCRIPTION

Basic description
small compact mound

Shape	Length	Width	Height	Surface area (sq m)
circular	45	42	2	124

Found	Preservation	Distortions
detected in GoogleEarth	high	minor digs of unknown origin on top

Excavated
no

Pottery	Other finds
7	no

DATING

Late Bronze Age	Early Iron Age	Hellenistic	Kushan and Kushan-Sasanian
Early Medieval	High Medieval	Post-Mongol	Pre-modern

Dating published elsewhere no

Bibliography
Rtveladze 1974, 74–75

Notes

Date of survey	Entered by
09.09.2010	Danielisová

IDENTITY

Site Code	Stride 2004		Rtveladze 1974	Arshavskaya et al. 1982
77	Uz-SD-237		B-038	no

Name of the site	Translation	District	Type of site
Egiztepa I	Twin mound	Kizirik	settlement

Alternative name of the site	Latitude	Longitude	Elevation (m.a.s.l.)
no	37.552236	67.233193	352

Location

3.2 km north of the Zang Canal, 2.2 km west of the Khaudag range; 4 km southeast of the village of Takiya

Topography

the site is situated in flat irrigated lowlands

DESCRIPTION

Basic description

flat mound slightly elevated in eastern-central part, otherwise very low

Shape	Length	Width	Height	Surface area (sq m)
	130	80	2	14399

Found	Preservation	Distortions
detected in GoogleEarth	high	no

Excavated

no

Pottery	Other finds
4	no

DATING

Late Bronze Age	Early Iron Age	Hellenistic	Kushan and Kushan-Sasanian
			X

Early Medieval	High Medieval	Post-Mongol	Pre-modern

Dating published elsewhere   no

Bibliography

Stride 2004, vol. 3, Uz-SD-237

Notes

few pottery; identification with Ikizaktepe uncertain; Stride placed the site to the place of the site of Shortepa I – 016 by mistake.

Date of survey	Entered by
09.09.2010	Stančo

IDENTITY

Site Code	Stride 2004	Rtveladze 1974	Arshavskaya et al. 1982
78	no	B-038	no

Name of the site	Translation	District	Type of site
Egiztepa II	Twin mound	Kizirik	settlement

Alternative name of the site	Latitude	Longitude	Elevation (m.a.s.l.)
no	37.550853	67.233004	351

Location

3 km north of the Zang Canal, 2.2 km west of the Khaudag range; 4 km southeast of the village of Takiya

Topography

the site is situated in flat irrigated lowlands

DESCRIPTION

Basic description

flat mound elevated in corners, pathway in the middle

Shape	Length	Width	Height	Surface area (sq m)
square	70	57	1	6693

Found	Preservation	Distortions
detected in GoogleEarth	high	no, partly covered with a vegetation

Excavated

no

Pottery	Other finds
6	no

DATING

Late Bronze Age	Early Iron Age	Hellenistic	Kushan and Kushan-Sasanian	X
Early Medieval	High Medieval	Post-Mongol	Pre-modern	

Dating published elsewhere   no

Bibliography

Arshavskaya et al. 1982, 135

Notes

few pottery; identification with Ikizaktepe uncertain

Date of survey	Entered by
09.09.2010	Stančo

IDENTITY

Site Code
79

Stride 2004
no

Rtveladze 1974
no

Arshavskaya et al. 1982
no

Name of the site
No name 19

Translation
no

District
Kizirik

Type of site
settlement?

Alternative name of the site
no

Latitude
37.581917

Longitude
67.183456

Elevation (m.a.s.l.)
354

Location
within the modern cemetery (20–21th c.), western margin of the village of Takiya (cemetery of Takiya-ota)

Topography
the site is situated in flat irrigated lowlands, within the modern cemetery of Takiya ota

DESCRIPTION

Basic description
irregular (uncertain) area within a modern cemetery; pottery traceable in its SE corner

Shape
unknown

Length
50

Width
50

Height

Surface area (sq m)
7398

Found
detected in GoogleEarth

Preservation
poor

Distortions
the site is covered with a modern cemetery

Excavated
no

Pottery
6

Other finds
no

DATING

Late Bronze Age	Early Iron Age	Hellenistic	Kushan and Kushan-Sasanian
Early Medieval	High Medieval	Post-Mongol	Pre-modern

Dating published elsewhere   no

Bibliography
no

Notes
no

Date of survey
10.09.2010

Entered by
Stančo

IDENTITY

Site Code	Stride 2004	Rtveladze 1974	Arshavskaya et al. 1982
80	no	B-037?	no

Name of the site	Translation	District	Type of site
No name 20	no	Kizirik	settlement

Alternative name of the site	Latitude	Longitude	Elevation (m.a.s.l.)
Talimaran Tepe (Stride 2004, by mistake)	37.592791	67.210551	362

Location

900 m northeast of the village of Takiya

Topography

the site is situated in flat irrigated lowlands

DESCRIPTION

Basic description

large compact mound square in ground plan, elevated in its NE and NW corners

Shape	Length	Width	Height	Surface area (sq m)
square	145	145	9	31170

Found	Preservation	Distortions
detected in GoogleEarth	high	no

Excavated

no

Pottery	Other finds
23	glass, bronze objects, coins

DATING

Late Bronze Age		Early Iron Age		Hellenistic	Kushan and Kushan-Sasanian	X
Early Medieval	X	High Medieval		Post-Mongol	X	Pre-modern	X

Dating published elsewhere   no

Bibliography

Rtveladze – Khakimov1973, 17; Rtveladze 1974, 78

Notes

this is the only bigger site in the former "2nd part of Yu. Akhunbabaev kolkhoz" where the site no. B-037 of Rtveladze is located (1974, 78); distances to the other sited, however, differs from the description – identification uncertain

Date of survey	Entered by
10.09.2010	Stančo

IDENTITY

Site Code
84

Stride 2004
no

Rtveladze 1974
no

Arshavskaya et al. 1982
no

Name of the site
No name 21

Translation
no

District
Sherabad

Type of site
architecture

Alternative name of the site
no

Latitude
37.625167

Longitude
67.085573

Elevation (m.a.s.l.)
362

Location
500 m west of the village of Saitabad

Topography

DESCRIPTION

Basic description

Shape

Length
5

Width
5

Height

Surface area (sq m)
188

Found

Preservation
not known

Distortions
no

Excavated
no

Pottery
no

Other finds
no

DATING

Late Bronze Age		Early Iron Age		Hellenistic	X	Kushan and Kushan-Sasanian	X
Early Medieval		High Medieval		Post-Mongol		Pre-modern	

Dating published elsewhere   Greco-Bactrian / Kushan (Urbanová 2011, 103–104)

Bibliography
Urbanová 2011

Notes

Date of survey
x.09.2006

Entered by
Stančo

IDENTITY

Site Code	Stride 2004	Rtveladze 1974	Arshavskaya et al. 1982
85	no	no	no

Name of the site	Translation	District	Type of site
No name 22	no	Sherabad	find spot

Alternative name of the site	Latitude	Longitude	Elevation (m.a.s.l.)
no	37.627539	67.089095	364

Location

northern part of the village of Saitabad; 250 m from the river of Kara Su

Topography

DESCRIPTION

Basic description

no visible traces on the surface (pottery deposit found accidentally in the depth of 1 m under the present surface during construction of a modern house)

Shape	Length	Width	Height	Surface area (sq m)
uncertain	3	3		20

Found	Preservation	Distortions
accidentally by local people, shown to us while excavating nearby Jandavlattepa	not known	no

Excavated

trial excavations in the place of accidental find carried out by K. Abdullaev in September 2005

Pottery	Other finds
no	no

DATING

Late Bronze Age	X	Early Iron Age		Hellenistic		Kushan and Kushan-Sasanian	
Early Medieval		High Medieval		Post-Mongol		Pre-modern	

Dating published elsewhere   no

Bibliography

Abdullaev – Stančo 2006, 20–21; Stančo 2018, 178

Notes

See fig. 5.3

Date of survey	Entered by
x.09.2005	Stančo

IDENTITY

Site Code	Stride 2004	Rtveladze 1974	Arshavskaya et al. 1982
86	no	no	no

Name of the site	Translation	District	Type of site
No name 23	no	Sherabad	architecture

Alternative name of the site	Latitude	Longitude	Elevation (m.a.s.l.)
no	37.622244	67.097466	366

Location

eastern part of the village of Saitabad; 120 m from the river of Kara Su

Topography

DESCRIPTION

Basic description

ruins of a house, vaulted structure made of mud-bricks

Shape	Length	Width	Height	Surface area (sq m)
rectangular	12	14		12

Found	Preservation	Distortions
field survey (K. Abdullaev in frame of the Czech-Uzbekistani expedition)	moderate	no

Excavated

no

Pottery	Other finds
no	no

DATING

Late Bronze Age		Early Iron Age		Hellenistic		Kushan and Kushan-Sasanian	
Early Medieval		High Medieval		Post-Mongol	X	Pre-modern	

Dating published elsewhere

Bibliography

Rtveladze – Khakimov 1973, 17; Rtveladze 1974, 78

Notes

Date of survey	Entered by
x.10.2002, x.09.2006	Stančo

IDENTITY

Site Code
87

Stride 2004
no

Rtveladze 1974
no

Arshavskaya et al. 1982
no

Name of the site
No name 24

Translation
no

District
Sherabad

Type of site
settlement

Alternative name of the site
no

Latitude
37.62126

Longitude
67.101269

Elevation (m.a.s.l.)
352

Location
southeastern part of the village of Saitabad

Topography

DESCRIPTION

Basic description

Shape
irregular

Length
30

Width
25

Height

Surface area (sq m)
655

Found

Preservation
not known

Distortions
no

Excavated
no

Pottery

Other finds
no

DATING

Late Bronze Age		Early Iron Age		Hellenistic		Kushan and Kushan-Sasanian	
Early Medieval		High Medieval		Post-Mongol		Pre-modern	

Dating published elsewhere   no

Bibliography

Notes

Date of survey
x.10.2002, x.09.2006

Entered by
Stančo

IDENTITY

Site Code	Stride 2004		Rtveladze 1974	Arshavskaya et al. 1982
88	no		no	no

Name of the site	Translation	District	Type of site
No name 25	no	Kizirik	tepa or kurgan

Alternative name of the site	Latitude	Longitude	Elevation (m.a.s.l.)
no	37.589859	67.138242	353

Location

5.5 km southeast of the site of Jandavlattepa

Topography

the site is situated in flat irrigated lowlands, close to the Sherabad River (left bank)

DESCRIPTION

Basic description

small compact mound, probably not a settlement (a kurgan?)

Shape	Length	Width	Height	Surface area (sq m)
circular	21	17	4	30

Found	Preservation	Distortions
detected in GoogleEarth	high	covered with a vegetation

Excavated

no

Pottery	Other finds
10	mud-bricks

DATING

Late Bronze Age		Early Iron Age		Hellenistic		Kushan and Kushan-Sasanian	
Early Medieval		High Medieval	X	Post-Mongol		Pre-modern	

Dating published elsewhere   no

Bibliography

no

Notes

Date of survey	Entered by
08.09.2010	Danielisová

IDENTITY

Site Code
89

Stride 2004
no

Rtveladze 1974
no

Arshavskaya et al. 1982
no

Name of the site
No name 26

Translation
no

District
Sherabad

Type of site
burial site?

Alternative name of the site
no

Latitude
37.614965

Longitude
67.026535

Elevation (m.a.s.l.)
365

Location
500 m northeast of the site of Taushkantepa

Topography

DESCRIPTION

Basic description

Shape	Length	Width	Height	Surface area (sq m)
oval	30	25		111

Found

Preservation
not known

Distortions
no

Excavated
no

Pottery
no

Other finds
no

DATING

Late Bronze Age	Early Iron Age	Hellenistic	Kushan and Kushan-Sasanian

Early Medieval	High Medieval	Post-Mongol	Pre-modern

Dating published elsewhere   no

Bibliography
no

Notes
probably site with a grave (graves?)

Date of survey
01.09.2009

Entered by
Stančo

241

IDENTITY

Site Code
94

Stride 2004
Uz-SD-160

Rtveladze 1974
B-106

Arshavskaya et al. 1982
160

Name of the site
Kurgan

Translation
no

District
Sherabad

Type of site
fortress

Alternative name of the site
Kafirkala (Rtveladze 1974; Arshavskaya et al. 1982; Stride 2004)

Latitude
37.685955

Longitude
67.012047

Elevation (m.a.s.l.)
440

Location
edge of the mountains and Sherabad, 50 m to the W from the bridge across the Sherbad Darya (Denau road)

Topography
elevated above the river valley

DESCRIPTION

Basic description
small fortress-like site on the summit of a natural mound with steep slopes (upper terrace), in the southern part the lower terrace

Shape
rectangular – irregular

Length
140

Width
75

Height

Surface area (sq m)
12538

Found
visually and literature

Preservation
moderate

Distortions
modern unpaved road and traces of a modern structure on the top (television transmitter)

Excavated
no

Pottery
21

Other finds
coin, ring, bones; mud bricks preserved within the entrance part (a buldozer-made section)

DATING

Late Bronze Age	Early Iron Age	Hellenistic	Kushan and Kushan-Sasanian
			X

Early Medieval	High Medieval	Post-Mongol	Pre-modern
X	X	X	X

Dating published elsewhere   Kushan, 10th–13th c., 18th–20th c. (Arshavskaya et al. 1982)

Bibliography
Kastal'skij 1930, 12; Parfyonov s.d., 174 no. 5: "Bekskaya gora" or "Kala Shirabadskogo beka"; Rtveladze 1980, 31–32; Arshavskaya et al. 1982, 134; Rtveladze 1987, 56; Stride 2004, Uz-SD-160

Notes
great view of all the Sherabad town and valley towards Tavka

Date of survey
02.09.2010

Entered by
Danielisová

IDENTITY

Site Code	Stride 2004		Rtveladze 1974	Arshavskaya et al. 1982
95	Uz-SD-160		B-106	160

Name of the site	Translation	District	Type of site
No name 27	no	Sherabad	fortress

Alternative name of the site	Latitude	Longitude	Elevation (m.a.s.l.)
Kafirkala (Rtveladze 1974; Arshavskaya et al. 1982; Stride 2004)	37.686653	67.010274	458

Location

edge of the mountains and Sherabad, 180 m to the NW from the bridge across the Sherbad Darya (Denau road)

Topography

elevated above the river valley

DESCRIPTION

Basic description

walled settlement – rectangular shape with towers-bastions in the NW and SW corners and the centre of western wall

Shape	Length	Width	Height	Surface area (sq m)
oblong; with eastern edge irregular	140	100		21338

Found	Preservation	Distortions
detected in GoogleEarth	high	in general well preserved, disturbed localy in several parts; electricity line

Excavated

no

Pottery	Other finds
24	no

DATING

Late Bronze Age		Early Iron Age		Hellenistic		Kushan and Kushan-Sasanian	X
Early Medieval	X	High Medieval		Post-Mongol	X	Pre-modern	X

Dating published elsewhere   no

Bibliography

See no. 94

Notes

Date of survey	Entered by
02.09.2010	Stančo

IDENTITY

Site Code
96

Stride 2004
no

Rtveladze 1974
no

Arshavskaya et al. 1982
no

Name of the site
No name 28

Translation
no

District
Sherabad

Type of site
settlement

Alternative name of the site
no

Latitude
37.685895

Longitude
67.009165

Elevation (m.a.s.l.)
465

Location
edge of the mountains and Sherabad, 250 m to the W from the bridge across the Sherbad Darya (Denau road)

Topography
promontory above the river valley of Sherabad Darya

DESCRIPTION

Basic description
fortified (walled) area

Shape	Length	Width	Height	Surface area (sq m)
irregular	360	290		147396

Found
field survey

Preservation
poor

Distortions
two cemeteries inside (Tatar Kabriston, Kosh-tigrmon Kabriston), localy disturbed, walls/ramparts well preserved

Excavated
no

Pottery
2

Other finds
no

DATING

Late Bronze Age	Early Iron Age	Hellenistic	Kushan and Kushan-Sasanian	X
Early Medieval	High Medieval	Post-Mongol	Pre-modern	

Dating published elsewhere   no

Bibliography
no

Notes
three cemeteries inside or around

Date of survey
02.09.2010

Entered by
Danielisová

IDENTITY

Site Code
97

Stride 2004
no

Rtveladze 1974
no

Arshavskaya et al. 1982
no

Name of the site
No name 29

Translation
no

District
Sherabad

Type of site
settlement

Alternative name of the site
no

Latitude
37.662184

Longitude
67.090431

Elevation (m.a.s.l.)
376

Location
580 m eastwards from village of Chukurkul

Topography
the site is situated in flat irrigated lowlands

DESCRIPTION

Basic description
small rectangular structure; mud-bricks immediately under the surface

Shape
rectangular

Length
44

Width
38

Height
2

Surface area (sq m)
2422

Found
detected in GoogleEarth

Preservation
high

Distortions
modern path across

Excavated
yes (visible traces of trenches)

Pottery
20

Other finds
no

DATING

Late Bronze Age		Early Iron Age		Hellenistic		Kushan and Kushan-Sasanian	X
Early Medieval		High Medieval		Post-Mongol		Pre-modern	

Dating published elsewhere   no

Bibliography
no

Notes
no

Date of survey
03.09.2010

Entered by
Danielisová

IDENTITY

Site Code **98**	Stride 2004 no	Rtveladze 1974 no	Arshavskaya et al. 1982 162

Name of the site
no name (Kuluksha cemetery)

Translation: no
District: Sherabad
Type of site: settlement

Alternative name of the site
Shortan-tepe? (Arshavskaya et al. 1982)

Latitude: 37.626913
Longitude: 67.004532
Elevation (m.a.s.l.): 375

Location
southern margin of village of Hurjoq

Topography
the site is situated in flat irrigated lowlands

DESCRIPTION

Basic description

Shape	Length	Width	Height	Surface area (sq m)
oblong	330	305		10995

Found: field survey
Preservation: poor
Distortions: the site is covered with a modern cemetery of the Kuluksha village

Excavated
no

Pottery: 16
Other finds: no

DATING

Late Bronze Age	Early Iron Age	Hellenistic	Kushan and Kushan-Sasanian X
Early Medieval X	High Medieval X	Post-Mongol	Pre-modern

Dating published elsewhere: 10th–12th c. (Arshavskaya et al. 1982)

Bibliography
Arshavskaya et al. 1982, 134

Notes
identification with one of the sites described in no. 162 of Arshavskaya et al. 1982 is uncertain

Date of survey: 01.10.2010
Entered by: Stančo

IDENTITY

Site Code	Stride 2004	Rtveladze 1974	Arshavskaya et al. 1982
99	Uz-SD-166	no	166

Name of the site	Translation	District	Type of site
Talashkantepa III	High mound	Sherabad	settlement

Alternative name of the site	Latitude	Longitude	Elevation (m.a.s.l.)
tomb of Khoja-Akkiyadaz (100k map)	37.584623	66.914732	364

Location

1.6 km east of the village of Talashkan, next to the road across the water canal

Topography

the site is situated in flat irrigated lowlands

DESCRIPTION

Basic description

oblong area with slightly elevated mound (tepa) in the western-central part

Shape	Length	Width	Height	Surface area (sq m)
rectangular	300	200	5	95487

Found	Preservation	Distortions
detected in GoogleEarth	moderate	water canal across the site (from NW to SE); Tomb-building in the NW part

Excavated

no

Pottery	Other finds
19	clay figurine (horse); fired mud bricks

DATING

Late Bronze Age		Early Iron Age		Hellenistic		Kushan and Kushan-Sasanian	X
Early Medieval		High Medieval	X	Post-Mongol		Pre-modern	

Dating published elsewhere   Early and High Medieval (Arshavskaya et al. 1982)

Bibliography

Stride 2004, vol. 3, Uz-SD-166

Notes

area given here forthe the Kushan phase given by guess

Date of survey	Entered by
05.09.2010	Stančo

IDENTITY

Site Code
100

Stride 2004
no

Rtveladze 1974
no

Arshavskaya et al. 1982
no

Name of the site
No name 30

Translation
no

District
Sherabad

Type of site
settlement?

Alternative name of the site
Koktash cemetery (100k map)

Latitude
37.692837

Longitude
67.139548

Elevation (m.a.s.l.)
381

Location
within the modern cemetery (20–21th c.), 450 m to the north from the village of Chinobod (NW from it), former "9. sovkhoz"

Topography
the site is surrounded by flat irrigated lowlands, within a modern cemetery

DESCRIPTION

Basic description
irregular (uncertain) area within a modern cemetery; pottery traceable in its SE corner

Shape
unknown

Length
60

Width
60

Height

Surface area (sq m)
5430

Found
detected in GoogleEarth

Preservation
poor

Distortions
the site is covered with a modern cemetery and bounded by a water canal in the south

Excavated
no

Pottery
15

Other finds
no

DATING

Late Bronze Age	Early Iron Age	Hellenistic	Kushan and Kushan-Sasanian	X
Early Medieval	High Medieval X	Post-Mongol X	Pre-modern	

Dating published elsewhere   no

Bibliography
no

Notes
no

Date of survey
06.09.2010

Entered by
Stančo

IDENTITY

Site Code
101

Stride 2004
no

Rtveladze 1974
no

Arshavskaya et al. 1982
no

Name of the site
No name 31

Translation
no

District
Sherabad

Type of site
settlement?

Alternative name of the site
no

Latitude
37.684752

Longitude
67.10417

Elevation (m.a.s.l.)
379

Location

Topography

DESCRIPTION

Basic description

Shape
unknown

Length
180

Width
200

Height

Surface area (sq m)
19194

Found

Preservation
not known

Distortions
no

Excavated
no

Pottery
8

Other finds
no

DATING

Late Bronze Age		Early Iron Age		Hellenistic		Kushan and Kushan-Sasanian	X
Early Medieval		High Medieval	X	Post-Mongol		Pre-modern	

Dating published elsewhere   no

Bibliography
Arshavskaya et al. 1982, 134

Notes

Date of survey
06.09.2010

Entered by
Stančo

IDENTITY

Site Code	Stride 2004		Rtveladze 1974	Arshavskaya et al. 1982
102	Uz-SD-161		no	161?

Name of the site

No name 32

Translation	District	Type of site
no	Sherabad	settlement

Alternative name of the site

Kukumas Joy (Arshavskaya et al. 1982, 134, no. 161); Kukumas-Ota

Latitude	Longitude	Elevation (m.a.s.l.)
37.64116	67.069492	374

Location

on the south-eastern margin of the village of Kishlok Bozor, within the modern cemetery (eastern one)

Topography

terrace above the river valley

DESCRIPTION

Basic description

small rectangular mound surrounded by the irregular area (pottery all across the modern cemetery)

Shape	Length	Width	Height	Surface area (sq m)
square (tepa), irregular (settlement)	62	62		2549

Found	Preservation	Distortions
visualy	poor	the site is covered with a modern cemetery

Excavated

no

Pottery	Other finds
no	lot of burnt bricks (small size)

DATING

Late Bronze Age		Early Iron Age		Hellenistic		Kushan and Kushan-Sasanian	
Early Medieval		High Medieval	X	Post-Mongol		Pre-modern	

Dating published elsewhere   10th–12th c. (Arshavskaya et al. 1982)

Bibliography

Arshavskaya et al. 1982, 135; Stride 2004, vol. 3, Uz-SD-161

Notes

identification with a site no. 161 uncertain

Date of survey	Entered by
08.09.2010	Stančo

IDENTITY

Site Code: **103**

Stride 2004: no

Rtveladze 1974: no

Arshavskaya et al. 1982: no

Name of the site: **No name 33**

Translation: no

District: Kizirik

Type of site: settlement?

Alternative name of the site: no

Latitude: 37.582619

Longitude: 67.171856

Elevation (m.a.s.l.): 352

Location: 1.2 km W from the village of Takiya

Topography: the site is situated in flat irrigated lowlands

DESCRIPTION

Basic description: unspecified flat area within a fields (not elevated); no structures, only pottery present

Shape: unknown

Length: 204

Width: 231

Height:

Surface area (sq m): 3656

Found: field survey

Preservation: poor

Distortions: original site not obvious, ploughed field

Excavated: no

Pottery: 7

Other finds: burnt bricks

DATING

Late Bronze Age	Early Iron Age	Hellenistic	Kushan and Kushan-Sasanian

Early Medieval	High Medieval	Post-Mongol	Pre-modern
	X		

Dating published elsewhere: no

Bibliography: no

Notes: no

Date of survey: 10.09.2010

Entered by: Stančo

IDENTITY

Site Code
105

Stride 2004
no

Rtveladze 1974
no

Arshavskaya et al. 1982
no

Name of the site
No name (within the cemetery of old Akkurgan village)

Translation
no

District
Sherabad

Type of site
settlement?

Alternative name of the site
no

Latitude
37.663728

Longitude
66.97137

Elevation (m.a.s.l.)
405

Location
in the centre of old village of Akkurgan

Topography
terrace above the flat irrigated lowlands, within a modern cemetery

DESCRIPTION

Basic description

Shape
unknown

Length
60

Width
115

Height

Surface area (sq m)
1960

Found

Preservation
not known

Distortions
no

Excavated
no

Pottery
13

Other finds
no

DATING

Late Bronze Age	Early Iron Age	Hellenistic	Kushan and Kushan-Sasanian
Early Medieval	High Medieval	Post-Mongol	Pre-modern

Dating published elsewhere   no

Bibliography
no

Notes

Date of survey
11.10.2010

Entered by
Stančo

263

IDENTITY

Site Code	Stride 2004		Rtveladze 1974	Arshavskaya et al. 1982
119	no		no	no

Name of the site	Translation	District	Type of site
No name 34	no	Sherabad	settlement?

Alternative name of the site	Latitude	Longitude	Elevation (m.a.s.l.)
Kattatepa – field to the west	37.667965	67.07791	380

Location

320 m to the W from the site of Kattatepa (010)

Topography

DESCRIPTION

Basic description

Shape	Length	Width	Height	Surface area (sq m)
irregular	70	90		544

Found	Preservation	Distortions
	not known	no

Excavated

no

Pottery	Other finds
10	no

DATING

Late Bronze Age		Early Iron Age		Hellenistic		Kushan and Kushan-Sasanian	
Early Medieval		High Medieval	X	Post-Mongol		Pre-modern	

Dating published elsewhere   no

Bibliography

Arshavskaya et al. 1982, 134; Stride 2004, Uz-SD-161

Notes

Date of survey	Entered by
20.09.2010	Stančo

IDENTITY

Site Code
120

Stride 2004
no

Rtveladze 1974
no

Arshavskaya et al. 1982
no

Name of the site
No name 35

Translation
no

District
Sherabad

Type of site
settlement?

Alternative name of the site
Gegirdak – cemetery

Latitude
37.64991

Longitude
67.068701

Elevation (m.a.s.l.)
381

Location

Topography

DESCRIPTION

Basic description

Shape
irregular

Length
77

Width
98

Height

Surface area (sq m)
578

Found
field survey

Preservation
not known

Distortions
no

Excavated
no

Pottery
13

Other finds
no

DATING

Late Bronze Age	Early Iron Age	Hellenistic	Kushan and Kushan-Sasanian

Early Medieval	High Medieval	Post-Mongol	Pre-modern

Dating published elsewhere   no

Bibliography
no

Notes

Date of survey
20.09.2010

Entered by
Stančo

IDENTITY

Site Code	Stride 2004	Rtveladze 1974	Arshavskaya et al. 1982
121	no	no	no

Name of the site

Sultan ota (Hermitage)

Translation	District	Type of site
no	Sherabad	settlement?

Alternative name of the site	Latitude	Longitude	Elevation (m.a.s.l.)
no	37.58022	67.13153	336

Location

on the cliff inside the Sherobod Darya valley

Topography

DESCRIPTION

Basic description

summit of a cliff in the river valley of Sherobod Darya (pottery), hermitage of Sultan Ota at the foot of the cliff

Shape	Length	Width	Height	Surface area (sq m)
irregular	50	107		333

Found	Preservation	Distortions
visualy / field survey	high	no

Excavated

no

Pottery	Other finds
2	no

DATING

Late Bronze Age	Early Iron Age	Hellenistic	Kushan and Kushan-Sasanian
Early Medieval	High Medieval	Post-Mongol	Pre-modern

Dating published elsewhere | no

Bibliography

no

Notes

just two ceramic sherds

Date of survey	Entered by
09.09.2010	Stančo

IDENTITY

Site Code
122

Stride 2004
no

Rtveladze 1974
no

Arshavskaya et al. 1982
151

Name of the site
Pastaktepa

Translation
Low mound

District
Sherabad

Type of site
ploughed settlement

Alternative name of the site
no

Latitude
37.698315

Longitude
67.075715

Elevation (m.a.s.l.)
385

Location
180 m S from the site of Gurintepa across the main road Sherobod – Kumkurgan

Topography

DESCRIPTION

Basic description
the site is now probably completely ploughed – no visible traces

Shape
unknown

Length
12

Width
10

Height

Surface area (sq m)
120

Found
field survey (Tušlová)

Preservation
not preserved

Distortions
completely ploughed

Excavated
no

Pottery
193

Other finds
no

DATING

Late Bronze Age		Early Iron Age		Hellenistic	X	Kushan and Kushan-Sasanian	
Early Medieval		High Medieval	X	Post-Mongol		Pre-modern	

Dating published elsewhere   Early Medieval (Arshavskaya et al. 1982)

Bibliography
Tušlová 2012a; Tušlová 2012b; here cf. Chapter 3.8.3

Notes
identified with a no name site with following localisation: allegedly 200 m to the south-east of Gilyambobtepa (i.e. our Gurintepa) (Arshavskaya et al. 1982, 133, no. 151), the tepa measured 12×10×3 m in the past, nowadays is completely destroyed

Date of survey
20.09.2010

Entered by
Stančo

IDENTITY

Site Code
123

Stride 2004
no

Rtveladze 1974
no

Arshavskaya et al. 1982
no

Name of the site
No name 36

Translation
no

District
Sherabad

Type of site
ploughed settlement

Alternative name of the site
no

Latitude
37.702063

Longitude
67.112085

Elevation (m.a.s.l.)
386

Location
1.8 km E from the village of Gurin, 380 m S from the main road Sherobod – Kumkurgan

Topography

DESCRIPTION

Basic description

Shape	Length	Width	Height	Surface area (sq m)
unknown	215	155		3003

Found
field survey (Tušlová)

Preservation
not preserved

Distortions
completely ploughed

Excavated
no

Pottery
no

Other finds
no

DATING

Late Bronze Age	Early Iron Age	Hellenistic	Kushan and Kushan-Sasanian

Early Medieval	High Medieval	Post-Mongol	Pre-modern
	X		

Dating published elsewhere   no

Bibliography
Tušlová 2012b

Notes

Date of survey
x.9.2010

Entered by
Tušlová

IDENTITY

Site Code
125

Stride 2004
no

Rtveladze 1974
no

Arshavskaya et al. 1982
no

Name of the site
Khojai Gambir-ota tepa

Translation
no

District
Sherabad

Type of site
settlement

Alternative name of the site
no

Latitude
37.633213

Longitude
67.024532

Elevation (m.a.s.l.)
376

Location
N from the village of Gambir, 250m W from the main Tashkent – Termez road

Topography
within the modern cemetery surrounded by irrigated lowlands

DESCRIPTION

Basic description
low shalow mound covered partly with vegetation and graves of Modern time

Shape
rectangular

Length
81

Width
96

Height
2

Surface area (sq m)
885

Found

Preservation
not known

Distortions
no

Excavated
no

Pottery
10

Other finds
no

DATING

Late Bronze Age	Early Iron Age	Hellenistic	Kushan and Kushan-Sasanian
Early Medieval	High Medieval	Post-Mongol	Pre-modern

Dating published elsewhere no

Bibliography
no

Notes

Date of survey
21.09.2010

Entered by
Stančo

IDENTITY

Site Code
126

Stride 2004
no

Rtveladze 1974
no

Arshavskaya et al. 1982
no

Name of the site
Qairogoch-ota tepa

Translation
no

District
Sherabad

Type of site
settlement and mausoleum

Alternative name of the site
no

Latitude
37.614084

Longitude
67.03956

Elevation (m.a.s.l.)
364

Location
SE end of the village of Topar

Topography

DESCRIPTION

Basic description
Principal building of the site is a mausoleum almost completely preserved. It was covered by mu during a flooding in the mid-20th c. and later cleaned by archaeologists.

Shape	Length	Width	Height	Surface area (sq m)
rectangular	120	95		897

Found

Preservation
not known

Distortions
no

Excavated
no

Pottery
no

Other finds
no

DATING

Late Bronze Age	Early Iron Age	Hellenistic	Kushan and Kushan-Sasanian

Early Medieval	High Medieval	Post-Mongol	Pre-modern
		X	X

Dating published elsewhere   17th–18th c. AD (Botirov – Khalikov 2006)

Bibliography
Botirov – Khalikov 2006

Notes

Date of survey
21.09.2010

Entered by
Stančo

IDENTITY

Site Code
127

Stride 2004
no

Rtveladze 1974
no

Arshavskaya et al. 1982
no

Name of the site
No name 37

Translation
no

District
Sherabad

Type of site
fortress

Alternative name of the site
no

Latitude
37.602641

Longitude
66.825805

Elevation (m.a.s.l.)
456

Location
2 km to NW from the end of the Sherobod Canal", former 18th Sovkhoz

Topography
flat steppe area close to the mountains and to the mountain road from Goz to Muzrabad

DESCRIPTION

Basic description
small compact rectangular mound

Shape	Length	Width	Height	Surface area (sq m)
rectangular	20	30	4	913

Found
reported by Shapulat Shaydullaev

Preservation
high

Distortions
three trenches in the northern part

Excavated
probably, but there is no publication known

Pottery
12

Other finds
mud-bricks and stone constructions

DATING

Late Bronze Age		Early Iron Age		Hellenistic		Kushan and Kushan-Sasanian	
Early Medieval		High Medieval	X	Post-Mongol		Pre-modern	

Dating published elsewhere   no

Bibliography
no

Notes
in the trenches are visible well preserved stone-made foundations and mud-bricks upper structures, even a vault

Date of survey
24.09.2010

Entered by
Stančo

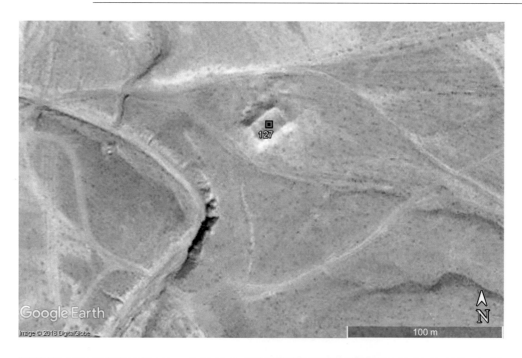

IDENTITY

Site Code
128

Stride 2004
no

Rtveladze 1974
no

Arshavskaya et al. 1982
no

Name of the site
Kishlok Bazar kabristoni

Translation
no

District
Sherabad

Type of site
settlement?

Alternative name of the site
no

Latitude
37.640363

Longitude
67.067744

Elevation (m.a.s.l.)
376

Location

Topography

DESCRIPTION

Basic description

Shape	Length	Width	Height	Surface area (sq m)
unknown	105	93		1027

Found

Preservation
not known

Distortions
no

Excavated
no

Pottery
13

Other finds
no

DATING

Late Bronze Age		Early Iron Age		Hellenistic		Kushan and Kushan-Sasanian	
Early Medieval		High Medieval	X	Post-Mongol		Pre-modern	

Dating published elsewhere   no

Bibliography
no

Notes

Date of survey
24.09.2010

Entered by
Stančo

IDENTITY

Site Code
129

Stride 2004
no

Rtveladze 1974
no

Arshavskaya et al. 1982
no

Name of the site
Chuyanchi ota kabristoni

Translation
no

District
Sherabad

Type of site
settlement?

Alternative name of the site
no

Latitude
37.664167

Longitude
67.035723

Elevation (m.a.s.l.)
403

Location

Topography

DESCRIPTION

Basic description

Shape	Length	Width	Height	Surface area (sq m)
unknown	60	240		1129

Found
field survey

Preservation
not known

Distortions
no

Excavated
no

Pottery
10

Other finds
no

DATING

Late Bronze Age	Early Iron Age	Hellenistic	Kushan and Kushan-Sasanian

Early Medieval	High Medieval	Post-Mongol	Pre-modern
	X	X	

Dating published elsewhere   no

Bibliography
no

Notes

Date of survey
02.11.2011

Entered by
Stančo

IDENTITY

Site Code
133

Stride 2004
no

Rtveladze 1974
no

Arshavskaya et al. 1982
no

Name of the site
Irjahangir-ota kabristoni

Translation
no

District
Muzrabad

Type of site
settlement

Alternative name of the site
Masoophirkhoja cemetery (100k topo)

Latitude
37.500296

Longitude
66.779969

Elevation (m.a.s.l.)
360

Location
within the cemetery of muzrabad close to the crossroad Sherabad – Muzarabad – Aktash

Topography
borderland of irrigated lowlands and steppe-hilly area

DESCRIPTION

Basic description
low irregular mound within modern cemetery

Shape
unknown

Length
130

Width
100

Height

Surface area (sq m)
60

Found
field survey

Preservation
low

Distortions
modern graves and waste, partly disrtubed by old building of a mosque

Excavated
no

Pottery
14

Other finds
no

DATING

Late Bronze Age		Early Iron Age		Hellenistic		Kushan and Kushan-Sasanian	
Early Medieval		High Medieval		Post-Mongol		Pre-modern	X

Dating published elsewhere   no

Bibliography
no

Notes

Date of survey
02.11.2011

Entered by
Stančo

284

IDENTITY

Site Code
135

Stride 2004
no

Rtveladze 1974
no

Arshavskaya et al. 1982
no

Name of the site
Khojakiyamiddin-ota kabristoni

Translation
no

District
Sherabad

Type of site
settlement?

Alternative name of the site
no

Latitude
37.654397

Longitude
66.929741

Elevation (m.a.s.l.)
412

Location
north-western part of Khojakiya village

Topography
the site is situated in flat irrigated lowlands, close to the hilly steppe area

DESCRIPTION

Basic description
flat location; pottery found only within a small part of the modern cemetery (eastern central part)

Shape
unknown

Length
1

Width
1

Height

Surface area (sq m)
39

Found
field survey

Preservation
low

Distortions
modern graves, partly disrtubed by old building of a mosque

Excavated
no

Pottery
7

Other finds
no

DATING

Late Bronze Age	Early Iron Age	Hellenistic	Kushan and Kushan-Sasanian
Early Medieval	High Medieval	Post-Mongol	Pre-modern X

Dating published elsewhere   no

Bibliography
no

Notes

Date of survey
02.11.2011

Entered by
Stančo

286

IDENTITY

Site Code
136

Stride 2004
no

Rtveladze 1974
no

Arshavskaya et al. 1982
no

Name of the site
No name 38

Translation
no

District
Sherabad

Type of site
settlement?

Alternative name of the site
no

Latitude
37.586755

Longitude
66.922606

Elevation (m.a.s.l.)
361

Location
1 km to SW from Bustan village

Topography
the site is situated in flat irrigated lowlands

DESCRIPTION

Basic description
plain fields, no morphological features, only pottery scattered around

Shape
unknown

Length
89

Width
136

Height
2

Surface area (sq m)
1233

Found
100k-topo maps 1980

Preservation
poor, not existent

Distortions
completely ploughed

Excavated
no

Pottery
6

Other finds
no

DATING

Late Bronze Age		Early Iron Age		Hellenistic		Kushan and Kushan-Sasanian	
Early Medieval	X	High Medieval		Post-Mongol		Pre-modern	

Dating published elsewhere   no

Bibliography
no

Notes
the site area corresponds to the pottery scatter not to the original size of the ploughed tepa

Date of survey
03.11.2011

Entered by
Stančo

IDENTITY

Site Code	Stride 2004	Rtveladze 1974	Arshavskaya et al. 1982
137	no	no	no

Name of the site	Translation	District	Type of site
No name 39	no	Sherabad	settlement?

Alternative name of the site	Latitude	Longitude	Elevation (m.a.s.l.)
no	37.585923	66.919631	362

Location

1.15 km to SW from Bustan village

Topography

the site is situated in flat irrigated lowlands

DESCRIPTION

Basic description

plain fields, no morphological features, only pottery scattered around

Shape	Length	Width	Height	Surface area (sq m)
unknown	138	112		1221

Found	Preservation	Distortions
100k-topo maps 1980	poor, not existent	completely ploughed

Excavated

no

Pottery	Other finds
6	no

DATING

Late Bronze Age		Early Iron Age		Hellenistic		Kushan and Kushan-Sasanian	
Early Medieval	X	High Medieval		Post-Mongol		Pre-modern	

Dating published elsewhere no

Bibliography

no

Notes

the site area corresponds to the pottery scatter not to the original size of the ploughed tepa

Date of survey	Entered by
05.11.2011	Stančo

IDENTITY

Site Code **138**	Stride 2004 no	Rtveladze 1974 no	Arshavskaya et al. 1982 no

Name of the site: **No name 40**

Translation: no

District: Sherabad

Type of site: settlement?

Alternative name of the site: no

Latitude: 37.652303

Longitude: 66.98933

Elevation (m.a.s.l.): 394

Location: 0.5 km east of the Akkurgan museum

Topography: the site is situated in flat irrigated lowlands / fields

DESCRIPTION

Basic description: plain fields / orchards, no morphological features, only pottery scattered around, some part found by local worker digging here during our survey; in the IKONOS image seems to be captured original mound in the northern corner of the playground

Shape: unknown

Length: 70

Width: 10

Height:

Surface area (sq m): 4153

Found: 100k-topo maps 1980

Preservation: poor, not existent

Distortions: completely ploughed

Excavated: no

Pottery: 1

Other finds: no

DATING

Late Bronze Age		Early Iron Age	X	Hellenistic		Kushan and Kushan-Sasanian	
Early Medieval	X	High Medieval		Post-Mongol		Pre-modern	

Dating published elsewhere: no

Bibliography: no

Notes: the site area corresponds to the pottery scatter not to the original size of the ploughed tepa

Date of survey: 05.11.2011

Entered by: Stančo

IDENTITY

Site Code	Stride 2004	Rtveladze 1974	Arshavskaya et al. 1982
139	no	no	no

Name of the site	Translation	District	Type of site
Toshtepa	Stone mound	Sherabad	settlement

Alternative name of the site	Latitude	Longitude	Elevation (m.a.s.l.)
no	37.682917	67.068466	386

Location

NW margin of Yangeyul village

Topography

the site is situated in flat irrigated lowlands, in the village

DESCRIPTION

Basic description

small compact mound

Shape	Length	Width	Height	Surface area (sq m)
circular	35	34	4	91

Found	Preservation	Distortions
100k-topo maps 1980	poor	small structure (a cowshed) in the sourhern part and on the slope; several pits here and there all around the surface

Excavated

no

Pottery	Other finds
1	no

DATING

Late Bronze Age		Early Iron Age		Hellenistic		Kushan and Kushan-Sasanian	
Early Medieval	X	High Medieval	X	Post-Mongol		Pre-modern	

Dating published elsewhere no

Bibliography

no

Notes

just a few ceramic sherds

Date of survey	Entered by
05.11.2011	Stančo

IDENTITY

Site Code	Stride 2004		Rtveladze 1974	Arshavskaya et al. 1982
140	no		no	no

Name of the site	Translation	District	Type of site
Kumirtepa	Coal mound	Kizirik	settlement

Alternative name of the site	Latitude	Longitude	Elevation (m.a.s.l.)
no	37.627304	67.197168	369

Location

0.66 km N from the "odd.no.4 savkh.no.7"

Topography

the site is situated in flat irrigated lowlands with cotton fields

DESCRIPTION

Basic description

simple low mound, partly covered with vegetation

Shape	Length	Width	Height	Surface area (sq m)
oval	33	30	3	74

Found	Preservation	Distortions
100k-topo maps 1980	moderate, not existent	traces of intensive cattle grazing

Excavated

no

Pottery	Other finds
1	mud-bricks (after short surface cleaning)

DATING

Late Bronze Age		Early Iron Age		Hellenistic		Kushan and Kushan-Sasanian	
Early Medieval		High Medieval		Post-Mongol		Pre-modern	

Dating published elsewhere   no

Bibliography

no

Notes

just a few ceramic sherds; the name of Kumirtepa was told to us by little local herder

Date of survey	Entered by
05.11.2011	Stančo

IDENTITY

Site Code
141

Stride 2004
no

Rtveladze 1974
no

Arshavskaya et al. 1982
no

Name of the site
No name 41

Translation
no

District
Kizirik

Type of site
settlement?

Alternative name of the site
no

Latitude
37.624971

Longitude
67.196129

Elevation (m.a.s.l.)
367

Location
0.37 km N from the "odd.no.4 savkh.no.7"

Topography
the site is situated in flat irrigated lowlands with cotton fields

DESCRIPTION

Basic description
plain fields, no morphological features, only pottery scattered around

Shape
unknown

Length
138

Width
110

Height
1

Surface area (sq m)
2171

Found
field survey

Preservation
poor, not existent

Distortions
completely ploughed

Excavated
no

Pottery
2

Other finds
no

DATING

Late Bronze Age		Early Iron Age		Hellenistic		Kushan and Kushan-Sasanian	
Early Medieval		High Medieval	X	Post-Mongol	X	Pre-modern	

Dating published elsewhere   no

Bibliography
no

Notes
found accidentally, the site area corresponds to the pottery scatter not to the original size

Date of survey
05.11.2011

Entered by
Stančo

IDENTITY

Site Code	Stride 2004	Rtveladze 1974	Arshavskaya et al. 1982
142	no	no	no

Name of the site: **No name 42**

Translation: no

District: Kizirik

Type of site: settlement?

Alternative name of the site: no

Latitude: 37.627181

Longitude: 67.193858

Elevation (m.a.s.l.): 367

Location: 0.52 km N from the "odd.no.4 savkh.no.7"

Topography: the site is situated in flat irrigated lowlands with cotton fields

DESCRIPTION

Basic description: plain fields, no morphological features, only pottery scattered around

Shape: unknown

Length: 176

Width: 176

Height: 1

Surface area (sq m): 1136

Found: field survey

Preservation: poor, not existent

Distortions: completely ploughed

Excavated: no

Pottery: 4

Other finds: no

DATING

Late Bronze Age		Early Iron Age		Hellenistic		Kushan and Kushan-Sasanian	
Early Medieval		High Medieval		Post-Mongol		Pre-modern	X

Dating published elsewhere: no

Bibliography: no

Notes: found accidentally, the site area corresponds to the pottery scatter not to the original size

Date of survey: 05.11.2011

Entered by: Stančo

IDENTITY

Site Code
143

Stride 2004
no

Rtveladze 1974
no

Arshavskaya et al. 1982
no

Name of the site
No name 43

Translation
no

District
Kizirik

Type of site
settlement?

Alternative name of the site
no

Latitude
37.630647

Longitude
67.190353

Elevation (m.a.s.l.)
366

Location
0.88 km north of the "odd.no.4 savkh.no.7"

Topography
the site is situated in flat irrigated lowlands with cotton fields

DESCRIPTION

Basic description
plain fields, no morphological features, only pottery scattered around

Shape
unknown

Length
5

Width
5

Height
1

Surface area (sq m)
600

Found
field survey

Preservation
poor, not existent

Distortions
completely ploughed

Excavated
no

Pottery
8

Other finds
no

DATING

Late Bronze Age		Early Iron Age		Hellenistic		Kushan and Kushan-Sasanian	
Early Medieval		High Medieval		Post-Mongol		Pre-modern	X

Dating published elsewhere   no

Bibliography
no

Notes
found accidentally, the site area corresponds to the pottery scatter not to the original size

Date of survey
05.11.2011

Entered by
Stančo

IDENTITY

Site Code
144

Stride 2004
no

Rtveladze 1974
no

Arshavskaya et al. 1982
no

Name of the site
No name 44

Translation
no

District
Kizirik

Type of site
settlement?

Alternative name of the site
no

Latitude
37.633724

Longitude
67.187965

Elevation (m.a.s.l.)
367

Location
1.2 km N from the "odd.no.4 savkh.no.7"

Topography
the site is situated in flat irrigated lowlands with cotton fields

DESCRIPTION

Basic description
plain fields, no morphological features, only pottery scattered around

Shape	Length	Width	Height	Surface area (sq m)
unknown	126	124	1	786

Found
100k-topo maps 1980

Preservation
poor, not existent

Distortions
completely ploughed

Excavated
no

Pottery
10

Other finds
no

DATING

Late Bronze Age	Early Iron Age	Hellenistic	Kushan and Kushan-Sasanian

Early Medieval	High Medieval	Post-Mongol	Pre-modern
			X

Dating published elsewhere   no

Bibliography
no

Notes
a mound marked in the 100k topomaps, today nothing remains, the site area corresponds to the pottery scatter not to the original size

Date of survey
05.11.2011

Entered by
Stančo

IDENTITY

Site Code **150**	Stride 2004 Uz-SD-235	Rtveladze 1974 B-034	Arshavskaya et al. 1982 no

Name of the site
Pashmaktepa

Translation	District	Type of site
(a sort of fruit) tepa	Sherabad	fire temple?

Alternative name of the site	Latitude	Longitude	Elevation (m.a.s.l.)
Pachmaktepa (Rtveladze 1974; Pidaev 1974)	37.614013	67.097801	358

Location
0.8 km SE from Jandavlattepa, south from Sidabad village

Topography
the site is situated in flat irrigated lowlands / fields

DESCRIPTION

Basic description

Shape	Length	Width	Height	Surface area (sq m)
unknown	49	57		15000

Found	Preservation	Distortions
in 1972 by Pidaev	poor, not existent	completely ploughed

Excavated
yes

Pottery	Other finds
55	fragment of a pestle

DATING

Late Bronze Age		Early Iron Age	X	Hellenistic		Kushan and Kushan-Sasanian	
Early Medieval		High Medieval		Post-Mongol		Pre-modern	

Dating published elsewhere   Achaemenid (Pidaev 1974; Rtveladze 1974)

Bibliography
Pidaev 1974, 33–38; Rtveladze 1974, 78; Tušlová 2012a; 2012b; Stride 2004, vol. 3, Uz-SD-235; see also chapter 3.8.6. in this volume (pp. 72–74)

Notes
checked by group of P. Tušlová during the field survey and total pick up´s around Jandavlattepa; size documented by Pidaev in 1972: diam. 30 m, height 3 m

Date of survey	Entered by
07.11.2011	Tušlová

IDENTITY

Site Code **152**	Stride 2004 no	Rtveladze 1974 no	Arshavskaya et al. 1982 no

Name of the site **No name 45**	Translation no	District Sherabad	Type of site ploughed settlement

Alternative name of the site no	Latitude 37.609559	Longitude 67.089863	Elevation (m.a.s.l.) 355

Location

Topography

the site is situated in flat irrigated lowlands / fields

DESCRIPTION

Basic description

Shape	Length	Width	Height	Surface area (sq m)
irregular	36	44		94

Found	Preservation	Distortions
100k-topo maps 1980	not known	no

Excavated

no

Pottery	Other finds
12	no

DATING

Late Bronze Age	Early Iron Age	Hellenistic	Kushan and Kushan-Sasanian
Early Medieval	High Medieval	Post-Mongol	Pre-modern

Dating published elsewhere no

Bibliography

Rtveladze 1974, 78; Pidaev 1974, 33–38; Tušlová 2012

Notes

checked by group of P. Tušlová during the field survey and total pick up´s around Jandavlattepa

Date of survey	Entered by
x.11.2011	Tušlová

IDENTITY

Site Code
153

Stride 2004
no

Rtveladze 1974
no

Arshavskaya et al. 1982
no

Name of the site
No name 46

Translation
no

District
Sherabad

Type of site
ploughed settlement

Alternative name of the site
no

Latitude
37.606761

Longitude
67.093518

Elevation (m.a.s.l.)
355

Location

Topography
the site is situated in flat irrigated lowlands / fields

DESCRIPTION

Basic description

Shape
irregular

Length
32

Width
39

Height

Surface area (sq m)
73

Found
100k-topo maps 1980

Preservation
not preserved

Distortions
completely ploughed

Excavated
no

Pottery
3

Other finds
no

DATING

Late Bronze Age	Early Iron Age	Hellenistic	Kushan and Kushan-Sasanian
Early Medieval	High Medieval	Post-Mongol	Pre-modern

Dating published elsewhere   no

Bibliography
Tušlová 2012b; see also chapter 3.8.6. in this volume (pp. 71–78)

Notes
checked by group of P. Tušlová during the field survey and total pick up´s around Jandavlattepa

Date of survey
x.11.2011

Entered by
Tušlová

IDENTITY

Site Code
154

Stride 2004
no

Rtveladze 1974
no

Arshavskaya et al. 1982
no

Name of the site
No name 47

Translation
no

District
Sherabad

Type of site
ploughed settlement

Alternative name of the site
no

Latitude
37.626063

Longitude
67.081182

Elevation (m.a.s.l.)
363

Location

Topography
the site is situated in flat irrigated lowlands / fields

DESCRIPTION

Basic description

Shape
irregular

Length
33

Width
34

Height

Surface area (sq m)
17000

Found
100k-topo maps 1980

Preservation
not preserved

Distortions
completely ploughed

Excavated
no

Pottery
57

Other finds
no

DATING

Late Bronze Age		Early Iron Age	X	Hellenistic		Kushan and Kushan-Sasanian	
Early Medieval		High Medieval		Post-Mongol		Pre-modern	

Dating published elsewhere   Kuchuk III – IV (Tušlová 2012a, 18–19)

Bibliography
Tušlová 2012a; 2012b; see also chapter 3.8.6. in this volume (pp. 71–78)

Notes
checked by group of P. Tušlová during the field survey and total pick up´s around Jandavlattepa

Date of survey
x.11.2011

Entered by
Tušlová

IDENTITY

Site Code **155**	Stride 2004 no	Rtveladze 1974 no	Arshavskaya et al. 1982 no

Name of the site
No name 48

Translation: no

District: Sherabad

Type of site: ploughed settlement

Alternative name of the site: no

Latitude: 37.620638

Longitude: 67.077585

Elevation (m.a.s.l.): 364

Location

Topography
the site is situated in flat irrigated lowlands / fields

DESCRIPTION

Basic description

Shape	Length	Width	Height	Surface area (sq m)
irregular	28	32	2	26000

Found: 100k-topo maps 1980

Preservation: not preseved

Distortions: completely ploughed

Excavated: no

Pottery: 45

Other finds: no

DATING

Late Bronze Age	Early Iron Age	X	Hellenistic	Kushan and Kushan-Sasanian
Early Medieval	High Medieval		Post-Mongol	Pre-modern

Dating published elsewhere: Kuchuk III – IV (Tušlová 2012a, 18–19)

Bibliography
Arshavskaya et al. 1982, 110–112 (with 3 ill.); Tušlová 2012a; 2012b; see also chapter 3.8.6. in this volume (pp. 71–78)

Notes
checked by group of P. Tušlová during the field survey and total pick up´s around Jandavlattepa

Date of survey: x.11.2011

Entered by: Tušlová

315

IDENTITY

Site Code
156

Stride 2004
no

Rtveladze 1974
no

Arshavskaya et al. 1982
no

Name of the site
No name 49

Translation
no

District
Sherabad

Type of site
ploughed settlement

Alternative name of the site
no

Latitude
37.620076

Longitude
67.081284

Elevation (m.a.s.l.)
363

Location

Topography
the site is situated in flat irrigated lowlands / fields

DESCRIPTION

Basic description

Shape	Length	Width	Height	Surface area (sq m)
irregular	20	23		14000

Found
100k-topo maps 1980

Preservation
not preserved

Distortions
completely ploughed

Excavated
no

Pottery
34

Other finds
no

DATING

Late Bronze Age	Early Iron Age	X	Hellenistic		Kushan and Kushan-Sasanian	
Early Medieval	High Medieval		Post-Mongol		Pre-modern	

Dating published elsewhere   Kuchuk III – IV (Tušlová 2012a, 18–19)

Bibliography
Tušlová 2012a; 2012b; see also chapter 3.8.6. in this volume (pp. 71–78)

Notes
checked by group of P. Tušlová during the field survey and total pick up´s around Jandavlattepa

Date of survey
x.11.2011

Entered by
Tušlová

317

IDENTITY

Site Code

157

Stride 2004

Uz-SD-617

Rtveladze 1974

no

Arshavskaya et al. 1982

no

Name of the site

Ota-Kul′ mulla ishan baba

Translation

no

District

Sherabad

Type of site

architecture

Alternative name of the site

Ataulla Said Vakkos (Arshavskaya et al. 1982)

Latitude

37.692883

Longitude

67.020908

Elevation (m.a.s.l.)

454

Location

Topography

hill top, above Sherabad Darya river valley

DESCRIPTION

Basic description

Shape	Length	Width	Height	Surface area (sq m)
unknown	30	30		187

Found

in publications (Arshavskaya et al. 1982)

Preservation

excellent (building reconstructed)

Distortions

modern graveyard around

Excavated

no

Pottery

5

Other finds

no

DATING

Late Bronze Age		Early Iron Age		Hellenistic		Kushan and Kushan-Sasanian	
Early Medieval		High Medieval	X	Post-Mongol		Pre-modern	

Dating published elsewhere   11th c. (Arshavskaya et al. 1982, 110–112)

Bibliography

Arshavskaya et al. 1982, 112–115 (with 4 ill.); Stride 2004, vol. 3, Uz-SD-613

Notes

pottery found during the second survey

Date of survey

11.11.2011

Entered by

Stančo

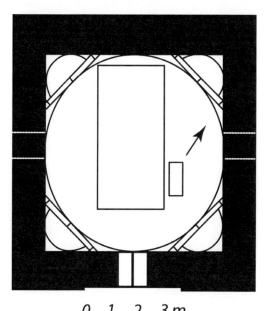

0 1 2 3 m

Ground plan of the building, drawn by P. Kazakova
after Arshavskaya et al. 1982, 112.

IDENTITY

Site Code
158

Stride 2004
no

Rtveladze 1974
no

Arshavskaya et al. 1982
no

Name of the site
No name 50

Translation
no

District
Sherabad

Type of site
ploughed settlement

Alternative name of the site
no

Latitude
37.587648

Longitude
66.908507

Elevation (m.a.s.l.)
367

Location

Topography

DESCRIPTION

Basic description

Shape
unknown

Length
55

Width
46

Height

Surface area (sq m)
188

Found
100k-topo maps 1980

Preservation
not preserved

Distortions
completely ploughed

Excavated
no

Pottery
8

Other finds
no

DATING

Late Bronze Age		Early Iron Age		Hellenistic		Kushan and Kushan-Sasanian	
Early Medieval	X	High Medieval		Post-Mongol		Pre-modern	X

Dating published elsewhere   no

Bibliography
no

Notes

Date of survey
11.11.2011

Entered by
Stančo

IDENTITY

Site Code	Stride 2004		Rtveladze 1974	Arshavskaya et al. 1982
159	no		no	no

Name of the site

Termez-ota mausoleum

	Translation	District	Type of site
	no	Sherabad	architecture

Alternative name of the site	Latitude	Longitude	Elevation (m.a.s.l.)
Khoja Isa (Arshavskaya et al. 1982)	37.67547	67.079806	379

Location

SE margin of Yakhteyul′ village and eastern margin of Dehkhanabad village

Topography

the site is situated in flat irrigated lowlands, within a large cemetery next to the village

DESCRIPTION

Basic description

Medieval mosque

Shape	Length	Width	Height	Surface area (sq m)
rectangular	20	9		102

Found	Preservation	Distortions
in publications (Arshavskaya et al. 1982)	excellent (building reconstructed)	modern graveyard around

Excavated

no

Pottery	Other finds
no	no

DATING

Late Bronze Age		Early Iron Age		Hellenistic		Kushan and Kushan-Sasanian	
Early Medieval		High Medieval	X	Post-Mongol		Pre-modern	

Dating published elsewhere   11th–13th c. (Arshavskaya et al. 1982, 112–115)

Bibliography

Arshavskaya et al. 1982, 132

Notes

restored in 2000, especially northern part (fifth); mulla informed us that in this area has been another ancient village called Bug (connected with famous Muslim scholar at–Termezi)

Date of survey	Entered by
11.11.2011	Stančo

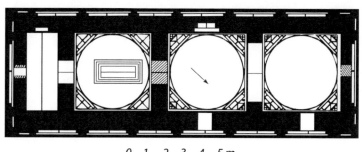

0 1 2 3 4 5 m

0 1 2 3 m

Ground plan and section of the building, drawn by
P. Kazakova after Arshavskaya et al. 1982, 113.

IDENTITY

Site Code	Stride 2004		Rtveladze 1974	Arshavskaya et al. 1982
160	no		no	no

Name of the site	Translation	District	Type of site
No name 51	no	Sherabad	ploughed settlement

Alternative name of the site	Latitude	Longitude	Elevation (m.a.s.l.)
no	37.582829	66.896313	368

Location

Topography

DESCRIPTION

Basic description

Shape	Length	Width	Height	Surface area (sq m)
unknown	20	20		1

Found	Preservation	Distortions
100k-topo maps 1980	not preserved	completely ploughed

Excavated

no

Pottery	Other finds
no	no

DATING

Late Bronze Age		Early Iron Age		Hellenistic		Kushan and Kushan-Sasanian	
Early Medieval		High Medieval		Post-Mongol		Pre-modern	

Dating published elsewhere | no

Bibliography

Rtveladze – Khakimov 1973, 18–19; Rtveladze 1974, 77; Pidaev 1974, 40–41; Pidaev 1978, 21

Notes

Date of survey	Entered by
11.11.2011	Stančo

IDENTITY

Site Code	Stride 2004	Rtveladze 1974	Arshavskaya et al. 1982
168	Uz-SD-147	no	147

Name of the site
No name 52

Translation: no

District: Sherabad

Type of site: ploughed settlement

Alternative name of the site: no

Latitude: 37.571222

Longitude: 66.909578

Elevation (m.a.s.l.): 358

Location
reportedly between the sites of Talashkan I and II; 100k map shows some feature in this place as well

Topography
the site is situated in flat irrigated lowlands

DESCRIPTION

Basic description
the site is now probably completely ploughed – no visible traces

Shape	Length	Width	Height	Surface area (sq m)
	30	20		1

Found
in publications (Arshavskaya et al. 1982)

Preservation
at the time of the survey not existent

Distortions
completely ploughed

Excavated
no

Pottery: no

Other finds: no

DATING

Late Bronze Age		Early Iron Age		Hellenistic		Kushan and Kushan-Sasanian	
Early Medieval		High Medieval		Post-Mongol	X	Pre-modern	

Dating published elsewhere   14th–15th c. AD (Arshavskaya et al. 1982)

Bibliography
Arshavskaya et al. 1982, 132; Stride 2004, vol. 3, Uz-SD-147

Notes
this site is known to us only from publications

Date of survey
not surveyed

Entered by
Stančo

IDENTITY

Site Code
169

Stride 2004
Uz-SD-234

Rtveladze 1974
B-029

Arshavskaya et al. 1982
no

Name of the site
Koshtepa 2 - western tepa

Translation
Double mound

District
Sherabad

Type of site
settlement

Alternative name of the site
no

Latitude
37.709845

Longitude
67.058025

Elevation (m.a.s.l.)
403

Location
eastern end of the village of Chagatay (?)

Topography

DESCRIPTION

Basic description

Shape
rectangular

Length
34

Width
38

Height

Surface area (sq m)
254

Found
detected in GoogleEarth

Preservation
not known

Distortions
no

Excavated
no

Pottery
no

Other finds
no

DATING

Late Bronze Age	Early Iron Age	Hellenistic	Kushan and Kushan-Sasanian
Early Medieval	High Medieval	Post-Mongol	Pre-modern

Dating published elsewhere   no

Bibliography
Rtveladze 1974, 77; Stride 2004, vol. 3, Uz-SD-234

Notes

Date of survey
17.09.2008

Entered by
Stančo

IDENTITY

Site Code
173

Stride 2004
Uz-SD-317

Rtveladze 1974
no

Arshavskaya et al. 1982
no

Name of the site
Bustan 1

Translation
no

District
Sherabad

Type of site
burial site

Alternative name of the site
no

Latitude
37.62489

Longitude
66.947781

Elevation (m.a.s.l.)
376

Location
6.5 km southwest of Sherabad on the left side of the road from Sherabad to Muzrabad

Topography

DESCRIPTION

Basic description

Shape
irregular

Length
165

Width
220

Height

Surface area (sq m)
42492

Found
in 1973 by Askarov

Preservation
not known

Distortions
not known

Excavated
no

Pottery
no

Other finds
no

DATING

Late Bronze Age	X	Early Iron Age		Hellenistic		Kushan and Kushan-Sasanian	
Early Medieval		High Medieval		Post-Mongol		Pre-modern	

Dating published elsewhere   Late Bronze Age

Bibliography
Askarov 1977, 57–68; Stride 2004, vol. 3, Uz-SD-317

Notes

Date of survey
not surveyed

Entered by
Stančo

IDENTITY

Site Code
174

Stride 2004
Uz-SD-317

Rtveladze 1974
no

Arshavskaya et al. 1982
no

Name of the site
Bustan 2

Translation
no

District
Sherabad

Type of site
burial site

Alternative name of the site
no

Latitude
37.623831

Longitude
66.946525

Elevation (m.a.s.l.)
370

Location
6.5 km southwest of Sherabad on the left side of the road from Sherabad to Muzrabad

Topography

DESCRIPTION

Basic description

Shape
irregular

Length
244

Width
316

Height

Surface area (sq m)
52129

Found
in 1973 by Askarov

Preservation
not known

Distortions
not known

Excavated
no

Pottery
no

Other finds
no

DATING

Late Bronze Age	X	Early Iron Age	Hellenistic	Kushan and Kushan-Sasanian
Early Medieval		High Medieval	Post-Mongol	Pre-modern

Dating published elsewhere   Late Bronze Age

Bibliography
Askarov 1977, 58; Stride 2004, vol. 3, Uz-SD-317

Notes

Date of survey
not surveyed

Entered by
Stančo

IDENTITY

Site Code
175

Stride 2004
Uz-SD-317

Rtveladze 1974
no

Arshavskaya et al. 1982
no

Name of the site
Bustan 4

Translation
no

District
Sherabad

Type of site
settlement

Alternative name of the site
no

Latitude
37.617797

Longitude
66.953439

Elevation (m.a.s.l.)
363

Location
6.5 km southwest of Sherabad on the left side of the road from Sherabad to Muzrabad

Topography

DESCRIPTION

Basic description

Shape
irregular

Length
116

Width
230

Height

Surface area (sq m)
38882

Found
in 1973 by Askarov

Preservation
not known

Distortions
not known

Excavated
excavated partially by Sherabad group of AI AS (Rakhmanov) in 1977

Pottery
no

Other finds
no

DATING

| Late Bronze Age | X | Early Iron Age | | Hellenistic | | Kushan and Kushan-Sasanian | |
| Early Medieval | | High Medieval | | Post-Mongol | | Pre-modern | |

Dating published elsewhere   Late Bronze Age

Bibliography
Askarov 1977, 58; Rakhmanov 1979; 1981; Askarov – Ruzanov 1990; Rakhmanov – Baratov 1995; Stride 2004, vol. 3, Uz-SD-317

Notes

Date of survey
not surveyed

Entered by
Stančo

IDENTITY

Site Code	Stride 2004		Rtveladze 1974	Arshavskaya et al. 1982
176	Uz-SD-317		no	no

Name of the site	Translation	District	Type of site
Bustan 5	no	Sherabad	burial site

Alternative name of the site	Latitude	Longitude	Elevation (m.a.s.l.)
no	37.610534	66.94729	364

Location

6.5 km southwest of Sherabad on the left side of the road from Sherabad to Muzrabad

Topography

DESCRIPTION

Basic description

Shape	Length	Width	Height	Surface area (sq m)
irregular	188	78		54435

Found	Preservation	Distortions
in 1973 by Askarov	not known	not known

Excavated

no

Pottery	Other finds
no	no

DATING

Late Bronze Age	X	Early Iron Age		Hellenistic		Kushan and Kushan-Sasanian	
Early Medieval		High Medieval		Post-Mongol		Pre-modern	

Dating published elsewhere	Late Bronze Age

Bibliography

Askarov 1977, 58–59; Askarov – Ruzanov 1990; Rakhmanov – Baratov 1995; Stride 2004, vol. 3, Uz-SD-317

Notes

Date of survey	Entered by
not surveyed	Stančo

IDENTITY

Site Code
177

Stride 2004
Uz-SD-366

Rtveladze 1974
no

Arshavskaya et al. 1982
no

Name of the site
Jarkutan necropolis 1

Translation
no

District
Sherabad

Type of site
burial site

Alternative name of the site
Jarkutan 2 (Askarov 1983)

Latitude
37.628415

Longitude
66.957282

Elevation (m.a.s.l.)
370

Location
4.8 km southwest of Sherabad on the left side of the road from Sherabad to Muzrabad

Topography

DESCRIPTION

Basic description
elongated tepa delimited by a road on the west and a ravine on the east side; NE–SW axis 340 m long; NE–SE 150 m

Shape
irregular oval

Length
308

Width
170

Height

Surface area (sq m)
54435

Found
1973 (Pidaev and Pilipko?)

Preservation
not known

Distortions
no

Excavated
1973–1990 excavations lead by Askarov, Ionesov, Shirinov, Baratov; 1994–2002 German-Uzbek excavations (Huff, Shaydullaev)

Pottery
no

Other finds
no

DATING

Late Bronze Age	X	Early Iron Age		Hellenistic		Kushan and Kushan-Sasanian	
Early Medieval		High Medieval		Post-Mongol		Pre-modern	

Dating published elsewhere   no

Bibliography
Ionesov 1996; Stride 2004, vol. 3, Uz-SD-366

Notes

Date of survey
not surveyed

Entered by
Stančo

339

IDENTITY

Site Code
178

Stride 2004
Uz-SD-366

Rtveladze 1974
no

Arshavskaya et al. 1982
no

Name of the site
Jarkutan necropolis 2

Translation
no

District
Sherabad

Type of site
burial site

Alternative name of the site
no

Latitude
37.627231

Longitude
66.958728

Elevation (m.a.s.l.)
370

Location
4.8 km southwest of Sherabad on the left side of the road from Sherabad to Muzrabad

Topography

DESCRIPTION

Basic description

Shape

Length

Width

Height

Surface area (sq m)
28142

Found
1973 (Pidaev and Pilipko?)

Preservation
not known

Distortions
no

Excavated
no

Pottery
no

Other finds
no

DATING

| Late Bronze Age | X | Early Iron Age | | Hellenistic | | Kushan and Kushan-Sasanian | |
| Early Medieval | | High Medieval | | Post-Mongol | | Pre-modern | |

Dating published elsewhere   no

Bibliography
Stride 2004, vol. 3, Uz-SD-366

Notes

Date of survey
not surveyed

Entered by
Stančo

341

IDENTITY

Site Code	Stride 2004		Rtveladze 1974	Arshavskaya et al. 1982
179	Uz-SD-366		no	no

Name of the site

Jarkutan necropolis 3

Translation	District	Type of site
no	Sherabad	burial site

Alternative name of the site	Latitude	Longitude	Elevation (m.a.s.l.)
Jarkutan 3 (Askarov 1983)	37.625785	66.958465	369

Location

4.8 km southwest of Sherabad on the left side of the road from Sherabad to Muzrabad

Topography

DESCRIPTION

Basic description

Shape	Length	Width	Height	Surface area (sq m)
				46893

Found	Preservation	Distortions
1973 (Pidaev and Pilipko?)	not known	no

Excavated

no

Pottery	Other finds
no	no

DATING

Late Bronze Age	X	Early Iron Age		Hellenistic		Kushan and Kushan-Sasanian	
Early Medieval		High Medieval		Post-Mongol		Pre-modern	

Dating published elsewhere   no

Bibliography

Pidaev 1974, 38–40; Stride 2004, vol. 3, Uz-SD-366

Notes

Date of survey	Entered by
not surveyed	Stančo

343

IDENTITY

Site Code
180

Stride 2004
Uz-SD-366

Rtveladze 1974
no

Arshavskaya et al. 1982
no

Name of the site
Jarkutan necropolis 4

Translation
no

District
Sherabad

Type of site
burial site

Alternative name of the site
Jarkutan 4 (Askarov 1983)

Latitude
37.62263

Longitude
66.960174

Elevation (m.a.s.l.)
368

Location
4.8 km southwest of Sherabad on the left side of the road from Sherabad to Muzrabad

Topography

DESCRIPTION

Basic description

Shape

Length

Width

Height

Surface area (sq m)
31199

Found
1973 (Pidaev and Pilipko?)

Preservation
not known

Distortions
no

Excavated
no

Pottery
no

Other finds
no

DATING

| Late Bronze Age | X | Early Iron Age | | Hellenistic | | Kushan and Kushan-Sasanian | |
| Early Medieval | | High Medieval | | Post-Mongol | | Pre-modern | |

Dating published elsewhere   no

Bibliography
Rtveladze 1974; Stride 2004, vol. 3, Uz-SD-366

Notes

Date of survey
not surveyed

Entered by
Stančo

IDENTITY

Site Code
181

Stride 2004
no

Rtveladze 1974
no

Arshavskaya et al. 1982
no

Name of the site
No name 53

Translation
no

District
Kizirik

Type of site
settlement

Alternative name of the site
no

Latitude
37.55994

Longitude
67.151232

Elevation (m.a.s.l.)
346

Location
200 m NW of Aysaritepa in the present day village Hokimishanov (Center Progres)

Topography

DESCRIPTION

Basic description
description given by Pidaev 1974, 39–40

Shape
unknown

Length

Width

Height

Surface area (sq m)
500

Found
field survey (Pidaev)

Preservation
destroyed by construction activities

Distortions
completely destroyed

Excavated
yes

Pottery
no

Other finds
no

DATING

| Late Bronze Age | | Early Iron Age | | Hellenistic | X | Kushan and Kushan-Sasanian | |
| Early Medieval | | High Medieval | | Post-Mongol | | Pre-modern | |

Dating published elsewhere   4th–1st c. BC (Pidaev 1974, 38–40)

Bibliography
Pidaev 1974, 38–40

Notes
according to Pidaev, local people had reported graves with ceramic pots

Date of survey
not surveyed

Entered by
Stančo

347

IDENTITY

Site Code
188

Stride 2004
no

Rtveladze 1974
B-21

Arshavskaya et al. 1982
no

Name of the site
Gummaz? (100k map)

Translation
no

District
Sherabad

Type of site
settlement

Alternative name of the site
kurgan Jelaktepa? (100k map)

Latitude
37.6481

Longitude
66.96732

Elevation (m.a.s.l.)
380

Location
2 km to the east of B-20 in the cotton fields

Topography
the site is situated in flat irrigated lowlands / fields

DESCRIPTION

Basic description
Surface max. 0.7 ha, height 2–2.5 m.

Shape
unknown

Length

Width

Height

Surface area (sq m)
7000

Found
in publications (Rtveladze 1974)

Preservation
at the time of the survey not existent

Distortions
completely ploughed

Excavated
no

Pottery
no

Other finds
coin of Kanishka

DATING

Late Bronze Age		Early Iron Age		Hellenistic		Kushan and Kushan-Sasanian	X
Early Medieval		High Medieval		Post-Mongol		Pre-modern	

Dating published elsewhere   Kushan period

Bibliography
Rtveladze 1974

Notes
this site is known to us only from publication of Rtveladze (1974, 76); no visible traces in the fields, not verified by field walking

Date of survey
not surveyed

Entered by
Stančo

IDENTITY

Site Code	Stride 2004	Rtveladze 1974	Arshavskaya et al. 1982
206	Uz-SD-317	no	no

Name of the site	Translation	District	Type of site
Bustan 6	no	Sherabad	burial site

Alternative name of the site	Latitude	Longitude	Elevation (m.a.s.l.)
no	37.616847	66.951086	366

Location

6.5 km southwest of Sherabad on the left side of the road from Sherabad to Muzrabad

Topography

the site is situated in flat irrigated lowlands / fields next to the Bustan Say

DESCRIPTION

Basic description

Shape	Length	Width	Height	Surface area (sq m)
irregular	310	377		93690

Found	Preservation	Distortions
in 1973 by Askarov	high	no

Excavated

excavated by Avanesova in 1990–2008 (ca. 500 objects).

Pottery	Other finds
no	

DATING

				Kushan and Kushan-Sasanian
Late Bronze Age	X	Early Iron Age	Hellenistic	
Early Medieval		High Medieval	Post-Mongol	Pre-modern

Dating published elsewhere   Late Bronze Age

Bibliography

Avanesova 1995; 2000; 2001; 2013; 2016; Avanesova – Lyonnet 1995; Avanesova – Tashpulatova 1999; Stride 2004, vol. 3, Uz-SD-317

Notes

Date of survey	Entered by
not surveyed	Stančo

5. The oasis in time and space: dynamics of the settlement pattern

L. Stančo

5.1 Settlement distribution

After four seasons of fieldwork in the Sherabad Oasis, our database included 125 archaeological sites,[63] of which only 14 belonged to a group of sites which we ourselves did not visit and surveyed, but we got the information about them from the scholarly literature and did not check them in the field for various reasons. Some sites were visited several times, several of them had been recorded even before the start of the systematic mapping during the Jandavlattepa excavations (2002–2006). Most, more precisely 78, of the 111 visited sites revealed ceramic finds, 70 out of these have given new dating information. In many cases, new dating either expands or slightly corrects chronological data suggested by scholars in the previous scholarly literature. About 36 sites, on the other hand, lack any solid chronolog-

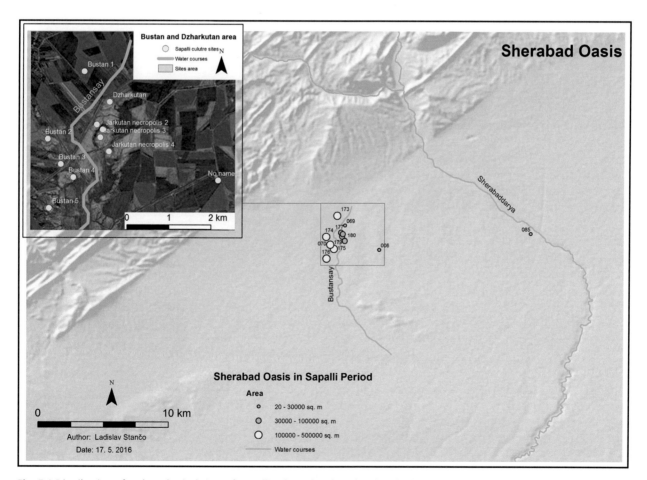

Fig. 5.1 Distribution of archaeological sites of Sapalli culture (LBA) in the Sherabad Oasis, map by author.

---

[63]   The first preliminary publication of the survey included only 93 sites (both in the oasis and in the piedmont steppe araea) that were studied by our team in 2008–2009, see Danielisová et al. 2010.

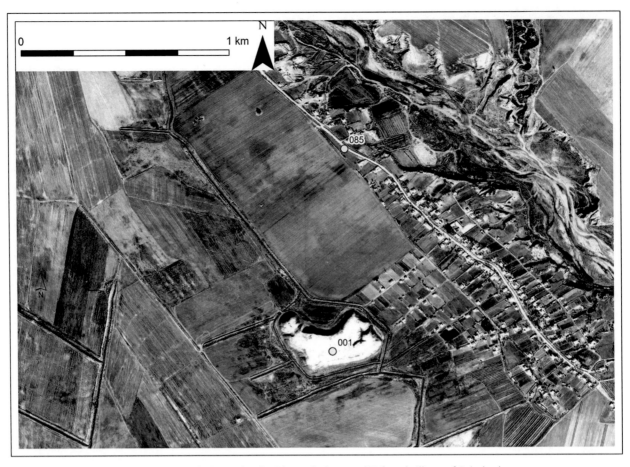

Fig. 5.2 Location of the Sapalli culture find spot (085) with Jandavlattepa (001) and village of Saitabad.

ical indications. It should be noted that we have also included sites situated in the former Kizirik District, since they form a homogenous unit with those in Sherabad District being part of the Sherabad Oasis or its irrigation system both in the past and today. Therefore, altogether 17 lowlands sites in our database out of the 125 belong to the former Kizirik District or lie on its border with the Angor District.

We gained the information about the altitude of the sites by measurements in the field using a geodetic GPS receiver, partly also by extracting data from Google Earth (which gave only very approximate, but sufficiently coherent data), and also from Soviet topographic maps. A clear boundary of our research area is formed by the steep ridges separating the fertile irrigated plains from hilly piedmont steppes, which forms a line running southwest – northeast. The line ranges from 360 m above sea level (site Irjahangir Ota), through 416 m (Anjirtepa) and 430 m (Sherabad), up to a point at an altitude of 420 m near Babatepa (**Fig. 1.2**). It should also be noted here that the lowest point of the district – the place where the river Sherabad Darya / Karasu leaves its territory – is situated at an altitude of 328 m.a.s.l. Thus below the altitude of the point at which Sherabad Darya leaves the mountains (430 m.a.s.l.) is located 126 sites (**Fig. 1**), which therefore could theoretically

be supplied by water, and their fields irrigated, from here.

At the current state of research, we are not able to determine the accurate dating of all known archaeological sites in the region. Among those that are firmly dated, we can recognise four sites of Sapalli culture (Late Bronze Age; if we count separately all subunits – as Bustan 1–7, for instance –, we come to the number of 14 sites including ten necropolises), ten sites of the Yaz period (Early Iron Age), eight sites of the Hellenistic period, 47 Kushan sites, 44 Early Medieval ones, while for the High Medieval period our database shows 26 sites only. The number of sites of Post-Mongol period decreases to a mere 14 sites. In the following subheading we deal with the respective chronological phases one by one and bring an overview of the settlement pattern and its dynamics, as well as brief historical implications. Each subheading is accompanied by a map of the oasis in the respective period. We do not provide all details on the individual sites here, since all the necessary information is given above in chapter 4.

We start the following overview with the Late Bronze Age. Unlike the piedmont steppe area and the upper reaches of the Sherabad Darya, in the Sherabad plains, there is no clear evidence of an earlier occupation. This situation, however, corresponds very well with that of the entire Surkhan Darya province lowlands.

5.2 Sapalli culture (Late Bronze Age)

The new survey has not brought any substantial additions to our knowledge of the Late Bronze Age in the Sherabad Oasis. The two main sites – Jarkutan and Bustan – were already well known and previously extensively studied by several expeditions. The publication of the digs results is, however, far from being complete.[64] The new French-Uzbek excavations at the site are essential as far as the transition from Late Bronze Age to Early Iron Age (Yaz I period) of the Sherabad area is concerned (Bendezu-Sarmiento – Lhuillier 2018). It is perfectly clear from the topography and morphology of these sites that they were supplied by water from the nearby stream of Bustan Say. Although nowadays completely dry, it was considered to be one of the ancient river beds of the Sherabad Darya (Askarov – Abdullaev 1983, 6) or its right-bank tributary. The other explanation says that the Bustan Say was a separate watercourse, which had dried due to the change of climate in the 2nd millennium BC (Stride 2004, vol. I, 126–127). Stride compares Bustansay with Karmaki and Kyzyldzhar in Mirshade in this respect (Stride 2004, 274, n. 154). In any case, the Late Bronze Age sites of western Sherabad Oasis were supplied by a natural water stream and seem not to employ any kind of artificial irrigation. As a matter of fact, in the case of Jarkutan and Bustan, one deals with a single cultural unit or micro-region, which has been divided by scholars into two sites or better to say chains of sites: Bustan on the right bank of the Bustan Say and Jarkutan on its left bank (**Fig. 5.1**). These were in their turn further subdivided into at least 11 individual units according to the two basic functions of various parts. Thus we have a number of necropolises Jarkutan 3 and 4, and Bustan 1, 2, 3, 5, 6, 7, as well as settlements of Jarkutan 1, 2 and Bustan 4 (Askarov 1977, 13).[65] The other sites are less important, mere find spots with Sapalli material. One of them (no. 6) is moreover situated quite close to the Jarkutan.

Fig. 5.3 Pottery assemblage of the Sapalli culture from the find spot in the village of Saitabad, photo by K. Abdullaev.

---

[64] The book of Askarov and Abdullaev (1983) remains the only monograph devoted to the site of Jarkutan, while the excavations of the Uzbek-German team working under the leadership of D. Huff and Sh. Shaydullaev at Jarkutan in the 1990s and at the beginning of the new century is still in preparation.

[65] It should be noted that the exact location of the individual parts of the Bustan site was not published – there is neither a general plan nor coordinates in the publications known to us. According to Askarov, the groups starts with Bustan 1 to the north of Jarkutan (Askarov 1977, 57), while Mustfakulov locates them to the south of it (Mustafakulov 1997, 28), an Sh. Shaydullaev insists that they are clustered to the west of Jarkutan. Thus, the location given in our map is approximate (based mainly on personal communication with Shapulat Shaydullaev and brief description in Askarov 1977, 57–59), and Bustan 7 is not indicated at all, since only published information about its location states that „the burial ground is situated in the middle reaches of the old Bustan river bed" (Mustafakulov 1997, 28). To confuse the matter even more, Mustafakulov mentions a site Bustan 8 without any further detail or reference (Mustafakulov 1997, 28). Note, that the site of Bustan 4, refered otherwise as a settlement, is listed among burial sites in Askarov – Ruzanov 1990, 6. Jarkutan, on the other hand, was firstly divided by Askarov into four parts that were in some cases further subdivided (Askarov 1983, 8). Jarkutan 1 is the most pronounced northern part of the settlement, the citadel (here no. 69), while Jarkutan 2 include all the rest of the settlement (here no. 178), which is subdivided in several individual mounds (Tepa I–VIII; see Huff 1997, 89, Abb. 6). Necropolises are numbered differently, but originally Askarov proposed only two parts (Jarkutan 3 and 4), with subdivision of the latter into 4a, 4b and 4v.

The only important addition to our knowledge of the Sapalli settlement pattern is a find spot (no. 85) in the village of Saitabad (**Fig. 5.2**). In this place, during the construction of a new house, local people found several well preserved vessels of the Sapalli period (**Fig. 5.3**). K. Abdullaev opened a small trench to find out what sort of a site this could be and found some more Sapalli pottery, but no specific remains of any structures or grave pits. Abdullaev believes that this situation was caused by extensive earthworks in 1960s, in other words, the original context, probably a grave pit, was according to him destroyed and the grave goods were removed and scattered around (Abdullaev – Stančo 2006, 20–21). This place deserves some more attention in the future.

It is therefore evident that Sapalli culture had in Sherabad Oasis only one main centre, which it is nec-essary to study together with the other more or less remote sites of the same period, especially with that of Sapallitepa (eponymous site of the Late Bronze Age culture) and with the smaller settlements in the piedmonts of Kugitang – Tilla Bulaq,[66] Ara Bulaq (Kaniuth 2007; Kaniuth et al. 2009; Kaniuth 2010) and a recently detected site at the village of Goz (Dvurechenskaya et al. 2014). In general, the sites of the Late Bronze Age in the Sherabad plain yielded an enor-mous amount of archaeological material and remain the most broadly studied topic in the given area. Very recently a few monographs on Bustan VI (Avanesova 2016 with a Russian verison of 2013), Late Bronze Age pottery and complex society (Luneau 2014), and burial rites (Teufer 2015), including an up-to-date bibliography on the LBA, have been published.

5.3 Yaz culture (Early Iron Age)

The period in question is a very complicated is-sue from an archaeological point of view in Central Asia in general. The conference *The Iron Age in Central Asia (2ⁿᵈ and 1ˢᵗ millennia BC)* that took place in June 2014 in Berlin tried to resolve some of the problems of nomenclature and a broader understanding of the period (but not chronology, since absolute chronology, despite being supported by ^{14}C data, still remains disputed).[67]

5.3.1 Yaz culture in the Sherabad plain – state of research

The situation in the study of the Yaz period is quite different from the Bronze Age (Sapalli culture) and – judging by the literature – somehow confusing. Shaydullaev (2002, 245–246) recognized in the Sher-abad irrigation area six sites with material of Yaz cul-ture (note that none of these is categorized as a burial site): Talashkantepa I, Pachmaktepa, no-name site in Angor, Jarkutan, Shortepa, and Jandavlattepa. One of them – the site in Angor – can be excluded, since it is situated in an area belonging most probably to an-other irrigation system at that time. This exclusion is exactly what Stride (2005, vol. 5, Fig. 62) has done.

This could be the case also for Shortepa, but there are some confusions about its identifications and location (Stride 2004, vol. 1, 42). In our database, there are two sites of this name, both of them located in the cen-tral part of the left-bank Sherabad plain, and, what is more important, both dated to the Kushan period and later only. The Shortepa in question is the site on the left bank of Kara-su, north of Angor.

Stride moreover, adopted the chronological sys-tem of the French team working in the area that calls the period in question protohistoric and divides it into two phases P1 and P2. According to this sys-tem Jarkutan ranks among the P1 sites, while three other sites (Talashkan, Pachmak and Jandavlattepa) are dated to P2 (Stride 2004, vol. 5, Fig. 62). Besides this, Stride lists the site of Aysaritepa among the Yaz period group (Stride 2004, vol. 3, 286), but only with general reference to Pidaev without a precise source. The occupation of Jarkutan is said to continue (Stride 2004, vol. 1, 285).

Some more confusion was introduced by Sarianidi and Koshelenko (1985, 188), who listed in their pub-lication a site called Pagmantepa, otherwise unknown. I suppose that in this case they just made a mistake in spelling the name of Pachmaktepa. Moreover, it is not clear what "No name tepa" is meant to be in their list,

---

[66] The project of LM University in Munich led by Kai Kaniuth has shown that this area was extensively exploited during the Sapalli culture period and was linked to the bigger sites in the plains (Kaniuth et al. 2011, esp. 280–281).
[67] The author presented a paper „New data on the Early Iron Age in the Sherabad District" at this event.

Sarianidi – Koshelenko 1985, 188	Shaydullaev 2002	Stride 2004	Current state of research[68]
Jandavlattepa	Jandavlattepa	Jandavlattepa (P2, no. 155)	Jandavlattepa (001)
Talashkan I	Talashkan I	Talashkan I (P2, no. 227)	Talashkan I (065)
Pagmantepa (Pachmaktepa?)	Pachmaktepa	Pachmaktepa (P2, no. 235)	Pachmaktepa (150)
No name	–	–	–
–	Jarkutan	Jarkutan (P1, no. 366)	Jarkutan (069)
–	Shortepa	Aysaritepa (P2, no. 344)	_[69]
–	Site in Angor	–	–
			Yalangoyoqota (026)
			No name (039)
			No name (138)
			No name (154)
			No name (155)
			No name (156)

since the literature is full of such no name *tepas* and without precise coordinates or detailed description one can just guess.

The table above shows the progress in our knowledge about the Yaz period in the Sherabad plain. Sites listed in the last column are dealt with further below.

5.3.2 New data for the Sherabad plain

Now, what has the Czech-Uzbek expedition added to the known Yaz culture data in the plains around Sherabad? The most important set of the data represents material, especially pottery assemblage, from the stratigraphic section of Jandavlattepa. Material from this sounding is currently being prepared by K. Abdullaev for publication in the second volume of Jandavlattepa excavation reports and we believe that it became one of the most important sequences of pottery in southern Central Asia, demonstrating very well the continuity from Yaz I to the Kushano-Sasanian period. For our purpose is it absolutely essential, since we gained a rich assemblage of pottery for comparison with the other, usually very limited complexes, be it from excavations or surface surveys.

5.3.3 Surroundings of Jandavlattepa in the Yaz culture period

Today, the plain around Jandavlattepa is completely flat and its fertile soil is exploited predominantly for extensive cotton cultivation. There are no visible traces of morphological anomalies indicating human activity in the past except for occasional circular spaces where the cotton grows poorly. These spaces may indicate insufficient irrigation of a particular area, but a much more likely explanation is that in such places, there had once been situated the remains of mud-brick structures, which were later destroyed by bulldozers and/or ploughed. A layer of hard-packed earth consequently does not allow the proper growing of cotton. Nonetheless, the surrounding of Jandavlattepa was dotted with small mounds in the recent past, as is well attested by Soviet topographic maps (1:100,000 scale), CORONA satellite images and the reports of local archaeologists. For our understanding of the complex of anthropogenic features surrounding Jandavlattepa is important the description given by Pidaev forty years ago:

"In the vicinity of the settlement of Jandavlattepa, numerous mounds are scattered. We have conducted small excavations on four of them. One of the mounds proved to be natural, and no traces of human activities were encountered here. The other three mounds have a cultural layer, but there are no clear traces of buildings. The excavated area turned out to be a carelessly compacted clay and mud bricks. Probably, on these mounds, small earthen platforms were erected to level the surface. Such platforms could be used in hot weather as a basis for light tents."[70]

As we can see, Pidaev surveyed four mounds around the site of Jandavlattepa in 1972: one of them he found to be a natural feature, three of them on the other hand revealed certain evidence of human activity. This was partly confirmed forty years later (in 2011) by the Czech-Uzbek team. The problem

---

[68] Numbers in brackets in this column indicate the identification code in the database of the Czech–Uzbek survey in the Sherabad District, i.e., also respective catalogue numbers in the present catalogue.

[69] There is not enough data to justify including this site between the Yaz culture settlement pattern.

[70] „В окрестностях городища Джандавлат-Тепе разбросаны многочисленные холмы. На четырех из них нами были произведены небольшие раскопки. Один из холмов оказался естественным, и никаких следов деятельности человека здесь не было обнаружено. На остальных трех холмах имеется культурный слой, но четких следов строений не зафиксировано. Вскрытая

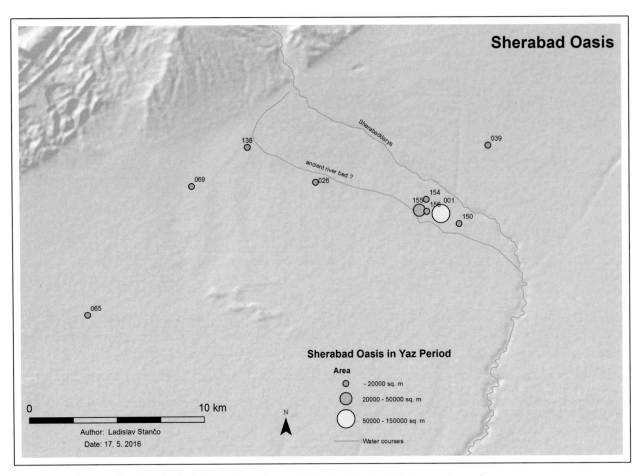

Fig. 5.4 Distribution of archaeological sites of Yaz culture (EIA) in the Sherabad Oasis, map by author.

is that we did not know where exactly the mounds studied by Pidaev had been situated or which of them he had surveyed and which one he had found natural, since the Pidaev publication lacks any coordinates or a site-plan. What we have done was simply verification of the topographic data given by the Old Russian military maps (Gen. shtab). The locations of six small mounds was surveyed, four of them systematically, two others just generally (**Figs. 3.51–56**). At four sites human activity was attested (Cf. here pp. 70–78), while two revealed no archaeological material (152, 153). One more mound – the only remaining one – had already been excavated by the Czech team in 2005, revealing a small mud-brick/pakhsa platform (Urbanová 2011). The same or a similar structure was described – but not shown in pictures – by Pidaev (1974). The image of CORONA was made roughly at the same time when he undertook his survey in 1972. Unfortunately, the imagery does not show all the features known from the maps.

On the contrary, the relief in the neighbourhood of the site looks far from being flat and levelled. It was not only uneven; the broken terrain was interlaced with dry river beds (**Fig. 3.53**).

5.3.4 Pachmaktepa

Pachmaktepa, excavated by Pidaev, revealed a substantial body of Yaz III/Kuchuk IV pottery. After the excavations the site virtually disappeared. It was precisely located (as we believe) by the surface survey of the Czech team in 2011. The only information we got was a vague description in Pideav's publication of 1974 saying that Pachmak is located 1 km southeast of Jandavlattepa next to the Saitabad village (Pidaev 1974, 33), and additionally we knew of a feature located approximately in the position mentioned by Pidaev documented on the old Soviet topographic maps and visible also on the CORONA images.

площадь оказалась небрежно забуртованной глиной и сырцовым кирпичом. Вероятно, на этих холмах возводили небольшие земляные платформы для выравнивания поверхности. Такие платформы могли быть использованы в жаркое время как основание для легких шатров" (Pidaev 1974, 33).

Fig. 5.5 Stone mortar from the early strata of Jandavlattepa and pestle from the surface survey in the area of former Pachmaktepa as exhibited in the Termez Archaeological Museum in 2013, photo by L. Stančo.

The localisation or – better to say – the verification of the original Pachmaktepa location was entrusted to archaeologist Petra Tušlová, who decided to cover an area of 400 × 400 m centred in the place of the above mentioned feature, to ensure the capturing of a complete image of the pottery scatter in the given area. Moreover, the method of total pick-up was employed on the spot with the highest density of pottery fragments. The results are clearly visible from the picture (**Fig. 3.55**). Surprisingly, the highest density was, according to the survey (see pp. 70–78 in this volume), attested not exactly in the place of the original small mound, but some 150 m to the west (on the original position only three fragments of Yaz III pottery were collected). How to explain this discrepancy? We are inclined to believe that the original location of Pachmaktepa was exactly in the position given by topographic maps and CORONA (**Fig. 3.51** and **3.53**). The recent large scale agricultural activities caused since the 1970s not only the intentional final destruction of the site, which was badly damaged by archaeological excavations, but also the moving of the remaining artefacts from their original position. We can imagine the use of bulldozers to remove earth from the mound to fill depressions in the surrounding surface and make the field as level as possible. In this case, the water canal today separating the highest density scatter must have been dug after this initial earthwork. The other explanation of the current situation is that there were also other parts inhabited or

used during the Yaz III period – not only the elevated points and mounds. For discussion on this possibility see below. Beside the Yaz pottery, another typical artefact belonging to the Yaz culture was found during the surface survey: a fragment of a black-stone pestle (**Fig. 5.5** and **Tab. 3.10, 9**), here seen as exhibited in Termez Archaeological Museum with a mortar from the lowest strata of the Jandavlattepa stratigraphic section). The three other locations detected from topographic maps (154, 155, 156) also revealed the Yaz III pottery complex, although in much fewer numbers (**Tab. 3.11** and **3.12**).

5.3.5 Yalangoyokotatepa

The site, called by locals at present Yalangoyokotatepa ("Mound of barefoot father"), is situated north of Gambir village, close to the town of Sherabad (coordinates: 37.634, 67.024). It had been detected in the satellite image (**Fig. 5.6**), and later on surveyed by the Czech-Uzbek team on 1st September 2009 (Danielisová et al. 2010, 78) and got the number 026 in our database system of the sites in the Sherabad District. It was previously mentioned only by Annaev (1988, 13), who, however, spoke of Niyazy-alangayaktepa or Kul'tepa, and reported the site location as 1 km to the north-east of Khosyattepa. It should be noted that Annaev did not link the site to the pre-Kushan periods. During the brief surface survey of the Czech-Uzbek team, a substantial amount of pottery of the Yaz III type was collected (**Fig. 6.1** and Pls. 6. XXII–XXIV). Without a doubt, the settlement was founded in the Achaemenid period. Although the site itself is well accessible, being located only 100 m from the main Tashkent – Termez road, it is unfortunately not suitable for archaeological excavations, since it forms a part of a modern Muslim cemetery of Khoja Gambirota (**Fig. 4.26a**). Moreover, a local mullah was buried on the top of the mound some time ago, thus the site became a sacred place for the local population. According to the pottery material, the site was inhabited until the Hellenistic/Kushan period. The later Medieval village had its centre some 150 m meters to the south. The most clearly visible part consists of a low shallow mound covered partly with low vegetation and graves of modern time with a modern structure on the top.

The ground-plan of this Yaz III period site is almost square measuring 37 × 39 m, with a ground elevation of 334.85 m and top elevation of 337.33 m (measured by TOPCON GMS2 receiver). By its ground-plan and size, Yalangoyokotatepa resembles Pachmaktepa. Also the orientation of the ground-plan is very similar to that of Pachmaktepa, at least as published by Pidaev, having edges – not the sides - oriented with main cardinal points (Pidaev 1974, 34, Ris. 2).

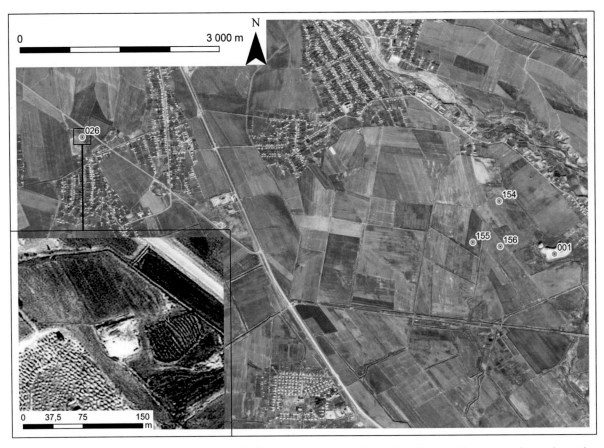

Fig. 5.6 Location of the newly discovered Jaz III site Yalangoyokotatepa close to the Sherabad-Termez road, map by author.

5.3.6 Other Yaz culture sites

The site no. 39 (no name) was surveyed by our team on 3rd September 2010 (**Fig. 4.39**). It is a small rounded mound (ca. 1,000 sq. m) in a moderate state of preservation, partly covered with vegetation. Here a large amount of badly preserved non-diagnostic pottery was found, which belong with all probability to the Yaz III period.

The site no. 138 (no name) is located in the irrigated fields next to modern orchards and a playground of the village of Navbog (**see Ch. 4 cat. no. 138**). It was surveyed on 3rd November 2011. There are no morphological features, only ceramics scattered around with a part found by a local worker digging here by accident during our survey. In the IKONOS – and in CORONA – image the remains of a mound in the northern corner of the present-day playground seems to be captured, while Google Earth already shows nothing in the same place any more. Pottery fragments belong to Yaz III.

5.3.7 Centre and its satellites

There are only a few well-researched Yaz period sites in Surkhandarya province. Among them,

a prominent position, from the point of view of complexity and study of the settlement pattern, is taken without a doubt by the site of Kiziltepa. What makes it unique is its interrelationship with small sites in its hinterland. These small sites, called Kizilcha (each with a serial number), were from the very beginning interpreted as small farms (Sagduallev 1987). These farms are clustered in three groups around the site of Kiziltepa, being located 200–1000 m (and not 250–550 m as stated by Sagdullaev 1987, 8) from the central settlement (Stančo 2018, fig. 21). Sagdullaev speaks of 14 sites, but admits that in the past, there were more of them around there judging from the pottery scatters in the area. He actually undertook a sort of surface survey, even if it was not in a totally systematic way. The better preserved mounds he described as follows: "Farmsteads of Kizilcha before excavations represented rectangular mounds 1–3 m in height, and with size of 45 × 25 m, 35 × 24 m, and 36 × 15 m. On the surface were collected pottery fragments dating to mid-1st millennium BC. The best-preserved mound of Kizilcha 6 has the size of 50 × 32 m and the height of 1.5–3 m" (Sagdullaev 1987, 9). Let us remind that the site of Kizilytepa evolved from the very beginning of the Yaz cultural sequence (be it in the middle of the 2nd millennium BC or later), and the foundation of the Kizilcha 6 (and probably also

360

of the other Kizilchas) already took place during the Yaz I (Sagdullaev 1987, 10).

How does this example of a developed settlement pattern and its chronology help us to understand the situation around the Jandavlattepa? In my opinion, we have almost the same scheme here. There is the central site dating from the Yaz I period (Jandavlattepa) and the group of small settlements, probably farmsteads, of Yaz III. These were once of the same size – or of a very similar one –, situated at similar distances from the centre and had also an analogical fate in modern times: in both regions these small mounds have been ploughed or otherwise destroyed.

In the Sherabad plains, there could have been one more similar central site with a satellite farmstead hinterland. According to Zapparov and Rtveladze, the fortress of Talashkan I used to be surrounded by unfortified structures. "Given these data, it is possible to suggest that Talashkantepa I was a fortress or citadel of a large settlement, since outside the walls were in some places found fragments of similar ceramics" (Zapparov – Rtveladze 1976, 23).

If this were true, we get a completely different picture of the Yaz period landscape in northern Bactria with a chain of central fortified sites with farmsteads grouped around them within a radius of ca. 1 km. This hypothesis should be verified by way of field walking and an intensive surface survey in the surroundings of Kuchuktepa, Talashkan and Bandykhan, which would be the missing link in the imaginary chain. The intensification of this system of central settlements surrounded by a group of farmsteads in the period Yaz III is not accidental. A similar system can be observed, although with a significantly greater density of sites in the very centre of the Achaemenid Empire, on the plains near Persepolis (Sumner 1986).

5.3.8 Irrigation systems in the Yaz period?

In the plain around Persepolis, there were, however, attested extensive irrigation systems, which could provide a water supply for such a dense settlement and irrigation for the fields (Sumner 1986, 13–17). How was the situation in the north-eastern province of the empire? There was some discussion about the water supply in the given period in Bactria. Sarianidi and Koshelenko presumed that all the settlements were situated close to streams (rivers, temporary streams, creeks) and from these water was taken and used both for household use and the irrigation of the fields, with the only exception of the late phase at Bolday, Vakhsh valley, Tajikistan (Sarianidi – Koshelenko 1985, 189). Sagdullaev, on the other hand, believed that the canals around Kiziltepa (remains of some of them were visible at the time of Sagdullaev's digs at Kizilcha) were used in the Yaz period already and there is actually no

reason to argue with him (Sagdullaev 1987, 8, canals marked on the fig. 1). In the case of Jandavlattepa, we can only speculate about the existence of a canal or an ancient river bed of the Sherabad Darya, which could provide the group of sites with water (Stančo 2018, Fig. 4). A complex irrigation system was not introduced to the Sherabad plain until the Kushan period (see Chapter 5.5 below).

5.3.9 Conclusions

At the moment, there are ten sites of the Yaz culture known in the lowlands of the Sherabad District: Jandavlattepa (no. 1), Talashkantepa I (no. 065), Pachmaktepa (no. 150), Yalangoyoqotatepa (no. 26), Jarkutan (no. 69), and five no-name sites (**Fig. 5.4**). Recent excavations at the principal site of the oasis – Jandavlattepa – have shown that this centre had been inhabited since the very early stages of Yaz I at least and then continuously until the Hellenistic period and later (Abdullaev – Stančo 2009; Abdullaev 2018). The Czech-Uzbek team, aside from work at Jandavlattepa, has found three more small sites around Jandavlattepa that revealed Yaz III material, and succeeded in discovering of precise location of Pachmaktepa (Tušlová 2012a, 18–19; Doležálková et al. 2012, 23–24), previously fully excavated (Pidaev 1974, 34–38), but for a long time lost, because the site was levelled by ploughing back in the 1980s. Our last contribution was the discovery of a new site of the Yaz III period close to the village of Gambir south of Sherabad (no. 26; Stančo 2018) and the finding of a no-name site (no. 39) and its dating to the same chronological phase. The other important discoveries have been made in the piedmont part of the Sherabad District, but these are dealt with elsewhere (Stančo et al. 2015). Moreover, a French team working at Jarkutan has quite recently attested the continuity of the inhabitation of this site during the Yaz I period (Bendezu-Sarmiento – Mustafakulov 2013, 215–229; Lhuillier et al. 2013, 365–366).

The general picture shows a very interesting situation and obvious change in the settlement structure compared to the Late Bronze Age. The Sherabad plain was still just sparsely inhabited, especially during the earliest stages of Yaz culture. Since the time period of this culture was considerably long, it is not surprising that settlements became gradually hierarchized. As the reason for the abandonment of the cluster at Bustan and Jarkutan at the very beginning of the Yaz I period is to be seen drying out of the Bustansay in this time caused most probably by climate change (Stride 2004, 126–127). The centre of the oasis seems to migrate to the location of the later Jandavlattepa. Here, the first traces of human activities predate the beginning of Yaz culture (find spot in the village of

Saitabad), but the exact place of the site itself seems not to have been inhabited until the Yaz I period (Abdullaev – Stančo 2009, 23). Exactly in this period we may encounter the last traces of human activity at Jarkutan, including several burials (Bendezu-Sarmiento 2013, 215–229). Even if we have only a few potsherds of Yaz I painted ware from the lowermost strata of Jandavlattepa stratigraphic section, we may assume that the settlement of the period in question was much larger: the location, where Yaz I material was found is situated in the part of the *tepa*, which is the lowest of all the site. Thus, in the other parts we may expect – or we can imagine – a similar or even thicker earliest strata.[71] From the spatial point of view it is remarkable that in the later phases of Yaz culture, especially during the Yaz III period, several new sites with symmetrical ground plan occurred. Their characteristics and the theories about the linkage to the principal site of the oasis are dealt with elsewhere (Stančo 2018). The specific distribution of the sites in the area of the present-day right-bank Sherabad Oasis allows us to speculate about the possibility of the existence of yet another ancient river bed of the Sherabad Darya / Karasu in this period. The other peculiarity is the occurrence of the first settlement on the left bank of the river (provided that the river bed was the same as

today). The simplicity of the settlement pattern contradicts the idea of a complicated irrigation system in this early stage of development of colonization of the area. We can imagine a simple water channel not longer than a few kilometres with an adequately simple system of water distribution for the small homesteads around the central place. Such a construction could have been organized by local people without the will and resources of a centralized state.

An exceptional phenomenon represents the site-fortress of Talashkan I flourishing in the Yaz III period. Both its location and ground-plan cannot be studied in isolation but only in relation to other EIA complexes. It seems to follow the line at the foot of steep mountain ranges, which was running from the Amu Darya region (Kuchuktepa) via Talashkan I, Jandavlattepa, and Bandikhan up to Kiziltepa in the north-east. It confirms the increase in population and the growing hierarchy of settlements in the so-called Achaemenid period. At the Talashkantepa I there was also found the earliest cooper object interpreted – with a question mark – as a coin (Rtveladze – Pidaev 1981, 14–15; ris. 2). So far it remains the only coin of the Achaemenid period from the regular archaeological excavations in the province of Surkhan Darya.[72]

5.4 Hellenistic and transitional period

Antiquity in Central Asia starts with the arrival of Alexander the Great and his armies to Bactria in 329 BC. Achaemenid satrapy of Bactria was conquered, subdued and the resistance of local princes and chieftains was gradually crushed. The Sherabad Oasis most probably played its role in the process, but archaeology brought to light no evidence of these events.

5.4.1 Archaeological data

In the following early historical period (referred to frequently as Hellenistic due to the predominant

foreign – western – influence in the broader region of Central Asia), there are known only eight sites in the Sherabad Oasis (**Fig. 5.7**): Jandavlattepa (001), Talashkantepa II (032), Yalangoyoqotatepa (026), and also Aysaritepa (042), Pastaktepa (122) and three sites without modern names, one of them situated near Jandavlattepa (084), one close to the site of Aysaritepa in the southern edge of the oasis (181), and the other at the area of a modern cemetery around the holy place called Termez-ata east of Sherabad (033). The accuracy of the picture is somehow obscured by the fact that we were not able to confirm the dating to the Hellenistic period in the case of two out of these eight sites by fieldwork. The archaeological material

---

[71] Numerous fragments of Yaz pottery (especially the Yaz III phase) were found displaced in later contexts at sector 20 of the same site. They had found their way up in the stratigraphy due to the postdeposition processes, reuse of soil (Včelicová 2015, 28; 57; 66; 81; fig. 33).

[72] The catalogue of the coin finds from the southern Uzbekistan of Rtveladze – Pidaev (1981) starts with the Greco-Bactrian coins only, except this uncertain piece, while on the territory of southern Tajikistan the famous Oxus treasure make an exception: it contains 60 pre-Hellenistic coins including 30 coins minted in the Achaemenid Empire (both centrally and by satraps and towns), cf. Zeymal' 1983, 18–26.

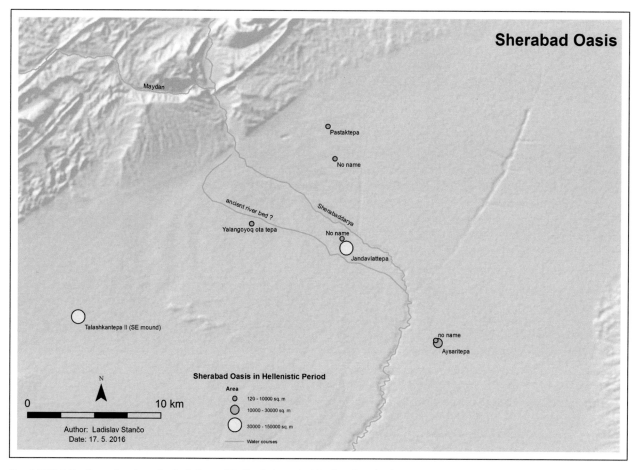

Fig. 5.7 Distribution of archaeological sites of Hellenistic period in the Sherabad Oasis, map by author.

collected by our team at Aysaritepa belongs only to the Kushan period and later, while the no-name site in its vicinity no more exists and its alleged location is covered by modern living houses. Thus, in the question of dating we have to trust Sh. Pidaev who briefly excavated both of them, but unfortunately did not fully published the material he gained (Pidaev 1974, 38–40).

Jandavlattepa seems to be the only settlement in the entire oasis that prolonged its life and functioning after the collapse of the Achaemenid Empire.[73] The stratigraphic section excavated by the Czech-Uzbek team shows cultural layers of the Seleucid and Greco-Bactrian periods respectively that are several meters thick. They yielded abundant archaeological material belonging to the given period (Abdullaev – Stančo 2009).[74] The evidence of ceramic material is further supported by coin finds of the Greco-Bactrian kings Euthydemus, Demetrius, Eucratides, and imitations of Heliocles that were found in the archaeological contexts at the site (Abdullaev 2011a, 172–173).

Jandavlattepa remained undoubtedly a centre of the oasis as it was during the Achaemenid period. Unfortunately, we cannot be more precise about the area of the settlement at this time, because the layers in question were examined at the single place – the eastern edge of the site. An indirect piece of evidence for the fact that the settlement area covered all the surface of Jandavlattepa may be served by the finds of Hellenistic pottery fragments at the so-called Citadel (westernmost part of the site; Včelicová 2015, 46–47 and 100). These finds, as well as the substantial height of the *tepa*, i.e., thickness of the cultural layers at the westernmost part of the site, indicate not only the size of the Hellenistic settlement, but also its importance compared to newly founded small forts at Kampyr-tepa and Old Termez. Let us note, however, that some functions of the cultural landscape of Jandavlattepa of the previous Achaemenid period were reduced or abandoned, as was the case of the small mounds surrounding the principal *tepa*, including Pachmaktepa (see previous subheading Nos. 150, 154, 155, 156).

---

[73] In fact, Jandavlattepa ranks among a few sites in the whole of the Surkhan Darya that prolonged continuously its life after Alexander. The situation of the other sites (Khalchayan, Termez, Khaytabadtepa) with probably the same fate is mostly more speculative than in this case, see Stride 2004, 315.
[74] The full report with complete material is currently being prepared for publication by K. Abdullaev. An earlier stratigraphic trench at almost the same place dug by Sh. Pidaev in 1993 has not been published yet.

363

The only exception may have been represented by the small mound situated to the north of Jandavlattepa, the so-called sector 30 of the Czech-Uzbek excavation project (Urbanová 2011, esp. 104 and fig. 2.4, 7). This small building was erected in the Greco-Bactrian or Kushan period.

The site of Yalangoyoqotatepa mentioned in the previous subheading most probably existed not only in the Achaemenid, but also in the Hellenistic period, since a part of the pottery finds belongs at least to the transitional period (late 4th c. BC). Anyway, it did not represent any important centre of the period. Its detailed research including excavations is prevented by the modern-day graveyard, which extends over the entire area of the site.

In the case of the settlement cluster at the modern village of Talashkan, an original circular Yaz III fortress (no. 65) had been abandoned and a new walled settlement was founded some 500 m to the north. In fact, there are two mounds very close to each other – they are separated by a ditch-like feature –, but only the south-eastern one (no. 32) yielded Hellenistic material. Its extent in the period in question is however, unknown. The other one (no. 72) was settled only in the Kushan period. This place had without a doubt a strategic position at the edge of the Sherabad Oasis on the way to the west: to the banks of the Amu Dayra, along its course, and further to Merv Oasis/Margiana. A similar role in the south of the oasis – on the way to the important Hellenistic fortresses protecting the crossings of the Amu Darya on the way to Bactra, i.e., those of Old Termez and Kampyrtepa – may have been played by the newly constructed walled site of Aysaritepa (no. 042), and its nearby satellite site (no. 181), if the dating of its earliest strata is correct.

Generally speaking, the settlements of the Hellenistic period known to us do not indicate any specific structure or hierarchy, except for some control functions of the middle-size sites situated in the marginal positions, as seen from the centre. The landscape potential was used only very haphazardly, the population did not grow and as far as we can judge from the available data, extensive irrigation systems had not yet been constructed.

The issue that should be analysed in the future is the relationship of the oasis, especially its centre at Jandavlattepa, to the recently found and partly already excavated Hellenistic fortresses situated not far to the north – at Kurganzol (Sverchkov 2013), Payon Kurgan (Abdullaev 2001), and Uzundara (Dvurechenskaya 2015), all in the present day Baysun District.

The sparsely settled Sherabad plain corresponds very well to the situation in the piedmont steppe area of the same district. By now, there are only a few settlements that can be dated to the given period. We may be certain about the site of Ghishttepa (Mokroborodov 2007) on the outskirts of Pashkhurt village and only hypothetically also Dabil Kurgan (Rtveladze 2013, 100), which is the main archaeological site of that village and of the whole piedmont area, ascribed to the Hellenistic period, since the relevant strata have not yet been excavated (Solov'ev personal communication, Autumn 2015). The early dating has been suggested tentatively by Rtveladze also for Maydan Kurgan located in the nearby piedmont village of Maydan (Rtveladze 2002, 106–107). For such a dating there is, however, absolutely no evidence neither in his survey material – as he admits himself –, nor in ours. Thus, Ghishttepa represents according to the current state of research only an isolated phenomenon in the piedmont steppe area, where otherwise some nomads may have lived at that time.

5.4.2 Historical implications

5.4.2.1 Alexander's campaign

The current state of research does not allow us to put forward any substantial historical conclusions. It is symptomatic that scholars dealing with campaigns of Alexander the Great almost omit the Sherabad Oasis, even though his army must have passed it on the way to Sogdiana one time at least. Exceptionally, Rtveladze had identified Talashkantepa I with the so-called town of Branchides (Sagdullaev – Rtveladze 1983, 50–60) mentioned by Curtius Rufus (VII, V, 27–35), but he himself refuted his own theory two decades later with convincing arguments (Rtveladze 2002, 70). We agree completely that Talashkantepa I does not fit to the Curtius account, but – on the other hand – there is absolutely no reason to exclude the site of Jandavlattepa from the "Branchides" discussion. Nevertheless, Jandavlattepa seems to be omitted,[75] except for a short note of Sagdullaev, who admits the site as a possible solution of the riddle (Sagdullaev in the foreword to Rtveladze 2002, 9). This fortified site was situated on the straight route from Bactra to Nautaca (modern Kitab/Shahrisabz) and Maracanda (modern Samarkand), it does not matter which way Alexander's army took across the river Oxus. The site is situated close to the place, where the Sherabad Darya leaves the mountain ranges and its upper valley provides the only easily penetrable road to the north, especially for armies with thousands of people, horses and flocks. Whoever wanted to go through it, must have passed off the Jandavlattepa, or evaded it on pur-

---

[75] Most recently see Rapin 2013, but he is concerned predominantly with events of the second and third years of Alexander's campaign in Central Asia (i.e., 328–327 BC).

pose: any army marching this way must have known the walled settlement at this site. Moreover, the abandonment of the smaller structures of the Achaemenid period around Jandavlattepa seems to confirm an idea expressed by Zapparov and Rtveladze a long time ago that most of the Achaemenid sites known to us were abandoned for good in the 4th c. BC. They connect it with the activities of Craterus, general of Alexander the Great, operating here in order to crush the rebelling local warlords (Zapparov – Rtveladze 1976, 24)[76], while Grenet and Rapin (2001, 82) are inclined to think that the main contribution to the abandonment of the old Achaemenid settlements in the province of the Surkhan Darya was made by one of the five units allocated by Alexander in the spring of 328, and that it was most probably the one led by Coenus and Artabazus. Stride, on the other hand, assumes that the situation was different: even if we have evidence of abandonment in some places,[77] there are other, frequently sizable Achaemenid sites (among them he mentions Jandavlattepa) that continued their existence after Alexander's campaign, and others that moved just slightly, a few hundred meters, such in the case of Talashkan (Stride 2004, vol. I, 312–313). In our opinion, if a settlement in a particular place changes its location, as Talashkan did, it means that something serious happened: the original one had been destroyed or damaged and was unsuitable for further use.

There is no separate geographic name of the Sherabad Oasis preserved in written sources of the Hellenistic period, there are some indications, however, that the broader region – a strip of land between the Amu Darya / Oxus and the Hissar Mountains was called Paretacene (Rtveladze 2002, 129–136).

5.4.2.2 Seleucids and Greco-Bactrian period (3rd c. and 1st half of the 2nd c. BC)

If the time of Alexander's campaign and the early Hellenistic period in the Sherabad Oasis is only scarcely researched, and we only speculate on the details of historical developments, the next three hundred years pose much more serious problems. Un-

like the Baysun District, where the last two decades witnessed important discoveries of Greco-Bactrian sites, in the Sherabad Oasis there were found neither new sites of the Hellenistic period, nor systematically investigated proper strata of the known sites. Some help is given by the catalogue of ancient coins (Rtveladze – Pidaev 1981) featuring all known coin finds at that time. Surprisingly, the period in question was very poorly represented: only nine coins of Greco-Bactrian kings was included, among them none from the Sherabad Oasis![78] The situation changed dramatically as shown not only by the example of Jandavlattepa (see above), but also Kampyrtepa and new sites in the Baysun District. The Jandavlattepa finds of Greco-Bactrian coins included, as stated above, mints of the most powerful rulers: Euthydemus[79], Demetrius, and Eucratides[80]. They attest the growing importance of a monetary economy in the Hellenistic period compared to the previous phase, but the amount of currency is still very low and we lack larger hoards or even individual finds from the countryside. This may of course be rather due to the state of research, but the discrepancy between Hellenistic and Kushan period is too striking to be accidental: Kushan coins are multiply more represented among the finds from Sherabad Oasis than the Greco-Bactrian ones (see next subheading).

5.4.2.3 The transitional period (2nd half of the 2nd c. and 1st c. BC)

There was of course a transitional period[81] between the "pure Hellenistic" and "pure Kushan" phase. It is, however, very difficult to detect the material of this period in the surface archaeological record. We consequently deal in this text with material dated to the period, which is characterised by typical coin finds known as imitations of Heliocles and associated numismatic material as "Transitional", while the later coins – and ceramics belonging to them –, we consider Kushan.

In the very beginning of the transitional period connected with the invasion of the nomadic tribes of Saka and Yue-zhi of Bactria one can expect some

---

[76] At that time, they were speaking about ten out of 17 known Achaemenid sites in northern Bactria (Zapparov – Rtveladze 1976, 24).

[77] He concludes that most of the abandoned sites were located in peripheral valleys and the process had nothing in common with Alexander's activities here, but was caused by salinization or other degradation of the soil and consequent worsening of agricultural production and at the same time this process was part of a transition from small-scale local agriculture in isolated valleys to large scale agriculture in the alluvial plain (Stride 2004, 314). In the Sherabad Oasis, however, there is no evidence of such a transition. The settlement pattern did not change substantially until the Kushan period.

[78] An overview of new finds of Hellenistic coins from Uzbekistan featuring 23 pieces only confirm the specific position of the Sherabad Oasis: while there are reported new finds from Termez, Kampyrtepa and even from Khayrabadtepa situated close to the Sherabad Oasis, no new find has been reported from the Sherabad plains (Abdullaev 2006).

[79] Yet another Euthydemus coin has been found by a German-Uzbek team working at Jandavlattepa in 1993, see Huff et al. 2001, 20, cf. also Abdullaev 2011a, 181.

[80] As Abdullaev (2011a, 181) points out, the square coin of Eucratides is the first find of this type north of the Amu Darya.

[81] The transitional period means the processes taking place in the 2nd half of the 2nd c. and 1st c. BC, during which the Greco-Macedonian rulers of Bactria lost the power on one hand and the nomad Yue-zhi clan leaders gradually established themselves in the newly subdued lands on the other.

abandonment phase (Stride 2004, vol. 1, 317). Unlike Khalchayan and Shortepa (Stride 2004, vol. 1, 317) in neighbouring regions, the sites of the Sherabad Oasis did not provide such data, although at Jandavlattepa this may be expected.

The copper imitations of Heliocles silver coins[82] from Jandavlattepa are of course part of this story. They belong to the transitional period and were minted by the "Barbarian" Yue-zhi chieftains or clan-leaders in the 2nd–1st c. BC.[83] Seven individual coins from the recent excavations at Jandavlattepa complemented an earlier small hoard from the sounding/section at the northernmost margin of the site of Akkurgan amounting also to seven pieces (Pidaev 1978, 58–59 and 71; Rtveladze – Pidaev 1981, 55–56). The higher occurrence of Heliocles imitations is, however, nothing specific about the Sherabad Oasis: the same

situation has been traced also in other regions of north-western Bactria, but not in north-eastern Bactria, in modern day Tajikistan.[84] The Sherabad Oasis seems to be a part of a domain of one of the Yue-zhi leaders, who minted these imitations, which circulated in a limited area only, corresponding roughly to the territory controlled by the given clan-leader. Note that Heliocles imitations from Jandavlattepa are assigned to early mints of this type (Abdullaev 2011a, 181), while the finds from Akkurgan are probably the latest ones (Rtveladze – Pidaev 1981, 33). Nevertheless, the pottery material from Akkurgan does not allow for dating of the contexts as early as the 1st c. BC, thus the imitations of Heliocles were probably deposited a long time after their minting and the site itself does not represent material culture of the transitional period.

5.5 Kushan and Kushano-Sasanian period (1st–4th c. AD)

In the Sherabad plains, there have been so far detected 51 settlements dated to the Kushan period, including the Kushano-Sasanian phase (**Fig. 5.8**). Ten additional Kushan sites have been identified in the neighbouring piedmonts by now, but we are not going to deal with them in the current publication, since this survey has not been finished yet and the data are not complete. The number of Kushan settlements corresponds very well to the overall figures given by Stride for the whole province of Surkhan Darya, including a comparison with the Greco-Bactrian phase. According to him, there were 23 Greco-Bactrian (or generally Hellenistic) sites and as many as 206 Kushan sites throughout the province including the Sherabad plain (Stride 2004, vol. 1, 322–323).[85]

The following table (p. 367) shows all the sites with the Kushan and Kushano-Sasanian strata in the Sherabad Oasis. The grey fields indicate the sites that continued their life from the transitional / Yue-zhi period, while the others were newly settled in the Kushan period. The names of the sites settled during

both the Kushan and Kushano-Sasanian periods are written in **boldface**, those newly settled in the Kushano-Sasanian phase are written in *italics*.

5.5.1 Irrigation system

The first important change compared to the earlier periods is obvious: there are a lot more settlements dispersed throughout the oasis. Perhaps it would be possible to say that only in this period something like an oasis was formed. An oasis means water and water means an oasis. At that time, the numerous inhabitants of the Sherabad plain, got access to water.[86] Under the patronage of the Kushan kings, a complicated and sophisticated system of canals was build bringing water – most probably from the Sherabad Darya itself – to all important sites. Or *vice versa*, along the newly constructed water canals new farms and walled settlements were founded. Dry dusty steppe was gradually changed to arable land in the anticipation of the rapid agricultural development of the Soviet

[82] For a detailed analysis and classification of these coins see Zeymal' 1983, 110–128.
[83] Some scholars suggest that the earliest types were minted by the Sakas, who invaded Bactria slightly earlier than the Yue-zhi (Abdullaev 2011a, 182).
[84] By 1981, there was known 58 coin finds of Heliocles' imitations (including the Akkurgan hoard) from the Surkhan Darya (Rtveladze – Pidaev 1981, 20), while from Tajikistan only several pieces were reported (Zeymal' 1983, 110–128).
[85] These figures are in sharp contrast with those from Eastern Bactria: in the plain of Ai Khanoum 133 sites of Hellenistic period have been detected, while for the Kushan period there are only 116 sites known (Stride 2004, vol. 1, 322–323).
[86] The idea of rapid development in irrigation system in the Kushan period has been stressed by Mukhamedjanov in 1968 and supported by evidence from all around southern Central Asia (Mukhamedjanov 1975).

366

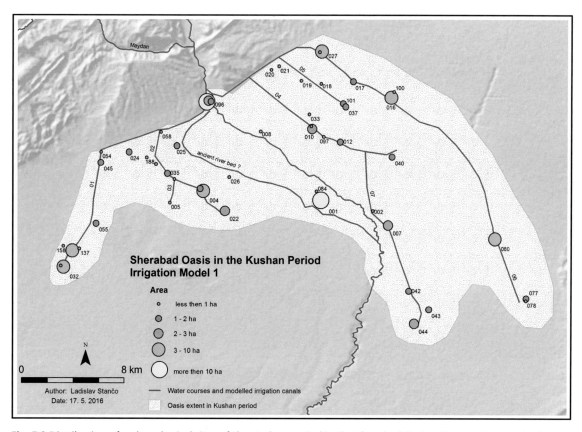

Fig. 5.8 Distribution of archaeological sites of the Kushan period in the Sherabad Oasis with Irrigation model 1, map by author.

Code	Name of site	Page		Code	Name of site	Page
001	Jandavlattepa			040	Shortepa	
002	Boshtepa			042	Aysaritepa	
004	Kulugshatepa			043	No name	
005	Aktepa			044	Teshiktepa	
007	Koshtepa II			045	No name	
008	Batyrabadtepa			054	Anjirtepa	
010	Kattatepa			055	Khalinchaktepa	
011	No name			058	Anjirtepa	
012	No name			061	No name	
016	Shortepa			063	Chalakurgan	
017	Shishtepa			072	Talashkantepa II	
018	Gilyambobtepa			077	Egiztepa I	
019	Gorintepa			078	Egiztepa II	
020	Dombratepa			080	No name	
021	Koshtepa 1			084	No name	
022	Iaushkantepa			094	Kurgan	
023	Tashlaktepa			095	No name	
024	Mozoroti Babatepa			096	No name	
025	Talagantepa			097	No name	
026	Yalangoyoq otatepa			098	no name (Hurjok cemetery)	
027	Babatepa			099	Talashkantepa III	
032	Talashkantepa II			100	No name	
033	No name			101	No name	
035	Chopan Ata			137	No name	
037	Ayritepa			158	No name	

era. Thus, we decided to create a model of an ancient irrigation system using and combining various data sources: the old maps, the satellite imagery and the settlement pattern.

5.5.1.1 Model 1 based on settlement pattern

Since remains of the ancient irrigation system has not been preserved in the research area,[87] we tried as a first step to sketch a probable model of the Kushan irrigation system that is based on the distribution of the settlements of the given period (**Fig. 5.8**). The model also takes into account the changing altitude of the research area. According to our model, the water was brought to the bigger sites by at least four, maybe even five main water canals. The places in between them were interwoven by smaller canals and filled with a checkerboard of fields in a very similar manner as today. The model estimates that the extent of the irrigated lands in the Sherabad Oasis of the Kushan period (including the surface of the sites) reached ca. 55,000 ha (**Fig. 5.8**).[88] This general figure is rather optimistic, since we must bear in mind that uneven steppe relief of that time did not allow the irrigation of the entire surface: no bulldozers levelled the landscape and deep ploughing did not yet exist. One can only guess the proportion of the irrigated fields and elevated dry areas throughout the oasis in the Kushan period and later.

Our map shows two long irrigation canals on the right bank of the present-day Sherabad Darya labelled 04/07 and 06. While the course of both canals we modelled according to the settlement pattern and slope (or rather plain) inclination, we are not sure about the end point, especially of the Canal No. 07. At the end of our model, there is situated settlement no. 44 (Teshiktepa), which seems to be locked by two branches of present day canals and thus it is very tempting to connect its irrigation with a hypothetical predecessor of the present-day Zang Canal, as Stride in his model did (Stride 2007, 106, fig. 4). The slope inclination between the point of departure at Haudag hills in the east and Teshiktepa in the west is very low: the drop is about 2 m within the length of 8.5 km, which would be a very difficult task for Kushan builders to maintain, unlike modern engineers. Thus, we prefer with some caution, the variant given here in the map showing a canal bringing water from the north. Note that our model would be valid only if the big collector canal called "Bol'shoy Zaur" did

not exist at that time (Bol'shoy Zaur is seen on every map in this chapter on the right as a prominent linear feature of the grey relief underlay oriented from NE to SW).

5.5.1.2 Model 2 based on historical maps

The second model (**Fig. 5.9**) is based on different assumptions. For now, we forget the settlement pattern having in mind that the picture of the pattern we have is incomplete anyway. Let us assume that some points discussed above were true: the collector canal Bol'shoy Zaur did not exist and the Zang Canal was built as a modern irrigation project and had no predecessor, at least in the same course it has nowadays. How to prove these hypotheses? Our primary sources – 100k topographic maps of the 1980s, satellite imagery of CORONA and IKONOS, and even actual landscape morphology does not help us in this respect. The only source (we know) capturing the landscape including water canals are older topographic maps. Unfortunately, the older Tsarist or Soviet maps were not accessible, and we had to rely on the U.S. Army maps compiled in 1952 at the scale of 1:250,000 from the USSR 1:200,000 scale maps of the General Staff of the Red Army from 1931–1937 and 1:500,000 scale from 1939 (J-42-C). Digitizing of the data answered both question we had: there was no big canal Zaur and the course of the Zang Canal was completely different leaving the area of the Town of Angor seemingly without water. Moreover, we got information of the course of many water canals throughout the Sherabad Oasis that no longer exist. They were built a long time before the collectivisation and construction of both backbone canals – the Big Sherabad Canal and the Zang Canal. The question is, when? To answer this question, we shall turn again to the settlement pattern as a subsidiary argument. It is not surprising that the canal network as partly preserved in the 1930s did not make sense in combination with the settlements of the Pre-Kushan period, but the same goes surprisingly also for the Pre-modern periods. The extent of the canal system was too large, too complicated and too dense to be used – and especially built – by a Medieval population (see maps of settlement pattern of the individual periods below in the following chapters). The settlement pattern of the Kushan period, on the other hand, works perfectly with the model based on the early 20th c. data. There are, however, some problems, which must be addressed

---

[87] There are several traces of canals that we have suspected to be the remains of ancient irrigation systems, but we actually have no evidence confirming this assumption. The human impact in the 20th c. was so strong that it is very unlikely to find the remains of the canals by the way of a simple surface survey or visual analysis of satellite images. More sophisticated tools, however, such as LIDAR or GPR may bring some new data on the historical landscape and relief with respect to water canals in particular, which are not visible on the present-day surface.

[88] Note that it was just in the Kushan period when the rotary quern stones became the principal technological means of grinding (Stančo 2018b).

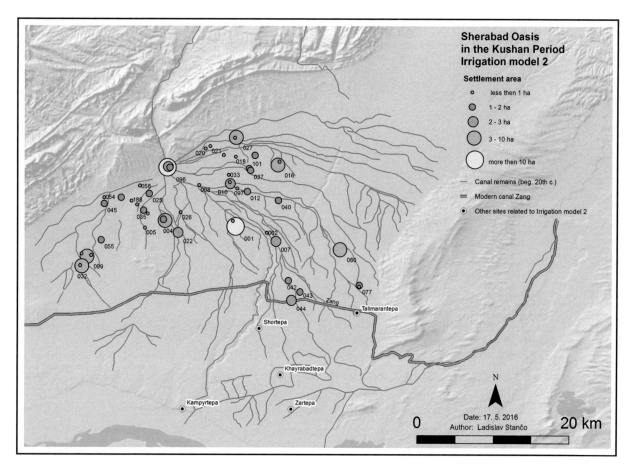

Fig. 5.9 Distribution of archaeological sites of the Kushan period in the Sherabad Oasis with Irrigation model 2, map by author.

in this respect. Firstly, there are several branches of the water canal system that does not supply any cluster of the Kushan or Early Medieval settlements, at least according to our current knowledge (it is especially the Aryk Istara and Aryk Yangi marked on the map). This can easily be explained by an insufficient state of research (which could always be the true), but also by the fact that the worst situation is in the Kizirik District, i.e., in the easternmost part of the Sherabad plain, where the large scale transformation of the landscape during the Soviet era was started earliest and the original relief has been changed most dramatically. The other option, however, how to explain the problem lies in the fact that we admit a combination of the historical and recent use of the same canals. In other words, the original Kushan Canals were cleaned up and maybe also extended in the Pre-modern period during the gradual colonization of the steppe by a settled population. Indeed, we can reasonably assume that some parts of the ancient water supply and irrigation system were exploited and thus also regularly cleaned during the entire post-Kushan history. This is exactly the case of other areas of southern Central

Asia depending on artificial water bringing systems, as for instance the Samarkand Oasis of Sogdiana. The ancient back-bone canals of this region, Bulungur and Dargom, today still fulfil their role as a main water supply of the Oasis, while the small branches of the system were abandoned, but still can be traced in the surrounding steppe (most recently Mantellini 2015; cf. his bibliography).

The other problematic issue concerns the extent of the Sherabad Oasis as such. In this book, we delimited the borders according to the natural barriers, the extent of the lands irrigated from one primary source, which is the Sherabad Darya, and additionally also according to the settlement pattern. If this second model is correct, we must admit that we were wrong on the initial "demarcation of the borders." In fact, the Sherabad Oasis seems to exceed the extent proposed by previous researchers (Masson 1974, 5; Staviski 1977, 47–56; Pidaev 1978, 16 and 18, tab. 1; Stride 2004, vol. I, 226–227, fig. 71),[89] and extends much farther to the south and west, and to the east probably as well which has been dealt with in the previous paragraph. If true, we have to count with the sites that

---

[89] Stride is the only scholar who admits theoretically the existence of a link between the Karasu / Sherabad Darya and the Angor irrigation system in Antiquity, see Stride 2004, vol. I, 226–227. It is noteworthy that Stride used the U.S. map of the 1950s, which shows exactly the situation he argues against (Stride 2004, vol. I, 227 and fig. 52).

were previously classified among the Zang Canal irrigation area (see all mentioned above and also Masson 1985, 258–259; Mukhamedjanov 1994, 257). These include such sites as Jalpaktepa, Kulaglitepa, several no name sites around Angor, but also the important walled settlements of Shortepa and Khayrabadtepa. This would of course completely change the spatial relations and functioning of the oasis in terms of an economic unit.

To further prove the second model of the canal system, we have compared the digitized canals with details of the historical relief and topography as preserved in the CORONA image. The task was not an easy one, since the U.S. map is not accurate and precise enough (as the description on the map itself admits), but after some adjustment we found out that individual sections of the canals drawn on the U.S. map match exactly the various natural features of the landscape captured in CORONA (irregular shapes of fields, for instance), and in some cases even parts of the water canals preserved at the turn of the 1960s and 1970s especially in the central and western part of the oasis.

We believe that the second model corresponds to historical reality better than the first one, and certainly better than the descriptions of the western and southern Surkhan Darya oases, as understood by our predecessors.

5.5.2 Settlement hierarchy

The other important change of the local settlement pattern that took place in the Sherabad Oasis during the Kushan period was an establishment of a clear hierarchy of the settlements with a leading position of one large central site.[90] This central fortified town was not surprisingly located at Jandavlattepa, once again. The second level of settlements, based on their size, is represented by Talashkan II (no. 032, Southeast mound), Talashkantepa III (099), Kulugshatepa (No. 004), Babatepa (No. 027), Shortepa (No. 016), and a no-name site located close to Takiya village (No. 80). The surface of these sites measure between 3 and 10 ha. These medium-sized settlements were fairly regularly distributed throughout the oasis. The third level consists of settlements ranging from 2 to 3 ha (five sites), the fourth level shows 15 sites having a surface area ranging from 1 to 2 ha, and the last level represents the 19 smallest units, smaller than 1 ha. Again, the smaller sites, hamlets and homesteads, were regularly distributed and not particularly clustered, which further attests to the irrigation system

model. The following table shows the direct distance between the sites of the second and third level and the central site of Jandavlattepa.[91]

Distance from	Distance to	Distance in km
Jandavlattepa	004	7.3
Jandavlattepa	007	4.5
Jandavlattepa	010	5.4
Jandavlattepa	016	8.9
Jandavlattepa	022	5.9
Jandavlattepa	027	11.2
Jandavlattepa	032	16.7
Jandavlattepa	044	10.9
Jandavlattepa	080	11.2
Jandavlattepa	095/096/094	10.2

The next table shows mutual distances between individual settlements of the oasis:

Distance from	Distance to	Distance in km
004	032	10.4
004	094/095/096	6.7
007	044	7.6
010	027	5.9
016	010	5.5
016	027	5.6
080	007	6.7
080	016	12.4
080	044	8.1
094/095/096	016	11.1

From these tables a certain system of measures is perfectly visible, suggesting a not accidental placing of newly founded settlements of various levels. As the distance 5.5–7.6 kms is very frequent and the exact distance of 6.7 km repeatedly occurs, we may assume this distance, or the average distance being counted from ten varied, but similar distances, which is 6.11 km, could be a unit of measurement. That applies a fortiori that the double rate also appears repeatedly. Thus we have distances of 10.4–12.4 km in seven cases with an average distance of 11.05 km (the exact half of it occurs three times). Six kilometres is about a 1–1.5 hour-long march. Moreover, we tried to test the mutual visibility of the sites while conducting the surface survey, and, where not blocked by modern houses and/or trees, the intervisibility between the sites being 6 km apart is very good (from Jandavlattepa to the site No. 007, for instance).[92]

---

[90] Or maybe two, it depends on the fact, what was the extent of Kafir Kala in Sherabad in the Kushan period.
[91] Measured in ArcMap.
[92] See Stančo 2018c for detailed analysis of the system of measuring units and its practical implications.

This settlement pattern and hierarchy of the Kushan period in the Sherabad Oasis corresponds roughly to a model observed by Stride in the surrounding of Dal'verzintepa and Khalchayan, in the north-eastern part of the Surkhan Darya province: there were two large settlements with a surface exceeding 40 ha (we do not have this category in the Sherabad plain), the next category comprises of sites of the size between 10 and 15 ha, typically located ca. 10 km from those major settlements. They have a regular plan, fortifications and citadel (corresponding to Jandavlattepa itself). The third category consists of sites that rarely exceed 3 ha in size. The pattern is complemented by smaller agricultural sites (Stride 2004, vol. 1, 324). A different situation has been observed in the Angor Oasis situated directly to the south of the Sherabad one and related supposedly to the irrigation system of the Zang Canal. The principal central site of Zartepa was surrounded by a number of smaller settlements, usually less then 1 ha in size and typically square or rectangular in their ground plan. Some of these sites were well fortified (Stride 2004, vol. 1, 325, fig. 49 and 71). Nonetheless, having in mind our second model of the irrigation system of the south western Surkhan Dayra province, we must judge the settlement pattern of the so called Angor or Zang Oasis very carefully.

If the river bed of the Sherabad Darya was indeed in the Kushan period situated west of Jandavlattepa, as suggested above in chapter 5.3, there would also be another advantage: it was not necessary to cross the river while travelling northwards from Termez and Zartepa in the south or westwards from Dal'verzintepa and Khalchayan in the east, to reach the principal site of the Sherabad Oasis – Jandavlattepa. At the current state of research, however, we prefer the model 2, where there is not only one backbone riverbed, but the whole complex of equally dimensioned canals covers most of the area of the oasis.

Even if we have quite a lot of data on settlements, there is an absolute lack of evidence about funeral rites, including spatial data: we have no idea where burial sites of the Kushan period population were situated. The only indirect evidence is represented by occasional finds of complete pottery forms, as in the case of an accidental find of a large body of typical Great Kushan ware (bowl, pots, lamps) that were reportedly found in one place close to the site of Babatepa and very well-preserved (Stančo 2015, 218–219). Such finds – unusually well preserved for living quarters and settlements in general – may indicate spots, where a burial grounds were situated: within several hundred meters of the main *tepa*, in this particular case to the west of it.

5.5.3 Historical implications

The impression of fundamental change we get looking at the maps of the Sherabad Oasis of the Hellenistic and Kushan period and the comparison of both can hardly be more striking. It is clear that something in the attitude towards the landscape and environment must have changed: The Sherabad steppe plain, formerly barely settled by a limited population with a few sites here and there in the oasis, transformed radically to a densely populated and apparently well irrigated area dotted with sites: a principal town (or two), fortified places, local centres, hamlets and fields. An agricultural oasis just emerged. The scale of the presumed irrigation system of this period seems to be too large to originate from a limited labour force and local authorities. It was rather a well-organized project ordered by a leadership of an administratively mature society and state: the Kushan realm. Moreover, the construction of the extensive irrigation system presupposes a certain degree of political and economic stability and peace in the region, hence in our view through a sort of *Pax Kushana*[93] could have ensured the right conditions for such a large and ambitious project.[94]

---

[93] The term was used by Aldrovandi and Hirata (2005), for instance, with a special emphasis on Buddhist art as a means of dissemination of the relevant ideas.

[94] Stride et al. (2009) discuss the relation between a central power of a sedentary nature and a nomadic society.

5.6 Early Medieval period (5th–8th c.)

The Early Medieval period in southern Central Asia is not a coherent time unit, it is rather an odd period starting after the collapse of something (i.e., the Kushan realm and its heirs, Kushano-Sasanians under the Sasanian supremacy) and before the beginning of something else (the rise of Islam). From the point of view of power games, the period starts with struggles between the Sasanid Iran and nomadic newcomers, whose waves once again flooded periodically southern Central Asia, which was at that time under the Sasanid control. It was V. M. Masson, who demanded the establishment of a more precise chronology of the Early Medieval period already in 1979, and considered as insufficient the general time span of the 5th–8th c. broadly established in scientific literature (Masson 1979, 4). If one tries to avoid the usage of the vague term "Early Medieval", some even stranger terms like "Turkic period" or "post-Kushan period" come to one's mind. None of them, however, characterises properly either the historical realities, or the changes in the society and material culture. The other option is given by the further subdivisions of the period, as done by Stride (2004, vol. I, 331), with the first phase labelled as "Hephtalite" (till 560 AD) and the second phase "(Sasano)-Turkic" (till 800).

The most comprehensive publication on any single historical period of the Surkhandarya province was devoted to Medieval settlements. The book *Srednevekovye pamyatniki Surkhandar'i* (Arshavskaya et al. 1982), lists only 35 sites in our research area (dated to the both Early and High Middle Ages), while our database contains 44 sites dated to the former period only. It is in this period when we can speak about Tokharistan instead of Bactria, as the Medieval written sources do. The earliest use of the term was reported from the year 383 AD (Arshavskaya et al. 1982, 21), however, recently introduced inscription mentioning Tokharistan is dated to the 2nd c. AD (Sims-Williams 2015).

5.6.1 Written sources

Soviet scholars argued that in the Persian Early Medieval sources one can find for the first time two separate names for the Sherabad Oasis. Al-Tabari and al-Balazhuri – they say – mention in their fa-

mous works the region of Guftan or Kuftan, while describing the campaigns of Qutaiba ibn Muslim to Tokharistan (Arshavskaya et al. 1982, 21; Pugachenkova –Rtveladze 1990, 123–124).[95] Neither Russian, nor English translation of Al-Baladhuri, however, contains the toponym *Guftan / Kuftan* (cf. al-Baladhuri; al-Balazuri). The only note on Guftan is in the footnote no. 69 of the Russian translation, which is simply the translator's commentary. Al-Tabari speaks of Kuftan as one of the principalities (besides Chaganian, Shuman and Akharun) on the right bank of the Amu Darya three times (at-Tabari 1150; 1162; 1180), but its geographic location is far from being clear.[96] Although Bartold admitted both the lower reaches of the Surkhan Darya or the Sherabad beg territory as a place of Guftan, Arshavskaya et al. argue for the lower and middle reaches of the Sherabad Darya, i.e., the Sherabad Oasis only (for both opinions see Arshavskaya et al. 1982, 21), while Kamaliddinov identified Kuftan with the piedmont settlement of Kugitang on the basis of the etymology of the name (Kamaliddinov 1993, 39–40).

Sasanian King of Kings Yazdegerd II (438–457) conquered Tokharistan for a short period of time towards the end of the first half of the 5th c. (Arshavskaya et al. 1985, 21), and, as described by Zeymal', "the Sasanian army laid waste territories subject to Kidarites and took fortresses" (Zeimal 1996, 124–125).

There is no exact moment when the Early Medieval period ends and the High Medieval, i.e., Islamic period, in western Central Asia began. The first raids of Arab troops went across the Amu Darya in 670s to the region of Bukhara and beyond with an occasional struggle for control of Termez. In the initial years of the 8th c. under Qutaiba ibn Muslim these incursions intensified, but their main concern was conquering northern Transoxiana: regions of Sogdiana, Khwarazm, Ferghana, and Chach. Some local rulers of principalities in Tokharistan voluntarily fought on the side of Qutaiba (as the ruler of Balkh did) and *Chagan khudat* (the ruler of Chaganiyan) even invited him to his country and to wage war against neighbours in Shuman (Dushanbe area) and Akharun (al-Baladhuri 419–420), both in present-day western Tajikistan (Jalilov 1996, 453). The Sherabad Oasis is not mentioned in Arabic / Persian sources of that time, but the area might have been affected

---

[95] Stride follows Soviet literature citing only secondary sources and not directly al-Baladhuri (Stride 2005, 134).
[96] A single piece of information that helps us in solving this question is the story of Musa making a sudden sortie from the Termez area into Kuftan in order to obatin plunder. This and the way back was completed during one night: Kuftan thus should be located within a couple of hours on horseback of Termez (at-Tabari 1162).

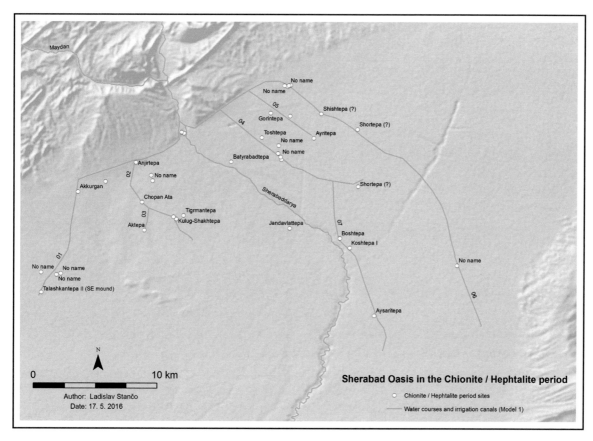

Fig. 5.10 Distribution of archaeological sites of Hephtalite period in the Sherabad Oasis, map by author.

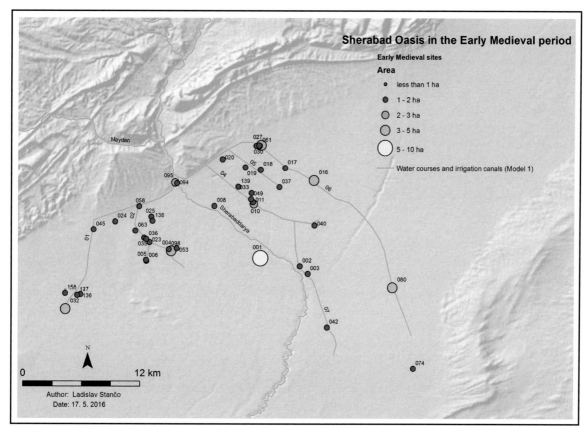

Fig. 5.11 Distribution of archaeological sites of Early Medieval period in the Sherabad Oasis, map by author.

by a struggle between Asad ibn Abdallah, Arab governor of Khorasan, and Türk kaghan Sulu,[97] who in the process attacked Chaganian, whose ruler had supported the Arabs (Jalilov 1996, 456). The present day province of Surkhan Darya was split into two main principalities at that time: Termez (Ta-mi of Chinese sources) and Chaganian (Ch'i-ngoh-yen-na). The Sherabad plain belonged most probably to the Termez principality, described by Xuanzang as follows: "*This country is 600 li* [194 km] *or so from east to west, and 400 li* [129 km] *or so from north to south. The capital, of the country is about 20 li* [6.5 km] *in circuit, extended from east to west, and narrow from north to south. There are about ten sangharmas with about one thousand monks. The stupas and the images of the honoured Buddha are noted for various spiritual manifestations. Going east we arrive at Ch'i-ngoh-yen-na*" (Xuanzang vol. I, 38–39).

5.6.2 Settlement pattern

The settlement pattern of the oasis did not change substantially compared to the previous Kushan and Late Kushan periods. According to our survey and to the previous scholarly research, 44 settlement sites are known throughout the oasis, 18 out of this number are mentioned in Arshavskaya et al. already (1982, 132–135).[98] Mainly following this source, Stride lists 21 sites in the territory, his figures concerning the right and left bank sites correspond proportionally to our own data: 23 sites on the left bank (Stride has 11) and 21 on the right bank (Stride has ten, see table above in the chapter 1.4; cf. Stride 2004, vol. I, 237–239). This almost equal division of the settlements on both banks of the river corresponds very well also to an even spatial distribution as seen on the map (**Fig. 5.11**). The overall picture given by the map is, however, somehow confusing, since some sites seem to have already been abandoned in the course of the 5th c., thus at the very beginning of the period in question (**Fig. 5.10**). This is first of all most probably the case of Jandavlattepa (Stančo 2011b, 52–52), but also of Kattatepa (010) and Aysaritepa (042), which is still less than 10% of the inhabited sites of the period. This contradicts to assumed catastrophic developments in the regions on the right bank of the Amu Darya, where "many towns were largely destroyed and whole oases laid waste during the last quarter of the fourth century and the beginning of the fifth" (Zeimal 1996, 130–131). Unfortunately, for none of these sites we have sufficient data to decide what the

immediate reason for the abandonment was. What these sites have in common is the fact that all three of them lay close to the river, let us say on one line or on one route of an army's march. On the way from Aysaritepa to Jandavlattepa lay two other sites: both of them seem to be settled only after the events we speculate of. In case of Boshtepa (002) it was resettled after some hiatus and in the case of Koshtepa I (003), the site was newly founded probably in the 5th c. A closer look makes it clear that during the 5th c. AD, proclaimed as an unstable time of decay, there were 37 inhabited sites in the oasis, which on the contrary indicates relative prosperity (compare really low numbers of inhabited sites in the Post-Mongol period and later, for instance – see below chapter 5.7) and implies that at least some of the irrigation systems build in the Kushan period were still in use.

5.6.3 Historical implications

The military events that possibly happened during the initial part of the period in question in the region may have been connected with the struggle between the Sasanian and Kidarite armies. The Kidarite invasion into Tokharistan took place either in the second half of the 4th century (Zeimal 1996, 125), or more probably it 420s–430s (Grenet 2002; Grenet 2005), which makes it one option to explain the above described development. The Yazdegerd II campaign against the Hephtalites in the 440s and 450s represents the other option. We are well aware of the speculative character of such suggestions, but one can imagine – looking at the map – an army advancing from the south (Bactra/Balkh or Taliqan) as far as the Sherabad Oasis, besieging its central site of Jandavlattepa, and one more walled settlement nearby (Kattatepa) serving as a last refuge for the local population. The third abandoned site – Aysaritepa – was simply the first site of the oasis on an army's march.

The excavations of Jandavlattepa yielded interesting situations that could well illustrate the sequence of events: there was a monumental building standing on the so-called citadel of this former principal site of the Kushano-Sasanian domains. This building was destroyed, probably in the 2nd half of the 4th c. (events connected with the Chionite invasion?), and within the ruins a wooden structure (post holes with circular ground plan remained) recalling a yurt was built. Even later this "yurt" was replaced by small houses of very poor quality masonry: compared to the previous

---

[97] The supremacy of the Türkit rulers over Tokharistan in the pre-islamic period is attested to also by the Chinese Buddhist pilgrim Xuanzang, who travelled through the region in the 630s and says that „*they have constituted twenty-seven states, divided by natural boundaries, yet as a whole dependent on the Tuh-kiueh tribes (Turks)*" (Xuanzang vol. I, 37–38).

[98] In that publication, there are mentioned altogether 29 sites of all the Medieval period in the Sherabad District including piedmonts (Arshavskaya et al. 1982. 132–135).

architectural standard these buildings appear rather pathetic (cf. Stančo 2011b, 53). Can we connect the "yurt" with the Chionite invasion in the middle of 4th c. and the poor houses with the return of refugees shortly after, or maybe with nomads gradually settling in the following decades? Again, this question remains speculative; we cannot answer it responsibly at the current state of research.

Let us turn to the case of the site of Kattatepa ("Big mound"), which was repeatedly identified with a centre mentioned in Medieval sources. According to Soviet scholarly literature (most recently Kamaliddinov 1993, 39–40), Kattatepa is identical to Khushvarag of the Arabo-Persian sources: the town should have flourish between the 5th and 8th century. As discussed above, the site was inhabited in the Kushano-Sasanian period and abandoned in the 5th c. at the latest and thus can hardly be identified with an important centre of the 5th–8th c. The only explanation for this inaccuracy seems to be confusion in names or rather inconsistent use of them in the scholarly literature. In isolated cases, the site of Khosyattepa (no. 052) is called also Kattatepa (Arshavskaya et al. 1982, 133, no. 158), and indeed, this site was at the height of its development in the Early Middle Ages. The extent of the settlement was enormous, especially taking into account remains in its neighbourhood that most probably once formed rabad of the town.

The narrow strip of land on the right bank of the present-day Sherabad Darya northwest of Jandavlattepa appears to have still not been inhabited during all the Early Medieval period, which raises questions about the reasons for this evident irregularity in the otherwise even settlement distribution. One of the possible answers is that it was in this period, when the waters of the river migrated from the ancient course to the modern one. The area in between the two was thus unstable and not suitable for the maintaining of any permanent settlements and agricultural activities. The other plausible answer is based on the same conditions as in the example above: the shifting of the riverbed took place sometime later and sites that had hypothetically existed were flooded and washed away, except for the large (and high) and thus stable site of Jandavlattepa.[99] The settlements we know north-west of Jandavlattepa, i.e., from the area close to the present-day right riverbank are in any case dated from the high Medieval period or later.

From the estimated surfaces of each and every site inhabited in this period we gain the cumulative sum of the inhabited area in total, which is 569,193 sq. m. This is almost the same as in the previous Kushano-Sasanian period 575,902 (sq. m), at least in the first half of the 5th c., when we have 539,177 sq. m of settlements, while later – after the abandonment of Jandavlattepa and Kattatepa, the surface area declined to 417,457 sq. m (72.5%). Bearing in mind this state of knowledge, we can hardly agree with the assertions that the Early Middle Ages was a period of decay: "*Le Haut Moyen Age commence vers la fin du IVe siècle, avec l'abandon de la majorité des sites de la période antique, et s'achève au cours du VIIIe siècle avec la fin de la conquête arabe*" (Stride 2004, vol. I, 331).

As stated above, most of the sites inhabited in the Early Medieval period prolonged their life from the previous Late Kushan/Kushano-Sasanian period. Among 44 sites, thirty represented this continuity. The only apparent change in the settlement pattern occurs in the far south-western margin of the oasis, around the sites Talashkan II and III, where several (a cluster of) new settlements appeared. As the new sites were probably mere hamlets, there is a problem with the central site of this cluster. In Achaemenid period, Talashkan I was local stronghold, later on during the Greco-Bactrian and Kushan periods its neighbour Talashkan II (both mounds) took over its function and became the local centre of the south-western border of the oasis. This site, more precisely its south-eastern mound, seems to have been occupied even in the Early Medieval phase (5th–7th c.), still forms a core of the cluster, but its successor Talashkan III, originally Kushan settlement, was inhabited in the High Medieval period. Our survey did not attest to the Early Medieval occupation at this site, as claimed by Arshavskaya et al. (1982, 135). Unlike the other centres of micro regions in this area, Talashkan migrated several times for unknown reasons.[100] One may suspect gradual changes in the water bringing system analogically to the shift of Sherabad Darya. The other parts of the region underwent only minor changes. The grey fields in the following table indicate the sites that were newly settled in the Early Medieval period. The other sites continued their life from the previous phase with sites clearly abandoned in the 5th c. written in **boldface**.[101]

99 The irregular shape of the site itself has led to speculation about the possible erosion of water which might wash away a part of north side of the settlement, see Huff et al. 2001, 219, for further discussion Stančo 2011a, 18 and note 5. We refuted this possibility bearing in mind the existence of Medieval sites in between the Jandavlattepa and the present-day river. However, this is in no way mutually exclusive, since the diversion of the river from its original course may have taken place far up the stream around Sherabad and the plain to the east of the site could be unaffected.
100 There is, however very good analogy in the neighbour Bandikhan area, where this shifting of settlement regularly happens from the Late Bronze Age to the Early Medieval period; cf. Boroffka 2009, 135.
101 Since most of the sites have only been studied by way of a surface survey, the gained archaeological material is limited and does not allow us to establish a chronology precise enough to decide in what part of the 5th or 6th century the given site was founded, inhabited, or abandoned. In this respect, lack of coin finds, especially of well-preserved ones, is one of the important lacks. Thus we are not able to describe the local history in detail.

Code	Name of site
001	**Jandavlattepa**
002	Boshtepa
003	Koshtepa I
004	Kulugshatepa
005	Aktepa
006	No name
008	Batyrabadtepa
010	**Kattatepa, the main tepa**
011	No name
016	Shortepa
017	Shishtepa
018	Gilyambobtepa
019	Gorintepa
020	Dombratepa
023	Tashlaktepa
024	Mozoroti babatepa
025	Talagantepa
027	**Babatepa (the main tepa)**
028	No name
029	Chopantepa
030	No name
032	Talashkantepa II (SE mound)

Code	Name of site
033	No name
035	Chopan Ata
036	Anjirtepa
037	Ayritepa
040	Shortepa
042	**Aysaritepa**
045	Akkurgan
049	Olleiortepa
053	Tigrmantepa
058	Anjirtepa
061	No name
063	Chalakurgan
074	Talimarantepa
080	No name
094	Kurgan
095	No name
098	no name (Hurjok cemetery)
136	No name
137	No name
138	No name
139	Toshtepa
158	No name

5.7 High Medieval period / pre-Mongol period

The rise of Islam in Central Asia is perceived as quite a significant turning point: from now on, almost everything is different. The change affects not only the prevalent religion itself, but also many aspects of daily life, material culture, art and architecture. The change in pottery production is so obvious that even a non-specialist is able to recognize typical ceramics of the period: the colourful glazures of Medieval wares are easy to distinguish among the surface material. The end of this period was abrupt: the flourishing cultures of Central Asia were literally erased from the face of the earth by Mongol armies in the early 13th c., which brought fatal destruction to cities, small towns, rural settlements, as well as irrigation systems.

What is very important to note is the fact that the archaeological sites (we do not claim them to be necessarily settlements in some cases), especially those on the left bank of the Sherabad Darya, have mostly just been found recently by a random surface survey, typically do not have any obvious topographic features, but are characterised only by scatters of pottery of the given period. This implies that only an intensive survey of the entire lowlands can bring a complete picture of the settlement pattern, which thus can be quite different from the current state of knowledge, as represented on the map here.

Our database contains 26 sites of the High Medieval period with the largest centre (No. 166) situated in the far south-western margin of the oasis

376

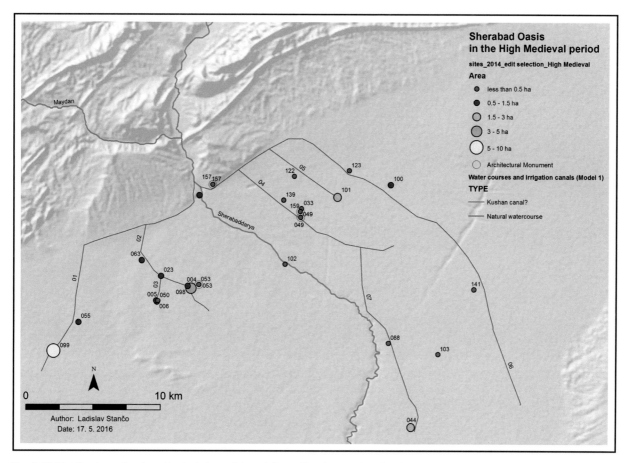

Fig. 5.12 Distribution of archaeological sites of the High Medieval period in the Sherabad Oasis, map by author.

(**Fig. 5.12**). The site of Talashkantepa III – or rather its core – has the form of a rectangle measuring 300 × 200 m. We observed plenty of archaeological material in the recently eroded water ravines (up to 2.5 m deep) on the western periphery of the site indicating that the lower quarters of the settlement (a rabat) are simply covered with soil due to the alluvial processes linked to the recent extensive agriculture and thus we can only guess the original size of the site. According to the surface material, Talashkan III seems to have been inhabited in the 10th–13th c., but predominantly in the last occupation phase, i.e., at the turn of the 12th and 13th c. before the Mongol conquest. Four out of the 26 sites are represented by single architectural monuments, two of them (Termez-ota mausoleum and Ota-Kul' mullah ishan baba /Ataula Said Vakkos) are still standing and in use. The cumulative sum of the sites' surfaces in the High Me-

Code	Name of the site
004	Kulugshatepa
005	Aktepa
006	No name
023	Tashlaktepa
033	No name
044	Teshiktepa
049	Olleiortepa
050	No name
053	Tugrmantepa
055	Khalinchaktepa
063	Chalakurgan
074	Talimarantepa
088	No name

Code	Name of the site
094	Kurgan / Kafirkala
098	No name (Hurjok cemetery)
099	Talashkantepa III
100	No name
101	No name
102	No name
103	No name
122	Pastaktepa
123	No name
139	Toshtepa
141	No name
157	Ota-Kul' mulla ishan baba
159	Termez-ota mausoleum

dieval period, as known up to now reaches 271,184 sq. m. The grey fields in the table (p. 377) (indicate the sites that were newly settled in the High Medieval period. We can see that 14 out of 26 Pre-Mongol sites (54%) were founded on greenfield sites, while only 12 sites demonstrate continuity with the previous Early Medieval period. Moreover, this continuity is apparent predominantly in the central part of the

oasis, i.e., in the core of the previously irrigated areas (up to 8 km from the site of Kafir-kala in Sherabad). Many sites on the periphery of the oasis, on the other hand, were abandoned, which could indicate the gradual or even abrupt collapse of the system of water canals that had been maintained for centuries. The total number of abandoned sites compared to the Early Medieval period is 32 (see the map).

5.8 Post-Mongol period

If we may have observed dramatic decrease in the number of inhabited sites during the High Medieval period, our evidence for the period after the devastating Mongol invasion resembles collapse of agricultural life along with both urban and rural life in the region. If we look at it in longer term, we see that this decline continued basically until the

beginning of the 20th century. Besides the destructive invasion, this long-term decline must have had some other reasons (be it political, economic or/and environmental), their combination, however, seems to stay close to the right answer.

Number of the sites belonging to this period and known to us by now is 14.[102] The cumulative

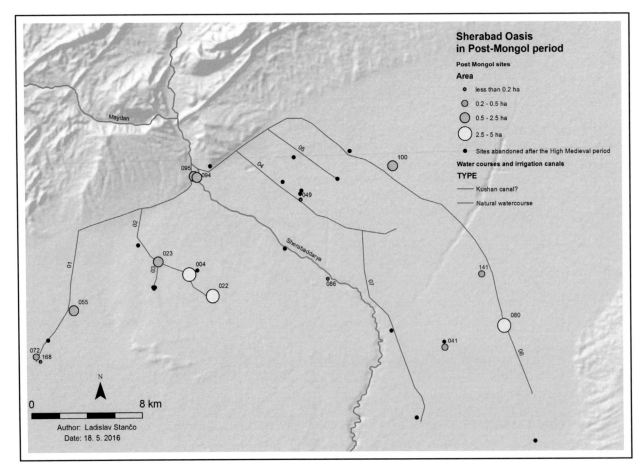

Fig. 5.13 Distribution of archaeological sites of Post-Mongol period in the Sherabad Oasis, map by author.

---

[102] Note that in this period we can find many sites in the piedmont steppe belt (north-western part of the oasis). In our database, there is 16 settlements of the given period, which is for the first time higher number than in the lowlands. Here we can probably

sum of the sites' surface in the Post-Mongol period is 166,152 sq. m. As is clearly seen on the map (**Fig. 5.13**), the Sherabad Oasis had changed dramatically. In this case, the map contains also black points indicating the sites abandoned after the High Medieval period. This helps us to reconstruct that the worst situation was in the area of the central north-

south axis of the oasis, especially on the left bank of the river, where no settlement escaped destruction. Moreover, the Post-Mongol distribution of the sites shows that probably only three main irrigation canals of our Model 1 survived (01, 02, and 06). The canal nr. 02 was able to provide the water for Kulugshatepa and Tauskhantepa.

5.9 Pre-modern period

The Pre-modern period is rather out of the scope of our research and the present chapter gives only general information on it that can help to understand the final stages in the development of the settlement pattern (**Fig. 5.14**). The town of Sherabad became a seat of the local governor in frame of the Bukhara caliphate, i.e., the beg (Sherabad beg), who

lived in the fort of Kafir Kala at the northern end of the town (no. 094). The town of the second half of the 19th c. was described by V. I. Lipskiy (1902) and local people, including beg and his entourage (**Fig. 5.15** and cover), photographed by Polish traveller and photographer L. Barscewski. Lipsky described the town as follows: "Sherabad (altitude 1,585 feet)

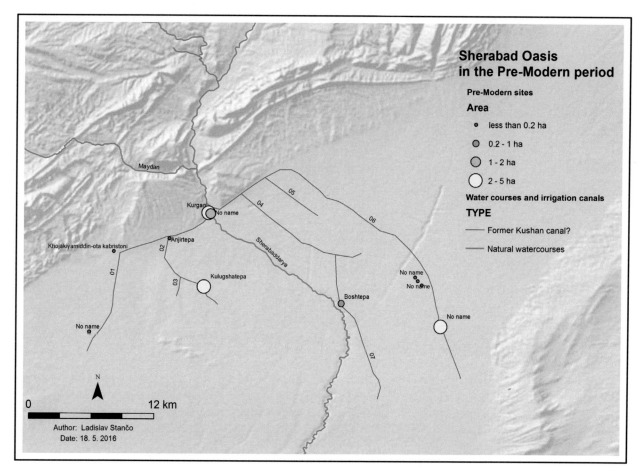

Fig. 5.14 Sherabad Oasis in the Pre-Modern period, map by author.

find one of clues for understanding of the dramatic change in the settlement pattern in the lowlands: part of population may have moved up into the steppe area.

represents important point of Southern Bukhara, because through it or past it, pass the roads to Eastern Bukhara. Moreover, it is situated close to the Afghan border, where the ferry over the Amu Darya is situated (Chushka-Guzar and Pata-Gissar). Besides, it represents important trading post. It is quite large, having a large bazaar, shops, inevitable fort that belong to beg. Judging from the remains of the structures and preserved moats, this fort had great importance in its time. ... What is bad about Sherabad, this is absence of good water; water of the small river that divides

Sherabad into two halves, has salty taste, and is suitable neither for tea, nor for drinking. ... Next day (August 28th) we visited the beg of Sherabad (Biy Mirza Jalyal') ..." (Lipskiy 1902, 310).

Besides the centre in Sherabad and its fort at Kafir Kala, several settlements existed in the oasis in 17th–19th c., among them Kulugshatepa, Boshtepa, Anjirtepa and No name *tepa* in the southeastern margin. The cumulative sum of the sites' surface in the Pre-modern period is 120,073 sq. m, which is less than the surface of one single Kushan centre of Jandavlattepa.

Fig. 5.15 Sherabad beg and his entourage in 1896, photo by Barscewski, from the archive of Igor Strojecki.

5.10 Sherabad Oasis nowadays

To analyse the current settlement pattern of the Sherabad Oasis is not our primary concern. We have, however, to present here some data relevant to the main topic, i.e., to historical settlements, especially dynamic of changes of the Sherabad Oasis landscape during the last century that affects greatly state of preservation of the archaeological sites.

The following table shows presence / absence of villages at various maps and satellite sources. For the dates of collection and compilation of individual maps, see above chapter 2.1.2. The settlements are sorted alphabetically. A number of modern settlements has

further been subdivided according to a simple key: individual organizing units used to get serial numbers and a nickname, such as "Sovkhoz imeni Lenina no. 7", with sovkhoz standing for a "state farm" in Russian. These basic units have usually several separate hamlets that received further serial number ("otd. No. XY" for a part of the whole sovkhoz settlement). The presence of the village / settlement in the given source is in the table indicated by either YES, or by the figure giving its surface area at the specific period.

The table brings forth some explanations of the processes that took place in the Sherabad plains in the sec-

| ID | Village | U.S. Army map txu-oclc-6559336-nj42-9 | CORONA | Map 100k--j42 | IKONOS |
		1930s	1970	1970s	2001
	Angor	Yes	Yes	Yes	Yes
33	Ak-kurgan	Yes	Yes	479	
47	Ak-zhar 2	No	Yes	109	370
	Ailli[103]	Yes		No	320 (other name)
17	Babatepa			32	98
	Besh-Kotan	Yes			
54	Betonzavod	No	No	86	
5	Bustan	No	Yes	69	
48	Bustan (NE)			228	367
	Chagatas (?)				
	Chukur-Kul'	Yes			
2	Dekhkanabad	No	Yes	77	
	Dekhkanabad (NE)			111	364
	Dzharty-Aryk	Yes			
	Gambyr	Yes			
9	Gegirdak			75	
	Gorin	Yes		228	
	Gilyam-Bob	Yes			
50	Guliston	No	Yes	883	1017
21	Istara 1	Yes	Yes	74	141
51	Istara 2	No	Yes	78	
53	Karmaki / Yangiyul'	No	Yes	192	506
	Khaudag				
34	Khodzha-Kiya			220	482
	Khurumsha	Yes			
	Khtay	Yes	No	No	No
55	Kiik	No	Yes	93	245
8	Kishlok-Bazar	Yes		101	
	Kuluksha	Yes			
32	Naubag	Yes		112	
22	Novbur			75	190
	PMK-52	No	No	Yes	
7	Rabotak	Yes[104]	No	174	352
67	Said-Abad	Yes		88	
25	Sarykh	No	Yes	71	
31	Seplan			112	
	Sherabad	Yes			
	Sokhta 1	Yes	No	No	No
	Sokhta 2	Yes	No	No	No
	Svkh. No. 6 Talimaran	No			
45	Svkh. No. 7 Im. Akhunbabaeva, odd. 1	No		166	

[103] Topo maps of Gen. shtab show in 1980s ruins of Ailli only.
[104] Rabotak was in 1930s marked on the spot of svkh. No. 8 Muradova.

ID	Village	U.S. Army map txu-oclc-6559336-nj42-9	CORONA	Map 100k--j42	IKONOS
		1930s	1970	1970s	2001
27	Svkh. No. 7 Im. Akhunbabaeva, odd. 2	No		114	
59	Svkh. No. 7 im. Akhunbabaeva, odd. 4			34	
44	Svkh. No. 7 Im. Akhunbabaeva, odd. 5	No		167	
38	Svkh. No. 7 Im. Akhunbabaeva, odd. 9	No		35	
	Svkh. Im. Frunze	No			
46	Sovkh. No. 6 Im. Lenina, otd. 7	No		198	
29	Sovkh. No. 6 Im. Lenina, otd. 8	No		28	
28	Sovkh. No. 6 Im. Lenina, otd. 10	No		42	
20	Svkh. No. 8 im. Muradova	Yes[105]	No	174	
14	Svkh. No. 9 im. Yusupova (N)	No[106]		49	167
4	Svkh. No. 9 im. Yusupova (S)	No[107]		92	320
68	Svkh. 10 im Kadirova	No		91	226
70	Svkh. 10 im Kadirova odd. 2	No		53	228
72	Svkh. Yangibad			352	849
30	Takiya	Yes		343	
	Talashkan	Yes			157
63	Tali-Maran	Yes		174	
71	Taskent	Yes		463	
3	Takuz			50	
10	Toragly			207	
	Yangiyul'	No	Yes	Yes	
1	Yakhtiyul'	Khurumsha	Yes	110	364
Ik54					128
Ik56					71
Ik57					21
Ik58					16
Ik60				no	350
Ik65					85
Ik66					59
Ik67					20
Ik68					22

ond half of the 20th c. It is clear that after the WW II the oasis undergone the greatest change in its history. Last remains of the ancient irrigation systems have been finally abandoned and the new project of the Great Sherabad Canal bringing water from the Surkhan Darya (Kumkurgan dam) has been started. Water is lifted through the water-pumps system about 28 m higher to reach the Sherabad plain. The construction was realised apparently in several steps causing gradual intensification of agricultural activities in the region.

[105] Marked as Rabotak.
[106] May be identical with older Sokhta (1).
[107] May be identical with older Sokhta (2).

In the first step, present-day Kizirik District has been provided with two main branches of water canal during the 1960s. As we can see, the old maps based on the field data collected in the 1930s (**Fig. 5.16**) show large area of bare land apparently of steppe character stretched between easternmost villages of the Sherabad settlement cluster on one hand, such as Rabotak and Istora, and Bandikhan on the other. Both CORONA images taken in late 1960s and in 1970s, and Soviet topographic maps compiled about ten years later bring evidence about rapid colonization process of this area. Open sources state that 14 new villages for agricultural labor force were founded (Khamraev et al. 2011). The fact that we do not possess detailed map of the northern Kizirik area before the WW II pose serious problem and obstacle for our understanding of the settlement pattern in this area. Exactly this territory seems to be drastically changed and only intensive surface survey may prove, if the virtual absence of the known archaeological sites in this part has been caused by the landscape changing processes, or it was really not settled in the past.

The second step prolonged the backbone Sherabad Canal to the town of Sherabad itself, changing completely centuries long practice of irrigation of the Sherabad Oasis from the – slightly salty – waters of the Sherabad Darya. This phase is well documented by maps of the "Gen. shtab" at the scale of 1:100,000. In the 1960s, only narrow strip of land at the foot of the mountain range, i.e., close to the course of the canal itself, has been intensively irrigated (as CORONA acquired in 1970 shows), while the rest of the eastern part and especially the western part of the oasis remained largely uncultivated. Note moreover that the original course of the canal was different between coordinates 37.741, 67.136 and 37.719, 67.058: the original canal was situated ca. 500 m to the south of the present one. There are some traces of this original canal still to be seen in the landscape and in the IKONOS satellite imagery, especially around Babatepa.

The third step brought the Great Sherabad Canal to the western part of the Sherabad Oasis, following the mountain range foot down to the south-west. As was dealt with above in the chapter 2.1.2, we have the sheet of 100k--j42-086 at our disposal, which shows the state of affairs after the building of southern Amu-Zang Canal (finished in 1973 according to online sources), but at the same time shortly before the construction of the Great Sherabad Canal. This event took place in late 1970s; hence, the sheet

200k--j42-19 from early 1980s contains the complete course of the canal already, as well as new settlements dispersed down the plain under the canal. The former map contains a number of features that we consider remains of ancient settlements (tepas) that are absent ten years later: the decade appears to have been disastrous to smaller monuments originally scattered over the steppe.

Digitized polygons based on the maps and satellite images (**Fig. 5.17** and **5.18**) allow us to compute basic statistics of the landscape and its dynamics. These attest clearly the rapid growth of the built-up areas throughout the plains. In 1970s, the surface of the villages in the Sherabad plains (with the Amu-Zang Canal as the southern border and the Big Sherabad Canal as the north one) covered area of 108 sq. km (or 10,904 ha) in 73 units.[108] The IKONOS image, which is about 30 years later (**Fig. 5.19** and **5.20**), shows the built-up areas of 193 sq. km (or 19,539 ha) in 119 units, it means growth of 78%! Paradoxically, the construction of the large water bringing system allowed for the expansion of cultivated areas that in its turn led to the rapid population growth associated with the expansion of built-up areas, covering the same valuable farmland.

These figures are quite striking and may sound even alarming concerning population growth, capacities of regional water sources necessary for both cotton fields' irrigation and covering of needs of the people living around. The consequences for archaeology and heritage protection are no less hazardous. According to the census in 2004, 25.2 thousand people lived in the town of Sherabad itself, while in the entire district (including piedmont steppe zone with Pashkhurt and other large villages) lived 134.7 thousand people. In Kizirik District lived in 2004 ca. 79.7 thousand people, among them 13.7 thousands in district centre Sariq.[109] These figures describe the same situation that has been captured by IKONOS imagery in 2001. In contrast, Karmysheva, who collected her ethnographic data in 1960s, states that in the region of the middle reaches of the Sherabad Darya, covering according to her 1,041 sq. km lived at that time 9.285 people in 21 settlements (Karmysheva 1976, 30–31, tab. 1).[110] We learn, moreover, that on the territory of the Sherabad Beg – including Termez and Jarkurgan – lived 1,108 Tajiks, 23,255 Uzbeks (78.7%), 4,165 Turkmens, 132 Arabs, 920 others (Karmysheva 1976, 32, tab. 2). Recent data claim that Uzbeks form as much as 95.6% of the Sherabad District inhabitants.

---

[108] With a unit, we mean either town, village, or individual part of a *sovkhoz*.

[109] Uzbek Wikipedia citing the same source gives similar, but not identical figures for Kizirik District: People, mainly ethnic Uzbeks, Tajiks, Turkmen, Tatar, Russian and other ethnic groups live there. The average population density of 1 sq. km is 236.4. The population of the town (Sariq) reaches 9.3 thousand people, and population living in countryside reaches 68.7 thousand people (2004).

[110] Note that in the upper Sherabad valley lived at the same time 18,034 people, i.e., twice the number of the inhabitants of the Sherabad plain (Karmysheva 1976, 30–31).

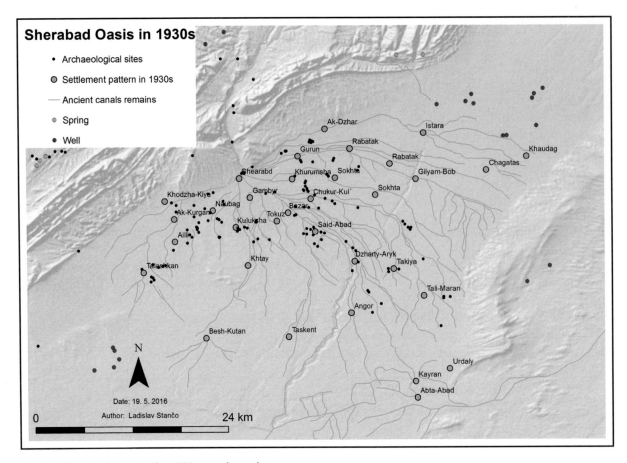

Fig. 5.16 Sherabad Oasis in the 1930s, map by author.

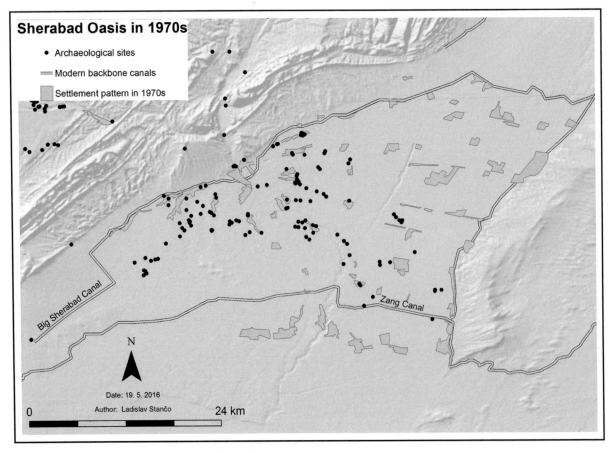

Fig. 5.17 Sherabad Oasis in the 1970s, map by author.

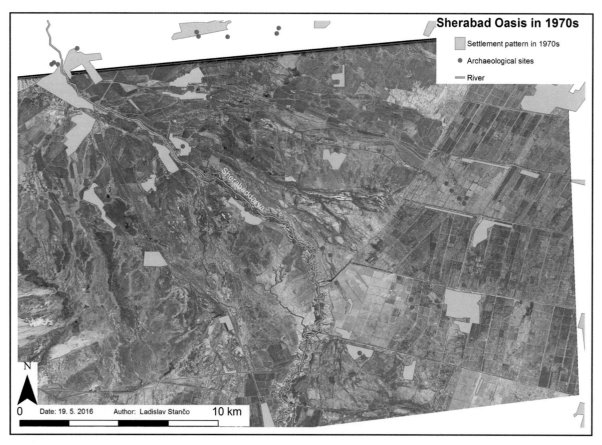

Fig. 5.18 Sherabad Oasis in the 1970s (detail with CORONA image underlay), map by author.

Fig. 5.19 Sherabad Oasis nowadays, map by author.

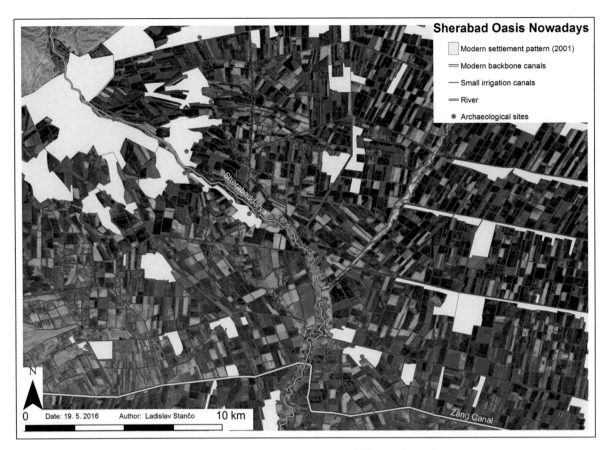

Fig. 5.20 Sherabad Oasis nowadays (detail with IKONOS imagery underlay), map by author.

6. Pottery from the extensive surface survey

M. Kobierská

6.1 Structure and description of the catalogue
Acquisition of the examined pottery assemblage

During the field survey of the Czech-Uzbekistani team in the Sherabad Oasis (2008–2010) 1,025 fragments of diagnostic pottery and small finds were collected from 54 sites, mostly *tepas*. Pottery, with 1,007 fragments, forms the main body of all the finds, with only few other pieces of small terracotta finds (seven figurines, seven tokens, two lamps and two beads). As the field survey was focused on chronological classification of the individual sites, predominantly the diagnostic fragments were collected, producing a high number of vessels rims – generally considered to be the most typologically and chronologically significant fragments – however pottery bases, body decorations or fragments with characteristic body treatment were collected as well.

The material processing

The pottery finds were being processed during each of the successive field seasons, proving to be an effective way of having work done, however, in retrospective it created difficulties with the uniformity of the gained data. The illustrations of diagnostic fragments as well as their photo documentation were undertaken during the three seasons by five different students of different school of data recording.[111] In result, the drawings, photographs, as well as the physical description of each shard, differs.

My task was to create unified and comprehensible study out of these heterogenous data, which would summarise the finds and their description into understandable table. Most of the data was possible to recover, however if they were not available from the first hand, or they were somehow unclear, I did not include them into the catalogue, simply not to provide false set of information.

Some of the shards were preliminary identified and classed already in the field by Shapulat Shaydullaev and Tokhtash Annaev, respected authorities on the material studies at the examined area. Their identifi-cations are also taken into account in the catalogue. Further parallels were sought in the abundant literature. Not all the shards were significant enough to be classed into established typologies, however, they are presented here as well to create complete picture. Perhaps our readers will recognize some of the material and see the links we did not succeed to find.

The catalogue division is based on the material from individual archaeological sites, with a list of the drawings and description of each of the sherds. Summary table of the proposed chronology of the individual sites based on the presented pottery follows each of the catalogue site entry.

Characteristics and quantification

The 2008–2011 Sherabad Oasis field survey assemblage consists of 1,025 pieces of diagnostic pottery fragments in total. By the term 'diagnostic' following terms are understood:

- significant fragments of vessels' rims and bases, as well as body fragments with surface treatment characteristic for specific period
- vessels' handles and their fragments
- fragments featuring decoration and/or extraordinary component (*e.g.*, a knob, an appliqué, *etc.*)
- terracotta lamps and their fragments
- 'tokens' and their fragments
- terracotta statuettes and their fragments
- terracotta beads and their fragments

Only eight items (less than 1%) from all the assemblage can be assessed as vessels whereof the whole profile is known. The rest of the set consists of more or less fragmentary vessels' pieces, which were – for sake of further evaluation and statistics – divided into groups. By far the greatest of them composes of rim fragments (64% of all items). Partial vessels' reconstruction was possible in 695 cases (*i.e.*, 68% of all items), when the vessels' base or rim diameter was conjecturable.

---

[111] Petra Belaňová, Věra Doležálková, Tereza Včelicová (Machačíková), Martin Odler and Alisher Shaydullaev.

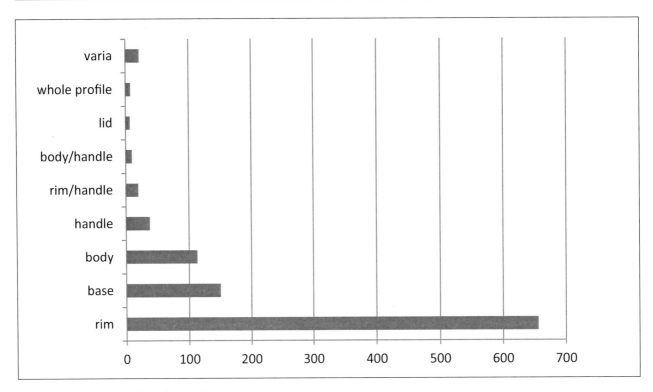

Diagram of body parts of the diagnostic pottery

The amount of items pertaining to a respective site varies considerably. A site with the highest number of documented potsherds (i.e., site 5) produced 60 diagnostic pieces. Eleven sites, on the other hand, are represented by only a single diagnostic item. Needless to say, the factor of frequency substantially affects the potency to plausibly estimate a site's dating. However, the average rate of ten items per site represents a rather convenient sample for re-examining.

Catalogue: notes and methods

The whole work follows a consistent scheme of reference to individual items: every individual item was assigned by a unique number (in Arabic figure). Item's order respects its pertinence to a site: sites were processed in a way that they form an ascending sequence (from 1 to 161).[112] Also within the individual sites, firm rules of succession were set: the respect of fraction characteristics is taken into account. Fractions' rate is sequenced as follows: whole profile – rim fragment – body fragment – handle – base fragment. In case an item is a combination of several fractions (e.g., rim fragment with a handle), it is assigned under the fraction of the higher rank. The sequence within the fractions' clusters was randomly chosen and usually reflects an order given in the primary documentation, if available.

Verbal definition as provided by the primary documentation data reflects the objective condition of the primary documentation. The physique form of the data, however, was slightly modified so that it follows a given integrating pattern. All dimensions are stated in meters.

Due to catalogue items voluminosity and repeatability, abbreviations are amply exerted. The complete list of abbreviations can be found at the outset of the catalogue. For better comprehensibility, abbreviations are marked in italics in the text.

There are four fabric quality categories sporadically distributed within the primary data: *Fine Ware* (FW), *Common Ware* (CW), *Kitchen Ware* (KW) and *Pithos* (P).[113] However, the data that has arisen from the primary examination are available for only 256 items, *i.e.,* for 25% of whole the set. Additionally, information about a presence of a red slip (RS) is given.

In order to simplify the concept and unify chronologically contemporary items, a simplified chronological scheme based on historical periods was applied (see Tab. below). Within the typological entries, period abbreviations are used extensively within the estimates.

As for the plates with drawings, all the items are displayed in identical scale 1:2.

---

[112] With an exception of the *miscellanea*, which are treated separately regardless of the site order.
[113] For further information on Sherabad wares' definition, see *e.g.,* Včelicová 2015, 26–29.

LIST OF CATALOGUE ABBREVIATIONS

(a) Measurements

bd	base diameter	ht	height	pth	preserved thickness
d	diameter	l	length	rd	rim diameter
est	estimated	max	maximum	th	thickness
ext	extant	pht	preserved height	w	width

(b) Descriptive (Form)

comp	complete	hdl	handle	pt	part(s)
ext	extant	hdld	handled	sec	section
fr	fragment	horiz	horizontal	spt	spout
frag	fragmentary	incmp	incomplete	vert	vertical
frr	fragments	p	preserved	vsl	vessel

(c) Compression Ridges (CR)

HM	hand made	smt	smooth	unbrn	unburnished
in	inner	sl	slip	WM	wheel made
out	outer	surf	surface(s)	WR	wheel-ridges
RS	red slip(ped)	TC	terracotta		

(d) Descriptive (Decoration)

burn	burnished	inc	incised	rng	running
crvl	curvilinear	lin	linear	rsd	residue(s)
dec	decorated / decoration	mon	monochrome	rsvd	reserved
eng	engobe	out	outer	undec	undecorated
gl	glaze / glazed	pol	polished		
in	inner	pnt	painted		

(a) Other

SSe   preliminarily datation estimate by Shapulat Shaydullaev

(b) Chronological scheme

Abbr.	PERIOD	ABSOLUTE CHRONOLOGY
PNE	Paleolithic – Neolithic – Early and Middle Bronze Age	2000 BC and earlier
LBA	Late Bronze Age	2000 BC–1500 BC
EIA	Early Iron Age	1500 BC–330 BC
HEL	Hellenistic period	330 BC–140 BC
TRA	Transitional phase	140 BC–0
KUS	Kushan	0–230 AD
LKU	Late Kushan and Kushano-Sassanian	230 AD–400 AD
EME	Early Medieval Age	400 AD–800 AD
HME	High Medieval Age = Pre-Mongol period	800 AD–1200 AD
LME	Late Medieval Age	1200 AD–1700 AD
PMO	Pre-modern	1700 AD–1920 AD

6.2 Catalogue of pottery from the extensive surface survey

SITE 1 (Jandavlattepa)[114]

1   Body *fr. Rd* ?, *pht* 0.045. *Rng* coal-black *sl, out surf rng dec:* skewed grid square motif. *SSe* EIA / HEL / TRA / KUS / LKU.

2   Body *fr. Rd* ?, *ext ht* 0.062. Ochre/brown fabric, yellowish *sl* on *out surf. SSe* EIA / HEL / TRA / KUS / LKU.

3   Body *fr. Rd* ?, *ext ht* 0.031. *Surf* ochre/brown. *Rsd* of coal on fracture. *SSe* EIA / HEL / TRA / KUS / LKU.

4   *Comp* base and *pt* of body. *Bd* 0.11, *ext ht* 0.042. Orange/brownish fabric, yellowish *sl* on *out surf, inc horiz lin dec* on *out surf. SSe* EIA / HEL / TRA / KUS / LKU.

Object #	PNE	LBA	EIA	HEL	TRA	KUS	LKU	EME	HME	LME	PMO
1			✓	✓	✓	✓	✓				
2			✓	✓	✓	✓	✓				
3			✓	✓	✓	✓	✓				
4			✓	✓	✓	✓	✓				

SITE 2 (Boshtepa)

5   Rim *fr. Rd* 0.09, *ext ht* 0.041. Brick-red fabric, *rsd* of *RS. CW.*

6   Rim *fr. Rd* 0.13, *ext ht* 0.038. Core and *surf* orange, *RS. CW.* Typological parallels R153 (Maxwell-Jones 2015). Period KUS / LKU. *SSe* 1ˢᵗ–4ᵗʰ c. AD.

7   *Hdl* and rim *fr. Rd* 0.14, *pht* 0.144. Yellow fabric core with orange margins, orange/yellow *surf, inc horiz lin dec* on *out surf.* Period PMO. *SSe* 19ᵗʰ c. AD.

8   Rim *fr. Rd* 0.2, *ext ht* 0.05. Brick-red fabric, ochre *eng* on *out surf.*

9   Rim *fr. Rd* 0.04, *ext ht* 0.016. Brick-red fabric, ochre *eng* on *surf.*

10   Rim *fr. Rd* 0.2, *ext ht* 0.05. Orange fabric, orange *eng* on *out surf,* strip of brown *sl* on *in surf.*

11   Rim *fr. Rd* 0.27, *ext ht* 0.035. Yellow/brown fabric, ochre *eng* on *surf.* Period LKU. *SSe* 3ʳᵈ and 4ᵗʰ c. AD.

12   Rim *fr. Rd* 0.36, *ext ht* 0.078. Orange/brick-red fabric, ochre *eng* on *out surf,* inclusion size up to 0.005. Typological parallels R4 (Maxwell-Jones 2015). Period EIA / HEL / LME / PMO, cf. Tušlová 2012b, tb. 11:6.

13   Rim *fr. Rd* 0.3, *ext ht* 0.141. Brick-red fabric, greenish/ochre *eng* on *surf.* Pink, ochre and brown stains on *in surf.* Typological parallels R29 (Maxwell-Jones 2015). Period LKU.

14   Rim *fr. Rd* 0.38, *ext ht* 0.081. Ochre fabric with brick-red margins, brick-red *surf.* Period HEL / TRA / LKU, cf. Zavyalov 2008.

15   Body *fr. Pht* 0.065. Rather deep comb *dec* on whole *surf,* pale brown fabric, *out surf* pale brown to orange/yellow.

16   Body *fr. Pht* 0.038. Fabric description identical to [15].

17   Body *fr* with *hdl. Pht* 0.078. Dark red/brown fabric, brownish to red *out surf, WR.*

18   Body *fr. Pht* 0.034. Brown fabric, concentric circles of lustrous brown, green and yellow *gl.*

19   Body *fr. Pht* 0.046. Orange/brown fabric, *in surf* yellow/ochre; yellow and white floral *sl* in *out surf.*

20   Body *fr. Pht* 0.044. Red fabric; *in surf* red and grey; *out surf* yellow and white *sl* and indistinctive chisel pattern.

21   Body *fr* of unsure orientation. *Pht* 0.108. Black fabric with grey stains; *out surf* red with grey stains; Plastic *rng dec.*

22   Body *fr. Pht* 0.037. Brown fabric; lustrous *gl* on *surf.*

23   Body *fr. Pht* 0.056. Brick-red fabric, core slightly paler.

---

[115] The site of Jandavlettepa was included simply for sake of completeness. It was, however, dealt with in detail in special publications. See, e.g., catalogue entry no. 1 in chapter 4.2 – Jandavlattepa.

24 Body *fr. Pht* 0.026. Fabric description identical to [23].

25 Body *fr. Pht* 0.043. Pale brown fabric; *out surf* pale brown to orange/yellow; rather deep comb *dec* on whole *surf.*

26 Body *fr. Pht* 0.033. For fabric description see [25].

27 Body *fr. Pht* 0.029. For fabric description see [25].

28 Body *fr. Pht* 0.032. For fabric description see [25].

29 Body *fr. Pht* 0.03. Orange fabric, *out surf* yellow/white with yellow *sl* and *crvl* comb *dec.*

30 Body *fr. Pht* 0.034. Brown fabric, yellowish *surf,* floral *dec* on *out surf.*

31 Body *fr. Pht* 0.096. Pale brown fabric, *out surf* pale brown to orange/yellow; occasional comb *dec* (grid).

32 Body *fr* with *hdl pt. Pht* 0.132. Yellow fabric with red margins, *in surf* red and grainy; orange *eng* on *out surf;* skewed grid *dec. SSe* PMO.

33 Body *fr. Pht* 0.059. Orange/red fabric, *in surf* half orange, half brown; shallow floral *dec.*

34 *Hdl fr. W* 0.054 × 0.023. Ochre to orange fabric; yellowish *sl.*

35 *Hdl fr. W* 0.055 × 0.02. For fabric description see [34].

36 *Hdl fr. W* 0.03 × 0.012. Brick-red fabric; *rsd* of ochre *eng. SSe* EIA / HEL / TRA / KUS / LKU.

37 *Hdl fr. W* 0.026 × 0.011. Carmine fabric. *SSe* EIA / HEL / TRA / KUS / LKU.

38 Base *fr. Bd* 0.09, *ext ht* 0.079. Dark red fabric, ochre *eng* on *out surf.*

Object #	PNE	LBA	EIA	HEL	TRA	KUS	LKU	EME	HME	LME	PMO
6						✓	✓				
7											✓
11							✓				
12			✓	✓						✓	✓
13							✓				
14				✓	✓		✓				
32											✓
36			✓	✓	✓	✓	✓				
37			✓	✓	✓	✓	✓				

SITE 3 (Koshtepa I)

39 Rim *fr. Rd* 0.08, *ext ht* 0.025. Brick-red fabric, ochre *eng* on *out surf.*

40 Rim *fr. Rd* 0.07, *ext ht* 0.037. Orange fabric, brick red on *surf.*

41 Rim *fr. Rd* 0.05, *ext ht* 0.046. Brick-red fabric; inclusion size up to 0.001.

42 Rim *fr. Rd* 0.21, *ext ht* 0.06. Brown fabric; ocre/green *eng* on *out surf;* inclusion size up to 0.001.

43 Rim *fr. Rd* 0.17, *ext ht* 0.076. Brown fabric and *out surf,* yellow/brown *in surf.*

44 Rim *fr. Rd* 0.33, *ext ht* 0.058. Brick-red fabric, ocre/greenish *eng* on *out surf.*

SITE 4 (Kulugshatepa)

45 Rim *fr. Rd* ?, *ext ht* 0.018. Very fine, pale brown/pinkish fabric, *RS.* Typological parallels R143/144 (Maxwell-Jones 2015); R212 (Puschnigg 2006); Bowls gr. 3A (5) (Včelicová 2015); Chasha 2 (Zavyalov 2008). Period KUS / LKU. *SSe* 1ˢᵗ–3ʳᵈ c. AD.

46 Rim *fr. Rd* ?, *ext ht* 0.028. Pale brown fabric, light blue *gl.* Typological parallels R125 (Maxwell-Jones 2015) (?). Period HEL / TRA.

47 Rim *fr. Rd* ?, *ext ht* 0.022. Pale brown fabric, blue/green *gl.* Period LKU, cf. Zavyalov 2008.

48 Rim *fr. Rd* ?, *ext ht* 0.029. Fine, pale brown fabric; coarse light blue *sl.* Period LKU, cf. Zavyalov 2008.

49 Rim *fr. Rd* 0.08, *ext ht* 0.025. Fine, pale brown fabric, *rsd* of dark brown *sl.*

50 Rim *fr. Rd* 0.065, *ext ht* 0.033. Coarse yellow/brown fabric, pale brown on fracture.

51 Rim *fr. Rd* 0.14, *ext ht* 0.026. Orange/brown fabric, brown and white *surf.* Typological parallels R4 (Maxwell-Jones 2015). Period HEL / TRA.

52 Rim *fr. Rd* 0.19, *ext ht* 0.028. Fine pale brown fabric.

53 Rim *fr. Rd* 0.13, *ext ht* 0.021. Orange/red fabric.

54 Rim *fr. Rd* 0.17, *ext ht* 0.019. Fine pale brown fabric; fine inclusions.

55 Rim *fr. Rd* ?, *ext ht* 0.018. Coarse brown/pale brown fabric.

56 Rim *fr. Rd* ?, *ext ht* 0.043. Orange fabric, pale brown core.

57 Rim *fr. Rd* 0.05, *ext ht* 0.053. Orange/brown fabric, brown and white *surf.*

58 Rim *fr. Rd* 0.22, *ext ht* 0.032. Red fabric, light brown *surf.* Typological parallels R81 (Puschnigg 2006); khozyaystvennye tagora 2g (Zavyalov 2008). Period LKU.

59 Rim *fr. Rd* 0.23, *ext ht* 0.032. Orange/brown fabric, dark *RS.* Period LKU, cf. Zavyalov 2008.

60 Rim *fr. Rd* 0.26, *ext ht* 0.021. Fine orange fabric, *RS.* Typological parallels R143/144 (Maxwell-Jones 2015); R212 (Puschnigg 2006); Bowls gr. 3A (5)

(Včelicová 2015); Chasha 2 (Zavyalov 2008). Period KUS / LKU. *SSe* 1ˢᵗ–3ʳᵈ c. AD.

61 Rim *fr. Rd* 0.27, *ext ht* 0.041. Fine, red fabric, pale yellow/brown *out surf.*

62 Rim *fr. Rd* 0.34, *ext ht* 0.038. Fine, pale orange/brown fabric. Typological parallels R129 (Maxwell-Jones 2015); *khozyaystvennye tagora* 1a (Zavyalov 2008); *tagora* (17) (Včelicová 2015). Period KUS / LKU. *SSe* 4ᵗʰ c. AD.

63 Rim *fr. Rd* 0.36, *ext ht* 0.021. Fine, pale yellow/brown fabric, light blue *gl.*

64 Rim *fr. Rd* 0.34, *ext ht* 0.046. Orange/red fabric, brown/grey *surf.* Typological parallels khumtscha 2 (Zavyalov 2008). Period LKU, cf. Tušlová 2012b, tb. 10:4.

65 Rim *fr. Rd* 0.2, *ext ht* 0.037. Yellow/brown fabric, red/pinkish on fracture.

66 Base *fr. Bd* 0.04, *ext ht* 0.031. Fine, grey fabric, black *sl* on *out surf.*

Object #	PNE	LBA	EIA	HEL	TRA	KUS	LKU	EME	HME	LME	PMO
45						✓	✓				
46				✓	✓						
47											✓
48											✓
51				✓	✓						
58							✓				
59							✓				
60						✓	✓				
62						✓	✓				
64							✓				

SITE 5 (Aktepa)

67 Rim *fr. Rd* 0.21, *ext ht* 0.028. Fine, pale orange fabric, originally *RS* (*in surf* and upper section of *out surf*), *pol dec* on *in surf.* Typological parallels R143/144 (Maxwell-Jones 2015); R212 (Puschnigg 2006); Bowls gr. 3A (5) (Včelicová 2015); Chasha 2 (Zavyalov 2008). Period KUS / LKU. *SSe* 1ˢᵗ–3ʳᵈ c. AD.

68 Rim *fr. Rd* 0.19, *ext ht* 0.019. Typological parallels R143/144 (Maxwell-Jones 2015); R212 (Puschnigg 2006); Bowls gr. 3A (5) (Včelicová 2015); Chasha 2 (Zavyalov 2008). Period KUS / LKU. *SSe* 1ˢᵗ–3ʳᵈ c. AD.

69 Rim *fr. Rd* 0.045, *ext ht* 0.028. Orange fabric, *rsd* of orange *sl* on *out surf.*

70 Rim *fr. Rd* 0.06, *ext ht* 0.018. Fine, pale orange fabric, yellowish *sl.*

71 Rim *fr. Rd* 0.09, *ext ht* 0.031. Fine, orange fabric, *rsd* of *RS* on *in surf*, yellowish *sl* on *out surf.*

72 Rim *fr. Rd* 0.21–0.22, *ext ht* 0.029. Orange/brown fabric, *rsd* of *RS* on *out surf.*

73 Rim *fr. Rd* 0.22, *ext ht* 0.026. Pale orange fabric; white/yellow *sl* on *out surf.*

74 Rim *fr. Rd* 0.22, *ext ht* 0.016. Fine, orange/grey fabric, *RS* on *in surf*, red/brownish *sl* on *out surf.*

75 Rim *fr. Rd* 0.12, *ext ht* 0.019.

76 Rim *fr. Rd* ?, *ext ht* 0.04. Disrupted surf, beige/orange fabric, paler on *surf.*

77 Rim *fr. Rd* 0.06, *ext ht* 0.029. Dark grey fabric.

78 Rim *fr. Rd* 0.28, *ext ht* 0.025. Orange fabric, yellowish *sl* on *in surf*, whitish *sl* on *out surf.* Typological parallels R129 (Maxwell-Jones 2015); Tagora (17) (Včelicová 2015). Period KUS / LKU. *SSe* 3ʳᵈ c. AD.

79 Rim *fr. Rd* 0.07, *ext ht* 0.028. Pale orange fabric, *rsd* of brown *sl.*

80 Rim *fr. Rd* 0.25, *ext ht* 0.053. Brownish/orangish fabric, white/yellow *sl* on *out surf.* Period KUS / LKU. *SSe* 3rd c. AD.

81 Rim *fr. Rd* 0.05, *ext ht* 0.051. Fine, pale orange fabric, *rds* of *RS*/brown *sl.*

82 Rim *fr. Rd* 0.17, *ext ht* 0.038. Brown/ochre fabric. Typological parallels R22 (Maxwell-Jones 2015); R194 (Puschnigg 2006). Period HEL / TRA / KUS / LKU. *SSe* 3rd c. AD.

83 Rim *fr. Rd* 0.18, *ext ht* 0.037. Orange fabric. Period KUS / LKU. *SSe* 3rd c. AD.

84 Rim *fr. Rd* 0.2, *ext ht* 0.052. Brick red fabric, black *sl* on *out surf.* Rim *fr. Rd* 0.18, *ext ht* 0.037. Orange fabric. Period KUS / LKU. *SSe* 3rd c. AD.

85 Rim *fr. Rd* 0.08, *ext ht* 0.041.

86 Rim *fr. Rd* 0.07, *ext ht* 0.045. Brick red fabric. Typological parallels R98 (Maxwell-Jones 2015); R165 (Puschnigg 2006). Period KUS / LKU. *SSe* 3rd c. AD.

87 Rim *fr. Rd* 0.08, *ext ht* 0.057. Orange/red fabric, *rds* of *RS* on *out surf.* Typological parallels R198 (Puschnigg 2006). Period KUS / LKU. *SSe* 3rd c. AD.

88 Rim *fr. Rd* 0.12, *ext ht* 0.025. Grey fabric, dark brick red *surf.* Cf.

89 Rim *fr. Rd* 0.11, *ext ht* 0.03. Beige fabric, orange *in surf.* Typological parallels R6 (Maxwell-Jones 2015). Period TRA / KUS / LKU. *SSe* 3rd c. AD.

90 Rim *fr. Rd* 0.33, *ext ht* 0.066. Orange fabric, yellow/white *sl* on *out surf.* Typological parallels R63 (Maxwell-Jones 2015). Period EIA / HEL / KUS / LKU, cf. Tušlová 2012b, tb. 14:1. *SSe* 3rd c. AD.

91 Rim *fr. Rd* 0.29, *ext ht* 0.073. Orange fabric, yellow *sl* on *out surf.* Typological parallels R56 (Maxwell-Jones 2015). Period HEL / TRA /KUS / LKU. *SSe* 3rd c. AD.

92 Rim *fr. Rd* 0.13, *ext ht* 0.025. Orange fabric, pale orange *surf.*

93 Rim *fr. Rd* 0.16, *ext ht* 0.016. Orange fabric, *RS* on both *surf. FW.*

94 Rim *fr. Rd* 0.1, *ext ht* 0.019. Orange/grey fabric, grey *surf.* Typological parallels R150 (Puschnigg 2006). Period KUS / LKU. *SSe* 3rd c. AD.

95 Rim *fr. Rd* 0.18, *ext ht* 0.025. Pale orange fabric; dark orange *sl* on *in* and partially *out surf*; orangish/whitish slip on *out surf.*

96 Rim *fr. Rd* 0.15, *ext ht* 0.021. Orange fabric; *rsd* of dark orange *sl.* Period LKU. *SSe* 3rd c. AD.

97 Rim *fr. Rd* 0.17, *ext ht* 0.027. Orange/brown fabric; yellowish *sl* on *out surf*; perforated. Typological parallels R39 (Puschnigg 2006)(?). Period KUS / LKU. *SSe* 3rd c. AD.

98 Rim *fr. Rd* 0.11, *ext ht* 0.097. Orange fabric; ochre/yellowish *surf.* Period HME. *SSe* 12th c. AD.

99 Rim *fr. Rd* 0.11, *ext ht* 0.061. Orange fabric; ochre/yellowish *surf.* Period HME. *SSe* 12th c. AD.

100 Rim *fr. Rd* 0.08, *ext ht* 0.075. Orange fabric. Period HME. *SSe* 12th c. AD.

101 Rim *fr. Rd* 0.17, *ext ht* 0.021. Orange fabric and *surf.*

102 Rim *fr. Rd* 0.18, *ext ht* 0.022. Brown/orange fabric; white/yellow *surf.*

103 Rim *fr. Rd* 0.09, *ext ht* 0.027. Pale orange/brown fabric; *rsd* of RS.

104 Rim *fr. Rd* 0.1, *ext ht* 0.027. Pale orange fabric and *surf.* Typological parallels Ref4 (Puschnigg 2006). Period KUS / LKU. *SSe* 3rd c. AD.

105 Rim *fr. Rd* 0.095, *ext ht* 0.023. Orange fabric; brownish *surf*, RS. Typological parallels R17 (Puschnigg 2006). Period LKU. *SSe* 3rd c. AD.

106 Rim *fr. Rd* 0.09, *ext ht* 0.026. Grey fabric; red/grey *surf.*

107 Rim *fr. Rd* 0.13, *ext ht* 0.029. Pale orange fabric; RS.

108 Rim *fr. Rd* 0.13, *ext ht* 0.03. Grey fabric; brick-red *in surf*; *out surf* grey with dark grey stripe below rim.

109 Rim *fr. Rd* 0.14, *ext ht* 0.029. Pale orange fabric. Typological parallels R83 (Puschnigg 2006). Period KUS / LKU. *SSe* 3rd c. AD.

110 Rim *fr. Rd* ?, *ext ht* 0.028. Pale orange fabric; brown *sl* on *in surf*; yellow/white *sl* on *out surf.*

111 Rim *fr. Rd* ?, *ext ht* 0.031. Beige/pale orange fabric; RS.

112 Rim *fr. Rd* ?, *ext ht* 0.029.

113 Hdl *fr. W* 0.018 × 0.013.

114 Body *fr. Pht* 0.079. Orange/pink fabric; yellowish *sl* and stains of runned-down brown *sl* on *out surf.*

115 Body *fr. Pht* 0.072. Orange/grey fabric; *in surf* grey to brown/orange; grey and *rsd* of black *sl* on *out surf. SSe* 12th c. AD.

116 Body *fr. Pht* 0.034. Beige/ochre fabric; pale brownish *sl* on *out surf. SSe* 12th c. AD.

117 Body *fr. Pht* 0.045. Orange/brown fabric; thin, dim orange *sl. SSe* 12th c. AD.

118 Base *fr. Bd* 0.05, *ext ht* 0.01. Orange fabric; pale orange *out surf* with *rsd* of RS.

119 Base *fr. Bd* 0.039, *ext ht* 0.008. Beige/ochre fabric.

120 Base *fr. Bd* 0.052, *ext ht* 0.021. Orange/brick-red fabric; *rsd* of orange *sl* on *in surf.*

121 Base *fr. Bd* 0.1, *ext ht* 0.025. Pale orange fabric; yellow *sl* on *out surf.*

122 Base *fr. Bd* 0.05, *ext ht* 0.022.

123 Base *fr. Bd* 0.09, *ext ht* 0.032.

124 Base *fr. Bd* 0.045, *ext ht* 0.019. Very fine, pale orange fabric; red *gl* with *pol* floral *dec* on *in surf.*

Object #	PNE	LBA	EIA	HEL	TRA	KUS	LKU	EME	HME	LME	PMO
67						✓	✓				
68						✓	✓				
78						✓	✓				
80						✓	✓				
82				✓	✓	✓	✓				
83						✓	✓				
84						✓	✓				
86						✓	✓				
87						✓	✓				
89					✓	✓	✓				
90			✓	✓		✓	✓				
91				✓	✓	✓	✓				
94						✓	✓				
96							✓				
97						✓	✓				
98									✓		
99									✓		
100									✓		
104						✓	✓				
105							✓				
109						✓	✓				
115									✓	✓	
116									✓	✓	
117									✓	✓	

SITE 6

125 Rim *fr. Rd* 0.165, *ext ht* 0.021. Corroded *in surf*; pink and red stains on *out surf. SSe* 12th–13th c. AD.

126 Body *fr. D* at bulge 0.08, *pht* 0.037. Brick-red fabric; ochre eng on surf.

127 Body *fr. Pht* 0.061. Brick-red fabric; ochre *eng* on *out surf. CW. SSe* 12th c. AD.

128 Body *fr. Pht* 0.074. For fabric description see [127]. *SSe* 12th c. AD.

129 *Hdl fr.* W 0.022 × 0.005. Orange fabric; ochre *eng* on *surf.*

130 Base *fr. Bd* 0.087, *ext ht* 0.011. Brick-red fabric; ochre *eng* on *out surf*; distinctive *WR*, roughing on base. *SSe* 12th–13th c. AD.

131 Base *fr. Bd* 0.12, *ext ht* 0.043. Brick-red/yellow fabric; creamy yellow *surf*; *HM* base. *CW/KW. SSe* 12th–13th c. AD.

132 Base *fr. Bd* 0.08, *ext ht* 0.041. Yellow fabric with brown spots; yellow *surf*; distinctive *WR*; impressed conch at the bottom. *SSe* 13th c. AD.

133 Base *fr. Bd* ?, *ext ht* 0.035. Brick-red/yellow fabric, *out surf* orange/brown. *SSe* 12th–13th c. AD.

Object #	PNE	LBA	EIA	HEL	TRA	KUS	LKU	EME	HME	LME	PMO
125									✓	✓	
127									✓	✓	
128									✓	✓	
130									✓	✓	
131									✓	✓	
132										✓	
133									✓	✓	

SITE 7 (Koshtepa II)

134 Rim *fr. Rd* 0.45, *ext ht* 0.135. Brown/yellow fabric; red *eng* on *out surf.* Typological parallels R81 (Puschnigg 2006); khazyaystvennye tagora 2g (Zavyalov 2008). Period LKU. *SSe* 4th c. AD.

135 Rim *fr. Rd* 0.12, *ext ht* 0.028. Brown fabric; ochre *surf*, *rsd* of *RS* on *in surf.* Typological parallels R157 (Maxwell-Jones 2015); R89 (Puschnigg 2006). Period TRA / KUS / LKU. *SSe* 4th c. AD.

136 Rim *fr. Rd* 0.08, *ext ht* 0.047. Brown fabric; ochre *eng* on *surf.* Period LKU. *SSe* 4th c. AD.

137 Rim *fr. Rd* 0.1, *ext ht* 0.035. Ochre fabric. Typological parallels R183 (Puschnigg 2006); *Chasha s peregribom* (Pindaev 1978). Period LKU. *SSe* 3rd and 4th c. AD.

138 Rim *fr. Rd* 0.4, *ext ht* 0.048. Orange fabric; ochre *eng* and *rsd* of *RS* on *surf.* Typological parallels R129 (Maxwell-Jones 2015); *khozyaystvennye tagora* 1a (Zavyalov 2008); *tagora* (17) (Včelicová 2015). Period KUS / LKU. *SSe* 4th c. AD.

Object #	PNE	LBA	EIA	HEL	TRA	KUS	LKU	EME	HME	LME	PMO
134							✓				
135					✓	✓	✓				
136				✓	✓	✓	✓	✓			
137							✓				
138							✓				

SITE 8 (Batyrabadtepa)

139 Rim *fr. Rd* 0.21, *ext ht* 0.057. Brown fabric; black *surf*; distinctive *WM.* Typological parallels R51 (Maxwell-Jones 2015). Period EIA / HEL / KUS / LKU. *SSe* KUS / LKU.

140 Rim *fr. Rd* 0.3, *ext ht* 0.03. Red-orange fabric. KUS / LKU.

141 Rim *fr. Rd* 0.34, *ext ht* 0.05. Orange fabric; *out surf* ochre/red. Typological parallels R12 (Maxwell-Jones 2015). Period LKU. *SSe* Kushan.

142 Rim *fr. Rd* 0.4, *ext ht* 0.133. Brick-red fabric; ochre, black and orange stains on *out surf.* Period LKU, cf. Zavyalov 2008.

143 Rim *fr. Rd* ?, *ext ht* 0.017. Brick-red fabric; ochre *eng* on both *surf. SSe* KUS / LKU.

144 Rim *fr. Rd* ?, *ext ht* 0.025. Orange fabric. *SSe* KUS / LKU.

145 Rim *fr. Rd* ?, *ext ht* 0.034. Brick-red fabric; ochre *eng* on *out surf*; *WR. SSe* KUS / LKU.

146 Rim *fr. Rd* 0.12, *ext ht* 0.015. Brick-red fabric. *SSe* KUS / LKU.

147 Rim *fr. Rd* 0.112, *ext ht* 0.027. Brick red fabric; ochre *eng* on *out surf.* Period KUS. *SSe* Kushan.

148 Rim *fr. Rd* 0.29, *ext ht* 0.042. Brick-red fabric; ochre *eng* of with *rsd* of *RS. SSe* KUS / LKU.

149 Rim *fr. Rd* 0.16, *ext ht* 0.027. Grey/black fabric; brick-red *surf. SSe* KUS / LKU.

150 Rim *fr. Rd* 0.08, *ext ht* 0.034. Brick-red fabric; ochre *eng* on *out surf. SSe* KUS / LKU.

151 *Hdl fr. W* 0.038 × 0.017. Brick-red fabric; ochre *eng* on both *surf. SSe* KUS / LKU.

152 *Hdl fr. W* 0.037 × 0.014. Orange fabric; ochre *eng* with *rsd* of *RS* on both *surf. SSe* KUS / LKU.

153 Body *fr. Pht* 0.062. Red fabric; *in surf* brown/red; *out surf* brown; inclusion size up to 0.002. *SSe* KUS / LKU.

154 Base *fr. Bd* 0.06, *ext ht* 0.008. Brick-red fabric; *out surf* ochre; *surf* sooted. *SSe* KUS / LKU.

155 Base *fr. Bd* 0.05, *ext ht* 0.021. Brick-red fabric; *WR. SSe* KUS / LKU.

156 Base *fr. Bd* 0.08, *ext ht* 0.018. Orange fabric; ochre *eng* on both *surf*, *WR. SSe* KUS / LKU.

Object #	PNE	LBA	EIA	HEL	TRA	KUS	LKU	EME	HME	LME	PMO
139			✓	✓		✓	✓				
140						✓	✓				
141							✓				
142							✓				
143						✓	✓				
144						✓	✓				
145						✓	✓				
146						✓	✓				
147						✓					
148						✓	✓				
149						✓	✓				
150						✓	✓				
151						✓	✓				
152						✓	✓				
153						✓	✓				
154						✓	✓				
155						✓	✓				
156						✓	✓				

SITE 9 (Khoja Qaptol Bobo)

157 Rim *fr. Rd* ?, *ext ht* 0.064. Coarse, dark grey fabric; beige, sporadically greenish on *surf*. Typological parallels R116 (Maxwell-Jones 2015). Period KUS / LKU. *SSe* 4th c. AD.

Object #	PNE	LBA	EIA	HEL	TRA	KUS	LKU	EME	HME	LME	PMO
157						✓	✓				

SITE 10 (Kattatepa)

158 *Compl vsl. Rd* 0.066, *ht* 0.052. *WR*; supposedly secondary used. Period LKU. *SSe* 3rd–4th c. AD.

159 Rim *fr. Rd* 0.08, *ext ht* 0.017. *SSe* LKU.

160 Rim *fr. Rd* 0.09, *ext ht* 0.054. Typological parallels R183 (Puschnigg 2006); *Chasha s peregribom* (Pindaev 1978). Period LKU. *SSe* 3rd and 4th c. AD.

161 Rim *fr. Rd* 0.1, *ext ht* 0.056. Period LKU. *SSe* 3rd–4th c. AD.

162 Rim *fr. Rd* 0.14, *ext ht* 0.034. Period LKU. *SSe* 3rd–4th c. AD.

163 Rim *fr. Rd* 0.09, *ext ht* 0.036. Black fabric; brown *surf*, *RS* on *surf*. Typological parallels R96 (Max-well-Jones 2015); R133 (Puschnigg 2006); *kuvshiny* IIa (Zavyalov 2008). Period LKU.

164 Rim *fr. Rd* 0.17, *ext ht* 0.057. Brick-red fabric; *RS* on *surf*. Period LKU. *SSe* 3rd–4th c. AD.

165 Rim *fr. Rd* 0.16, *ext ht* 0.046. *RS* on *surf*, *WR*.

166 Rim *fr. Rd* 0.08, *ext ht* 0.025. *RS* on *surf*. Period LKU. *SSe* 3rd–4th c. AD.

167 Rim *fr. Rd* 0.12, *ext ht* 0.024. Dark brown fabric; ochre *eng* on *out surf*. *SSe* 3rd–4th c. AD.

168 Rim *fr. Rd* 0.1, *ext ht* 0.021. *RS*; *WR*.

169 Rim *fr. Rd* 0.07, *ext ht* 0.023. *RS*. *SSe* 3rd–4th c. AD.

170 Rim *fr. Rd* 0.24, *ext ht* 0.042. Brick-red fabric. Period LKU. *SSe* 3ʳᵈ–4ᵗʰ c. AD.

171 Rim *fr. Rd* 0.25, *ext ht* 0.064. *RS*. Typological parallels *Tagora* (12) (Včelicová 2015).

172 Rim *fr. Rd* ?, *ext ht* 0.087. Brick-red *out surf; WR*. Period LKU. *SSe* 3rd and 4ᵗʰ c. AD.

173 Rim *fr. Rd* 0.4, *ext ht* 0.038. Brown *in surf.* Period LKU, cf. Zavyalov 2008).

174 Rim *fr. Rd* 0.34, *ext ht* 0.07. Typological parallels *khum* 1 (Zavyalov 2008). Period LKU / EME, cf. Tušlová 2012b, tb. 13:7.

175 Rim *fr. Rd* 0.3, *ext ht* 0.034.

176 Rim *fr. Rd* 0.22, *ext ht* 0.039. Brick-red fabric; ochre *eng* on *surf.* Period LKU. *SSe* 3ʳᵈ and 4ᵗʰ c. AD.

177 Rim *fr. Rd* 0.1, *ext ht* 0.046. *Rsd* of *RS; WR*.

178 Rim *fr. Rd* 0.16, *ext ht* 0.032. Brick-red fabric; *out surf* ochre; *rsd* of *RS* on *in surf.* Typological parallels R99 (Maxwell-Jones 2015); R198 (Puschnigg 2006). Period TRA / KUS / LKU. *SSe* 3ʳᵈ–4ᵗʰ c. AD.

179 Rim *fr. Rd* 0.15, *ext ht* 0.023. Brick-red fabric; ochre *eng* on both *surf; rsd* of *RS*. Period LKU. *SSe* 3ʳᵈ–4ᵗʰ c. AD.

180 Rim *fr. Rd* 0.18, *ext ht* 0.04. *RS*. Period LKU. *SSe* 3ʳᵈ–4ᵗʰ c. AD.

181 Body *fr. Pht* 0.11. *RS; WR*.

182 Body *fr. Pht* 0.086. Painted *dec* (red stripe). Period LKU. *SSe* 3ʳᵈ–4ᵗʰ c. AD.

183 Body and *hdl fr. Pht* 0.103. *RS*.

184 Base *fr. Bd* 0.06, *ext ht* 0.011. *RS; WR*.

185 Base *fr. Bd* 0.11, *ext ht* 0.032. *In surf* unpreserved.

Object #	PNE	LBA	EIA	HEL	TRA	KUS	LKU	EME	HME	LME	PMO
159						✓	✓				
160							✓				
161							✓				
162							✓				
163							✓				
164							✓				
165							✓				
166							✓				
167							✓				
169							✓				
170							✓				
172							✓				
173							✓				
174							✓	✓			
176							✓				
177							✓				
178					✓	✓	✓				
179							✓				
180							✓				
182							✓				

SITE 11

186 Rim *fr. Rd* 0.07, *ext ht* 0.045. Orange fabric; *in surf* yellow; dark red *eng* on *out surf; WR*. Typological parallels R91 (Maxwell-Jones 2015). Period LKU / EME.

187 Rim *fr. Rd* 0.1, *ext ht* 0.03. Orange fabric; *out surf* carmine red. Typological parallels R132 (Puschnigg 2006). Period KUS / LKU, cf. Tušlová 2012b, tb. 8:8. *SSe* 3ʳᵈ–4ᵗʰ c. AD.

188 Rim *fr. Rd* 0.1, *ext ht* 0.024. Brick-red fabric.

189 Rim *fr. Rd* 0.09, *ext ht* 0.015.

190 Rim *fr. Rd* 0.06, *ext ht* 0.028. Ochre fabric; black *eng* on *out surf;* inclusion size up to 0.0005; distinctive *RW*. Period KUS. *SSe* 1ˢᵗ c. AD.

191 Rim *fr. Rd* 0.18, *ext ht* 0.04. Brick-red fabric; ochre *eng* on *out surf.*

192 Rim *fr. Rd* 0.21, *ext ht* 0.035. Typological parallels R153 (Maxwell-Jones 2015). Period KUS / LKU. *SSe* 1ˢᵗ–4ᵗʰ c. AD.

Object #	PNE	LBA	EIA	HEL	TRA	KUS	LKU	EME	HME	LME	PMO
186							✓	✓			
187						✓	✓				
190						✓					
192						✓	✓				

SITE 12

193 Rim *fr. Rd* 0.12, *ext ht* 0.027. Fine, orange/reddish fabric.

194 Rim *fr. Rd* 0.17, *ext ht* 0.03. Fine, pale brown fabric.

195 Rim *fr. Rd* 0.15, *ext ht* 0.021. Brown fabric, darker on *in surf.*

196 Rim *fr. Rd* 0.15, *ext ht* 0.037. Brown poriferous fabric; greenish brown on *out surf.* Typological parallels R156 (Maxwell-Jones 2015). Period HEL / TRA.

197 Rim *fr. Rd* 0.19, *ext ht* 0.02. Fine, yellow/brown fabric, reddish on fracture.

198 Rim *fr. Rd* 0.14, *ext ht* 0.019. *Out surf* grey/greenish; *in surf* orange/brownish; tiny inclusions.

199 Rim *fr. Rd* 0.1, *ext ht* 0.017. Yellow/brownish fabric; *RS.* Period LKU. *SSe* 3rd and 4th c. AD.

200 Rim *fr. Rd* 0.25, *ext ht* 0.021. Red fabric, yellow/brownish on fracture. Typological parallels R127 (Maxwell-Jones 2015); R214 (Puschnigg 2006); *blyuda* 2 (Zavyalov 2008). Period LKU. *SSe* 4th c. AD.

201 Rim *fr. Rd* 0.24, *ext ht* 0.028. Dark red fabric; pale brown *surf*, tiny inclusions. Typological parallels R125 (Maxwell-Jones 2015); Fishplate (1) (Včelicová 2015). Period HEL / TRA.

202 Rim *fr. Rd* 0.25, *ext ht* 0.034. Reddish and yellow/brownish fabric. Period LKU, cf. Zavyalov 2008.

203 Rim *fr. Rd* 0.34, *ext ht* 0.051. Fine orange fabric; brown/yellow *sl* on *out surf*, *inc crvl dec* on *in surf.* Typological parallels R136 (Maxwell-Jones 2015); R13 (Puschnigg 2006). Period LKU.

204 Rim *fr. Rd* 0.03, *ext ht* 0.018. Grey fabric; tiny orange/reddish inclusions.

205 Rim *fr. Rd* ?, *ext ht* 0.028. Pinking/brown fabric; *out surf* yellow/brownish.

206 Rim *fr. Rd* 0.08, *ext ht* 0.03. Dark brown fabric; *out surf* pale brown; tiny inclusions.

207 Lid *fr* with *hdl. Max hdl d* 0.05, *ext ht* 0.028. Orange/reddish fabric, brown on fracture.

208 Base *fr. Bd* 0.05, *ext ht* 0.021. Poriferous pale brown/orangish fabric.

Object #	PNE	LBA	EIA	HEL	TRA	KUS	LKU	EME	HME	LME	PMO
196				✓	✓						
199							✓				
200							✓				
201				✓	✓						
202							✓				
203							✓				

SITE 16 (Shortepa)

209 Rim *fr. Rd* 0.18, *ext ht* 0.029. *RS* on *out surf.* Period LKU. *SSe* 4th c. AD.

210 Rim *fr. Rd* 0.06, *ext ht* 0.025. Brown fabric, ochre on *surf.* Period LKU. *SSe* 4th c. AD.

211 Rim *fr. Rd* 0.06, *ext ht* 0.037. *Eng* on *surf.* Period LKU. *SSe* 4th c. AD.

212 Rim *fr. Rd* 0.08, *ext ht* 0.045. Ochre fabric. Typological parallels R132 (Puschnigg 2006). Period KUS / LKU, cf. Tušlová 2012b, tb. 8:8. Period LKU. *SSe* 3rd–4th c. AD.

213 Rim *fr. Rd* 0.2, *ext ht* 0.033. Brick-red fabric. Period LKU. *SSe* 4th c. AD.

214 Rim *fr. Rd* 0.19, *ext ht* 0.037. Brown fabric; ochre *eng* with *rsd* of *RS* on *out surf.* Period LKU. *SSe* 4th c. AD.

215 Rim *fr. Rd* ?, *ext ht* 0.051. Brick-red fabric; unsure orientation. Period LKU. *SSe* 4th c. AD.

216 Rim *fr. Rd* 0.11, *ext ht* 0.03. Orange fabric; *out surf* yellow. Period LKU. *SSe* 4th c. AD.

217 Rim *fr. Rd* 0.12, *ext ht* 0.03. *RS*; *WR*. Typological parallels R12 (Puschnigg 2006) Period LKU. *SSe* 4th c. AD.

218 Rim *fr. Rd* 0.08, *ext ht* 0.028. Typological parallels R103 (Maxwell-Jones 2015). Period KUS / LKU. *SSe* 4th c. AD.

219 Rim *fr. Rd* 0.14, *ext ht* 0.023. Brown fabric, ochre *eng*. Period LKU. *SSe* 4th c. AD.

220 Rim *fr. Rd* 0.11, *ext ht* 0.028. Typological parallels R153 (Maxwell-Jones 2015). Period KUS / LKU. *SSe* 1st–4th c. AD.

221 Rim *fr. Rd* 0.09, *ext ht* 0.029. *RS* on *out surf*. Period LKU. *SSe* 4th c. AD.

222 Rim *fr. Rd* 0.13, *ext ht* 0.031. Brown fabric; *in surf* ochre; brown *eng* on *out surf*. Period LKU. *SSe* 4th c. AD.

223 Rim *fr. Rd* 0.11, *ext ht* 0.037. Yellow fabric. Period LKU. *SSe* 4th c. AD.

224 Rim *fr. Rd* 0.1, *ext ht* 0.049. Period LKU. *SSe* 4th c. AD.

225 Rim *fr. Rd* 0.14, *ext ht* 0.02. Typological parallels Chasha 6a (Zavyalov 2008). Period LKU. *SSe* 4th c. AD.

226 Rim *fr. Rd* 0.16, *ext ht* 0.017. Black/grey fabric; *rsd* of black *sl*. Period LKU. *SSe* 4th c. AD.

227 Rim *fr. Rd* 0.18, *ext ht* 0.023. Typological parallels Chasha 6a (Zavyalov 2008). Period LKU. *SSe* 4th c. AD.

228 Rim *fr. Rd* 0.17, *ext ht* 0.02. Grey fabric; ochre *eng* on *surf*. Typological parallels R5 (Maxwell-Jones 2015). Period EIA / LKU. *SSe* 4th c. AD.

229 Rim *fr. Rd* 0.24, *ext ht* 0.014. Brown fabric; *out surf* grey. Typological parallels R127 (Maxwell-Jones 2015); R214 (Puschnigg 2006); *blyuda* 2 (Zavyalov 2008). Period LKU. *SSe* 4th c. AD.

230 Rim *fr. Rd* 0.1, *ext ht* 0.026. Eng on *surf*.

231 Rim *fr. Rd* 0.34, *ext ht* 0.067. Brown fabric; *RS* on *in surf*; ochre *eng* on *out surf*. Typological parallels R134 (Maxwell-Jones 2015); *khozyaystvennye tagora* 1d (Zavyalov 2008) (?). Period KUS / LKU. *SSe* 4th c. AD.

232 Rim *fr. Rd* 0.36, *ext ht* 0.025. *Eng* on *surf*.

233 Rim *fr. Rd* ?, *ext ht* 0.023. Brown fabric; ochre *eng* on *out surf*; ochre *eng* and *rsd* of *RS* on *in surf*; unsure orientation.

234 Rim *fr. Rd* ?, *ext ht* 0.028. Brick-red fabric.

235 Rim *fr. Rd* ?, *ext ht* 0.013. Brick-red fabric; ochre *eng* on *surf*.

236 Rim *fr. Rd* ?, *ext ht* 0.012. Typological parallels Chasha 6a (Zavyalov 2008). Period LKU. *SSe* 4th c. AD.

237 Rim *fr. Rd* ?, *ext ht* 0.012.

238 Rim *fr. Rd* ?, *ext ht* 0.107.

239 Body and *hdl fr. Pht* 0.067.

240 Body *fr. Pht* 0.026. Brick-red fabric; ochre *eng* on *out surf*; *in surf* unpreserved.

241 Body *fr. Pht* 0.02. Brown fabric; ochre *eng* on *surf*.

242 Body *fr. Pht* 0.042. Orange fabric; ochre *eng* on *surf*.

243 *Hdl fr. W* 0.024 × 0.019. Brick-red fabric; yellow *eng* on *surf*.

244 *Hdl fr. W* 0.031 × 0.016. Brown fabric; ochre *eng* on *surf*.

245 *Hdl fr. W* 0.038 × 0.016. Brick-red fabric; ochre *eng* on *surf*.

246 *Hdl fr. W* 0.034 × 0.015. For fabric description see [245].

247 *Hdl fr. W* 0.029 × 0.01. For fabric description see [244].

248 Base *fr. Bd* ?, *ext ht* 0.008. Brick-red fabric; ochre *eng* on *out surf*; *in surf* unpreserved.

249 Base *fr. Bd* ?, *ext ht* 0.031. Brick-red fabric.

250 Base *fr* (?). *Bd* ?, *ext ht* 0.023. Brick-red fabric; supposedly shattered base *fr*.

251 Base *fr. Bd* 0.04, *ext ht* 0.007. Brick-red fabric; *in surf* unpreserved.

252 Base *fr. Bd* 0.04, *ext ht* 0.026. Brick-red fabric; ochre *eng* on *out surf*; *in surf* unpreserved.

253 Base *fr. Bd* 0.06, *ext ht* 0.018. Brick-red fabric; ochre *eng* on *in surf*; impressed conch on the bottom.

254 Base *fr. Bd* 0.11, *ext ht* 0.027. Ochre *eng* on *surf*.

255 Base *fr. Bd* 0.11, *ext ht* 0.034.

256 Base *fr. Bd* 0.11, *ext ht* 0.021. WR.

257 Base *fr. Bd* 0.12, *ext ht* 0.049.

Object #	PNE	LBA	EIA	HEL	TRA	KUS	LKU	EME	HME	LME	PMO
209							✓				
210							✓				
211							✓				
212						✓	✓				
213							✓				
214							✓				
215							✓				
216							✓				

Object #	PNE	LBA	EIA	HEL	TRA	KUS	LKU	EME	HME	LME	PMO
217							✓				
218						✓	✓				
219							✓				
220						✓	✓				
221							✓				
222							✓				
223							✓				
224							✓				
225							✓				
226							✓				
227							✓				
228			✓				✓				
229							✓				
236							✓				

SITE 17 (Shishtepa)

258 Rim *fr. Rd* 0.35, *ext ht* 0.055. Brick-red fabric.
259 Rim *fr. Rd* 0.4, *ext ht* 0.053. Brick-red fabric; yellowish/ochre *sl* on *out surf*, *rsd* of brown/white *sl* on *in surf*. Typological parallels *storage jars* gr. 2(5) (Včelicová 2015). Period LKU / EME, cf. Tušlová 2012b, tb. 14:3.
260 Rim *fr. Rd* 0.42, *ext ht* 0.074. Orange fabric; yellowish on *surf*; plastic *crvl dec*. Period LKU. *SSe* 2nd half of 3rd c. AD.
261 Rim *fr. Rd* 0.09, *ext ht* 0.025. Brick-red fabric.
262 Rim *fr. Rd* 0.09, *ext ht* 0.038. Brown/red fabric; yellow/brown *surf*.

263 Rim *fr. Rd* 0.07, *ext ht* 0.026. Orange fabric; *sl* (darker *on out surf*).
264 Rim *fr. Rd* 0.065, *ext ht* 0.017. Pale orange fabric, brownish on *out surf*; RS.
265 Rim *fr. Rd* 0.23, *ext ht* 0.061. Red/greyish fabric, grey on fracture.
266 Rim *fr. Rd* 0.28, *ext ht* 0.03. Dark red fabric; orange *gl*; *in surf* unpreserved.
267 Rim and *hdl fr. Rd* 0.03, *ext ht* 0.027, *hdl w* 0.028 × 0.013. Orange fabric; *RS* on both *surf*.
268 Body *fr. Pht* 0.036. Pale orange fabric; yellow stain on *out surf*.

Object #	PNE	LBA	EIA	HEL	TRA	KUS	LKU	EME	HME	LME	PMO
259							✓	✓			
260							✓				
264							✓				
267							✓				
268							✓				

SITE 18 (Gilyambobtepa)

269 Rim *fr. Rd* ?, *ext ht* 0.042. Brown fabric; ochre *eng*.
270 Rim *fr. Rd* ?, *ext ht* 0.041. Brick-red fabric; ochre *eng* on *out surf*; upper part sooted; inclusion size up to 0.005.

271 Rim *fr. Rd* ?, *ext ht* 0.031. Pale brown fabric, *out surf* dark brown. Typological parallels Chasha 6a (Zavyalov 2008). Period LKU. *SSe* 4th c. AD.
272 Rim *fr. Rd* 0.2, *ext ht* 0.149. Grey fabric, *out surf* red. Period KUS / LKU / EME. *SSe* Kushan / EME.

273 Rim *fr. Rd* 0.16, *ext ht* 0.107. Brown/orange fabric, *in surf* orange; ochre *eng* on *out surf*; stain of *RS*. Period LKU. *SSe* 4th c. AD.

274 Rim *fr. Rd* 0.18, *ext ht* 0.031. *RS*. Typological parallels R142 (Maxwell-Jones 2015); R1 (Puschnigg 2006); Bowls gr. 2 (1) (Včelicová 2015). Period KUS / LKU. *SSe* 3rd and 4th c. AD.

275 Rim *fr. Rd* 0.13, *ext ht* 0.035. *RS* on *out surf*. Typological parallels R142 (Maxwell-Jones 2015); R1 (Puschnigg 2006); Bowls gr. 2 (1) (Včelicová 2015). Period KUS / LKU. *SSe* 3rd and 4th c. AD.

276 Rim *fr. Rd* 0.14, *ext ht* 0.028. Brown fabric; brown *eng* on *out surf*; red *eng* on *in surf*.

277 Rim *fr. Rd* 0.1, *ext ht* 0.029. Brown fabric; ochre *eng* on *out surf*.

278 Rim *fr. Rd* 0.1, *ext ht* 0.043. Sandwich fabric: brown margins, orange core; brown on *surf*.

279 Rim *fr. Rd* 0.09, *ext ht* 0.042. Brick-red fabric.

280 Rim *fr. Rd* 0.09, *ext ht* 0.049. Brick-red fabric; ochre *eng* on *out surf*. Typological parallels R27 (Puschnigg 2006) Period LKU.

281 Rim *fr. Rd* 0.16, *ext ht* 0.048. Brick-red fabric; ochre *eng* on *in surf*. Typological parallels Chasha 6a (Zavyalov 2008). Period LKU. *SSe* 4th c. AD.

282 Rim *fr. Rd* 0.4, *ext ht* 0.077. Brick-red fabric; red *eng* on *out surf*. Typological parallels R128 (Puschnigg 2006). Period LKU.

283 Rim *fr. Rd* 0.4, *ext ht* 0.045. Brown fabric; ochre *eng* on *surf*. Typological parallels R56 (Maxwell-Jones 2015). Period LKU.

284 Rim *fr. Rd* 0.1, *ext ht* 0.036. Ochre fabric; *RS*.

285 Rim *fr. Rd* 0.09, *ext ht* 0.037. Yellow fabric; brown *sl* on *out surf*.

286 Rim *fr. Rd* 0.07, *ext ht* 0.032. Orange fabric; *RS* on *out surf*.

287 Body *fr. Pht* 0.031. Brick-red fabric; ochre *eng* on *surf*.

288 Body *fr. Pht* 0.051. Brown fabric; *RS* on *out surf*.

289 *Hdl fr. Pht* 0.033, *w* 0.04 × 0.011. Orange fabric; ochre *eng* on *out surf*; *rsd* of *RS*.

290 *Hdl fr. Pht* 0.029, *w* 0.041 × 0.012. Orange/yellow fabric; ochre *eng* on *surf*; *rsd* of *RS* in upper part.

291 Base *fr. Bd* 0.04, *ext ht* 0.016. Brown fabric; *RS* on *out surf*.

292 Base *fr. Bd* 0.11, *ext ht* 0.048. Sandwich fabric: orange margins, yellow core; yellow *surf*; attached nib.

Object #	PNE	LBA	EIA	HEL	TRA	KUS	LKU	EME	HME	LME	PMO
271							✓				
272						✓	✓	✓			
273							✓				
274						✓	✓				
275						✓	✓				
280							✓				
281							✓				
282							✓				
283				✓	✓	✓	✓				

SITE 19 (Gorintepa)

293 Rim *fr. Rd* ?, *ext ht* 0.052. Red fabric with inclusions; *in surf* orange; *out surf* panned. Period LKU. *SSe* end of 3rd–beginning of 4th c. AD.

294 Rim *fr. Rd* ?, *ext ht* 0.037. Orange/red fabric; ochre *eng* on *out surf*. Period LKU. *SSe* end of 3rd–beginning of 4th c. AD.

295 Rim *fr. Rd* ?, *ext ht* 0.026. *RS*. Period LKU. *SSe* end of 3rd–beginning of 4th c. AD.

296 Rim *fr. Rd* ?, *ext ht* 0.026. Orange fabric; *in surf* yellow; ochre *eng* on *out surf*. Period LKU. *SSe* end of 3rd–beginning of 4th c. AD.

297 Rim *fr. Rd* 0.106, *ext ht* 0.033. *RS*. Typological parallels R153 (Maxwell-Jones 2015). Period KUS / LKU. *SSe* 1st–4th c. AD.

298 Rim *fr. Rd* 0.46, *ext ht* 0.08. Red/brown fabric; ochre *eng* on *out surf*. *SSe* LKU / EME.

299 *Handle fr. W* 0.043 × 0.016. Orange fabric; creamy yellow *surf*. Period LKU. *SSe* end of 3rd–beginning of 4th c. AD.

300 Body and *hdl fr*, *horiz sec. Hdl w* 0.019 × 0.014. Orange fabric; *in surf* creamy yellow; *RS*. Period LKU. *SSe* end of 3rd–beginning of 4th c. AD.

Object #	PNE	LBA	EIA	HEL	TRA	KUS	LKU	EME	HME	LME	PMO
293							✓				
294							✓				
295							✓				
296							✓				
297						✓	✓				
298							✓	✓			
299							✓				
300							✓				

SITE 22 (Taushkantepa)

301 Rim *fr. Rd* 0.4, *ext ht* 0.073. Brick-red fabric; ochre *eng* on *out surf.*

302 Rim *fr. Rd* 0.4, *ext ht* 0.087. For fabric description see [301]. Typological parallels R79 (Maxwell-Jones 2015). Period HEL / TRA.

303 Rim *fr. Rd* 0.22, *ext ht* 0.05. Red fabric, *out surf* brown; inclusion size up to 0.007. Typological parallels R83 (Maxwell-Jones 2015); *storage jars* gr. 4A/B (5) (Včelicová 2015); *khumtscha* 1 (Zavyalov 2008). Period KUS / LKU.

304 Rim *fr. Rd* ?, *ext ht* 0.087. Sandwich fabric: brick-red margins, black core; brown *eng* on *surf*; limestone inclusion size up to 0.005.

305 Rim *fr. Rd* ?, *ext ht* 0.035. Carmine fabric, *in surf* brick-red; ochre *eng* on *out surf.* Period KUS / LKU. *SSe* 3rd and 4th c. AD.

306 Rim *fr. Rd* 0.16, *ext ht* 0.016. Brick-red fabric; *rsd* of *RS* on *out surf.*

307 Rim *fr. Rd* 0.19, *ext ht* 0.065. For fabric description see [306]. Typological parallels R111 (Maxwell-Jones 2015). Period KUS / LKU. *SSe* 3rd and 4th c. AD.

308 Rim *fr. Rd* 0.08, *ext ht* 0.053. Brick-red fabric. Typological parallels R132 (Puschnigg 2006). Period KUS / LKU, cf. Tušlová 2012b, tb. 8:8. *SSe* 3rd–4th c. AD.

309 Body *fr. Pht* 0.097. Brick-red fabric; *rsd* of *RS* on *out surf*, *CR.* Period KUS / LKU. *SSe* 3rd and 4th c. AD.

310 *Hdl fr. W* 0.035 × 0.011. Brick-red fabric, ochre *surf.*

Object #	PNE	LBA	EIA	HEL	TRA	KUS	LKU	EME	HME	LME	PMO
302				✓	✓						
303						✓	✓				
305						✓	✓				
307						✓	✓				
308						✓	✓				
309						✓	✓				

SITE 23 (Tashlaktepa)

311 Rim *fr. Rd* 0.26, *ext ht* 0.04. Pale red fabric; yellow *eng* on *out surf*, *WR.* Period KUS / LKU. *SSe* 4th c. AD.

312 Rim *fr. Rd* 0.12, *ext ht* 0.028. Grey fabric, *out surf* red, *in surf* brown. Period EME. *SSe* 7th–8th c. AD.

313 Rim *fr. Rd* 0.04, *ext ht* 0.026. Orange fabric; white *eng* on *surf.* Period EME. *SSe* 7th–8th c. AD.

314 Rim *fr. Rd* 0.09, *ext ht* 0.022. Pale brown fabric; yellow *eng* on *surf.* Period EME. *SSe* 7th–8th c. AD.

315 Rim *fr. Rd* 0.23, *ext ht* 0.084. Grey fabric, *out surf* brown, *in surf* grey/purple; inclusion size up to 0.003. Period EME. *SSe* 7th–8th c. AD.

316 Rim *fr. Rd* 0.4, *ext ht* 0.088. Red fabric; ochre *eng* on *out surf*; inclusion size up to 0.002.

317 Rim *fr. Rd* 0.2, *ext ht* 0.116. Brick-red fabric; ochre *eng* on *out surf.* Typological parallels R86 (Maxwell-Jones 2015). Period LKU / EME. *SSe* 7th and 8th c. AD.

318 Body *fr. Pht* 0.056. Brick-red fabric.

319 Body *fr. Pht* 0.103. Brick-red fabric, *out surf* orange/yellow. Period EME. *SSe* 7th–8th c. AD.

320 Body *fr. Pht* 0.024. Brick-red fabric, *in surf* ochre; blue and white *gl* on *out surf.* Period EME. *SSe* 7th–8th c. AD.

321 Body *fr. Pht* 0.021. Yellow fabric. Period EME. *SSe* 7th–8th c. AD.

322 Body *fr. Pht* 0.025. Brick-red fabric. Period EME. *SSe* 7th–8th c. AD.

323 *Hdl fr. W* 0.042 × 0.015. Brick-red fabric; yellow *eng* on *surf.* Period EME. *SSe* 7th–8th c. AD.

324 *Hdl fr. W* 0.044 × 0.015. Pale red fabric; yellow *eng* on *surf.* Period EME. *SSe* 7th–8th c. AD.

325 Base *fr. Bd* 0.1, *ext ht* 0.058. Brick-red fabric; *WR.* Period EME. *SSe* 7th–8th c. AD.

326 Base *fr. Bd* 0.15, *ext ht* 0.06. Brick-red fabric; ochre *eng* on *out surf; WR.* Period EME. *SSe* 7th–8th c. AD.

327 Base *fr. Bd* ?, *ext ht* 0.013. Period EME. *SSe* 7th–8th c. AD.

328 Base *fr. Bd* 0.06, *ext ht* 0.016. Dark orange/red fabric.

Object #	PNE	LBA	EIA	HEL	TRA	KUS	LKU	EME	HME	LME	PMO
311							✓				
312								✓			
313								✓			
314								✓			
315								✓			
316							✓	✓			
317							✓	✓			
319								✓			
320								✓			
307								✓			
321								✓			
322								✓			
323								✓			
324								✓			
325								✓			
326								✓			
327								✓			

SITE 24 (Mozoroti baba tepa)

329 Rim *fr. Rd* 0.34, *ext ht* 0.124. Typological parallels R18 (Maxwell-Jones 2015). Period LKU.

330 Rim *fr. Rd* 0.4, *ext ht* 0.077. Ochre *eng* on both *surf.* Typological parallels R29 (Maxwell-Jones 2015). Period LKU.

331 Rim *fr. Rd* 0.07, *ext ht* 0.029. Inclusion size up to 0.001; *WR.* Typological parallels R183 (Puschnigg 2006); *Chasha s peregribom* (Pindaev 1978). Period LKU. *SSe* 3rd and 4th c. AD.

332 Rim *fr. Rd* 0.1, *ext ht* 0.02. *RS* on both *surf.*

333 Rim *fr. Rd* 0.08, *ext ht* 0.054. *RS; WR.*

334 Rim *fr. Rd* 0.22, *ext ht* 0.067. Ochre *eng* and *rsd* of *RS* on both *surf; WR.*

335 Rim *fr. Rd* 0.25, *ext ht* 0.091. Ochre *eng* on both *surf; WR.* Period LKU. *SSe* 3rd and 4th c. AD.

336 Rim *fr. Rd* 0.38, *ext ht* 0.049. Ochre *eng* on both *surf.*

337 Rim *fr. Rd* 0.34, *ext ht* 0.107. For fabric description see [336]. Period LKU / EME. *SSe* 3rd–4th c. AD / 7th–8th c. AD.

338 Rim *fr. Rd* 0.04, *ext ht* 0.04. *RS* on both *surf.*

339 Rim *fr. Rd* 0.06, *ext ht* 0.019. For fabric description see [338].

340 Rim fr. Rd 0.12, ext ht 0.017. For fabric description see [338]. Typological parallels R143/144 (Maxwell-Jones 2015); R212 (Puschnigg 2006); Bowls gr.

3A (5) (Včelicová 2015); Chasha 2 (Zavyalov 2008). Period KUS / LKU. *SSe* 1st–3rd c. AD.

341 Rim *fr. Rd* 0.12, *ext ht* 0.019. For fabric description see [338].

342 Rim *fr. Rd* 0.17, *ext ht* 0.036. Ochre *eng* on both *surf.* Typological parallels R5 (Maxwell-Jones 2015). Period EIA / LKU. *SSe* 4th c. AD.

343 Rim *fr. Rd* 0.16, *ext ht* 0.036. *RS* on *in surf.*

344 Rim *fr. Rd* 0.34, *ext ht* 0.054. Sandwich fabric: red margins, black core; red/brown *surf;* supposedly *HM.* Typological parallels R128 (Maxwell-Jones 2015). Period TRA / KUS / medieval. *SSe* medieval.

345 Rim *fr. Rd* 0.2, *ext ht* 0.022. Typological parallels R55 (Puschnigg 2006). Period LKU.

346 Rim *fr. Rd* ?, *ext ht* 0.057. Grey fabric, *out surf* red; red and black *sl* stripe on *in surf;* inclusion size up to 0.005. Typological parallels R83 (Maxwell-Jones 2015); *storage jars* gr. 4A/B (5) (Včelicová 2015); *khumtscha* 1 (Zavyalov 2008). Period KUS / LKU.

347 Rim *fr. Rd* ?, *ext ht* 0.057. Brick-red fabric; *WR.*

348 Body *fr. Pht* 0.038.

349 *Hdl fr. Pht* 0.101, *w* 0.023 × 0.023.

350 *Hdl fr. Pht* 0.066, *w* 0.023 × 0.011.

351 *Hdl fr. Pht* 0.028, *w* 0.031 × 0.01.

352 *Hdl fr. Pht* 0.038, *w* 0.03 × 0.015. *RS.*

353 *Hdl fr. Pht* 0.026, *w* 0.016 × 0.008. *RS.*

354 Knob *fr. Max th* 0.046. Brick-red fabric, ochre *surf.*

355 Base *fr. Bd* 0.062, *ext ht* 0.012. Spiral *WR* on *in surf.*

356 Base *fr. Bd* 0.13, *ext ht* 0.035.

357 Base *fr. Bd* 0.07, *ext ht* 0.03. Brick-red fabric.

358 Base *fr. Bd* 0.15, *ext ht* 0.034.

Object #	PNE	LBA	EIA	HEL	TRA	KUS	LKU	EME	HME	LME	PMO
329							✓				
330							✓				
331							✓				
334					✓						
335							✓				
340						✓	✓				
342			✓				✓				
344					✓	✓		✓	✓	✓	
345							✓				
346						✓	✓				

SITE 25 (Talagantepa)

359 Rim *fr. Rd* ?, *ext ht* 0.016. Ochre fabric; black *sl* on *surf.* Period KUS. *SSe* 1st c. AD.

360 Rim *fr. Rd* ?, *ext ht* 0.014. Ochre fabric; inclusion size up to 0.003. Period KUS. *SSe* 1st c. AD.

361 Rim *fr. Rd* ?, *ext ht* 0.016. *RS* on both *surf.* Period KUS. *SSe* 1st c. AD.

362 Rim *fr. Rd* ?, *ext ht* 0.014. For fabric description see [361]. Typological parallels R143/144 (Maxwell-Jones 2015); R212 (Puschnigg 2006); Bowls gr. 3A (5) (Včelicová 2015); Chasha 2 (Zavyalov 2008). Period KUS / LKU. *SSe* 1st–3rd c. AD.

363 Rim *fr. Rd* ?, *ext ht* 0.025. For fabric description see [361]. Period KUS. *SSe* 1st c. AD.

364 Rim *fr. Rd* ?, *ext ht* 0.024. For fabric description see [361]. Typological parallels R153 (Maxwell-Jones 2015). Period KUS / LKU. *SSe* 1st–4th c. AD.

365 Rim *fr. Rd* 0.19, *ext ht* 0.059. Brick-red fabric; red *eng* on *out surf.* Typological parallels R88 (Maxwell-Jones 2015). Period LKU / EME. *SSe* EME.

366 Rim *fr. Rd* 0.22, *ext ht* 0.031. *Burn* on *in* side; *RS.* Typological parallels R143/144 (Maxwell-Jones 2015); R212 (Puschnigg 2006); Bowls gr. 3A (5) (Včelicová 2015); Chasha 2 (Zavyalov 2008). Period KUS / LKU. *SSe* 1st–3rd c. AD.

367 Rim *fr. Rd* 0.17, *ext ht* 0.018. Brown fabric; ochre *eng* on *surf.* Period KUS. *SSe* 1st c. AD.

368 Rim *fr. Rd* 0.13, *ext ht* 0.03. Period KUS. *SSe* 1st c. AD.

369 Rim *fr. Rd* 0.16, *ext ht* 0.03. Brown fabric; ochre *eng* on *out surf.* Period KUS / LKU (cf. Zavyalov 2008). *SSe* 1st c. AD.

370 Rim *fr. Rd* 0.12, *ext ht* 0.054. Orange fabric; ochre *eng* and *rsd* of *RS* on *out surf.* Typological parallels R14 (Maxwell-Jones 2015). Period EME. *SSe* EME.

371 Rim *fr. Rd* 0.4, *ext ht* 0.063. Orange fabric; red stains on fracture. Typological parallels *khum* 1 (Zavyalov 2008). Period KUS / LKU / EME, cf. Tušlová 2012b, tb. 13:7.

372 Rim *fr. Rd* 0.36, *ext ht* 0.067. Red fabric. Typological parallels R81 (Maxwell-Jones 2015). Period HEL / TRA / KUS. *SSe* 1st c. AD.

373 Rim *fr. Rd* 0.42, *ext ht* 0.074. Brick-red fabric; yellow *eng* on *surf*; *RS* in upper part. Period KUS. *SSe* 1st c. AD.

374 Rim *fr. Rd* 0.11, *ext ht* 0.03. Orange fabric; *out surf* ochre; *rsd* of *RS* on *in surf*. Period KUS. *SSe* 1st c. AD.

375 Rim *fr. Rd* 0.12, *ext ht* 0.031. Ochre fabric; *rsd* of *RS*. Period KUS. *SSe* 1st c. AD.

376 Rim *fr. Rd* 0.11, *ext ht* 0.036. Brown fabric; black *sl* on *out surf*; *RS* on *in surf*. Period KUS. *SSe* 1st c. AD.

377 Rim *fr. Rd* 0.09, *ext ht* 0.046. Grey/black fabric; *out surf* red. Period KUS. *SSe* 1st c. AD.

378 Rim *fr. Rd* 0.07, *ext ht* 0.049. Orange fabric, *in surf* yellow; *rsd* of *RS* on *surf*; ochre *eng* on *out surf*. Period KUS. *SSe* 1st c. AD.

379 Rim *fr. Rd* 0.28, *ext ht* 0.137. Brick-red fabric; yellow *eng* on *out surf*; inclusion size up to 0.005. Period KUS. *SSe* 1st c. AD.

380 Rim *fr. Rd* 0.19, *ext ht* 0.017. Pink/red fabric; yellow *eng* on *surf*; unsure orientation. Period KUS. *SSe* 1st c. AD.

381 Body *fr. Pht* 0.063. Pink fabric; yellow *eng* on *out surf*. Period KUS. *SSe* 1st c. AD.

382 Body *fr. Pht* 0.034. Brick-red fabric, *out surf* brown, *in surf* ochre. Period KUS. *SSe* 1st c. AD.

383 Body *fr. Pht* 0.036. Brick-red fabric; *rsd* of *RS*; yellow *eng* on *out surf*. Period KUS. *SSe* 1st c. AD.

384 Body *fr. Pht* 0.027. Brown fabric, *in surf* ochre; yellow *eng* on *out surf*. Period KUS. *SSe* 1st c. AD.

385 Body *fr. Pht* 0.025. *RS* on *out surf*. Period KUS. *SSe* 1st c. AD.

Object #	PNE	LBA	EIA	HEL	TRA	KUS	LKU	EME	HME	LME	PMO
359						✓					
360						✓					
361						✓					
362						✓	✓				
363						✓					
364						✓	✓				
365							✓	✓			
366						✓	✓				
367						✓					
368						✓					
369						✓	✓				
370								✓			
371						✓	✓	✓			
372				✓	✓	✓					
373						✓					
374						✓					
375						✓					
378						✓					
379						✓					
380						✓					
381						✓					
382						✓					
383						✓					
384						✓					
385						✓					

SITE 26 (Yalangoyoq ota tepa)

386 Rim *fr. Rd* 0.34, *ext ht* 0.072. Brick-red fabric; ochre *eng* and *rsd* of *RS* on *out surf*, *WR*. Typological parallels R65 (Maxwell-Jones 2015). Period EIA, cf. Tušová 2012b, tb. 14:1. *SSe* 6th–5th c. BC.

387 Rim *fr. Rd* 0.35, *ext ht* 0.062. Brick-red fabric, *out surf* ochre. Typological parallels R58 (Maxwell-Jones 2015). Period EIA / LKU, cf. Tušlová 2012b, tb. 14:1. *SSe* 6th–5th c. BC.

388 Rim *fr. Rd* 0.1, *ext ht* 0.019. Brick-red fabric, ochre *eng* on both *surf*. Typological parallels R94 (Puschnigg 2006); Bowls gr. 1A (3) (Včelicová 2015). Period LKU.

389 Rim *fr. Rd* 0.1, *ext ht* 0.03. Ochre *eng* on *out surf*.

390 Rim *fr. Rd* 0.11, *ext ht* 0.026. Ochre *eng* on *in surf*.

391 Rim *fr. Rd* 0.08, *ext ht* 0.025. *RS* on both *surf*.

392 Rim *fr. Rd* 0.07, *ext ht* 0.028. Brick-red fabric; *rsd* of ochre *eng* on both *surf*.

393 Rim *fr. Rd* 0.08, *ext ht* 0.019. Very fine, beige/orange fabric.

394 Rim *fr. Rd* 0.1, *ext ht* 0.033. Ochre *eng* on *out surf*.

395 Rim *fr. Rd* 0.11, *ext ht* 0.022. Pale beige fabric; *WR* on *out surf*.

396 Rim *fr. Rd* 0.11, *ext ht* 0.017. Ochre *eng* on *out surf*. Typological parallels R94 (Puschnigg 2006); Bowls gr. 1A (3) (Včelicová 2015). Period LKU.

397 Rim *fr. Rd* 0.11, *ext ht* 0.019. Ochre *eng* on both *surf*. Typological parallels R153 (Maxwell-Jones 2015). Period KUS / LKU. *SSe* 1st–4th c. AD.

398 Rim *fr. Rd* 0.22, *ext ht* 0.038. Orange fabric; ochre and red stains on *surf*; *HM* attachments.

399 Rim *fr. Rd* 0.2, *ext ht* 0.04. Orange fabric, *out surf* beige.

400 Rim *fr. Rd* 0.09, *ext ht* 0.069. Typological parallels R184 (Puschnigg 2006). Period LKU. *SSe* 4th c. AD.

401 Rim *fr. Rd* 0.24, *ext ht* 0.048. Pale beige fabric; partially burned; quartz inclusion size up to 0.001.

402 Rim *fr. Rd* 0.11, *ext ht* 0.031. *Rsd* of *RS* on *out surf*. Typological parallels R142 (Maxwell-Jones 2015); R1 (Puschnigg 2006); Bowls gr. 2 (1) (Včelicová 2015). Period KUS / LKU. *SSe* 3rd and 4th c. AD.

403 Rim *fr. Rd* 0.19, *ext ht* 0.019. Brick-red fabric; ochre *eng* on *out surf*. Typological parallels R137 (Maxwell-Jones 2015); R100 (Puschnigg 2006). Period HEL / TRA / KUS / LKU.

404 Rim *fr. Rd* 0.11, *ext ht* 0.024. Brick-red fabric; *WR*.

405 Rim *fr. Rd* 0.16, *ext ht* 0.028. Brick-red fabric; *HM* attachments. Typological parallels R4 (Maxwell-Jones 2015). Period HEL / TRA.

406 Rim *fr. Rd* 0.12, *ext ht* 0.023. Typological parallels R153 (Maxwell-Jones 2015). Period KUS / LKU. *SSe* 1st–4th c. AD.

407 Rim *fr. Rd* 0.18, *ext ht* 0.024. Very fine, dark orange fabric.

408 Rim *fr. Rd* 0.15, *ext ht* 0.023. Ochre *eng* on *out surf*. Typological parallels R142 (Maxwell-Jones 2015); R1 (Puschnigg 2006); Bowls gr. 2 (1) (Včelicová 2015). Period KUS / LKU. *SSe* 3rd and 4th c. AD.

409 Rim *fr. Rd* ?, *ext ht* 0.024.

410 Rim *fr. Rd* ?, *ext ht* 0.028. *Rsd* of *RS* on *out surf*.

411 Rim *fr. Rd* 0.25, *ext ht* 0.039. Brick-red fabric; ochre *eng* on *out surf*. Typological parallels R62 (Maxwell-Jones 2015). Period EIA / HEL, cf. Tušová 2012b, tb. 14:1.

412 Rim *fr. Rd* ?, *ext ht* 0.041. For fabric description see [411]. Typological parallels R17 (Puschnigg 2006). Period LKU. *SSe* 3rd c. AD.

413 Rim *fr. Rd* 0.26, *ext ht* 0.035. Fine, yellow/orange fabric. Typological parallels R156 (Maxwell-Jones 2015). Period HEL / TRA / LKU, cf. Tušová 2012b, tb. 8:2.

414 Rim *fr. Rd* ?, *ext ht* 0.024. Fine, pale brown fabric, *out surf* beige/grey.

415 Rim *fr. Rd* 0.29, *ext ht* 0.032. Brick-red fabric; ochre *eng* on *surf*.

416 Rim *fr. Rd* 0.16, *ext ht* 0.039. Brick-red fabric; yellow stains. Typological parallels R173 (Maxwell-Jones 2015). Period LKU / EME.

417 Rim *fr. Rd* 0.11, *ext ht* 0.044. Ochre fabric, *in surf* brick-red; *WR*. Period LKU. *SSe* 4th c. AD.

418 Rim *fr. Rd* 0.16, *ext ht* 0.029. Fine, dark red fabric. Typological parallels in Zavyalov (2008). Period LKU.

419 Rim *fr. Rd* 0.15, *ext ht* 0.03. Pale orange fabric; ochre *eng* on both *surf*. Typological parallels R153 (Maxwell-Jones 2015). Period KUS / LKU. *SSe* 1st–4th c. AD.

420 Rim *fr. Rd* 0.16, *ext ht* 0.038. Orange fabric; *out surf* yellow.

421 Rim *fr. Rd* 0.17, *ext ht* 0.04. *SSe* LKU.

422 Rim *fr. Rd* 0.16, *ext ht* 0.021. Orange fabric; ochre *eng* on *out surf*. Typological parallels R173 (Maxwell-Jones 2015). Period LKU / EME.

423 Rim *fr. Rd* ?, *ext ht* 0.06. Brick-red fabric; ochre *eng* on *out surf*.

424 Rim *fr. Rd* ?, *ext ht* 0.062. Coarse, yellow/brown fabric.

425 Body *fr. Pht* 0.026. Brick-red fabric; ochre *eng* on *out surf*.

426 Knob *fr* (?). *Max th* 0.017. For fabric description see [425].

427 *Hdl fr. W* 0.035 × 0.011. Brick-red fabric, ochre *surf*.

428 Base *fr. Bd* 0.09, *ext ht* 0.014. *RS* on *in surf*.

429 Base *fr. Bd* ?, *ext ht* 0.033. Dark red fabric, partially orange.

430 Base *fr. Bd* 0.08, *ext ht* 0.023.

431 Base *fr. Bd* 0.06, *ext ht* 0.027. Brick-red fabric; ochre *eng* on *out surf.*

432 Base *fr. Bd* 0.055, *ext ht* 0.039. Brick-red fabric; *RS* on *out surf. SSe* 2nd half of the 4th c. AD.

433 Base *fr. Bd* 0.05, *ext ht* 0.031.

434 Base *fr. Bd* 0.06, *ext ht* 0.032.

Object #	PNE	LBA	EIA	HEL	TRA	KUS	LKU	EME	HME	LME	PMO
397						✓	✓				
400							✓				
402						✓	✓				
403				✓	✓	✓	✓				
405				✓	✓						
406						✓	✓				
408						✓	✓				
411			✓	✓							
412							✓				
413				✓	✓		✓				
416							✓	✓			
417				✓	✓	✓	✓	✓			
418							✓				
419						✓	✓				
421							✓				
422							✓	✓			
432							✓				

SITE 27 (Babatepa)

435 Rim *fr. Rd* 0.14, *ext ht* 0.054. *RS.* Typological parallels R168 (Maxwell-Jones 2015). Period KUS.

436 Rim fr. Rd 0.11, ext ht 0.027. Brick-red fabric.

437 Rim *fr. Rd* 0.22, *ext ht* 0.043. Sandwich fabric: red margins, brown core; dark red/black *surf.*

438 Rim *fr. Rd* 0.23, *ext ht* 0.048. Brick-red fabric; ochre *eng* on *pt* of *out surf*, inclusion size up to 0.002.

439 Rim *fr. Rd* 0.4, *ext ht* 0.084. Brick-red fabric; ochre *eng* on *surf.*

440 Rim *fr. Rd* 0.19, *ext ht* 0.047. Ochre fabric; two *pnt* red stripes; red stains. Typological parallels R191 (Puschnigg 2006). Period LKU.

441 Rim *fr. Rd* 0.17, *ext ht* 0.03. Period LKU. *SSe* 3rd–4th c. AD.

442 Rim *fr. Rd* 0.17, *ext ht* 0.044. Brick-red fabric; ochre *eng* on *out surf.*

443 Body *fr. Pht* 0.037. *RS* on both *surf; burn.*

444 Base *fr. Bd* ?, *ext ht* 0.09. Brick-red fabric; ochre *eng* on *out surf;* white grainy base; *in surf* grainy; inclusion size up to 0.003.

Object #	PNE	LBA	EIA	HEL	TRA	KUS	LKU	EME	HME	LME	PMO
435						✓					
440							✓				
441							✓				

SITE 32 (Talashkantepa II)

445 Rim *fr. Rd* 0.16, *ext ht* 0.036. Typological parallels R153 (Maxwell-Jones 2015). Period KUS / LKU. *SSe* 1st–4th c. AD.
446 Rim *fr. Rd* 0.2, *ext ht* 0.037. Typological parallels in Zavyalov (2008). Period LKU.
447 Rim *fr. Rd* 0.26, *ext ht* 0.041. Period LKU, cf. Zavyalov 2008.
448 Rim *fr. Rd* 0.2, *ext ht* 0.064. Typological parallels R111 (Maxwell-Jones 2015). Period KUS / LKU.
449 Rim *fr. Rd* 0.16, *ext ht* 0.039.
450 Rim *fr. Rd* 0.38, *ext ht* 0.067.
451 Rim *fr. Rd* 0.4, *ext ht* 0.042. Typological parallels R129 (Maxwell-Jones 2015); *khozyaystvennye tagora* 1a (Zavyalov 2008); *tagora* (17) (Včelicová 2015). Period KUS / LKU. *SSe* 4th c. AD.
452 Rim *fr. Rd* 0.12, *ext ht* 0.037.
453 Rim *fr. Rd* 0.11, *ext ht* 0.042.
454 Rim *fr. Rd* 0.1, *ext ht* 0.043. Typological parallels R91 (Maxwell-Jones 2015). Period LKU / EME.
455 Rim *fr. Rd* 0.48, *ext ht* 0.052. Typological parallels R133 (Maxwell-Jones 2015); *tagora* (16) (Včelicová 2015). Period KUS / LKU. *SSe* 1st c. AD.
456 Rim *fr. Rd* 0.08, *ext ht* 0.038. Period LKU. *SSe* 4th c. AD.
457 Rim *fr. Rd* 0.2, *ext ht* 0.045. Typological parallels R88 (Maxwell-Jones 2015). Period LKU / EME. *SSe* EME.
458 Rim *fr. Rd* 0.18, *ext ht* 0.095.
459 Rim *fr. Rd* 0.03, *ext ht* 0.052.
460 Rim *fr. Rd* 0.24, *ext ht* 0.103. Typological parallels R83 (Maxwell-Jones 2015); *storage jars* gr. 4A/B

(5) (Včelicová 2015); *khumtscha* 1 (Zavyalov 2008). Period KUS / LKU.
461 Rim *fr. Rd* 0.3, *ext ht* 0.11. Period HEL / TRA / LKU, cf. Zavyalov 2008.
462 Rim *fr. Rd* 0.12, *ext ht* 0.024.
463 Rim *fr. Rd* 0.14, *ext ht* 0.067.
464 Rim *fr. Rd* 0.22, *ext ht* 0.032. Typological parallels R136 (Maxwell-Jones 2015); R13 (Puschnigg 2006) Period LKU.
465 Rim *fr. Rd* 0.18, *ext ht* 0.04. Typological parallels R148 (Maxwell-Jones 2015). Period HEL / TRA. Cf. Maxwell-Jones (2015).
466 Rim *fr. Rd* 0.1, *ext ht* 0.051.
467 Rim *fr. Rd* 0.12, *ext ht* 0.05.
468 Rim *fr. Rd* 0.4, *ext ht* 0.092. Typological parallels *khum* 1 (Zavyalov 2008). Period LKU / EME, cf. Tušlová 2012b, tb. 13:7.
469 Rim *fr. Rd* 0.46, *ext ht* 0.055. Period LKU, cf. Zavyalov 2008.
470 Rim *fr. Rd* 0.2, *ext ht* 0.082.
471 Rim *fr. Rd* 0.12, *ext ht* 0.044.
472 Rim *fr. Rd* 0.11, *ext ht* 0.042. Typological parallels R96 (Maxwell-Jones 2015); R133 (Puschnigg 2006); *kuvshiny* IIa (Zavyalov 2008). Period LKU.
473 Body *fr. Pht* 0.038.
474 Body *fr. D* at upper fracture 0.14, *pht* 0.061.
475 Base *fr. Bd* 0.06, *ext ht* 0.047.
476 Base *fr. Bd* 0.055, *ext ht* 0.025.
477 Base *fr. Bd* 0.04, *ext ht* 0.029. Used secondary after breakage.
478 Base *fr. Bd* 0.045, *ext ht* 0.009.

Object #	PNE	LBA	EIA	HEL	TRA	KUS	LKU	EME	HME	LME	PMO
445						✓	✓				
446							✓				
447							✓				
448						✓					
450					✓	✓					
451						✓	✓				
454							✓	✓			
455							✓				
456				✓	✓	✓	✓	✓			
457							✓	✓			
460						✓	✓				
461				✓	✓		✓				
464							✓				
465				✓	✓						
468							✓	✓			
469							✓				
472							✓				

SITE 33

479 *Comp vsl. Rd* 0.18, *bd* 0.12, *ht* 0.187.
480 *Compl vsl. Rd* 0.03, *bd* 0.07, *ht* 0.24. Typological parallels R253 (Puschnigg 2006). Period LKU.
481 Rim *fr. Rd* 0.23, *ext ht* 0.046. Ochre *eng* on *surf.* Typological parallels R142 (Maxwell-Jones 2015); R1 (Puschnigg 2006); Bowls gr. 2 (1) (Včelicová 2015). Period KUS / LKU. *SSe* 3rd and 4th c. AD.
482 Rim *fr. Rd* 0.13, *ext ht* 0.041. *WR.* Typological parallels R175 (Puschnigg 2006). Period LKU.
483 Rim *fr. Rd* 0.13, *ext ht* 0.034. Brick-red fabric; *RS* on both *surf*; *WR.* Typological parallels R175 (Puschnigg 2006). Period LKU.
484 Rim *fr. Rd* 0.13, *ext ht* 0.03. Creamy brown fabric; *in surf* ochre.
485 Rim *fr. Rd* 0.06, *ext ht* 0.089. Typological parallels R165 (Puschnigg 2006). Period HEL / TRA / LKU. *SSe* 2nd–1st c. BCE.
486 Rim and *hdl fr. Rd* 0.16, *ext ht* 0.066. Adherent *hdl* attachment. Typological parallels R5 (Maxwell-Jones 2015). Period EIA / LKU. *SSe* 4th c. AD.
487 Rim *fr. Rd* 0.28, *ext ht* 0.043. Corrupted; probably adherent.
488 Rim *fr. Rd* 0.35, *ext ht* 0.06. Pale brown fabric, ochre *eng* on *surf*; *WR.* Typological parallels R116 (Maxwell-Jones 2015). Period KUS / LKU. *SSe* 4th c. AD.

489 Rim *fr. Rd* 0.4, *ext ht* 0.078. Typological parallels R121 (Maxwell-Jones 2015). Period LKU. *SSe* 4th c. AD.
490 Rim *fr. Rd* 0.4, *ext ht* 0.058. Typological parallels R78 (Maxwell-Jones 2015). Period KUS.
491 Rim *fr. Rd* 0.4, *ext ht* 0.036.
492 Rim *fr. Rd* 0.33, *ext ht* 0.099. Typological parallels *khumtscha* 2 (Zavyalov 2008). Period LKU / HME, cf. Zavyalov 2008; Tušlová 2012b, tb. 9:6.
493 Rim *fr. Rd* ?, *ext ht* 0.065. Coarse, brick-red fabric, *out surf* red/black; inclusion size up to 0.003; *HM.*
494 Body *fr. Pht* 0.043. Period HME. *SSe* 12th c. AD.
495 Body *fr. Pht* 0.04. *SSe* LKU.
496 Body and *hdl fr. Pht* 0.087.
497 Lid (?) knob. *Max d* 0.044, *ext ht* 0.031. Fine, beige clay, reddish on fracture.
498 Base *fr. Bd* 0.23, *ext ht* 0.09. *WR.*
499 Base *fr. Bd* 0.24, *ext ht* 0.017. Brick-red fabric; *in surf* unpreserved.
500 Base *fr. Bd* 0.024, *ext ht* 0.079. *RS*; spiral *WR* on *in surf. SSe* 2nd–1st c. BC.
501 Base *fr. Bd* 0.035, *ext ht* 0.036. *RS*; stem attached after jiggering. *SSe* end of 3rd–beginning of 4th c. AD.
502 Base *fr. Bd* 0.145, *ext ht* 0.13.
503 Base *fr. Bd* 0.048, *ext ht* 0.072. *WR*; impressed conch at the bottom.

Object #	PNE	LBA	EIA	HEL	TRA	KUS	LKU	EME	HME	LME	PMO
480							✓				
481						✓	✓				
482							✓				
483							✓				
485				✓	✓		✓				
486			✓				✓				
488						✓	✓				
489							✓				
490						✓					
492							✓		✓		
494									✓		
495							✓				
500				✓	✓						
501							✓				

SITE 35 (Chopan Ata)

504 Rim *fr. In rd* (without moulding) 0.26, *ext ht* 0.037. Typological parallels R83 (Maxwell-Jones 2015); *storage jars* gr. 4A/B (5) (Včelicová 2015); *khumtscha* 1 (Zavyalov 2008). Period KUS / LKU.
505 Rim *fr. Rd* 0.17, *ext ht* 0.053. Brown/orange fabric with inclusions; depression 0.007 in *d*. Typological parallels R11 (Maxwell-Jones 2015); *Pots* gr. 9 (4) (Včelicová 2015). Period HEL / TRA.
506 Rim *fr. Rd* 0.12, *ext ht* 0.04. Orange fabric, yellowish orange *surf*; shallow cuts on *surf*. Typological parallels R17 (Puschnigg 2006). Period LKU. *SSe* 3rd c. AD.

507 Rim *fr. Rd* 0.24, *ext ht* 0.049. Orange fabric, ochre/yellow *surf*; *inc crvl dec* on *out surf*. Typological parallels R1 (Puschnigg 2006). Period LKU, cf. Zavyalov 2008.
508 Rim *fr. Rd* 0.19, *ext ht* 0.027. Red/orange fabric, ochre/yellow *surf*.
509 Rim *fr. Rd* 0.4, *ext ht* 0.063. Coarse, orange/grey fabric with inclusions; ochre/yellow *sl* on *out surf*. Typological parallels R84 (Maxwell-Jones 2015); *storage jars* gr. 4C (Včelicová 2015); *khum* 3 (Zavyalov 2008). Period LKU. *SSe* late Kushan.

Object #	PNE	LBA	EIA	HEL	TRA	KUS	LKU	EME	HME	LME	PMO
504						✓	✓				
505				✓	✓						
506							✓				
507							✓				
509							✓				

SITE 35/36

510 Body *fr. Pht* 0.079. Pale orange/brown fabric; perforated (d of perforation 0.008).

SITE 36 (Anjirtepa)

511 Body *fr. Pht* 0.05. Brick-red fabric; ochre *sl* and partially worn off *RS*; three tree-shaped impressions.
512 Body *fr. Pht* 0.025. Brick-red fabric, dark brick-red *surf*.

513 Body *fr. Pht* 0.05. Brick-red fabric; ochre *sl* on *out surf*.

SITE 37 (Ayritepa)

514 Rim *fr. Rd* ?, *ext ht* 0.033. Beige fabric, dark brown on fracture.
515 Rim *fr. Rd* ?, *ext ht* 0.021. Fine, dark red fabric, paler on *out surf*.
516 Rim *fr. Rd* ?, *ext ht* 0.027. Pale brown fabric; orange *sl*.
517 Rim *fr. Rd* 0.31, *ext ht* 0.067. Dark red fabric, yellow/brown on *out surf*. Typological parallels R56 (Maxwell-Jones 2015). Period HEL / TRA /KUS / LKU. *SSe* 3rd c. AD.
518 Rim *fr. Rd* 0.25, *ext ht* 0.056. Reddish brown fabric, *out surf* beige.
519 Rim *fr. Rd* 0.15, *ext ht* 0.061. Coarse, dark brown fabric; burned on *out surf*. Typological parallels R41 (Maxwell-Jones 2015). Period HEL / TRA.

520 Rim *fr. Rd* 0.19, *ext ht* 0.069. Beige fabric, orange on fracture.
521 Rim *fr. Rd* 0.1, *ext ht* 0.03. Orange fabric, pale brown on *out surf*. Typological parallels R98 (Maxwell-Jones 2015); R165 (Puschnigg 2006). Period KUS / LKU. *SSe* 3rd c. AD.
522 Rim *fr. Rd* 0.11, *ext ht* 0.022. Pale orange fabric; *RS*.
523 Rim *fr. Rd* 0.12, *ext ht* 0.024. Very fine, pale brown fabric.
524 Rim *fr. Rd* 0.13, *ext ht* 0.019. Fine, pale beige fabric.
525 Rim *fr. Rd* 0.08, *ext ht* 0.027. Fine, pale brown fabric.

526 Rim *fr. Rd* 0.08, *ext ht* 0.024. For fabric description see [525]. Typological parallels R132 (Puschnigg 2006). Period KUS / LKU, cf. Tušlová 2012b, tb. 8:8. *SSe* 3ʳᵈ–4ᵗʰ c. AD.

527 Rim *fr. Rd* 0.06, *ext ht* 0.028. Reddish brown fabric.

528 Rim *fr. Rd* 0.05, *ext ht* 0.016. Dark brown fabric, *out surf* pinkish beige.

529 Rim *fr. Rd* 0.09, *ext ht* 0.02. Very fine, pale brown fabric; *RS*.

Object #	PNE	LBA	EIA	HEL	TRA	KUS	LKU	EME	HME	LME	PMO
517				✓	✓	✓	✓				
519				✓	✓						
521						✓	✓				
526						✓	✓				

SITE 38

530 Rim *fr. Rd* 0.12, *ext ht* 0.022. Pale brown *out surf*; brown *in surf*.

SITE 40 (Shortepa)

531 Rim *fr. Rd* ?, *ext ht* 0.034. Orange fabric; ochre *eng* on *surf*.

532 Rim *fr. Rd* ?, *ext ht* 0.027. Orange fabric; *RS* on both *surf*.

533 Rim *fr. Rd* ?, *ext ht* 0.021. *RS* on both *surf*. Typological parallels R142 (Maxwell-Jones 2015); R1 (Puschnigg 2006); Bowls gr. 2 (1) (Včelicová 2015). Period KUS / LKU. *SSe* 3ʳᵈ and 4ᵗʰ c. AD.

534 Rim *fr. Rd* ?, *ext ht* 0.031. Orange fabric, ochre on *surf*; unsure orientation.

535 Rim *fr. Rd* ?, *ext ht* 0.022. Orange fabric, *out surf* brick-red, *in surf* unpreserved; unsure orientation.

536 Rim *fr. Rd* ?, *ext ht* 0.018. Brown fabric; ochre *eng* on *out surf*.

537 Rim *fr. Rd* ?, *ext ht* 0.02. Brick-red fabric; *rsd* of ochre *eng*.

538 Rim *fr. Rd* ?, *ext ht* 0.012. Brick-red fabric; *RS* on both *surf*.

539 Rim *fr. Rd* 0.11, *ext ht* 0.04.

540 Rim *fr. Rd* 0.1, *ext ht* 0.035. Orange fabric; ochre *eng* on *surf*.

541 Rim *fr. Rd* 0.12, *ext ht* 0.019. Brick-red fabric, *in surf* orange.

542 Rim *fr. Rd* 0.05, *ext ht* 0.028. Brick-red fabric; ochre *eng* on *surf*.

543 Rim *fr. Rd* 0.05, *ext ht* 0.02. Brick-red fabric; *RS* on *in surf*.

544 Rim *fr. Rd* 0.3, *ext ht* 0.028. Brick-red fabric; orange *eng* on *surf*. Typological parallels R133 (Maxwell-Jones 2015). Period KUS / LKU.

545 Rim *fr. Rd* 0.4, *ext ht* 0.075. Sandwich fabric: orange margins/brown core; *in surf* orange; ochre *eng* on *out surf*. Period LKU / EME, cf. Tušlová 2012b, tb. 4:3.

546 Rim *fr. Rd* 0.13, *ext ht* 0.027. Black fabric, *out surf* brick-red, *in surf* brown.

547 Rim *fr. Rd* 0.12, *ext ht* 0.027. Brick-red/orange fabric, *out surf* brick-red, *in surf* orange. Typological parallels R77 (Puschnigg 2006). Period LKU.

548 Rim *fr. Rd* 0.15, *ext ht* 0.035. *RS* on both *surf*. Typological parallels R153 (Maxwell-Jones 2015). Period KUS / LKU. *SSe* 1ˢᵗ–4ᵗʰ c. AD.

549 Rim *fr. Rd* 0.11, *ext ht* 0.015. Brick-red fabric; ochre on *surf*.

550 Rim *fr. Rd* 0.14, *ext ht* 0.026. *RS* on both *surf*. Typological parallels R142 (Maxwell-Jones 2015); R1 (Puschnigg 2006); Bowls gr. 2 (1) (Včelicová 2015). Period KUS / LKU. *SSe* 3ʳᵈ and 4ᵗʰ c. AD.

551 Rim *fr. Rd* 0.1, *ext ht* 0.036. Dark brown fabric. Period KUS. *SSe* Kushan.

552 Body *fr. Pht* 0.032. Orange fabric; ochre *eng* on *out surf*; *WR*. Period LKU. *SSe* 3ʳᵈ and 4ᵗʰ c. AD.

553 *Hdl fr. W* 0.023 × 0.014. Brown fabric.

554 *Hdl fr. W* 0.015 × 0.013.

555 Base *fr. Bd* 0.12, *ext ht* 0.027.

556 Base *fr. Bd* 0.08, *ext ht* 0.027.

Object #	PNE	LBA	EIA	HEL	TRA	KUS	LKU	EME	HME	LME	PMO
533						✓	✓				
544						✓	✓				
545							✓	✓			
547							✓				
548						✓	✓				
550						✓	✓				
551						✓					

SITE 41

557 Rim *fr. Rd* ?, *ext ht* 0.047. Dark brown/red fabric. Typological parallels R56 (Maxwell-Jones 2015). Period HEL / TRA /KUS / LKU. *SSe* 3rd c. AD.
558 Rim *fr. Rd* 0.34, *ext ht* 0.053. Orange/red fabric, *out surf* beige; plastic *lin dec* on *out surf.*

559 Rim *fr. Rd* 0.34, *ext ht* 0.058. Pale brown fabric, red on fracture; light blue *gl* on *in surf.* Period LKU, cf. Zavyalov 2008.
560 Rim *fr. Rd* ?, *ext ht* 0.031. Coarse, dark red fabric, pale brown/beige on *surf.*
561 Rim *fr. Rd* 0.1, *ext ht* 0.024. Dark brown fabric, paler on *out surf.*

Object #	PNE	LBA	EIA	HEL	TRA	KUS	LKU	EME	HME	LME	PMO
557				✓	✓	✓	✓				
559							✓				✓

SITE 42 (Aysaritepa)

562 Rim *fr. Rd* ?, *ext ht* 0.029. Black/red fabric, grey/white on *surf*; potsherd axially cut in halves.
563 Rim *fr. Rd* 0.05, *ext ht* 0.015. Greyish orange fabric.
564 Rim *fr. Rd* 0.1, *ext ht* 0.015. Porous greyish red fabric.
565 Rim *fr. Rd* 0.065, *ext ht* 0.024. Orange fabric; beige *sl.*
566 Rim *fr. Rd* 0.1, *ext ht* 0.036. Black/red fabric; large quartz inclusions; alternating black and red stripe *dec* on *in surf.*

567 Rim *fr. Rd* 0.12, *ext ht* 0.024. Orange fabric.
568 Rim *fr. Rd* 0.12, *ext ht* 0.023. Orange fabric; *out surf* white.
569 Rim *fr. Rd* 0.13, *ext ht* 0.03. Grey fabric. Period KUS. *SSe* Kushan.
570 Rim and *hdl fr. Rd* 0.11, *ext ht* 0.03. Dark red fabric, beige on *surf.*
571 Base *fr. Bd* 0.075, *ext ht* 0.01. Fine, dark grey fabric.
572 Base *fr. Bd* 0.09, *ext ht* 0.039. Coarse, grey fabric.

Object #	PNE	LBA	EIA	HEL	TRA	KUS	LKU	EME	HME	LME	PMO
569						✓					

412

SITE 43

573 Rim *fr. Rd* 0.15, *ext ht* 0.029. Pale brown fabric, *out surf* yellow. Typological parallels R17 (Puschnigg 2006). Period LKU. *SSe* 3ʳᵈ c. AD.

574 Rim *fr. Rd* 0.14, *ext ht* 0.028. Dark red fabric.

575 Rim *fr. Rd* 0.07, *ext ht* 0.044. Orange/red fabric, brown on *surf*. Period LKU. *SSe* 4ᵗʰ c. AD.

576 Rim *fr. Rd* 0.1, *ext ht* 0.015. Orange/red fabric, *out surf* yellow/brown.

577 Rim *fr. Rd* 0.06, *ext ht* 0.026. Coarse, orange fabric.

578 Rim *fr. Rd* 0.085, *ext ht* 0.026. Fine, pale brown fabric, orange on fracture. Typological parallels R103 (Maxwell-Jones 2015). Period KUS / LKU. *SSe* 4ᵗʰ c. AD.

579 Rim *fr. Rd* 0.21, *ext ht* 0.027. Pale brown fabric, reddish on fracture. Period LKU, cf. Zavyalov 2008.

580 Rim *fr. Rd* 0.24, *ext ht* 0.042. Orange/red fabric, brown on *surf*.

581 Rim *fr. Rd* 0.28, *ext ht* 0.036. Dark red fabric. Typological parallels *Chasha* 5 (Zavyalov 2008). Period LKU.

582 Rim *fr. Rd* 0.21, *ext ht* 0.048. Sandwich fabric: dark red/light brown margins, black core; quartz inclusion size up to 0.005. Typological parallels R83 (Maxwell-Jones 2015); *storage jars* gr. 4A/B (5) (Včelicová 2015); *khumtscha* 1 (Zavyalov 2008). Period KUS / LKU.

583 Rim *fr. Rd* ?, *ext ht* 0.025. Orange/red fabric with inclusions.

584 Rim *fr. Rd* ?, *ext ht* 0.051. Coarse, brown fabric, greyish on *surf*; quartz inclusion size up to 0.006. Typological parallels R84 (Maxwell-Jones 2015); *storage jars* gr. 4C (Včelicová 2015); *khum* 3 (Zavyalov 2008). Period LKU. *SSe* late Kushan.

585 Base *fr. Bd* 0.06, *ext ht* 0.011. Dark brown fabric, *out surf* green/grey.

586 Base *fr. Bd* 0.04, *ext ht* 0.017. Red fabric; dark *RS*.

587 Base *fr. Bd* 0.08, *ext ht* 0.017. Very fine, black fabric.

Object #	PNE	LBA	EIA	HEL	TRA	KUS	LKU	EME	HME	LME	PMO
573							✓				
575				✓	✓	✓	✓	✓			
578						✓	✓				
579							✓				
581							✓				
582						✓	✓				
584							✓				

SITE 45

588 Rim *fr. Rd* 0.17, *ext ht* 0.033. Brick-red fabric. Period KUS / LKU (cf. Zavyalov 2008). *SSe* 1ˢᵗ c. AD.

589 Rim *fr. Rd* 0.14, *ext ht* 0.029. RS on *in surf*.

590 Rim *fr. Rd* 0.11, *ext ht* 0.047. Typological parallels R91 (Maxwell-Jones 2015). Period LKU / EME.

591 Rim *fr. Rd* 0.18, *ext ht* 0.021. RS on both *surf*. Typological parallels R143/144 (Maxwell-Jones 2015); R212 (Puschnigg 2006); Bowls gr. 3A (5) (Včelicová 2015); *Chasha* 2 (Zavyalov 2008). Period KUS / LKU. *SSe* 1ˢᵗ–3ʳᵈ c. AD.

592 Rim *fr. Rd* 0.21, *ext ht* 0.023.

593 Rim *fr. Rd* 0.32, *ext ht* 0.019. Ochre *eng* on both *surf*.

594 Rim *fr. Rd* 0.4, *ext ht* 0.085.

595 Rim *fr. Rd* 0.2, *ext ht* 0.069. Brick-red fabric.

596 Rim *fr. Rd* 0.22, *ext ht* 0.032. Ochre *eng* on both *surf*.

597 Body *fr. Pht* 0.047. RS on *out surf*.

598 Body *fr. Pht* 0.06. Dark red fabric, *in surf* pale red; ochre *eng* on *out surf*.

599 Hdl *fr. W* 0.033 × 0.01. Brick-red fabric; ochre *eng* on *out surf*.

600 Hdl *fr. W* 0.017 × 0.011. Brick-red fabric.

Object #	PNE	LBA	EIA	HEL	TRA	KUS	LKU	EME	HME	LME	PMO
588						✓	✓				
590							✓	✓			
591						✓	✓				
594			✓								

SITE 48 (south-east mound of Kattatepa)

601 *Comp* lid. Lid *d* 0.09, *ht* 0.034. Fine, grey/beige fabric.
602 Rim *fr. Rd* ?, *ext ht* 0.012. Dark orange, green/beige on *surf.*
603 Rim *fr. Rd* 0.06, *ext ht* 0.02. Dark brown/red fabric. Typological parallels R96 (Maxwell-Jones 2015); R133 (Puschnigg 2006); *kuvshiny* IIa (Zavyalov 2008). Period LKU.

604 Rim *fr. Rd* 0.08, *ext ht* 0.054. Orange/brown fabric with inclusions, grey/beige on *surf*; moulding on *surf.*
605 Rim *fr. Rd* 0.12, *ext ht* 0.013. Dark orange fabric; *RS.*
606 Rim *fr. Rd* 0.31, *ext ht* 0.074. Brown/orange fabric; *in surf* burned. Typological parallels R121 (Maxwell-Jones 2015). Period LKU. *SSe* 4th c. AD.
607 Base *fr. Bd* 0.142, *ext ht* 0.135. Beige fabric; orange stains.

Object #	PNE	LBA	EIA	HEL	TRA	KUS	LKU	EME	HME	LME	PMO
603							✓				
606							✓				

SITE 49 (Olleiortepa)

608 Rim *fr. Rd* ?, *ext ht* 0.017. Black, green and white *gl* (floral *dec*); *rsd* of *gl* on *out surf.*

SITE 50

609 Rim *fr. Rd* ?, *ext ht* 0.02. Orange fabric, creamy ochre on *surf.*
610 Body *fr. Pht (in)* 0.031. Orange fabric, *in surf* yellow; yellow *gl* on *out surf*; *WR*; unsure orientation.

611 Body *fr. Pht* 0.02. Orange fabric, *in surf* yellow; yellow *gl* on *out surf*; unsure orientation.
612 Base *fr. Bd* 0.08, *ext ht* 0.036. Orange fabric, creamy/yellow on *out surf*; distinctive *WR.*

SITE 52 (Khosyattepa)

613 Rim *fr. Rd* ?, *ext ht* 0.019. Brick-red fabric; ochre *eng* and *rsd* of *RS* on *out surf.*
614 Rim *fr. Rd* ?, *ext ht* 0.015. For fabric description see [613]. Typological parallels R143/144 (Maxwell-Jones 2015); R212 (Puschnigg 2006); Bowls gr.

3A (5) (Včelicová 2015); Chasha 2 (Zavyalov 2008). Period KUS / LKU. *SSe* 1st–3rd c. AD.
615 Rim *fr. Rd* 0.11, *ext ht* 0.028. Brick-red fabric; inclusion size up to 0.002.
616 Body *fr. Pht* 0.018. Orange fabric; yellow *eng* on both *surf.*

Object #	PNE	LBA	EIA	HEL	TRA	KUS	LKU	EME	HME	LME	PMO
614						✓	✓				

SITE 53 (Tigrmantepa)

617 Rim *fr. Rd* 0.25, *ext ht* 0.027. Brick-red fabric.

618 Base *fr. Bd* ?, *ext ht* 0.047. Brown fabric; ochre *eng* on *surf.*

SITE 54 (Anjirtepa)

619 Body *fr. Pht* 0.04. Brick-red fabric; *RS* on *out surf.* Period LKU. *SSe* 4th c. AD.

620 Base *fr. Bd* 0.08, *ext ht* 0.062. Period LKU. *SSe* 4th c. AD.

621 Base *fr. Bd* 0.09, *ext ht* 0.02. Brick-red fabric. Period LKU. *SSe* 4th c. AD.

Object #	PNE	LBA	EIA	HEL	TRA	KUS	LKU	EME	HME	LME	PMO
619							✓				
620							✓				
621							✓				

SITE 55 (Khalinchaktepa)

622 Rim *fr. Rd* 0.38, *ext ht* 0.079. Brown fabric; ochre *eng* on *surf.* Period LKU. *SSe* 4th c. AD.

623 Rim and *hdl fr. Rd* 0.09, *ext ht* 0.03. Ochre fabric; ochre *eng* on *surf.* Typological parallels R21 (Puschnigg 2006). Period LKU.

624 Rim *fr. Rd* 0.17, *ext ht* 0.042. Typological parallels R142 (Maxwell-Jones 2015); R1 (Puschnigg 2006); Bowls gr. 2 (1) (Včelicová 2015). Period KUS / LKU. *SSe* 3rd and 4th c. AD.

625 Rim *fr. Rd* 0.1, *ext ht* 0.015. Brick-red fabric; ochre *eng* on *out surf.*

626 Rim *fr. Rd* ?, *ext ht* 0.033. For fabric description see [625]. Period LKU. *SSe* 3rd–4th c. AD.

627 Body *fr. Pht* 0.056. Orange fabric; white, black and partially blue *gl* and *inc dec* on *in surf*; stripe of white *gl* on *out surf*; unsure orientation. Period HME. *SSe* 12th c. AD.

628 Body *fr. Pht* 0.031. Orange fabric; ochre *eng* on *surf.* Period HME. *SSe* 12th c. AD.

629 *Hld fr.* W 0.035 × 0.018.

630 Base *fr. Bd* 0.05, *ext ht* 0.011. Brick-red fabric.

Object #	PNE	LBA	EIA	HEL	TRA	KUS	LKU	EME	HME	LME	PMO
622							✓				
623							✓				
624						✓	✓				
626							✓				
627									✓		
628									✓		

SITE 58 (Anjirtepa)

651 Rim *fr. Rd* 0.1, *ext ht* 0.029. Brown fabric; ochre eng on surf; *HM*. Period HME. *SSe* 12th c. AD.

652 Rim *fr. Rd* 0.1, *ext ht* 0.017. Brick-red fabric; ochre eng on out surf. *SSe* LKU.

653 Rim *fr. Rd* 0.14, *ext ht* 0.043. Brown fabric; ochre eng on out surf; rsd of RS on in surf.

654 Rim *fr. Rd* ?, *ext ht* 0.023. Typological parallels R153 (Maxwell-Jones 2015). Period KUS / LKU. *SSe* 1st–4th c. AD.

655 Rim *fr. Rd* ?, *ext ht* 0.019. Brown fabric; ochre eng on surf. Period LKU. *SSe* 3rd–4th c. AD.

656 Body *fr. Pht* 0.018. Unsure orientation. Period LKU. *SSe* 3rd–4th c. AD.

657 *Hdl fr.* W 0.025 × 0.011. Brick-red fabric. Period LKU. *SSe* 3rd–4th c. AD.

Object #	PNE	LBA	EIA	HEL	TRA	KUS	LKU	EME	HME	LME	PMO
651									✓		
652							✓				
654						✓	✓				
655							✓				
656							✓				
657							✓				

SITE 61

658 Rim *fr. Rd* 0.24, *ext ht* 0.079. Brick-red fabric; ochre *eng* on *surf.* Typological parallels R27 (Maxwell-Jones 2015). Period HEL / TRA.
659 Rim *frr. Rd* ?, *ext ht* 0.094. Sandwich fabric: red margins/black core; ochre *eng* on *surf.*

660 Rim *fr. Rd* ?, *ext ht* 0.052. Brown fabric.
661 Body *fr. Pht* 0.04. Orange fabric, *out surf* ochre, *in surf* unpreserved, unsure orientation.

Object #	PNE	LBA	EIA	HEL	TRA	KUS	LKU	EME	HME	LME	PMO
658				✓	✓						

SITE 63 (Chalakurgan)

664 Rim *fr. Rd* 0.24, *ext ht* 0.046. Black fabric, red on *surf.*
665 Rim *fr. Rd* 0.15, *ext ht* 0.018. Brown fabric; ochre *eng* on *surf.*
666 Rim *fr. Rd* ?, *ext ht* 0.047. Brick-red fabric; ochre *eng* on *surf.*
667 Rim *fr. Rd* ?, *ext ht* 0.034. Brown fabric; ochre *eng* on *out surf*, *in surf* unpreserved.
668 Rim *fr. Rd* ?, *ext ht* 0.027. *RS* on both *surf.*

669 Rim *fr. Rd* ?, *ext ht* 0.014. Brick-red/orange fabric, *in surf* orange, *out surf* brick-red.
670 Rim *fr. Rd* ?, *ext ht* 0.015. Brown fabric, *out surf* ochre, *in surf* orange; fine *gl.*
671 Body *fr. Pht* 0.028. Brick-red fabric; ochre *eng* on *out surf.*
672 Body *fr. Pht* 0.032. Brick-red fabric; *RS* on *out surf.*
673 Body *fr. Pht* 0.012. Yellow fabric.

SITE 71

674 Rim *fr. Rd* 0.37, *ext ht* 0.055. Dark orange/reddish fabric, out surf beige.

SITE 72 (north-west mound of Talashkantepa)

675 Rim *fr. Rd* 0.38, *ext ht* 0.042. Orange fabric; *out surf* partially beige. Typological parallels R127 (Maxwell-Jones 2015). Period LKU.
676 Rim *fr. Rd* 0.16, *ext ht* 0.034. Fine, pale brown fabric; *RS.* Typological parallels R25 (Puschnigg 2006). Period LKU.
677 Rim *fr. Rd* 0.08, *ext ht* 0.013. Orange fabric, yellow/brown on *surf.*
678 Rim *fr. Rd* 0.07, *ext ht* 0.046. Fine, grey fabric, black on *in surf*, *inc dec* on *out surf.* Typological parallels Period PMO, cf. Tušlová 2012b, tb. 4:1.

679 Rim and *hdl fr. Rd* 0.08, *ext ht* 0.08. Dark red fabric; *WR.* Period HME / LME, cf. Tušlová 2012b, tb. 2:5. *SSe* Late medieval.
680 Rim *fr. Rd* ?, *ext ht* 0.029. Brown fabric; *inc dec.*
681 Body fr. *Pht* 0.192. Beige fabric; partially red stains on *surf.*
682 Base *fr. Bd* 0.108, *ext ht* 0.013. Coarse, dark red fabric.

Object #	PNE	LBA	EIA	HEL	TRA	KUS	LKU	EME	HME	LME	PMO
675							✓				
676							✓				
678											✓
679										✓	✓	

SITE 75

683 Rim *fr. Rd* 0.26, *ext ht* 0.088.
684 Rim *fr. Rd* 0.18, *ext ht* 0.032. Typological parallels R142 (Maxwell-Jones 2015); R1 (Puschnigg 2006); Bowls gr. 2 (1) (Včelicová 2015). Period KUS / LKU. *SSe* 3rd and 4th c. AD.
685 Rim *fr. Rd* 0.2, *ext ht* 0.018. Typological parallels R143/144 (Maxwell-Jones 2015); R212 (Puschnigg 2006); Bowls gr. 3A (5) (Včelicová 2015); Chasha 2 (Zavyalov 2008). Period KUS / LKU. *SSe* 1st–3rd c. AD.

686 Rim *fr. Rd* 0.2, *ext ht* 0.016. Typological parallels R143/144 (Maxwell-Jones 2015); R212 (Puschnigg 2006); Bowls gr. 3A (5) (Včelicová 2015); Chasha 2 (Zavyalov 2008). Period KUS / LKU. *SSe* 1st–3rd c. AD.
687 Body and *hdl fr. Pht* 0.066.
688 Body *fr. Pht* 0.047.
689 Base *fr. Bd* 0.06, *ext ht* 0.025.

Object #	PNE	LBA	EIA	HEL	TRA	KUS	LKU	EME	HME	LME	PMO
683								✓			
684						✓	✓				
685						✓	✓				
686						✓	✓				

SITE 77 (Egiztepa I)

690 Rim *fr. Rd* 0.18, *ext ht* 0.025. Dark red fabric.
691 Rim *fr. Rd* 0.12, *ext ht* 0.038. Reddish brown fabric.

692 Rim *fr. Rd* ?, *ext ht* 0.023. Dark red fabric; greyish *RS*.
693 Base *fr. Bd* 0.04, *ext ht* 0.015. For fabric description see [692].

SITE 78 (Egiztepa II)

694 Rim *fr. Rd* ?, *ext ht* 0.03. Dark brown/red fabric.
695 Rim *fr. Rd* 0.34, *ext ht* 0.038. For fabric description see [694]. Typological parallels R175 (Maxwell Jones 2015). Period HEL / TRA.
696 Rim *fr. Rd* 0.2, *ext ht* 0.031. Dark brown fabric, *in surf* reddish.

697 Rim *fr. Rd* 0.12, *ext ht* 0.026. Very fine, dark red fabric; finely *pol*.
698 Rim *fr. Rd* 0.09, *ext ht* 0.016. Very fine, dark red fabric, *in surf* brownish.
699 Base *fr. Bd* 0.05, *ext ht* 0.015. Dark brown, partially reddish fabric; tiny quartz inclusions.

Object #	PNE	LBA	EIA	HEL	TRA	KUS	LKU	EME	HME	LME	PMO
695				✓	✓						

SITE 79

700 *Comp vsl. Rd* 0.42, *ht* 0.08.
701 Rim *fr. Rd* 0.13, *ext ht* 0.068.
702 Body and *hdl fr.* Body *pht* 0.039.

703 Body *fr. Pht* 0.041.
704 Base *fr. Bd* 0.1, *ext ht* 0.087.
705 Base *fr. Bd* 0.09, *ext ht* 0.066.

SITE 80

706 Rim *fr. Rd* 0.3, *ext ht* 0.05. Dark orange fabric. Typological parallels R132 (Puschnigg 2006). Period LKU.
707 Rim *fr. Rd* 0.36, *ext ht* 0.032. Pale orange fabric, *surf* beige.
708 Rim *fr. Rd* 0.28, *ext ht* 0.015.
709 Rim and *hdl fr. Rd* 0.09, *ext ht* 0.047. Typological parallels R21 (Puschnigg 2006). Period LKU.
710 Rim *fr. Rd* 0.12, *ext ht* 0.025. Black fabric with inclusions, *surf* red.
711 Rim *fr. Rd* 0.13, *ext ht* 0.018. Typological parallels R137 (Maxwell-Jones 2015); R100 (Puschnigg 2006). Period HEL / TRA / KUS / LKU.
712 Rim *fr. Rd* 0.26, *ext ht* 0.057. Orange fabric; beige *sl.* Typological parallels R54 (Maxwell-Jones 2015). Period EIA / HEL.
713 Rim *fr. Rd* 0.14, *ext ht* 0.053. Dark orange fabric, *surf* ochre; brown inclusions of considerable size; burned; *HM.*
714 Rim *fr. Rd* 0.12, *ext ht* 0.03.
715 Rim *fr. Rd* 0.1, *ext ht* 0.026.
716 Rim *fr. Rd* 0.06, *ext ht* 0.04. Dark orange fabric; grey *sl* on *out surf.* Typological parallels R132 (Pus-

chnigg 2006). Period KUS / LKU, cf. Tušlová 2012b, tb. 8:8. *SSe* 3rd–4th c. AD.
717 Rim *fr. Rd* 0.08, *ext ht* 0.026. Typological parallels R103 (Maxwell-Jones 2015). Period KUS / LKU. *SSe* 4th c. AD.
718 Rim *fr. Rd* 0.07, *ext ht* 0.019. Typological parallels R96 (Maxwell-Jones 2015); R133 (Puschnigg 2006); *kuvshiny* IIa (Zavyalov 2008). Period LKU.
719 Rim *fr. Rd* 0.07, *ext ht* 0.03. Typological parallels R98 (Maxwell-Jones 2015); R165 (Puschnigg 2006). Period KUS / LKU. *SSe* 3rd c. AD.
720 Rim *fr. Rd* ?, *ext ht* 0.028. *HM.*
721 Rim *fr. Rd* ?, *ext ht* 0.024.
722 Rim *fr. Rd* ?, *ext ht* 0.037. Green/blue *gl.*
723 Lid *fr. Rd* 0.16, *ext ht* 0.015.
724 Body *fr. Pht* 0.039.
725 Body (?)/rim (?) *fr. Ht* 0.022.
726 Base *fr. Bd* 0.09, *ext ht* 0.018. Beige fabric; crackled green *gl* on *in surf.*
727 Base *fr. Bd* 0.16, *ext ht* 0.035. Orange fabric; beige *sl* on *out surf.*
728 Base *fr. Bd* 0.1, *ext ht* 0.037. Orange fabric, *surf* beige.

Object #	PNE	LBA	EIA	HEL	TRA	KUS	LKU	EME	HME	LME	PMO
706							✓				
709							✓				
711				✓	✓	✓	✓				
712			✓	✓							
716						✓	✓				
717						✓	✓				
718							✓				
719						✓	✓				

SITE 88

729 Rim *fr. Rd* 0.41, *ext ht* 0.078. Fine orange/red fabric, *out surf* pale yellow/brown; *inc dec* on *in* rim. *SSe* medieval.
730 Rim and *hdl fr. Rd* ?, *ext ht* 0.104, *hdl w* 0.035 × 0.015. Very fine, pale yellow/brown fabric; *inc lin dec* on *out surf.*

731 Rim *fr. Rd* 0.27, *ext ht* 0.068. Brown fabric, yellow/brown on *surf; inc* geometric *dec* on *out surf.* Typological parallels R81 (Maxwell-Jones 2015). Period HEL / TRA.
732 Rim *fr. Rd* 0.23, *ext ht* 0.046. Fine, pale yellow/brown fabric, red on fracture; *inc dec. SSe* HME / LME.

733 Rim *fr. Rd* 0.014, *ext ht* 0.103. Grey/black fabric. Period HME / LME, cf. Tušlová 2012b, tb. 2:7, Galieva 2014.

734 Rim *fr. Rd* ?, *ext ht* 0.04. Fine, pale yellow/brown fabric, darker on fracture; *inc dec* on *in surf.*

735 Rim *fr. Rd* 0.17, *ext ht* 0.029. Red fabric, surf pale yellow/brown.

736 Rim *fr. Rd* 0.13(?), *ext ht* 0.016. Fine, orange fabric.

737 *Hdl fr. W* 0.037 × 0.017. Fine, pale yellow/brown fabric.

738 Base *fr. Bd* 0.07, *ext ht* 0.023. Very fine, orange/brown fabric.

Object #	PNE	LBA	EIA	HEL	TRA	KUS	LKU	EME	HME	LME	PMO
731				✓	✓						
732									✓	✓	
733									✓	✓	

SITE 94 (Kurgan)

745 Rim and *hdl fr. Rd* 0.08, *ext ht* 0.051, *w* 0.058 × 0.028. Pale orange fabric.

746 Rim *fr. Rd* ?, *ext ht* 0.045. Fine, red fabric, surf brown/yellow; *inc crvl dec.* Period LKU. *SSe* 2nd half of 3rd c. AD.

747 Rim *fr. Rd* ?, *ext ht* 0.05. Coarse fabric, brown/yellow on *out surf*, orange on *in surf.*

748 Rim *fr. Rd* ?, *ext ht* 0.03. Very fine, pale brown fabric; green, blue and black *gl* on *in surf*; cyan *gl* on *out surf.*

749 Rim *fr. Rd* 0.36, *ext ht* 0.057. Fine, pale brown/yellow/red fabric. Period LKU, cf. Tušlová 2012b, tb. 6:7.

750 Rim *fr. Rd* 0.23, *ext ht* 0.06. Coarse, reddish fabric, *in surf* black. Typological parallels R175 (Puschnigg 2006). Period LKU.

751 Rim *fr. Rd* 0.2, *ext ht* 0.041. Fine, pale orange fabric, *in surf* darker. Period KUS. *SSe* Kushan/medieval.

752 Rim *fr. Rd* 0.44, *ext ht* 0.037. Very fine, pale yellow/brown fabric, orange on fracture; *inc dec* on rim. Typological parallels R158 (Maxwell-Jones 2015). Period HEL / TRA.

753 Rim *fr. Rd* 0.2-0.24, *ext ht* 0.035. Grey fabric; blue, green and black *gl.* Period EME (cf. Tušlová 2012b, tb. 3:4).

754 Rim *fr. Rd* 0.15, *ext ht* 0.02. Fine, pale brown/yellow fabric, orange on fracture. Typological parallels R75 (Puschnigg 2006). Period LKU.

755 Rim *fr. Rd* 0.13, *ext ht* 0.02. Fine, brown/yellow fabric; white *gl* on *out surf*, green/blue *gl* on *in surf.* Cf. Zavyalov 2008, 163: 76.2.

756 Rim *fr. Rd* 0.13, *ext ht* 0.018. Coarse, yellow/orange fabric.

757 Rim *fr. Rd* 0.045, *ext ht* 0.016. Fine, red fabric, *surf* brown/yellow.

758 Rim *fr. Rd* 0.05, *ext ht* 0.03. Coarse, orange/brown fabric.

759 Rim *fr. Rd* 0.08, *ext ht* 0.023. Fine, pale yellow/brown fabric. Typological parallels R98 (Maxwell-Jones 2015); R165 (Puschnigg 2006). Period KUS / LKU. *SSe* 3rd c. AD.

760 Rim *fr. Rd* 0.07, *ext ht* 0.028. Pale yellow/brown fabric; brown *sl.*

761 Spout *fr. L* 0.063, spout *d* at the knob 0.022. Coarse, pale brown fabric.

762 Base *fr. Bd* 0.12, *ext ht* 0.011. Fine, pale brown fabric; green purple and white *gl.*

763 Base *fr. Bd* 0.05, *ext ht* 0.016. Pale brown fabric; green and blue *gl.*

764 Base *fr. Bd* 0.045, *ext ht* 0.009. Fine, brown/yellow fabric; dark *RS.*

765 Base *fr. Bd* 0.07, *ext ht* 0.064. Fine, beige fabric; cyan and black *gl* on upper part.

Object #	PNE	LBA	EIA	HEL	TRA	KUS	LKU	EME	HME	LME	PMO
746							✓				
749							✓				
750							✓				
752				✓	✓						
753								✓			
754							✓				
759						✓	✓				

SITE 95

766 *Comp vsl. Rd* 0.27, *bd* 0.08, *ht* 0.084. Very fine, pale yellow/brown fabric; *WR*.

767 Rim *fr. Rd* 0.16, *ext ht* 0.025. Very fine, pale red fabric. Cf. Zavyalov 2008, 163: 76.2.

768 Rim *fr. Rd* 0.18, *ext ht* 0.019. Fine, pale yellow/brown fabric, black and blue *gl*. Period EME (cf. Tušlová 2012b, tb. 3:4).

769 Rim *fr. Rd* 0.12, *ext ht* 0.024. Coarse, brick-red fabric.

770 Rim *fr. Rd* 0.19, *ext ht* 0.04. Fine, pale brown fabric.

771 Rim *fr. Rd* 0.07, *ext ht* 0.026. Very fine, pale orange fabric; *rsd* of brown *sl* on *in surf.*

772 Rim *fr. Rd* 0.1, *ext ht* 0.026. Fine, orange fabric; orange *sl*. Cf. Zavyalov 2008, 163: 76.2. Period LKU.

773 Rim *fr. Rd* 0.1, *ext ht* 0.029. Fine, pale brown fabric; *hdl* broken away.

774 Rim *fr. Rd* 0.11, *ext ht* 0.033. Fine, orange/brown fabric; *rsd* of RS.

775 Rim *fr. Rd* 0.12, *ext ht* 0.035. Fine, dark red fabric, *out surf* coarse, brown/grey.

776 Rim *fr. Rd* 0.24, *ext ht* 0.042. Very fine, pale orange fabric, *surf* brown/yellow.

777 Rim *fr. Rd* 0.28, *ext ht* 0.027. Fine, pale grey fabric; brown and green *gl* on *in surf.* Period LKU (?), cf. Zavyalov 2008.

778 Rim *fr. Rd* 0.25, *ext ht* 0.056. Very fine, pale yellow/brown fabric, orange on fracture.

779 Rim *fr. Rd* 0.34, *ext ht* 0.064. Fine, pale brown fabric; blue *gl* (floral and geometric *dec*). Cf. Zavyalov 2008, 185: 98.12(?).

780 Rim *fr. Rd* 0.34, *ext ht* 0.045. Fine, orange fabric. Typological parallels R133 (Maxwell-Jones 2015). Period LKU.

781 Rim *fr. Rd* 0.35, *ext ht* 0.0243 Fine, pale yellow/brow fabric, pinkish on *surf; inc lin dec* on *out* rim. Cf. Zavyalov 2008, 165: 78.16.

782 Rim *fr. Rd* 0.35, *ext ht* 0.065. Fine, pale yellow/brown fabric, pinkish on fracture; *inc crvl dec* on *out* rim; *WR*.

783 Rim *fr. Rd* 0.36, *ext ht* 0.05. Fine, pale yellow/brown fabric, pinkish on fracture; *inc crvl dec* on *out* rim.

784 Rim *fr. Rd* 0.38, *ext ht* 0.075. Fine, pale yellow/brown fabric; distinctive *WR*.

785 Rim *fr. Rd* 0.38, *ext ht* 0.055. Grey fabric, *out surf* orange; quartz inclusion size up to 0.004. Cf. Zavyalov 2008, 179: 92.20. Typological parallels R84 (Maxwell-Jones 2015); *storage jars* gr. 4C (Včelicová 2015); *khum* 3 (Zavyalov 2008). Period LKU. *SSe* late Kushan.

786 Rim *fr. Rd* 0.26, *ext ht* 0.058. Coarse fabric, dark red on *surf; in surf* burned; white inclusion size up to 0.005.

787 Rim *fr. Rd* 0.18, *ext ht* 0.055. Black fabric, dark red on *surf;* inclusion size up to 0.003. Cf. Zavyalov 2008, 166: 79.36(?).

788 Base *fr. Bd* 0.11, *ext ht* 0.04. Coarse, pale orange fabric; white and black *gl* (floral and solar motives).

789 Base *fr. Bd* 0.1, *ext ht* 0.073. Fine, pale brown fabric; white and blue *gl* on *in surf;* cuts and ledges – probably defects in manufacture.

Object #	PNE	LBA	EIA	HEL	TRA	KUS	LKU	EME	HME	LME	PMO
768								✓			
772							✓				
777							✓				
780							✓				
785							✓				

SITE 96

790 Rim *fr. Rd* 0.25(?), *ext ht* 0.053. Coarse pale brown fabric, dark red on fracture.

791 *Hdl fr. Pht* 0.04, *w* 0.023 × 0.013.

SITE 98 (Hurjok cemetery)

792 Rim *fr. Rd* 0.415, *ext ht* 0.17. Fine, beige fabric, orange on fracture. Typological parallels R109 (Maxwell-Jones 2015). Period LKU.

793 Rim *fr. Rd* 0.37, *ext ht* 0.088. Fine, orange fabric, white on *out surf*; plastic *dec* on rim.

794 Rim *fr. Rd* 0.32, *ext ht* 0.064. Coarse, orange fabric with grey core; quartz inclusions.

795 Rim *fr. Rd* 0.24, *ext ht* 0.033. Coarse, dark brown fabric with quartz inclusions; white/pinkish *sl*. Cf. Zavyalov 2008, 184: 97.11. Typological parallels R83 (Maxwell-Jones 2015); *storage jars* gr. 4A/B (5) (Včelicová 2015); *khumtscha* 1 (Zavyalov 2008). Period KUS / LKU.

796 Rim *fr. Rd* 0.28, *ext ht* 0.028. Pale beige fabric; orange, brown and green *gl* on *in surf*. Cf. Zavyalov 2008, 163: 76.7(?).Period LKU (?).

797 Rim *fr. Rd* 0.13, *ext ht* 0.016. Fine, brown/orange fabric; orange *sl*. Cf. Zavyalov 2008, 169: 82.11(?).Typological parallels R94 (Puschnigg 2006); Bowls gr. 1A (3) (Včelicová 2015). Period LKU.

798 Rim and *hdl fr. Rd* ?, rim *ht* 0.046. Coarse, grey/brown fabric; quartz and fine ceramics inclusions (approximately 0.002); twisted *hdl*.

799 Body and *hdl fr. Pht* 0.158. Very fine, pale brown fabric, *out surf* white, sporadically red stains; *inc dec* on *out surf*.

800 Body *fr. Pht* 0.097. Fine, pale brown/yellow fabric; compound floral motives stamped (details badly preserved); traces of impressed fingers.

801 Base *fr. Bd* 0.08, *ext ht* 0.021. Beige fabric; cyan, black and white *gl* on *in surf* (floral motive).

802 Base *fr. Bd* 0.06, *ext ht* 0.035. Pale beige fabric; light blue *gl* on *in surf*; vertical *lin dec* on *out surf*; *HM*.

803 Base *fr. Bd* 0.055, *ext ht* 0.032. Very fine, pale brown fabric, darker on *surf*. Cf. Zavyalov 2008, 180: 93.25.

804 Base *fr. Bd* 0.04, *ext ht* 0.015. Pale brown fabric; white *gl* on *in surf*.

805 Base *fr. Bd* 0.1, *ext ht* 0.026. Fine, pale beige fabric, orange on fracture; green, yellow and black *gl* on *in surf* (geometric motive).

806 Base *fr. Bd* 0.1, *ext ht* 0.049. Fine, orange/beige fabric; *in surf* badly preserved; bossed.

807 Base (?) *fr. Bd* 0.11, *ext ht* 0.058. Beige fabric, *out surf* pale yellow/brown; unsure orientation.

Object #	PNE	LBA	EIA	HEL	TRA	KUS	LKU	EME	HME	LME	PMO
792							✓				
795						✓	✓				
797							✓				

SITE 99 (Talashkantepa III)

808 Rim *fr. Rd* 0.45, *ext ht* 0.052.

809 Rim *fr. Rd* 0.45, *ext ht* 0.046.

810 Rim *fr. Rd* 0.42, *ext ht* 0.087. Beige fabric, in surf orange.

811 Rim *fr. Rd* 0.34, *ext ht* 0.05.

812 Rim *fr. Rd* 0.29, *ext ht* 0.096.

813 Rim *fr. Rd* 0.34, *ext ht* 0.085. Typological parallels *khumtscha* 1 (Zavyalov 2008). Period LKU.

814 Rim *fr. Rd* ?, *ext ht* 0.085

815 Rim *fr. Rd* ?, *ext ht* 0.087. Typological parallels R56 (Maxwell-Jones 2015). Period HEL / TRA / KUS / LKU. *SSe* 3rd c. AD.

816 Rim *fr. Rd* 0.14, *ext ht* 0.044. Typological parallels R99 (Maxwell-Jones 2015); R198 (Puschnigg

2006). Period TRA / KUS / LKU. *SSe* 3rd–4th c. AD.

817 Rim and *hdl fr. Rd* ?, *ext ht* 0.046, *hdl w* 0.029 × 0.012.

818 Rim *fr. Rd* ?, *ext ht* 0.039.

819 Rim *fr. Rd* ?, *ext ht* 0.035.

820 Rim *fr. Rd* ?, *ext ht* 0.036. White/yellow fabric. Plastic *dec*.

821 Rim (?) *fr. Rd* ?, *w* 0.044.

822 Body *fr. Pht* 0.063. *Inc* floral *dec*.

823 Body *fr. Pht* 0.069. *Inc* floral *dec*.

824 Base *fr. Bd* 0.12, *ext ht* 0.033.

825 Base *fr. Bd* 0.12, *ext ht* 0.042.

826 Base *fr. Bd* ?, *ext ht* 0.017.

Object #	PNE	LBA	EIA	HEL	TRA	KUS	LKU	EME	HME	LME	PMO
812								✓	✓	✓	
813							✓				
815				✓	✓	✓	✓				
816					✓	✓	✓				

SITE 100

827 Rim *fr. Rd* 0.45, *ht* 0.122. Coarse, yellow/brown/orange fabric, brown on fracture.

828 Rim *fr. Rd* 0.38, *ext ht* 0.055. Pale brown fabric, darker on fracture.

829 Rim *fr. Rd* 0.17, *ext ht* 0.083. Orange fabric, *out surf* yellow/brown.

830 Rim and *hdl fr. Rd* 0.19, *ext ht* 0.056, *w* 0.033 × 0.011. Fine, brown fabric; *inc dec* on *out surf*. Period LKU. *SSe* 4ᵗʰ c. AD.

831 Rim and *hdl fr. Rd* 0.05, *ext ht* 0.03, *w* 0.031 × 0.022. Grey/brown fabric with brown inclusions. Typological parallels R21 (Puschnigg 2006). Period LKU.

832 Rim *fr. Rd* 0.08, *ext ht* 0.022. Pale brown fabric; cyan, blue and green *gl* (*lin dec*).

833 Rim *fr. Rd* 0.19, *ext ht* 0.05. Yellow/brown fabric, red on fracture; *dec* rim.

834 Rim and *hdl fr. Rd* 0.11, *ext* rim *ht* 0.031. Orange/brown fabric, *out surf* yellow/brown; rivet-imitating *hdl*.

835 Rim *fr. Rd* 0.11, *ext ht* 0.037. Fine, orange/brown fabric.

836 Rim *fr. Rd* 0.42, *ext ht* 0.154. Dark grey/brown fabric.

837 Knob. Max *d* 0.066, *ht* 0.034. Very coarse, brown fabric.

838 Body *fr.* Max *d* 0.046, p*ht* 0.047. Pale brown fabric. Cf. Zavyalov 2008, 160: 72. кубки 2.

839 Base *fr. Bd* 0.06, *ext ht* 0.046. Pale brown/orange fabric; white and blue *gl* (dots) on *in surf*.

840 Base *fr. Bd* 0.07, *ext ht* 0.047. Orange fabric; light brown *sl*.

841 Base *fr. Bd* 0.065, *ext ht* 0.051. Brown/orange fabric.

Object #	PNE	LBA	EIA	HEL	TRA	KUS	LKU	EME	HME	LME	PMO
830							✓				
831							✓				

SITE 101

842 Rim *fr. Rd* 0.17, *ext ht* 0.073. Orange fabric; beige *sl*.

843 Rim *fr. Rd* 0.18, *ext ht* 0.04. Worn, beige *sl*.

844 Rim *fr. Rd* 0.18, *ext ht* 0.049. Orange fabric; beige *sl*.

845 Rim *fr. Rd* 0.14, *ext ht* 0.057. *Out surf* beige, *in surf* orange.

846 Rim *fr. Rd* 0.055, *ext ht* 0.036. Typological parallels R21 (Puschnigg 2006). Period LKU.

847 Rim *fr. Rd* ?, *ext ht* 0.027. Orange fabric; *out surf* beige.

848 Base *fr. Bd* 0.05, *ext ht* 0.02.

849 Base *fr. Bd* 0.075, *ext ht* 0.048. Grey/orange fabric, *surf* beige.

Object #	PNE	LBA	EIA	HEL	TRA	KUS	LKU	EME	HME	LME	PMO
846							✓				

SITE 103

850 Rim *fr. Rd* 0.34, *ext ht* 0.054. Orange fabric; *surf* beige.
851 Lid *fr. Rd* 0.18, *ext ht* 0.022.
852 Vsl *fr. D* 0.07, *p ht* 0.137. Orange fabric; *surf* beige.
853 Base *fr. Bd* 0.11, *ext ht* 0.082. Pale orange fabric, *surf* beige.

854 Base *fr. Bd* 0.08, *ext ht* 0.028. Pale orange fabric; green and white *gl* on *in surf.*
855 Base *fr. Bd* 0.11, *ext ht* 0.049. Pale orange fabric.
856 Base *fr. Bd* 0.36, *ext ht* 0.043. Orange fabric, *in surf* white; worn-off *surf.*

SITE 105 (cemetery of old Akkurqon village)

857 Rim *fr. Rd* 0.04, *ext ht* 0.015. Yellow/brown fabric, beige on fracture.
858 Rim *fr. Rd* ?, *ext ht* 0.019. Beige fabric, *out surf* yellow/brown.

859 Rim *fr. Rd* ?, *ext ht* 0.03. Beige fabric.
860 Base *fr. Bd* 0.11, *ext ht* 0.07. Orange/pink fabric; orange *sl.*

SITE 119

898 Rim *fr. Rd* 0.21, *ext ht* 0.031. Pale brown fabric, *surf* yellow. Cf. Zavyalov 2008, 163: 76.7.
899 Rim *fr. Rd* 0.2, *ext ht* 0.033. Pale beige fabric, orange on fracture; *inc crvl dec* on *out* lip. Cf. Zavyalov 2008, 187: 100.6.

900 Rim *fr. Rd* 0.25, *ext ht* 0.018. White/yellow fabric, orange on fracture. Cf. Zavyalov 2008, 185: 98.20(?).
901 Rim *fr. Rd* 0.3, *ext ht* 0.019. Orange fabric; *RS*(?). Cf. Zavyalov 2008, 185: 98.17. Typological parallels Plate (9) (Včelicová 2015). Period HEL / TRA.

Object #	PNE	LBA	EIA	HEL	TRA	KUS	LKU	EME	HME	LME	PMO
901				✓	✓						

SITE 120

902 Rim *fr. Rd* 0.37, *ext ht* 0.044. Beige fabric, orange/brown on fracture. Typological parallels R125 (Maxwell-Jones 2015). Period HEL / TRA.
903 Rim *fr. Rd* 0.08, *ext ht* 0.019. Grey/brown fabric, red/brownish on fracture.
904 Rim *fr. Rd* 0.09, *ext ht* 0.07. White/yellow fabric, beige on fracture. Cf. Zavyalov 2008, 175: 88.9(?).

905 Rim *fr. Rd* 0.1, *ext ht* 0.055. Pale orange fabric, *out surf* white; plastic *dec* on lip.
906 Rim *fr. Rd* 0.1, *ext ht* 0.05. Beige fabric, *surf* white; plastic *dec* on lip.
907 Base *fr. Bd* 0.075, *ext ht* 0.04. Beige fabric; blue and black *gl* (*lin dec*).
908 Base *fr. Bd* 0.1, *ext ht* 0.025. Beige fabric; white, black and green/blue *gl.*

Object #	PNE	LBA	EIA	HEL	TRA	KUS	LKU	EME	HME	LME	PMO
902				✓	✓						

SITE 125 (Khojai Gambir-ota tepa)

911 Rim *fr. Rd* ?, *ext ht* 0.02. Yellow/grey fabric.
912 Rim *fr. Rd* ?, *ext ht* 0.031.
913 Rim *fr. Rd* 0.2, *ext ht* 0.04. Orange fabric, *surf* yellow. Cf. Zavyalov 2008, 169: 82.17(?). Period LKU.

914 Rim *fr. Rd* 0.09, *ext ht* 0.035. Pale orange fabric, *out surf* yellow. Cf. Zavyalov 2008, 163: 76.22.
915 Rim *fr. Rd* 0.16, *ext ht* 0.039. For fabric description see [908].

916 Rim *fr. Rd* 0.12, *ext ht* 0.028. Fine, orange/yellow fabric. Cf. Zavyalov 2008, 163: 76.2.
917 Rim *fr. Rd* 0.38, *ext ht* 0.069. Very fine, orange fabric, *surf* yellow. Cf. Zavyalov 2008, 172: 85.10.
918 Base *fr. Bd* 0.08, *ext ht* 0.031. Fine, beige/brown fabric.

919 Base *fr. Bd* 0.14, *ext ht* 0.032. Orange/dark brown fabric; *inc lin dec* on *out surf.*
920 Base *fr. Bd* 0.06, *ext ht* 0.011. Pale orange/beige fabric.

Object #	PNE	LBA	EIA	HEL	TRA	KUS	LKU	EME	HME	LME	PMO
913							✓				

SITE 127

921 Rim *fr. Rd* ?, *ext ht* 0.03. Pale brown fabric, light blue *gl.*

922 Rim *fr. Rd* ?, *ext ht* 0.03. Very coarse, orange/grey fabric.

SITE 128 (Kishlok Bazar kabristoni)

923 Rim *fr. Rd* ?, *ext ht* 0.03. Orange/brown fabric, *in surf* black and brown/white.
924 Rim *fr. Rd* 0.24, *ext ht* 0.024. Dark brown fabric; partially burned. Cf. Zavyalov 2008, 164: 77.18.
925 Base *fr. Bd* 0.11, *ext ht* 0.022. Yellow/orange fabric.

926 Base *fr. Bd* 0.06, *ext ht* 0.031. Coarse, dark red, partially beige fabric.
927 Base *fr. Bd* ?, *ext ht* 0.089. Coarse, grey/green fabric. Pugachenkova – Rtveladze 1978, 16.

SITE 129 (Chuyanchi ota kabristoni)

928 *Comp vsl. Rd* 0.34, *bd* 0.25, *ht* 0.093. Pale brown fabric; *inc crvl dec* on *in* lip.
929 Rim *fr. Rd* 0.4, *ext ht* 0.137. Fine, pale orange fabric. Typological parallels R177 (Maxwell-Jones 2015). Period HEL / TRA.

930 Rim *fr. Rd* ?, *ext ht* 0.015. Pale brown fabric; cyan *gl.*
931 Rim *fr. Rd* 0.18, *ext ht* 0.035. Grey/brown fabric. Cf. Zavyalov 2008, 163: 76.32. Typological parallels R34 (Maxwell-Jones 2015). Period LKU.

Object #	PNE	LBA	EIA	HEL	TRA	KUS	LKU	EME	HME	LME	PMO
929				✓	✓						
931							✓				

SITE 133 (Irjahangir-ota kabristoni)

937 Rim *fr. Rd* 0.26, *ext ht* 0.035.
938 Rim *fr. Rd* 0.3, *ext ht* 0.033.
939 Rim *fr. Rd* 0.32, *ext ht* 0.058.
940 Rim *fr. Rd* 0.12, *ext ht* 0.061. Period LKU. *SSe* 4th c. AD.

941 Rim *fr. Rd* 0.09, *ext ht* 0.047.
942 Rim *fr. Rd* 0.09, *ext ht* 0.048.
943 Base *fr. Bd* 0.07, *ext ht* 0.034.
944 Base *fr. Bd* 0.07, *ext ht* 0.024.

Object #	PNE	LBA	EIA	HEL	TRA	KUS	LKU	EME	HME	LME	PMO
940							✓				

SITE 135 (Khojakiyamiddin-ota kabristoni)

951 Body *fr. Pht* 0.057.

952 Base *fr. Bd* 0.11, *ext ht* 0.057.

SITE 136

953 Base *fr. Bd* 0.12, *ext ht* 0.012.

IN BETWEEN SITES 136 AND 137

954 Rim *fr. Rd* 0.33, *ext ht* 0.051.

SITE 138

955 Rim *fr. Rd* 0.28, *ext ht* 0.042. Typological parallels R63 (Maxwell-Jones 2015). Period EIA / HEL, cf. Tušlová 2012b, tb. 14:1.

Object #	PNE	LBA	EIA	HEL	TRA	KUS	LKU	EME	HME	LME	PMO
955			✓	✓							

SITE 139 (Toshtepa)

956 Rim *fr. Rd* 0.34, *ext ht* 0.041.

SITE 141

957 Rim *fr. Rd* 0.21, *ext ht* 0.025. Cf. Zavyalov 2008, 163: 76.7.

958 Body *fr. Pht* 0.056.

SITE 142

959 Rim *fr. Rd* ?, *ext ht* 0.018.
960 Rim *fr. Rd* 0.2, *ext ht* 0.014.

961 Base *fr. Bd* 0.08, *ext ht* 0.019.
962 Base *fr. Bd* 0.1, *ext ht* 0.056.

SITE 143

963 Rim *fr. Rd* 0.2, *ext ht* 0.043.
964 Rim *fr. Rd* 0.2, *ext ht* 0.043.
965 Rim *fr. Rd* 0.26, *ext ht* 0.019. Cf. Zavyalov 2008, 163: 76.7.
966 Rim *fr. Rd* 0.28, *ext ht* 0.027. Cf. Zavyalov 2008, 163: 76.7. Period LKU.

967 Rim *fr. Rd* 0.3, *ext ht* 0.034. Cf. Zavyalov 2008, 163: 76.7. Period LKU.
968 Body *fr. Pht* 0.048.
969 *Spt fr.* Ht 0.03, l 0.053.
970 Base *fr. Bd* 0.1, *ext ht* 0.014.

Object #	PNE	LBA	EIA	HEL	TRA	KUS	LKU	EME	HME	LME	PMO
966							✓				
967							✓				

SITE 144

971 Rim *fr. Rd* 0.28, *ext ht* 0.02.

SITE 157 (Ota-Kul' mulla ishan baba)

991 Body and *hdl fr. Ext ht* 0.116.
992 Base *fr. Bd* 0.13, *ext ht* 0.054.

MISCELLANEA

Teraccotta Tokens

1008 Token. *D*±0.02. Orange/brown fabric; beige *sl* on one *surf.*
1009 Token. *D* ±0.023. Orange fabric; yellowish *sl* on one *surf.*
1010 Token. *D* ±0.033. Pale brown fabric; smooth on *surf.*
1011 Token. *D* ±0.026. Brick orange fabric. Cf. Annaev 1988, tab. XX.

1012 Token. *D* ±0.033. Red/orange fabric, fracture: yellow core/red margins. Cf. Annaev 1988, tab. XX.
1013 Token. *D* ±0.055. Rough, brown fabric. Cf. Annaev 1988, tab. XX, XXI.
1014 Token. *D* ±0.075. Brick-red fabric; ochre *eng* on *out surf.*

Teraccotta Lamps

1015 lamp. *Bd* 0.036, *max ht* 0.03. Fine fabric. Cf. Pugachenkova 1989, 84, 85.

1016 lamp. *Bd* 0.038, *pht* 0.026. Brown/orange fabric, *HM*. Cf. Pugachenkova 1989, 84, 85.

Teraccotta Statuettes

1017 Zoomorphic statuette *fr. Max* dimensions 0.077 × 0.043 × 0.062. Cf. Masson 1976, 56.
1018 Statuette *fr. Max* dimensions 0.06 × 0.038 × 0.047. Cf. Masson 1976, 56.
1019 Zoomorphic statuette *fr. Max* dimensions 0.095 × 0.048 × 0.038. Cf. Masson 1976, 56; Pugachenkova – Rtveladze 1978, 68: 40.7.
1020 Zoomorphic statuette. *Max* dimensions 0.128 × 0.07 × 0.061. Cf. Masson 1976, 56, 105.

1021 Anthropomorphic statuette *fr. Max* dimensions 0.046 × 0.036.
1022 Statuette *fr. Max* dimensions 0.042 × 0.023 × 0.013. Pale brown fabric. Cf. Masson 1976, 56.
1023 Statuette/appliqué *fr. Max* dimensions 0.05 × 0.015 × 0.014. Dark orange fabric, ochre/orange on out surf; dark stone and charcoal inclusions.

Terracota Beads

1024 Bead. D 0.02, ht 0.018. Cf. Masson 1976, 56.

1025 Bead. D 0.025, ht 0.015. Cf. Pugachenkova 1989, 62; Annaev 1988, tab. XX.

The overview of the sites with possible estimated dating based on the pottery:

Site	Number of individuals	PNE	LBA	EIA	HEL	TRA	KUS	LKU	EME	HME	LME	PMO
1	4			✓	✓	✓	✓	✓				
2	9			✓	✓	✓	✓	✓			✓	✓
4	10				✓	✓	✓	✓				✓
5	24			✓	✓	✓	✓	✓		✓	✓	
6	7									✓	✓	
7	5				✓	✓	✓	✓	✓			
8	18			✓	✓		✓	✓				
9	1						✓	✓				
10	20					✓	✓	✓	✓			
11	4						✓	✓	✓			
12	6				✓	✓		✓				
16	22			✓			✓	✓				
17	5							✓	✓			
18	9				✓	✓	✓	✓	✓			
19	8						✓	✓	✓			
22	6				✓	✓	✓	✓				
23	17							✓	✓			
24	10			✓		✓	✓	✓	✓	✓	✓	
25	25				✓	✓	✓	✓	✓			
26	17			✓	✓	✓	✓	✓	✓			
27	3						✓	✓				
32	17				✓	✓	✓	✓	✓			
33	14			✓	✓	✓	✓	✓		✓		
35	5				✓	✓	✓	✓				
37	4				✓	✓	✓	✓				
40	7						✓	✓	✓			
41	2				✓	✓	✓	✓				✓
42	1						✓					
43	7				✓	✓	✓	✓	✓			
45	4			✓		-	✓	✓	✓			
48	2							✓				
52	1						✓	✓				
54	3							✓				
55	6						✓	✓		✓		
58	6						✓	✓		✓		
61	1				✓	✓						
72	4							✓		✓	✓	✓
75	4						✓	✓	✓			
78	1				✓	✓						
80	9			✓	✓	✓	✓	✓				

Site	Number of individuals	PNE	LBA	EIA	HEL	TRA	KUS	LKU	EME	HME	LME	PMO
88	3				✓	✓				✓	✓	
94	7				✓	✓	✓	✓	✓			
95	5							✓	✓			
98	3						✓	✓				
99	4				✓	✓	✓	✓	✓	✓	✓	
100	2							✓				
101	1							✓				
119	1				✓	✓						
120	1				✓	✓						
125	1							✓				
129	2				✓	✓		✓				
133	1							✓				
138	1			✓	✓							
143	2							✓				

Site 1, 2

TABLE I

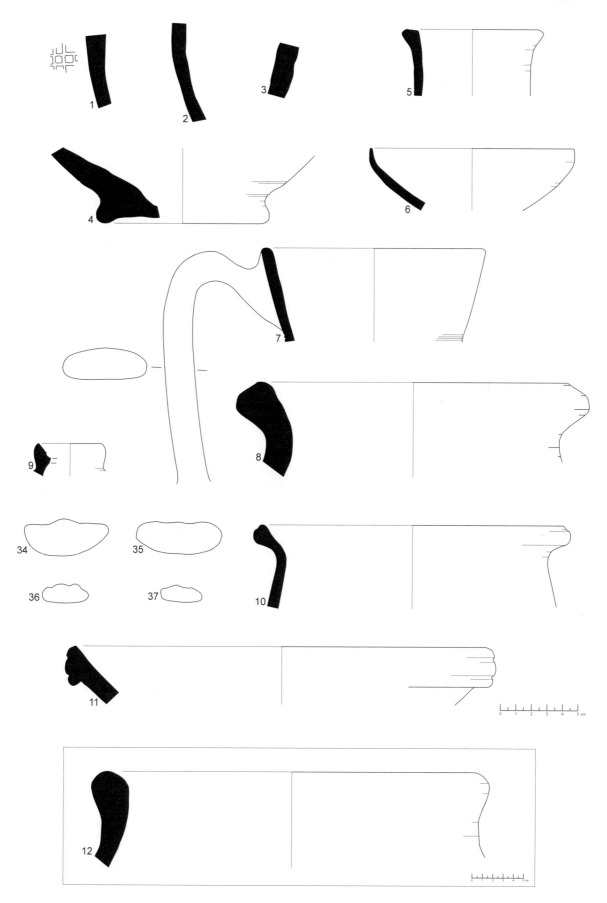

Site 2   TABLE II

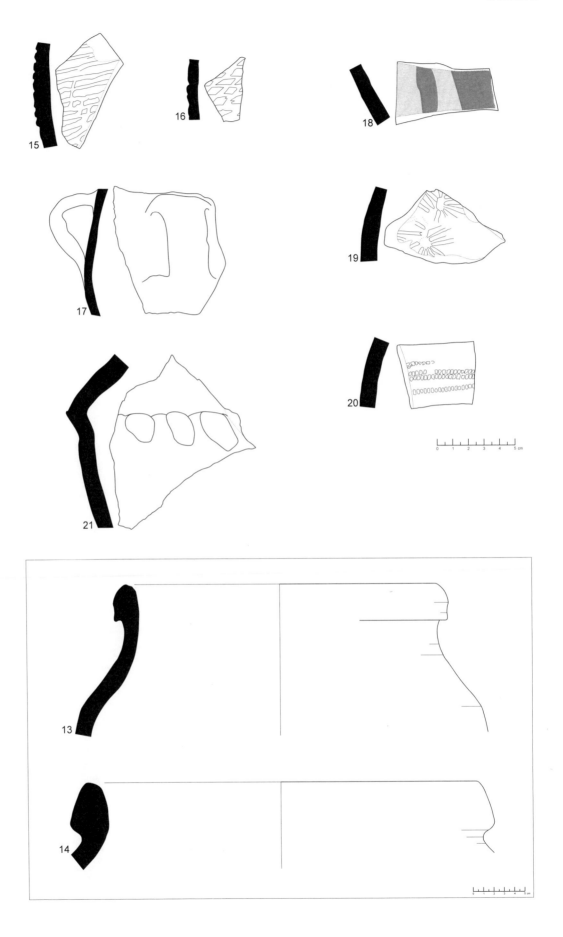

Site 2, 3, 4

TABLE III

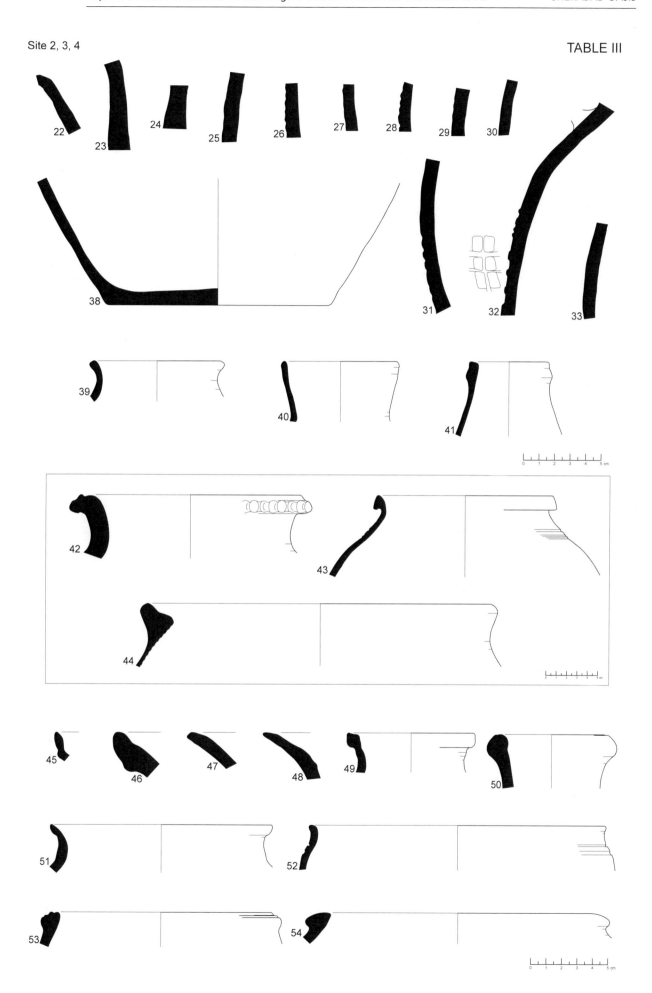

Site 4, 5

TABLE IV

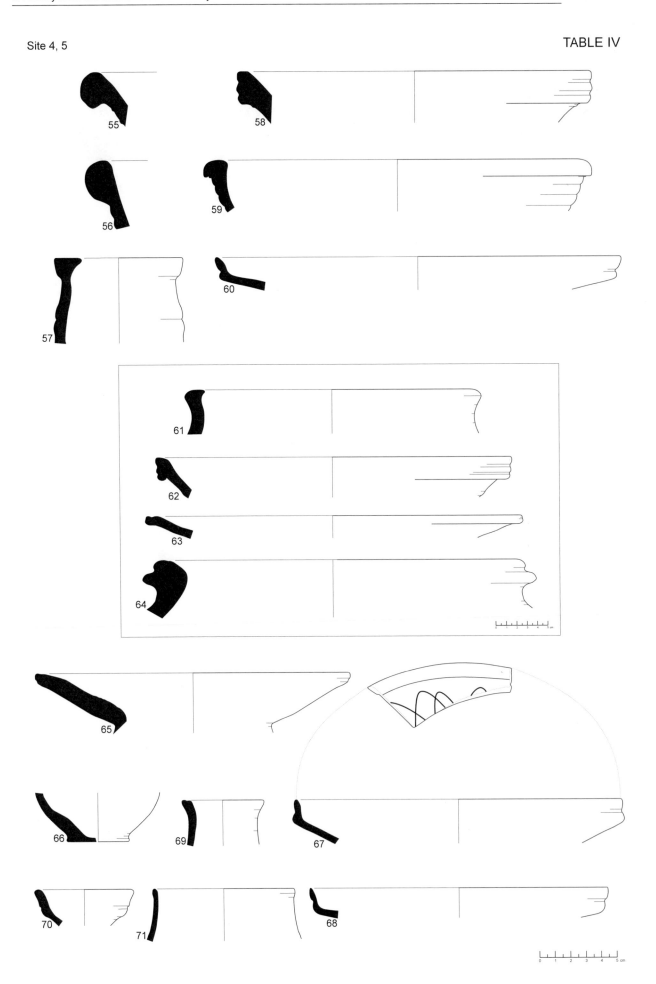

Site 5

TABLE V

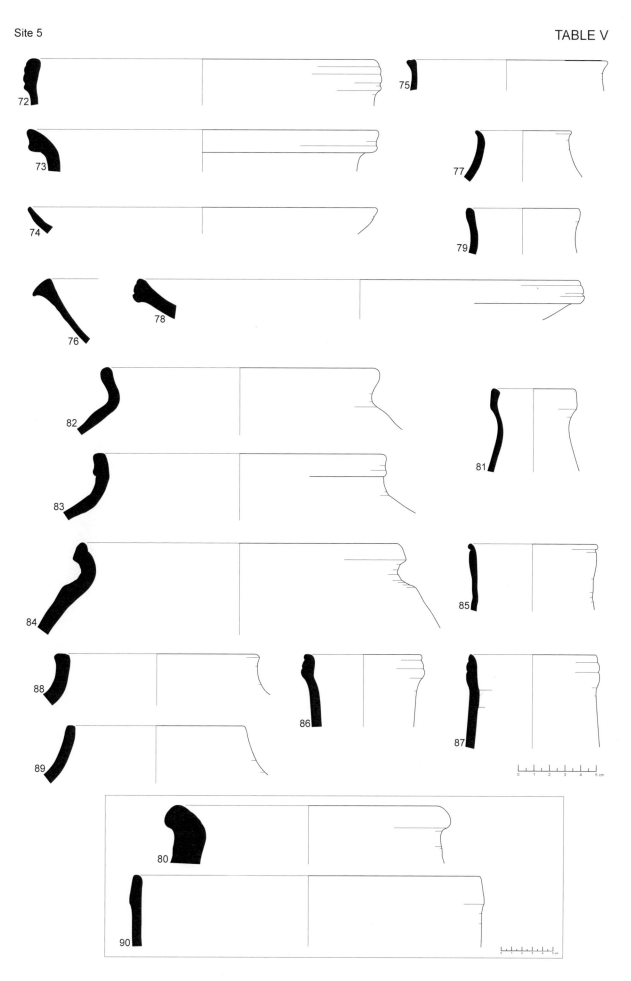

Site 5

TABLE VI

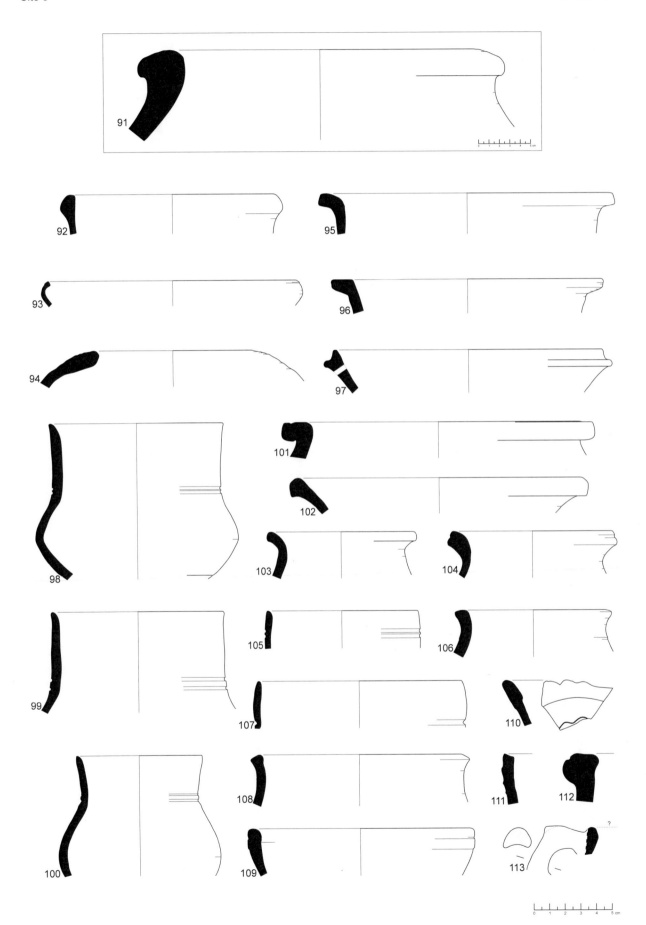

Site 5, 6, 7

TABLE VII

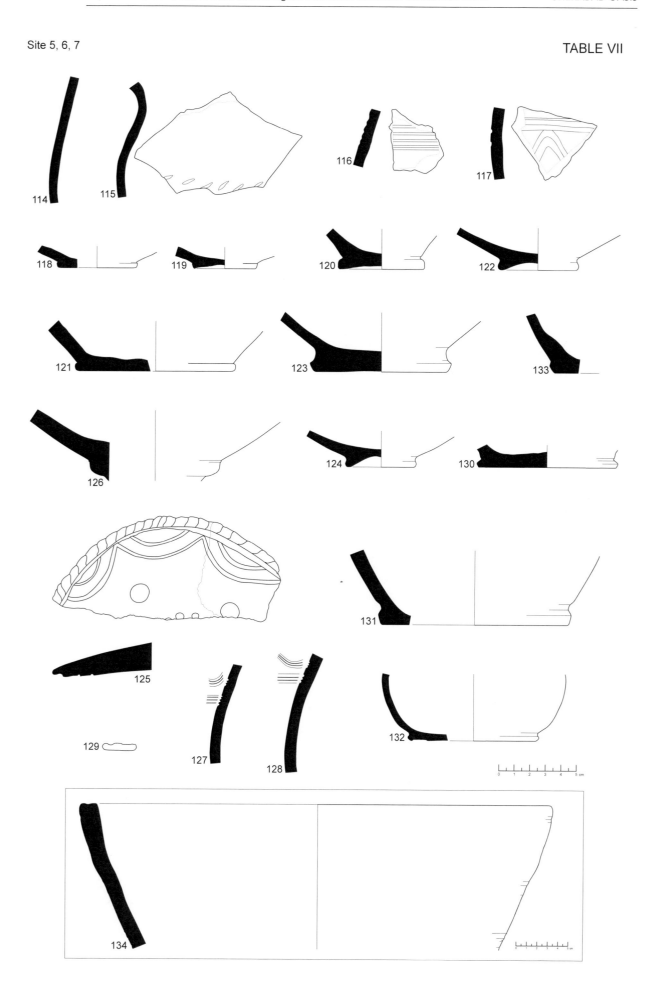

Site 7, 8 TABLE VIII

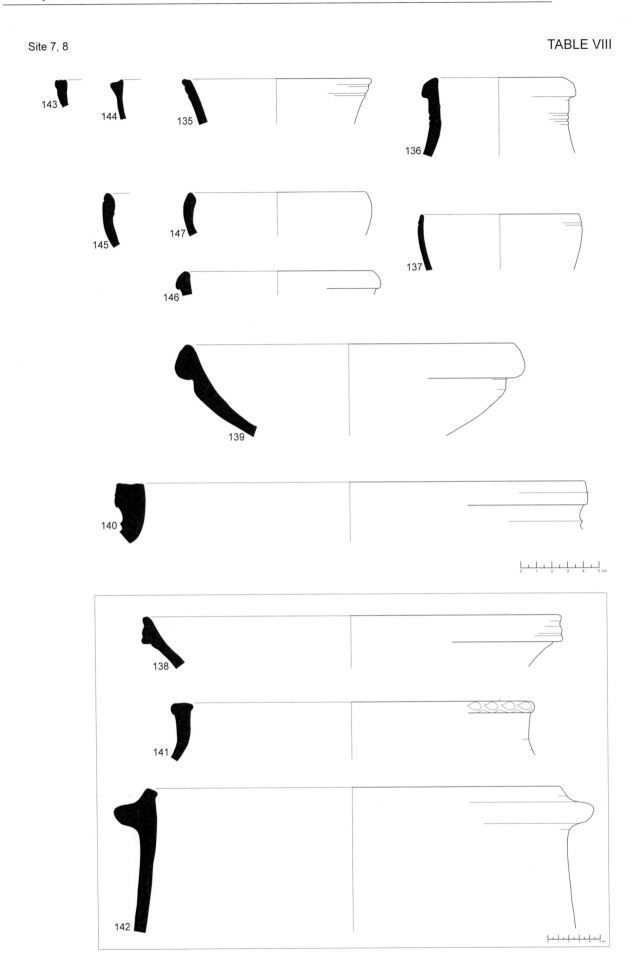

Site 8, 9, 10

TABLE IX

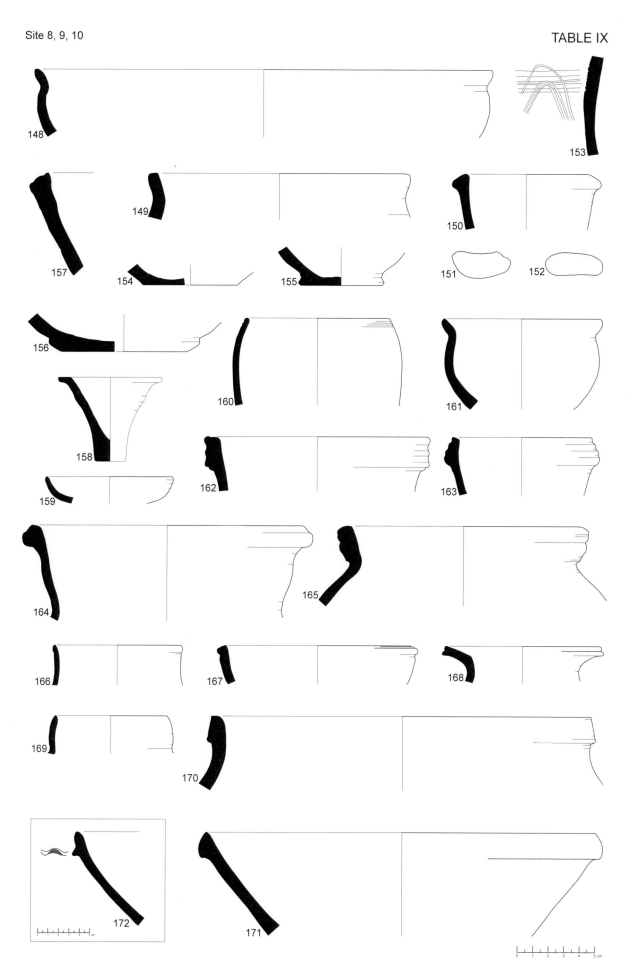

Site 10

TABLE X

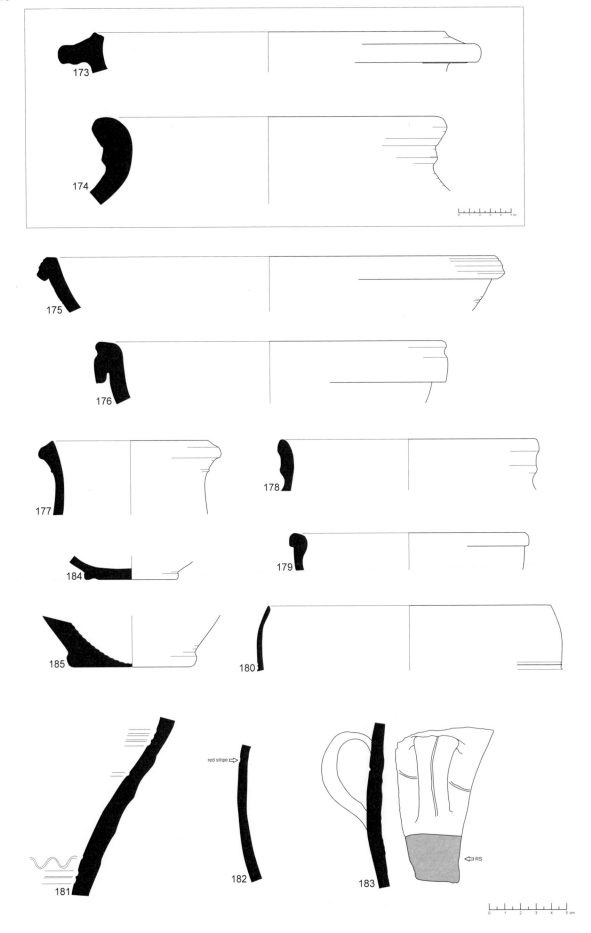

Site 11, 12, 16

TABLE XI

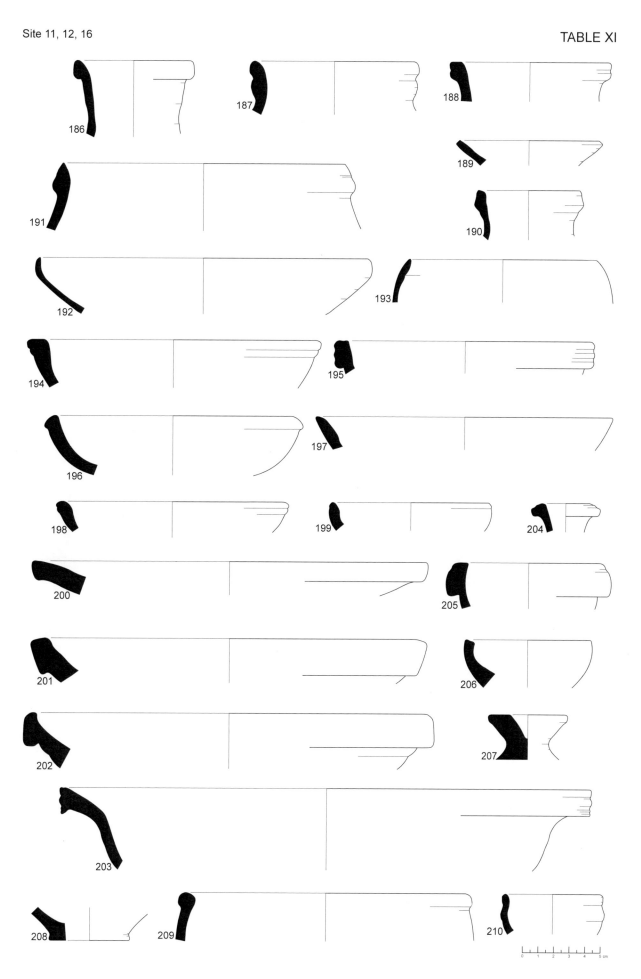

Site 16

TABLE XII

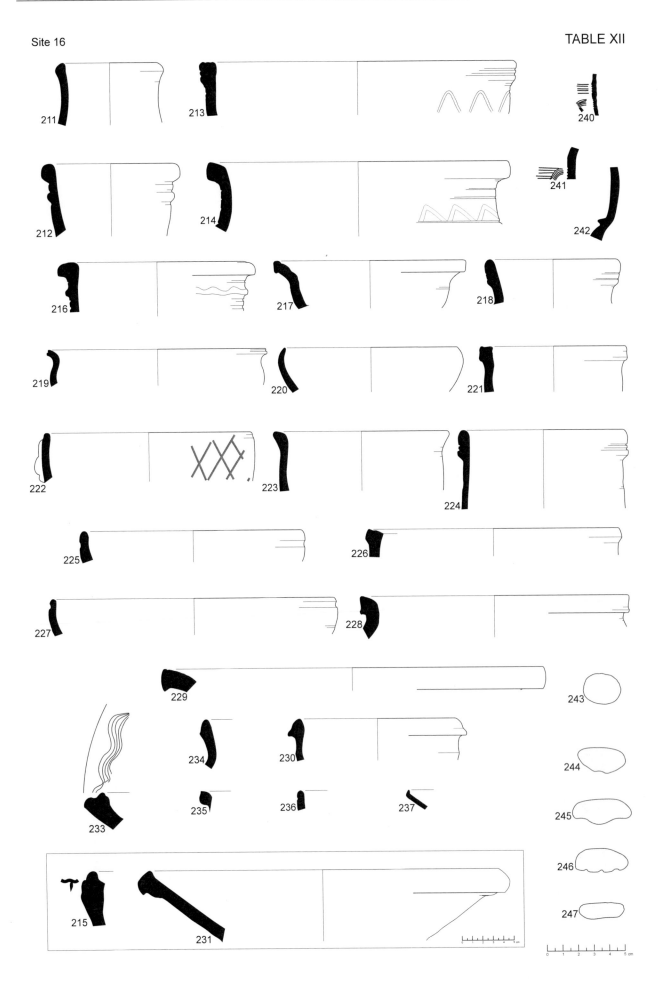

Site 16, 17

TABLE XIII

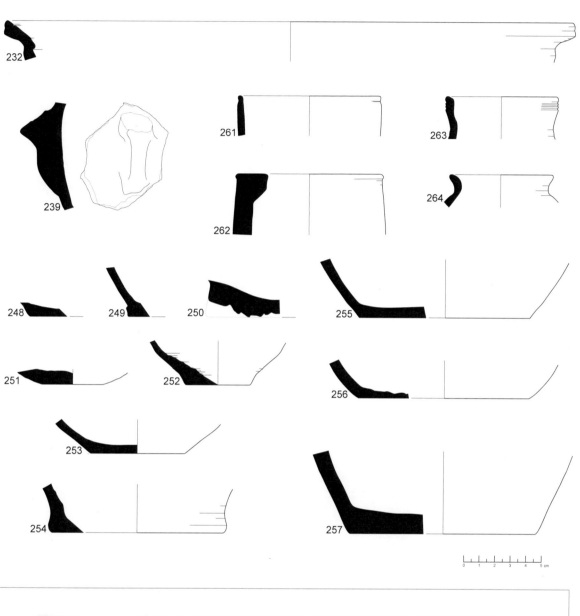

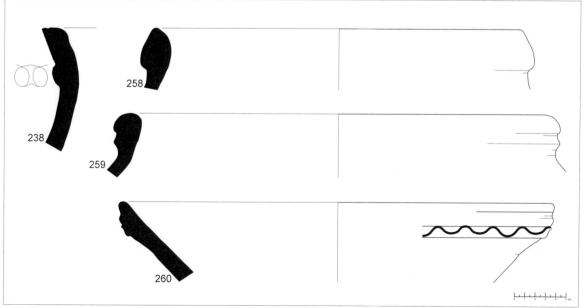

Site 17, 18

TABLE XIV

Site 18, 22

TABLE XV

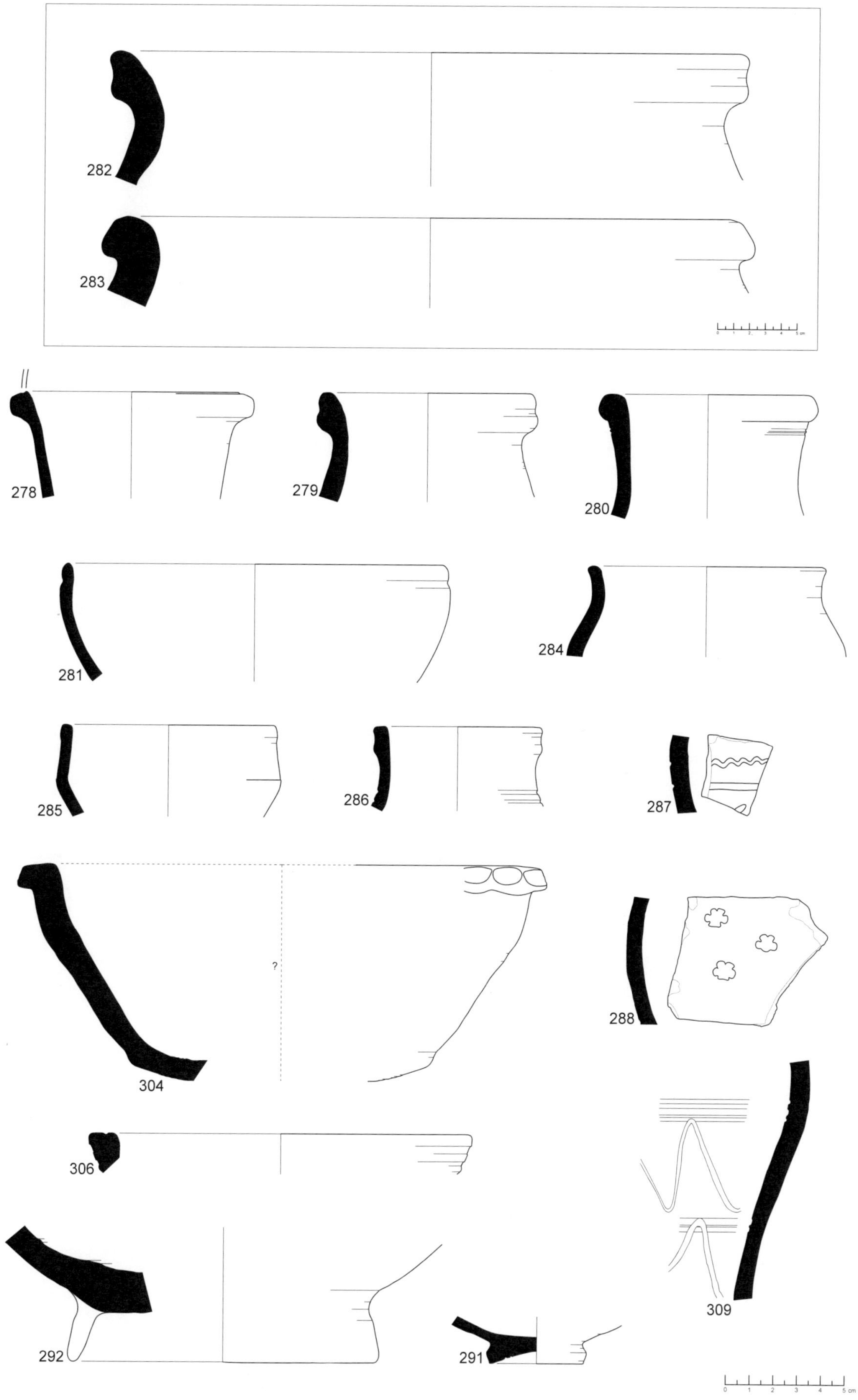

282

283

278

279

280

281

284

285

286

287

304

?

288

306

309

292

291

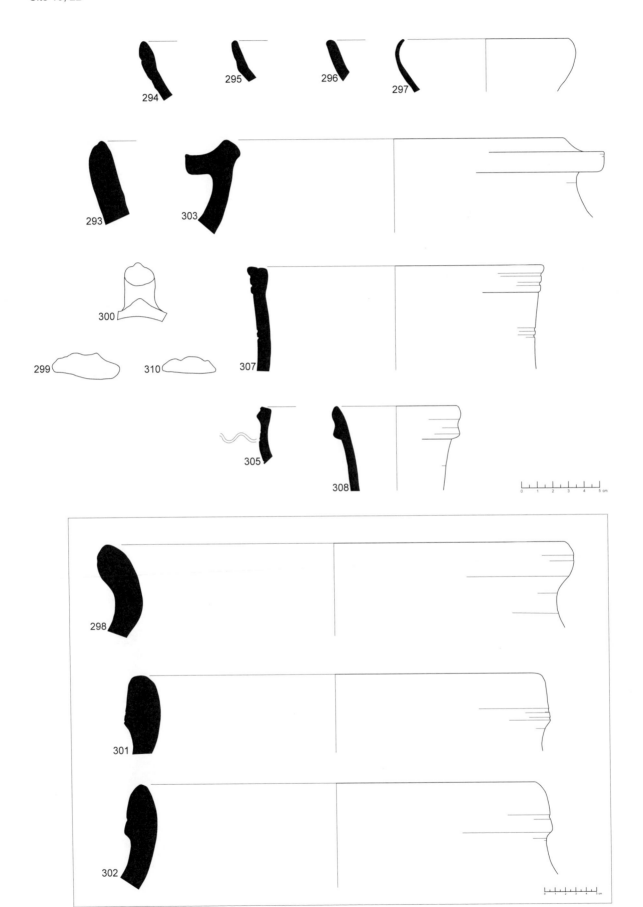

Site 23

TABLE XVII

315

316

311

312

313

314

317

318

319

323

324

320

321

325

327

322

326

328

Site 24   TABLE XVIII

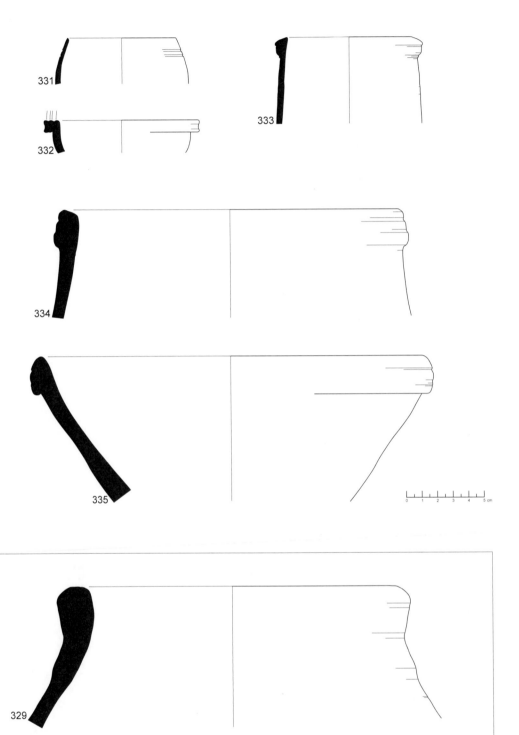

Site 24

TABLE XIX

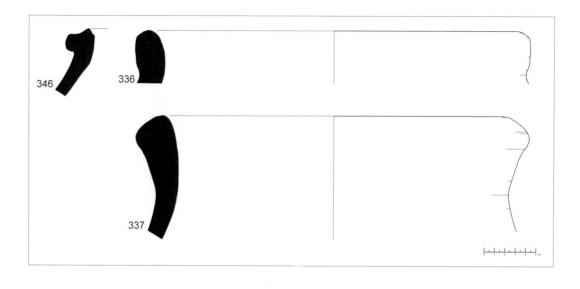

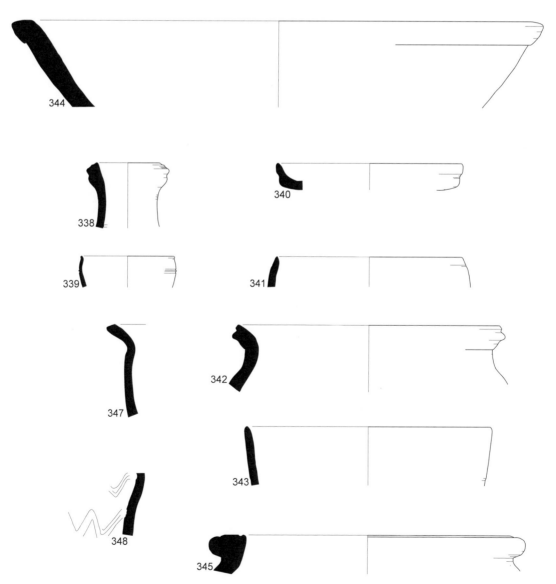

Site 24, 25

TABLE XX

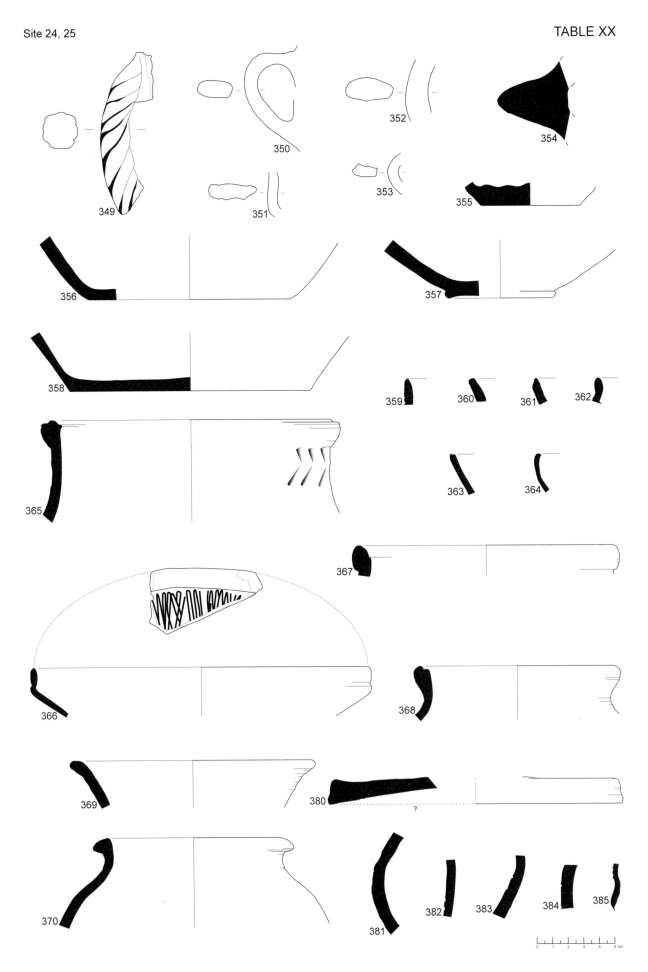

Site 25

TABLE XXI

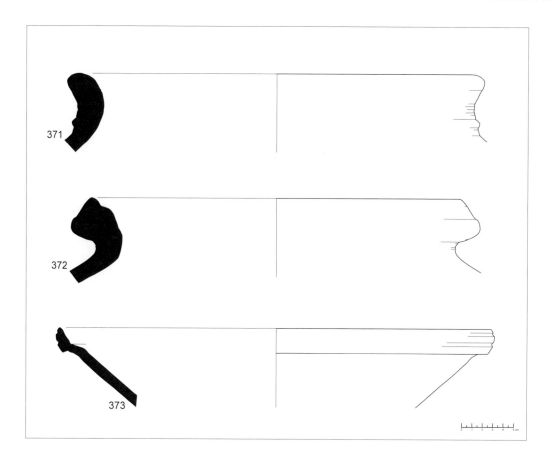

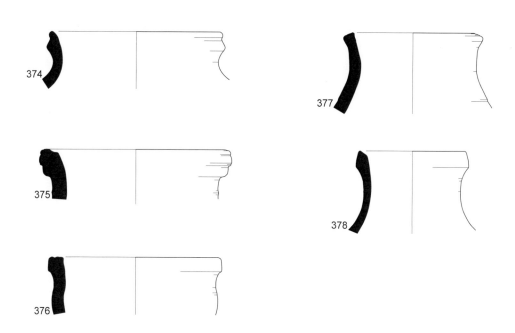

Site 25, 26

TABLE XXII

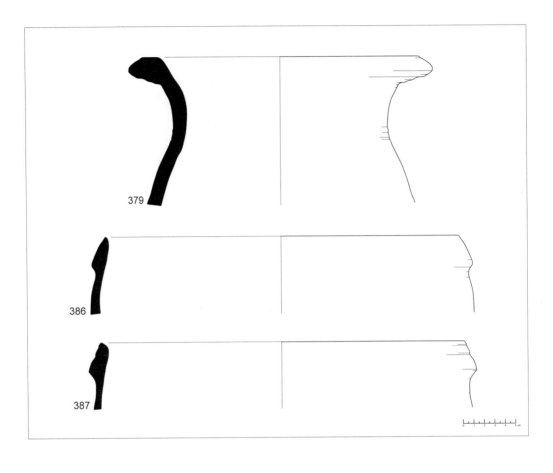

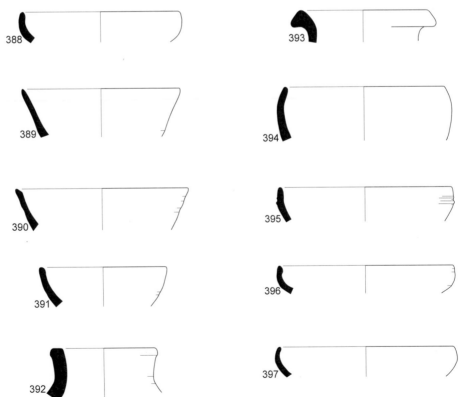

Site 26

TABLE XXIII

Site 26, 27

TABLE XXIV

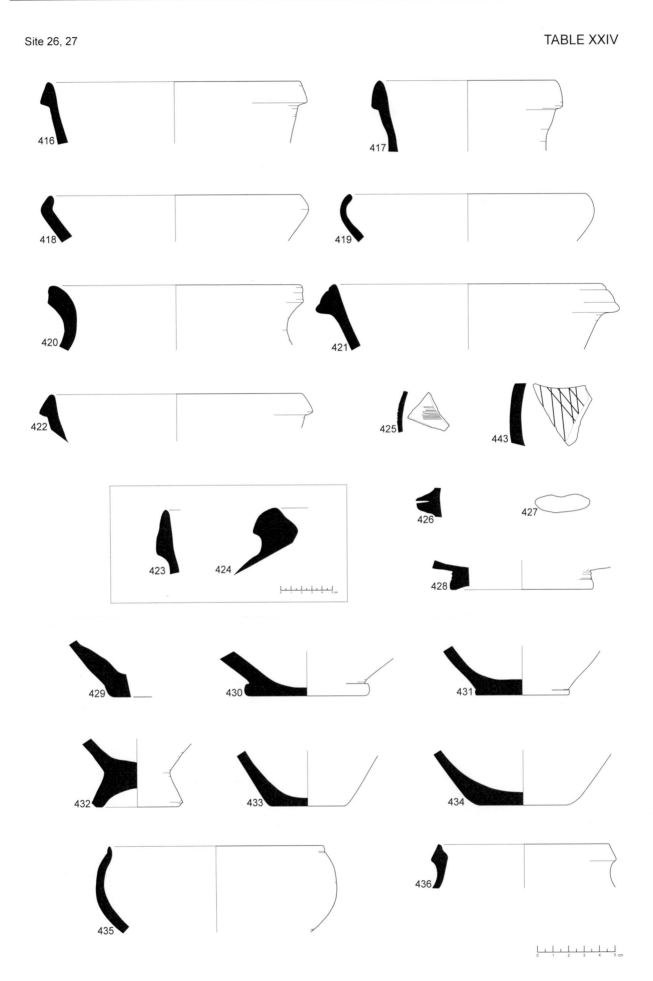

Site 27, 32

TABLE XXV

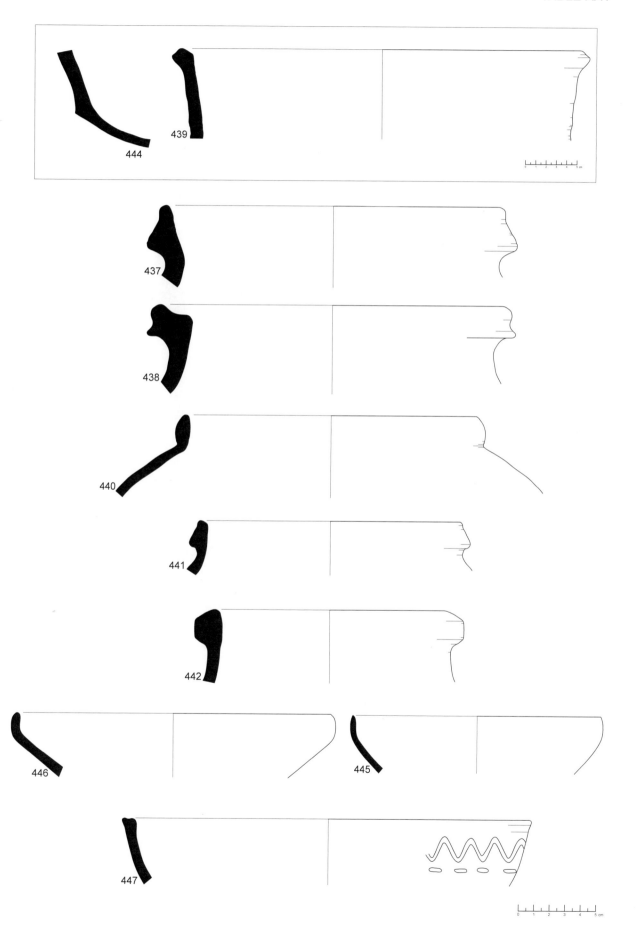

Site 32   TABLE XXVI

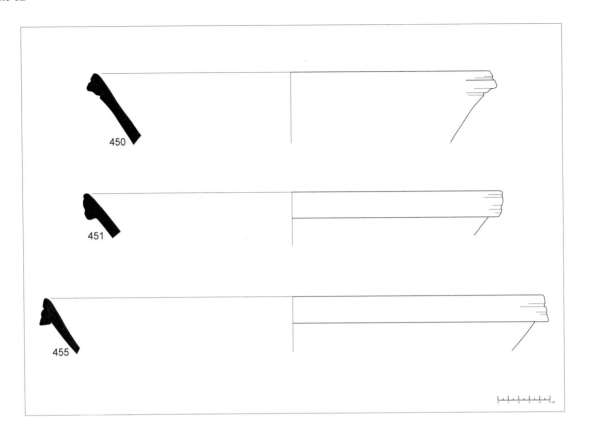

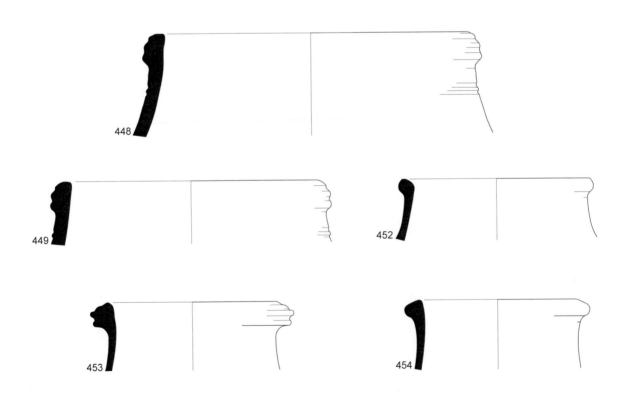

Site 32

TABLE XXVII

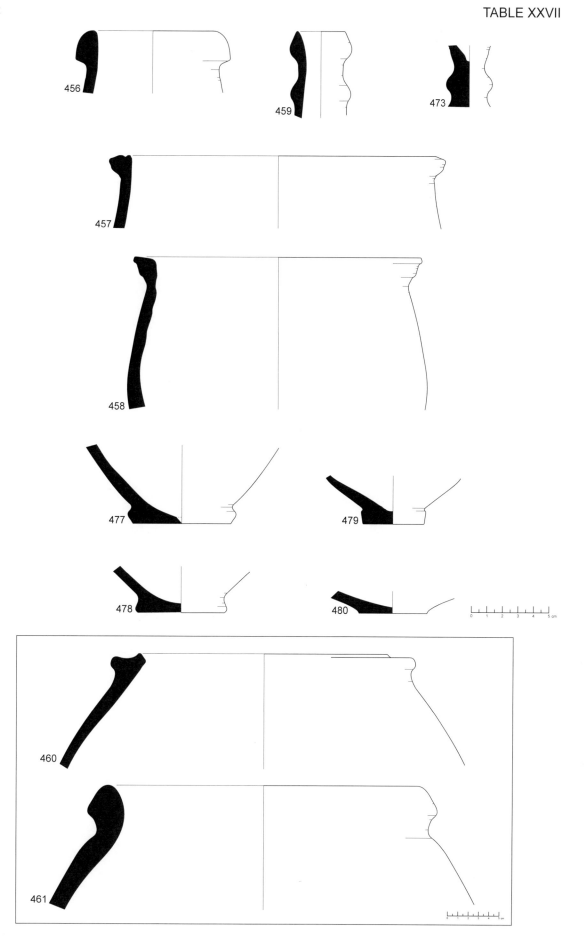

Site 32

TABLE XXVIII

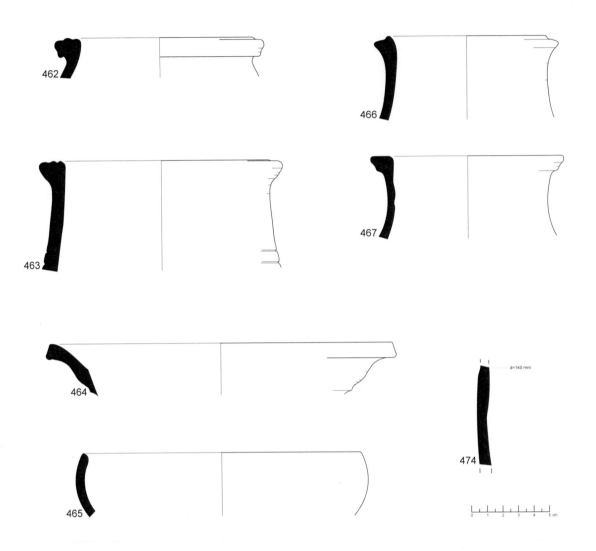

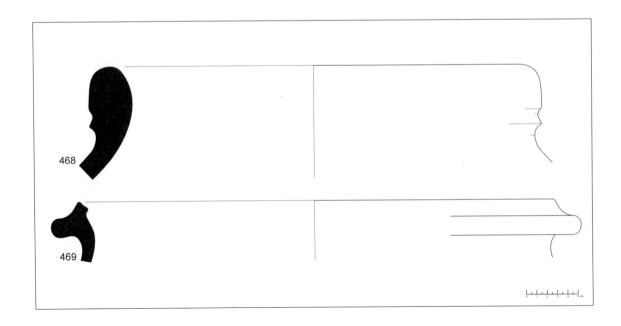

TABLE XXIX

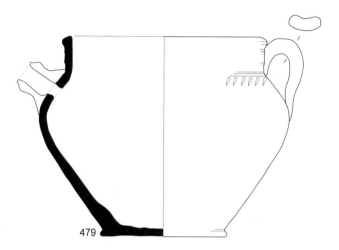

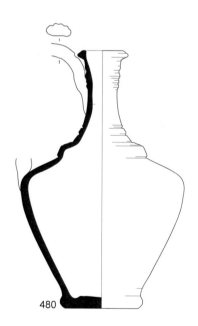

Site 32, 33

TABLE XXX

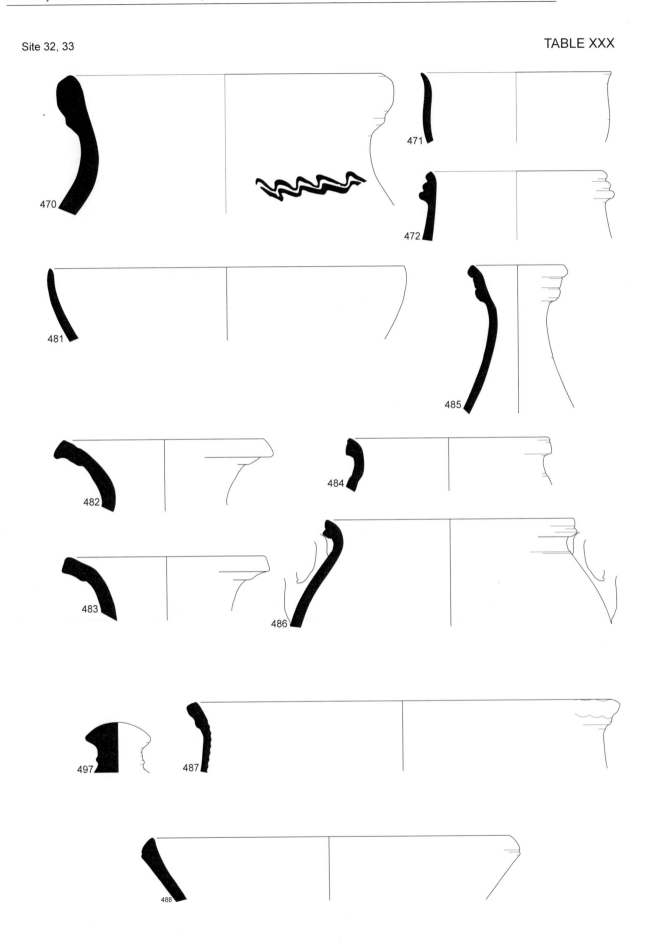

Site 33

TABLE XXXI

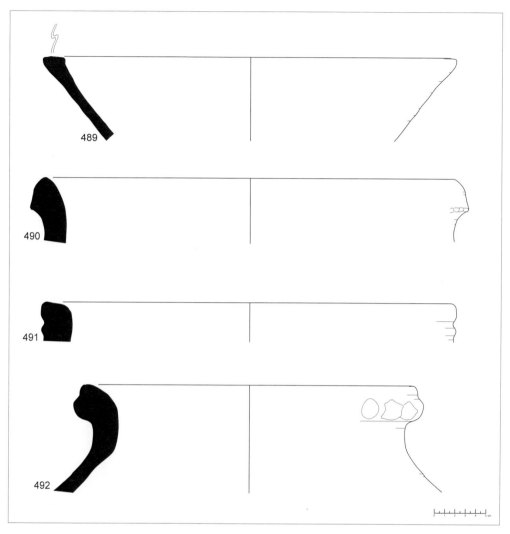

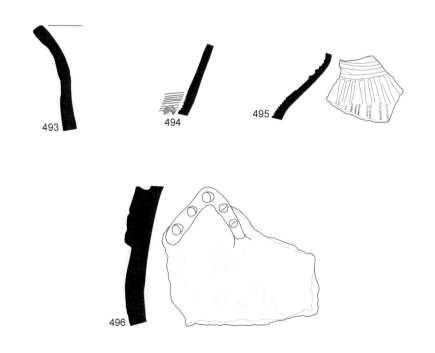

Site 33, 35, 36

TABLE XXXII

Site 35, 37

TABLE XXXIII

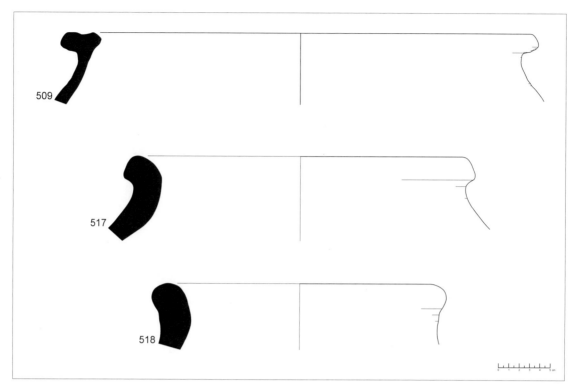

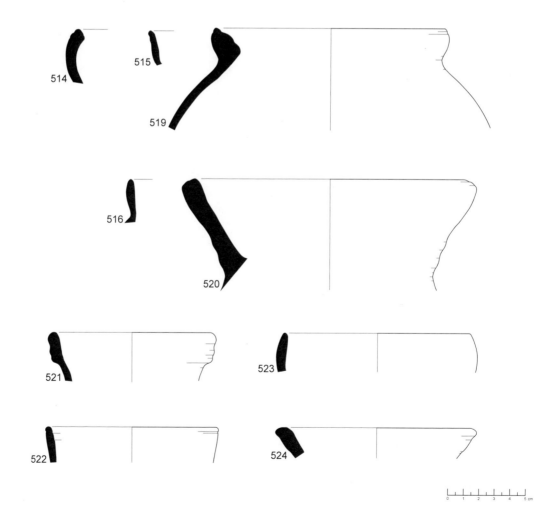

Site 37, 38, 40 TABLE XXXIV

Site 40, 41, 42

TABLE XXXV

Site 43, 45

TABLE XXXVI

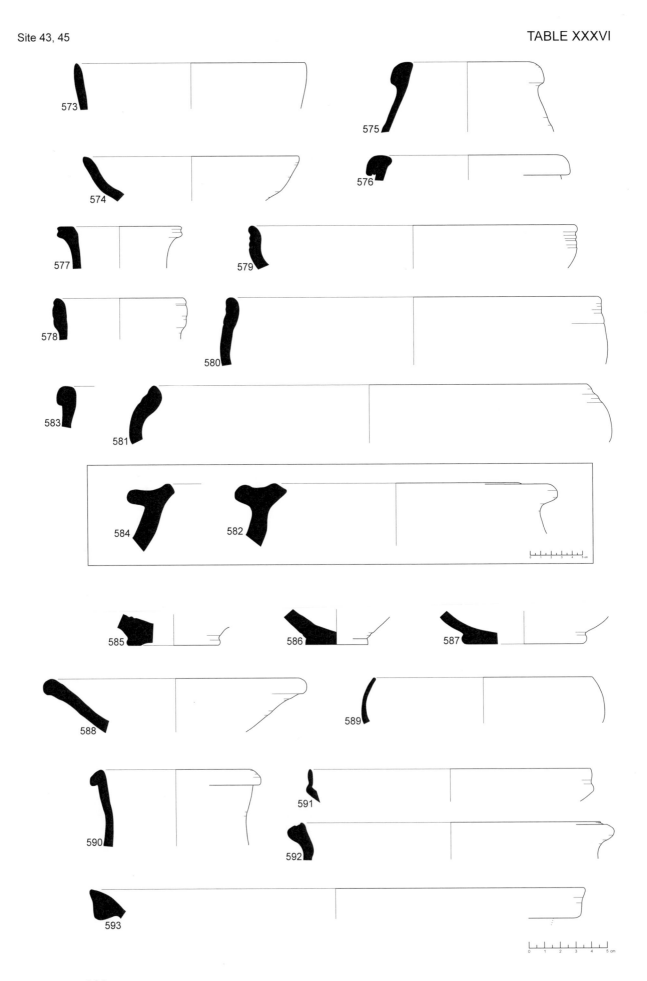

Site 45, 48

TABLE XXXVII

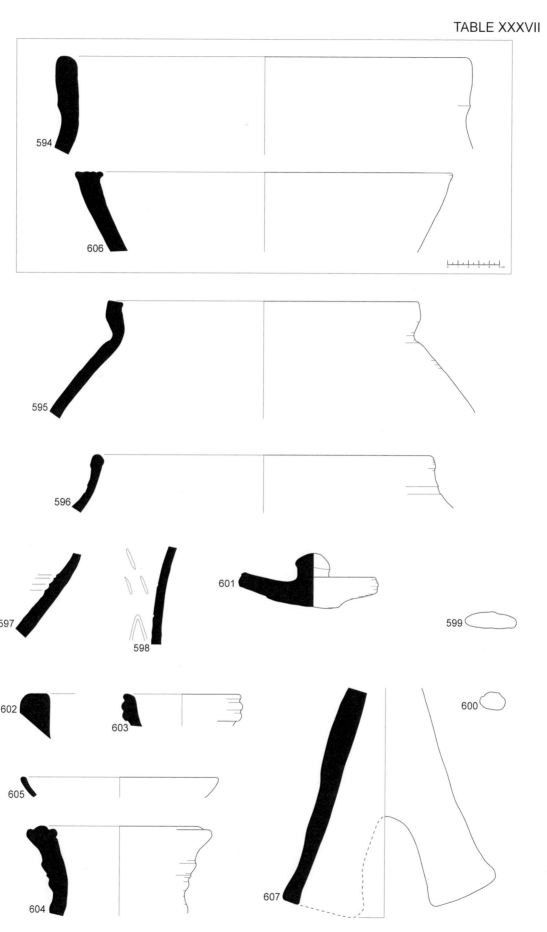

Site 49, 50, 52, 53, 54, 55, 58

TABLE XXXVIII

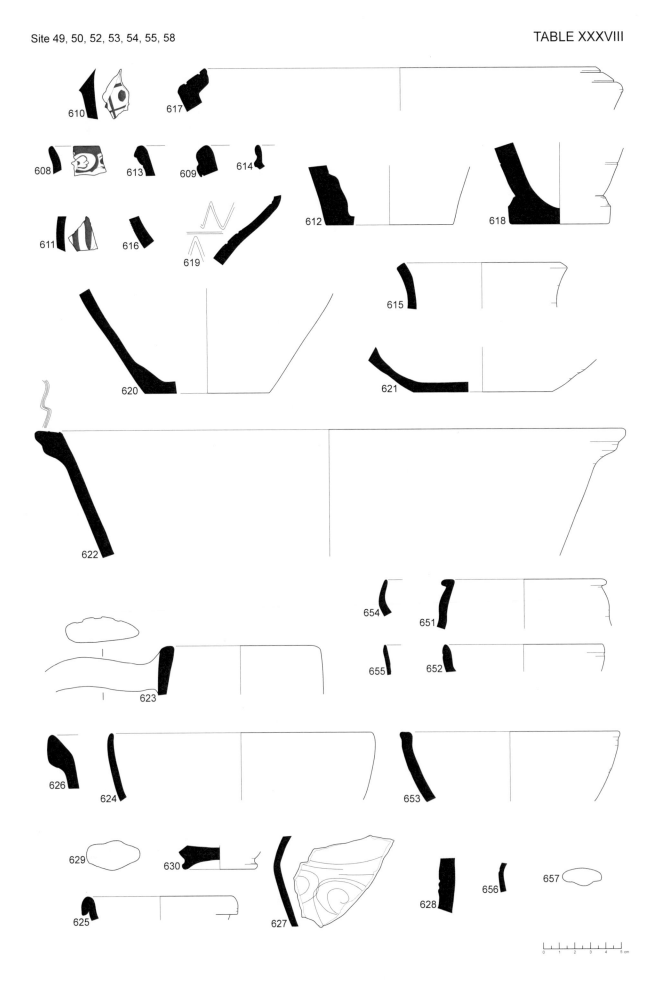

Site 61, 63, 71, 72

TABLE XXXIX

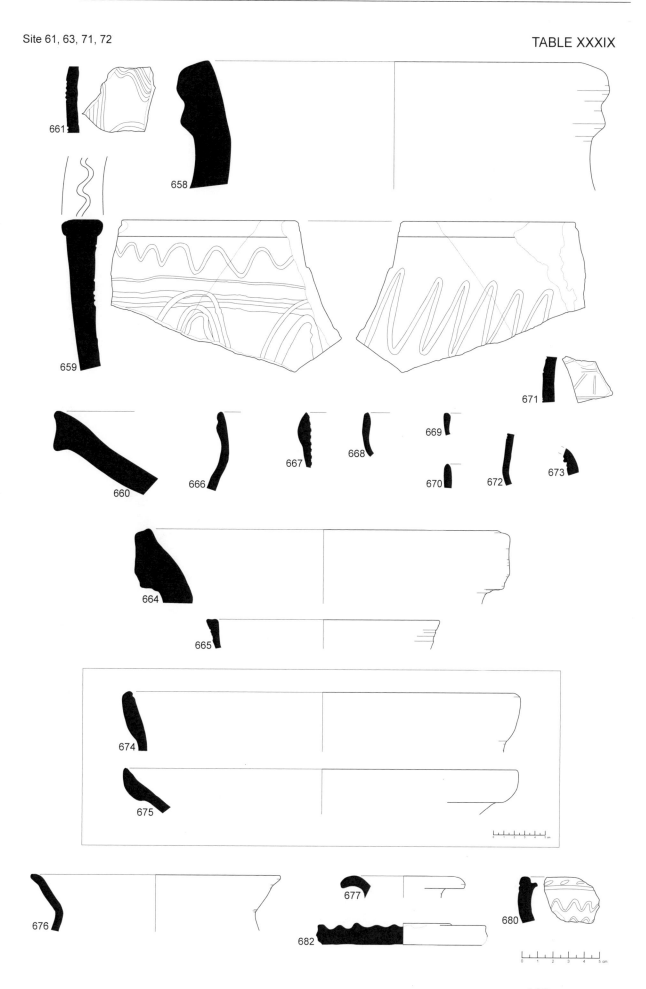

M. Kobierská

Site 72, 75, 77, 78

TABLE XL

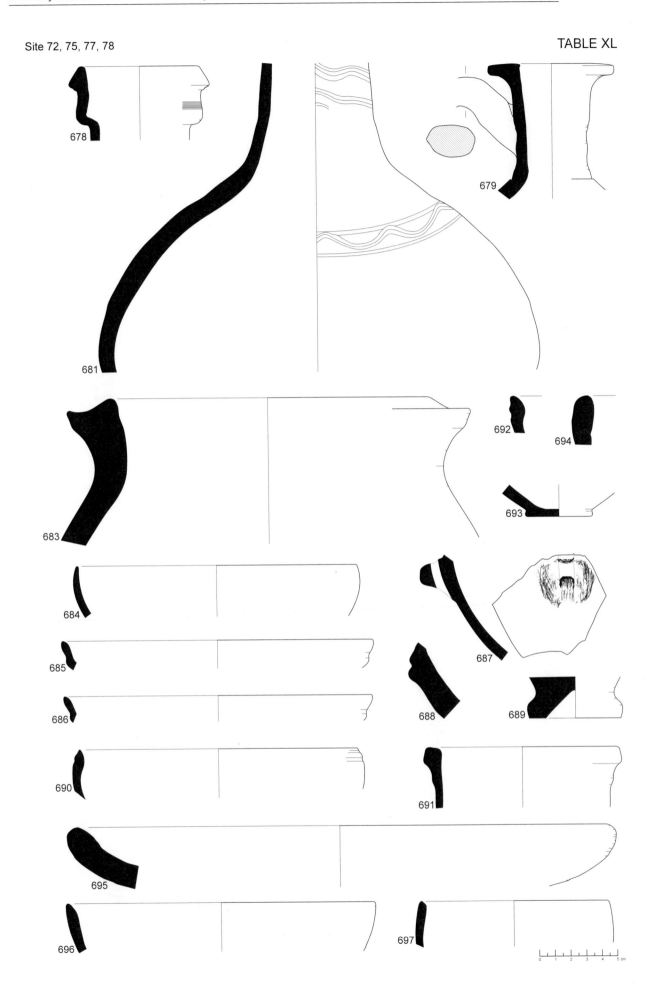

Site 78, 79, 80

TABLE XLI

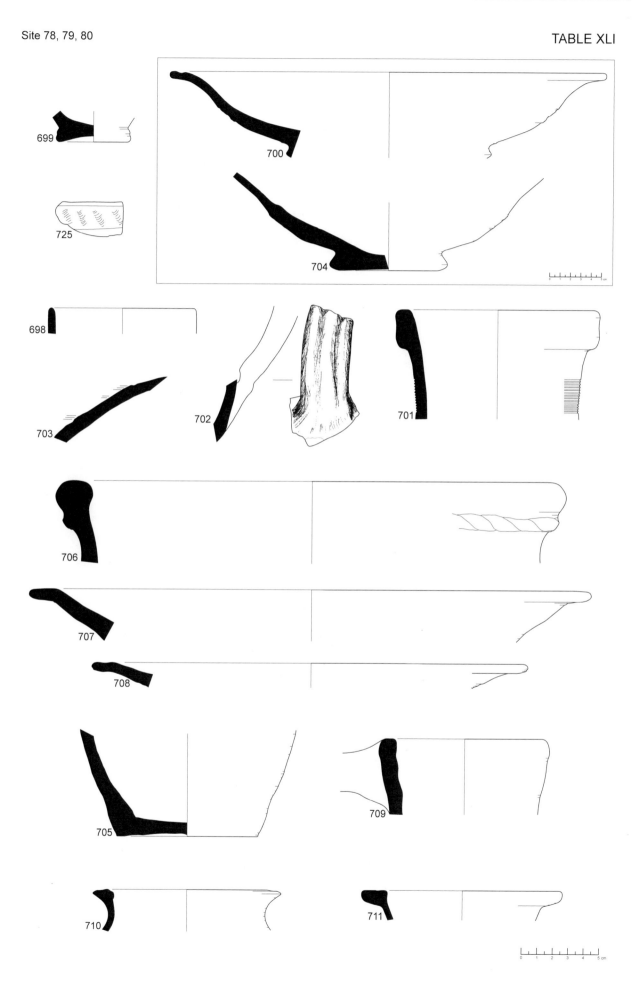

Site 80, 88

TABLE XLII

Site 88, 94

TABLE XLIII

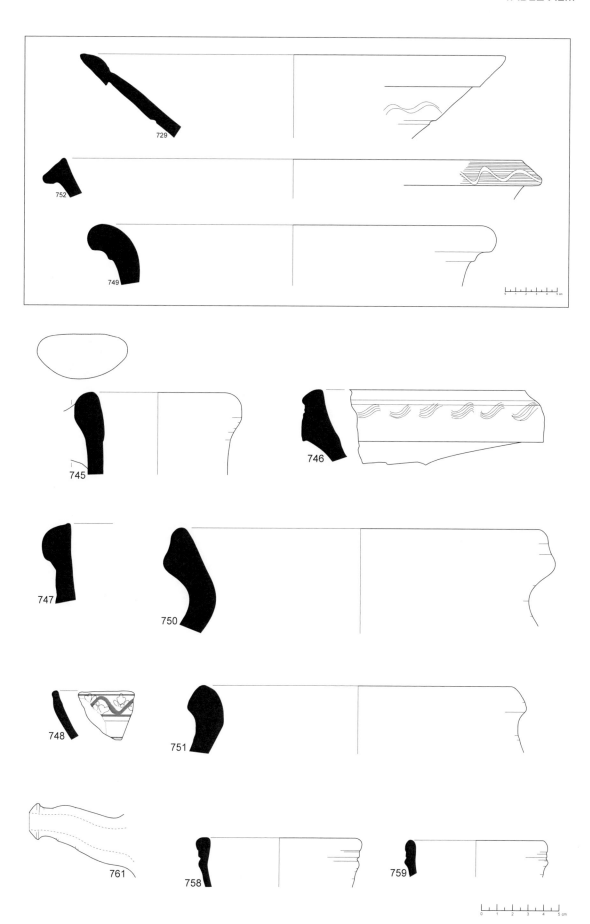

Site 94, 95

TABLE XLIV

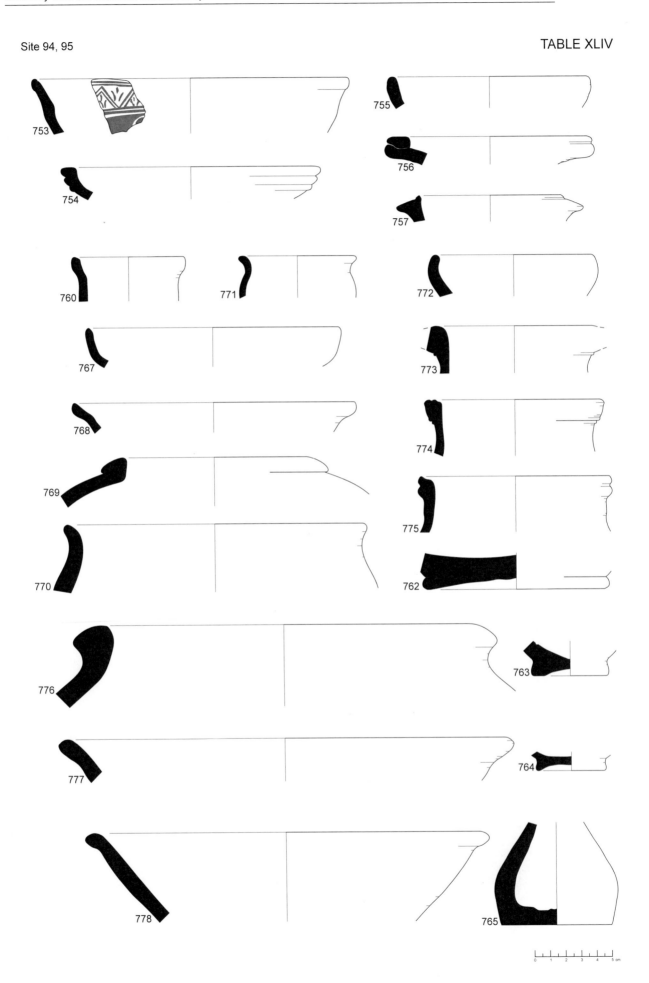

Site 95, 96

TABLE XLV

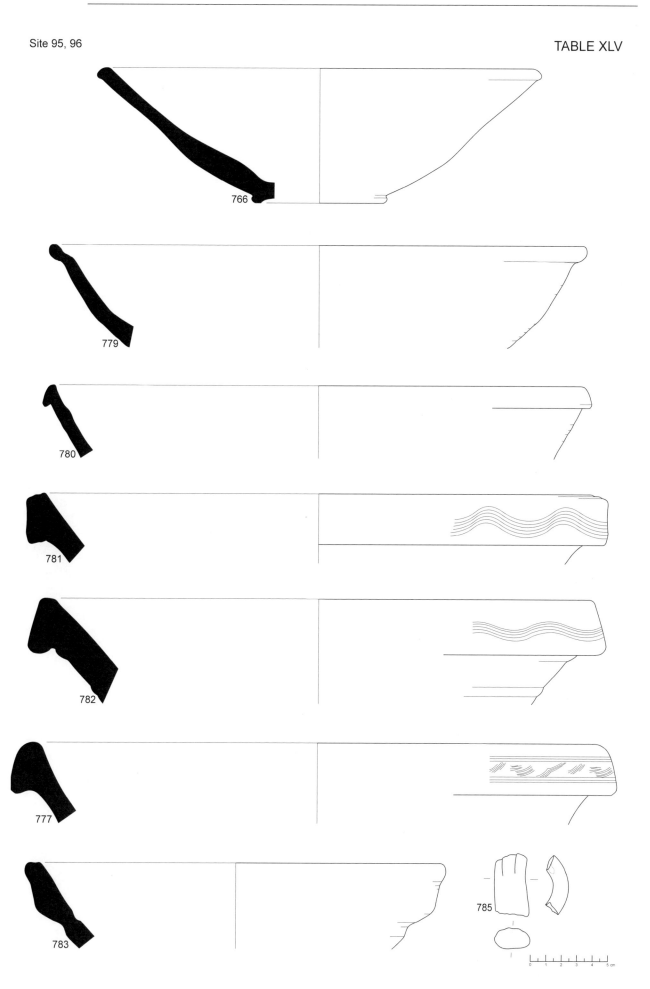

Site 95

TABLE XLVI

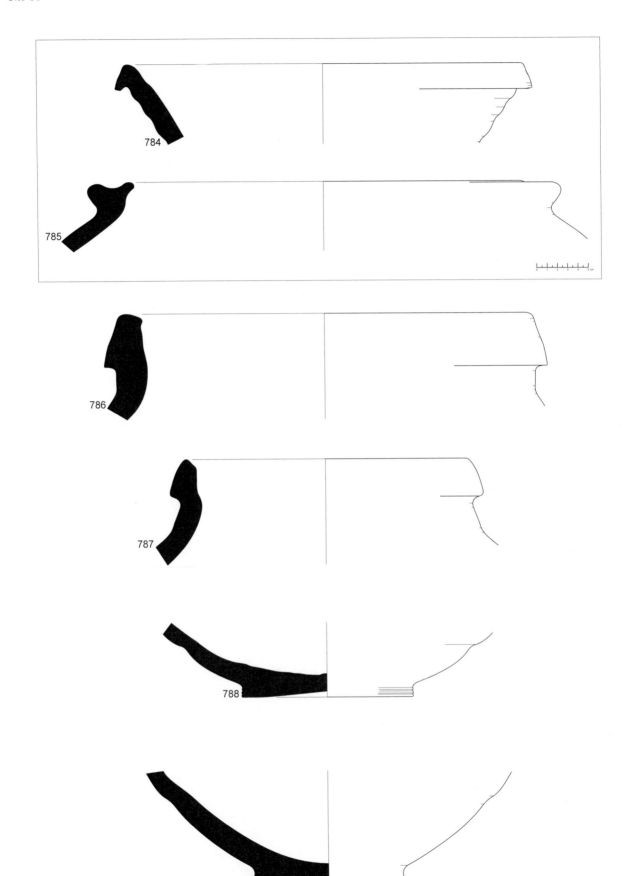

Site 98

TABLE XLVII

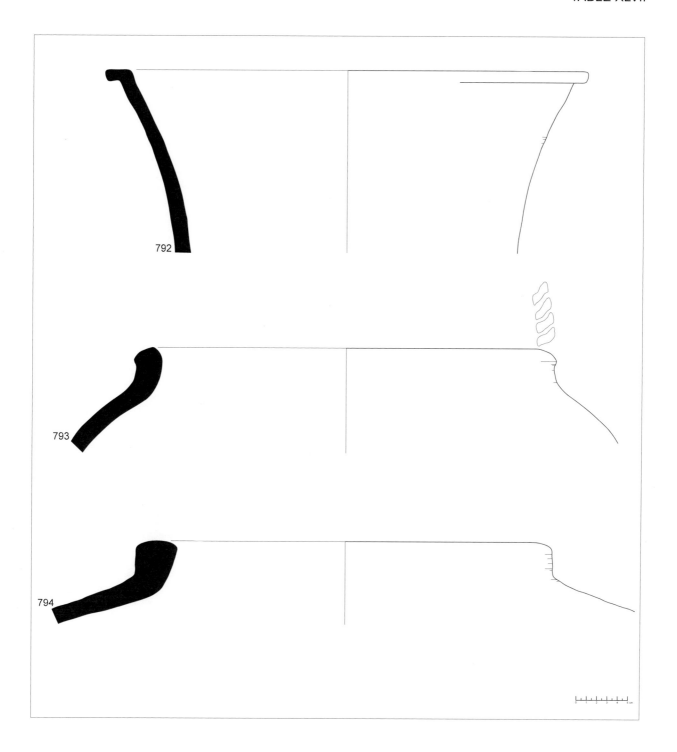

Site 98

TABLE XLVIII

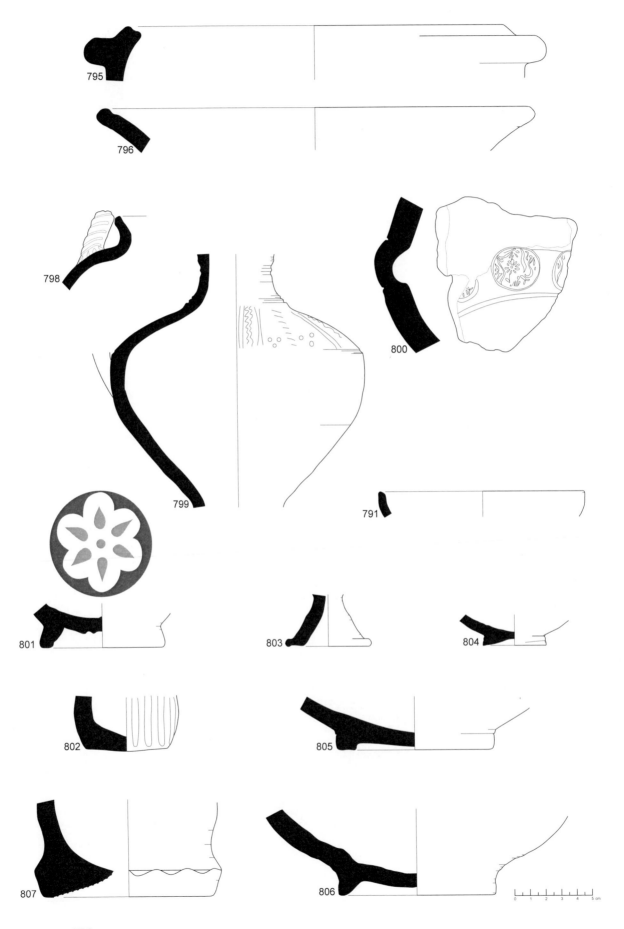

Site 99

TABLE XLIX

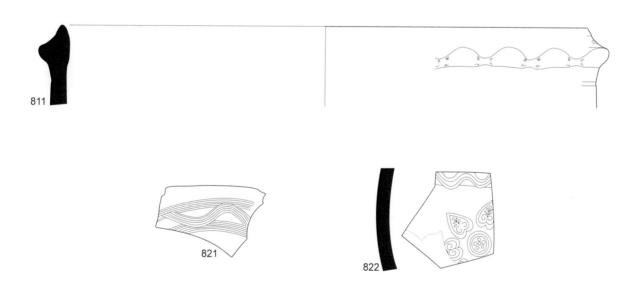

Site 99   TABLE L

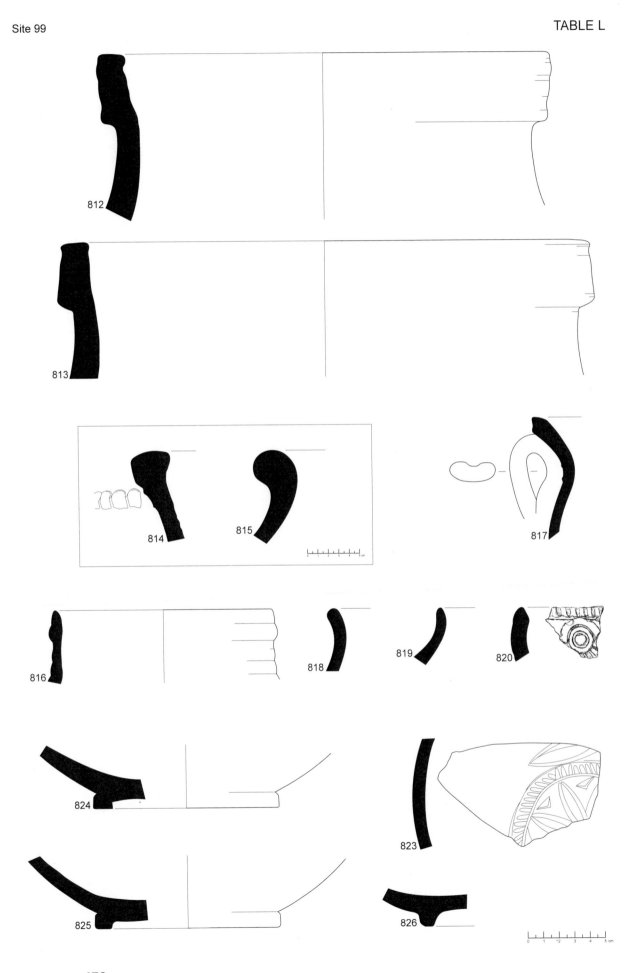

TABLE LI

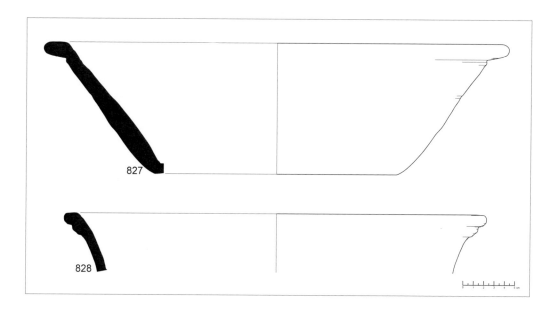

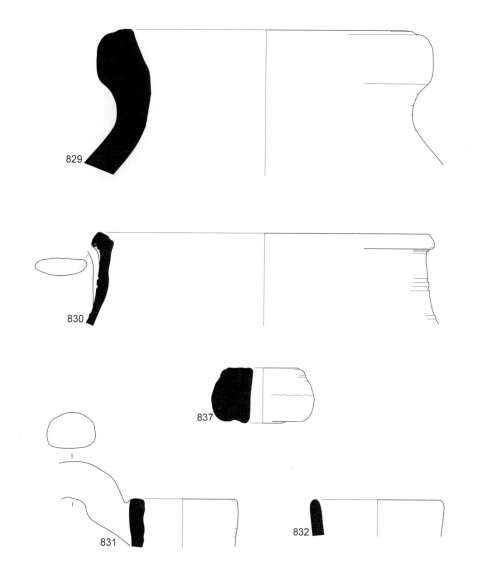

Site 100

TABLE LII

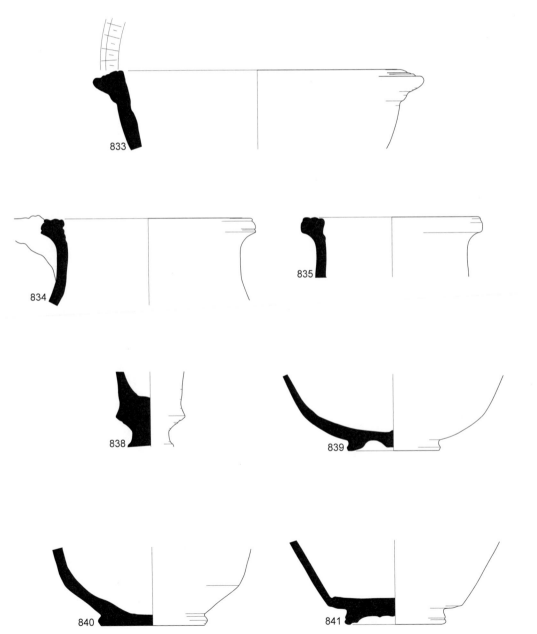

Site 101, 103

TABLE LIII

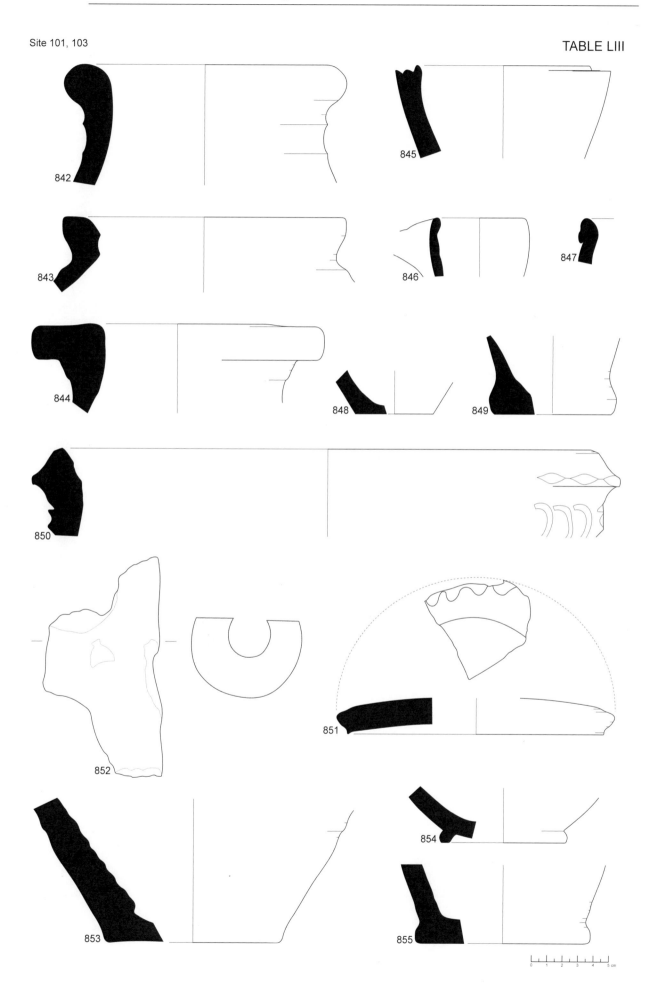

Site 105, 119, 120   TABLE LIV

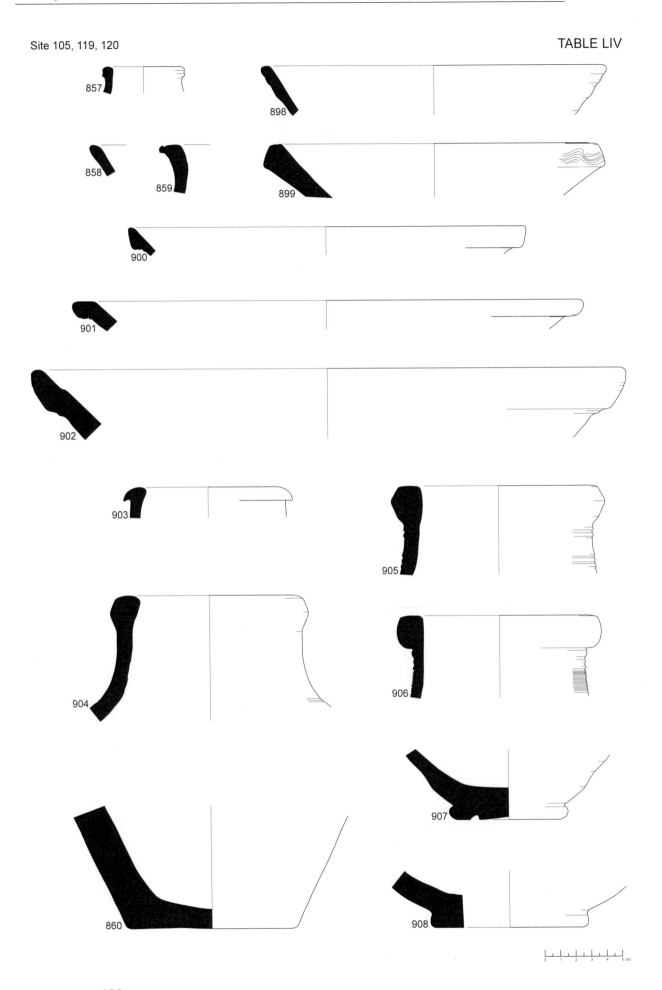

Site 125, 127, 128, 129

TABLE LV

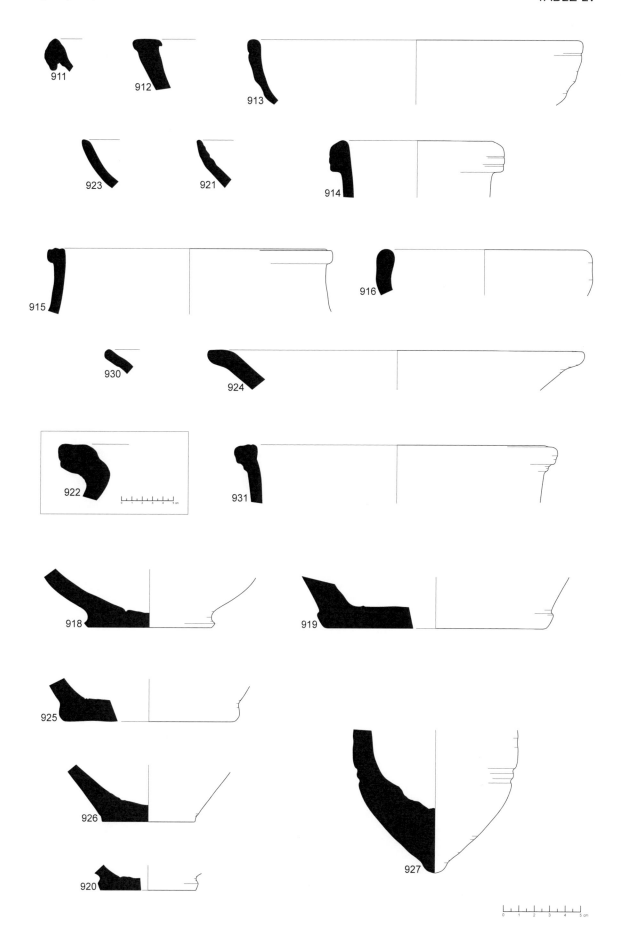

Site 125, 129

TABLE LVI

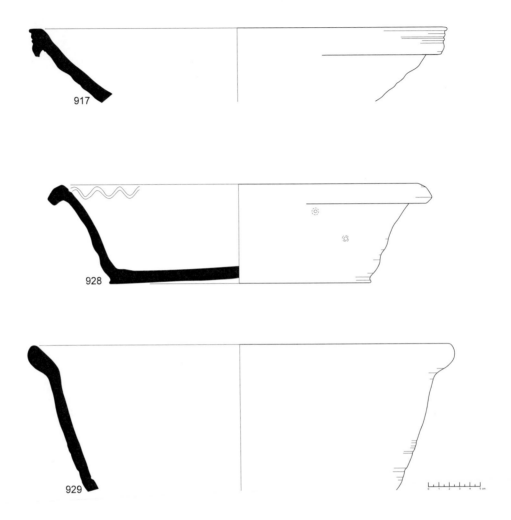

917

928

929

Site 133

TABLE LVII

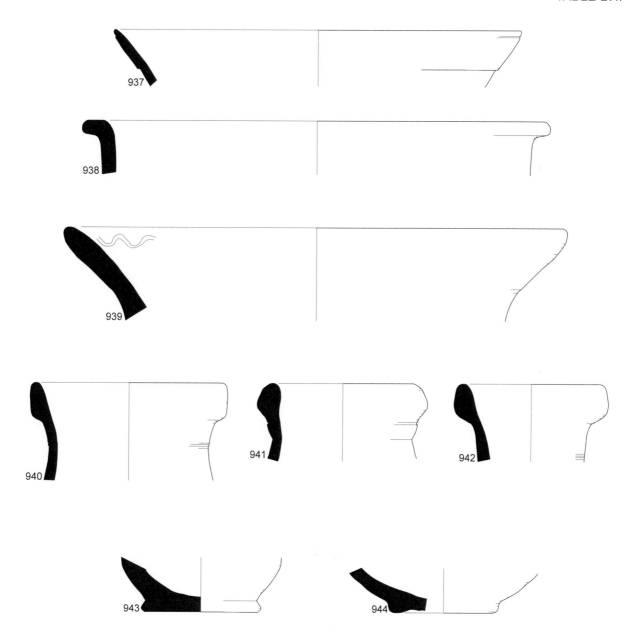

M. Kobierská

Site 135, 136, 136/137, 138, 139, 141, 142, 143 TABLE LVIII

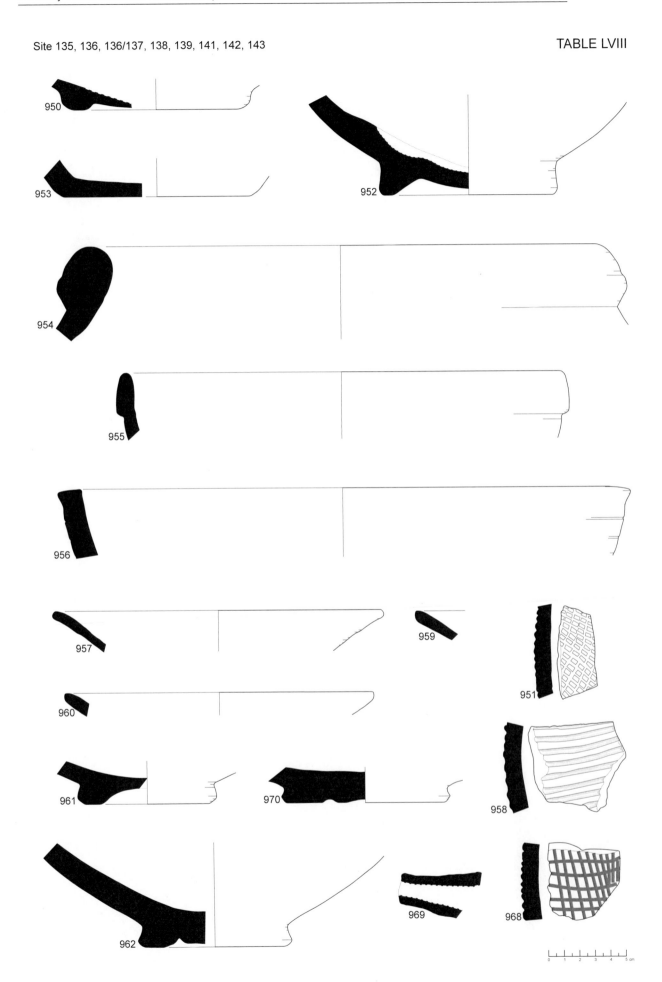

TABLE LIX

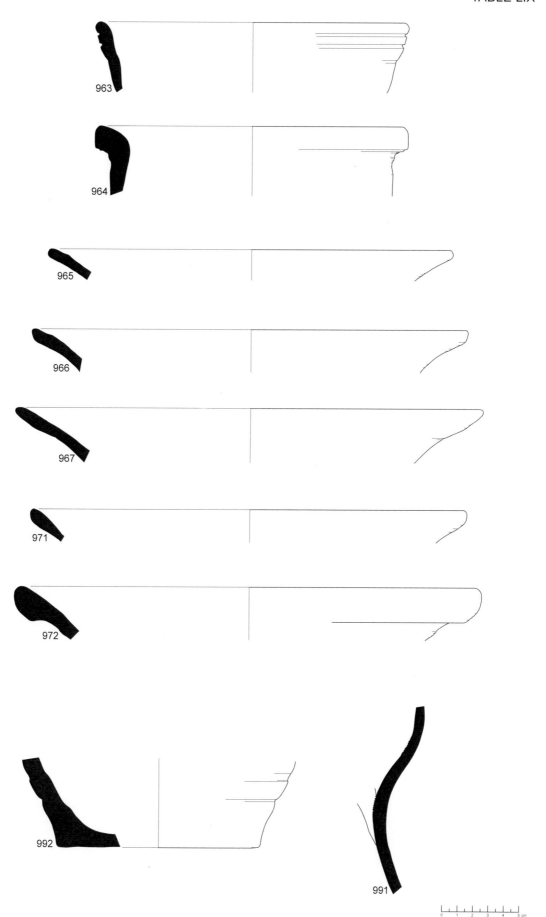

Miscellanea: tokens, lamps, terracottas, beads

TABLE LX

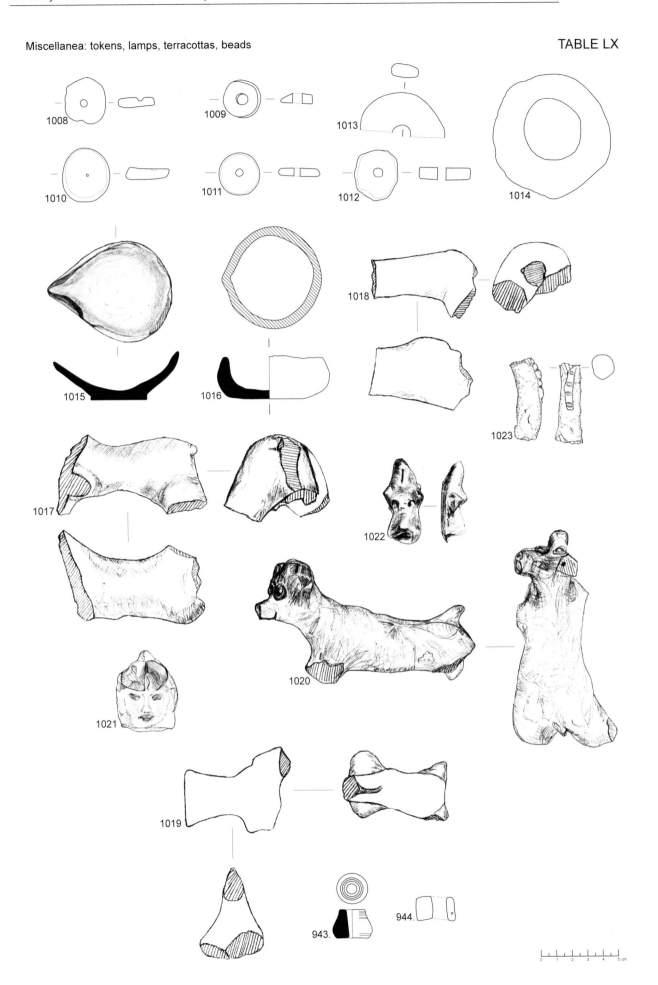

7. Conclusions

Ladislav Stančo

Since the very beginning of our field work, we used to perceive the landscape surrounding the town of Sherabad in the southern Uzbekistan as an oasis. Indeed, in most of its history, the region was an oasis in terms we defined in the Introduction. However, our study has shown, that the real oasis in this area was created only in the Kushan period. Current state of research attests that in the prehistory, especially in the Late Bronze Age, the Sherabad steppe plains were settled sporadically here and there and people exploited only limited – partly seasonal – surface water sources, mostly the small stream of Bustan, as was the case of the main settlement cluster with Jarkutan and Bustan sites. The Early Iron Age brought gradual change in the structure of settlements. It was in this period, when the main centre of the region moved from Jarkutan and based at the site known to us as Jandavlattepa. Surprisingly, Hellenistic, i.e., Seleucid and Greco-Bactrian, period did not change much this picture. While to the south of the river Oxus / Amu Darya the number of settlements grown dramatically (as the example of Ai Khanum area shows clearly), here the settlement pattern changed only slightly and the population did not grow at all. The region may have had some strategic importance being located on the main route to the north (to Kashka Darya basin, Maracanda / Samarkand and beyond). Besides Jandavlattepa, only several sites were settled in the Hellenistic period for sure. The Sherabad plains must have served as a buffer zone between nomadic tribes that had gradually occupied the steppes beyond the mountains and threatened settled population of Bactria.

Some of these nomadic newcomers – the Kushans, or rather a conglomerate of peoples of local origin and nomadic descent – turned to be most successful settlers and farmers in the whole history of the Sherabad Oasis. In the Kushan and Kushano-Sasanian period, across the plains, sophisticated irrigation system was constructed, bringing the water to several substantial settlements (towns) and numerous smaller ones (villages, farms, hamlets). Population of Tokharistan, as was called former territory of Bactria in the Late Kushan period at the latest, was growing rapidly, as did production, and exploitation of the landscape. Material culture, especially in the Kushano-Sasanian period, shows traces of Iranian, but also Mediterranean influences.

Surpisingly, at least concerning previous research, the extensive agricultural activities did not decrease in the following Early Medieval period. What seems to have changed was the organization of the society that became less centralized and more fragmented compare to the Kushan period. We incline to identifying important historical milestones in the abrupt changes of the settlement pattern in both mentioned historical periods (see chapters 5.5 and 5.6), the reality may have been, however, quite different. High Medieval period with coming of Islam and related acculturation, and renewed ties to Iran, meant substantial changes in material culture. From 9th c. onwards the glazed pottery and new decorative techniques and repertoire facilitate the dating of archaeological record. The settlement pattern attests to further decrease of sites number and their distribution suggests gradual decline of the irrigation system (cf. chapter 5.7). Some religious structures of that period, on the other hand, became the first monuments of the Sherabad Oasis that have survived to the present days, including their functioning. The Mongol invasion at the beginning of the 13th c. was a final blow for most of the Central Asiatic oases. Consequent re-settlement was very tedious and it was not until the 19th and especially the 20th century, when the number of the sites and population exceeded that of the Kushan period. The Soviet collectivisation and extensive agriculture caused first broadening of the oasis since the 4th c. AD, complete change of the former irrigation system by bringing waters from the Surkhan river valley, but also destruction of the archaeological sites throughout the oasis.

There are several phenomena – or their absence – worth mentioning as very preliminary general conclusions. First point concerns necropolises: at present, we know only ten sites in the entire Sherabad Oasis interpreted as burial sites. All of them belong to Late Bronze Age, i.e., Sapalli culture and are closely related to each other, at least spatially. Most recent excavations at the citadel of Jarkutan has brought to light several Early Iron Age burials (see chapter 5.3) that change the traditional opinion about absence of the graves of this period. The real absence of analogical data from the later periods we ascribe to the extensive cultivation of the lowlands in the last forty years. Some new data are to be expected only from intensive surface survey. It should be noted in this respect that our knowledge of burial sites in the piedmont steppes of northwestern Sherabad District (i.e., outside the oasis itself) has changed only quite recently and only due to the intensive field survey (Stančo et al. 2015).

As staeted above, extensive irrigation systems were with all probability introduced to the Sherabad Oasis only in the Kushan period, not before. The earlier cultures used here only very basic systems of water supply, which did not allow expansion of agricultural areas and thereby population growth.[115] The increase in the number of settlements in the Kushan period is so striking that even without concrete and clear evidence of irrigation canals can be argued that in the first centuries AD already, some extensive irrigation

systems were constructed. Another important component in providing water for settlements in the oasis could has been the river itself, or better to say, waters of the hypothetical original riverbed circumfluous Jandavlattepa from the west. This hypothesis, however, cannot be proved in the present state of research.

While discussing the anthropogenic features surrounding Jandavlattepa we shall underline also other specific point. The so far isolated find of Sapalli pottery assemblage in the Saitabad village mentioned above (see chapter 5.2) has shown that the plains around Jandavlattepa could have been settled in this early stage in greater scale. It is well possible that the area around the site – forming once much more uneven terrain than how it appears nowadays – was dramatically changed in the recent past by both intensive agriculture and alluvial processes (they, in their turn, were also caused by the modern agriculture, as we suppose). Intensive field survey and randomly placed trenches in seemingly not interesting agricultural landscape could be one of the methods that could still bring many new and perhaps surprising information about the development of settlement pattern in the Sherabad Oasis. This task, however, remains for the future research.

---

[115] We admit an existence of certain irrigation in the Late Bronze Age, but limited to the immediate vicinity of the principal sites, i.e., Jarkutan and Bustan.

8. Bibliography

Abdullaev, B. N. 1977: Raskopki pozdnikh pogrebeniy mogil'nika Dzharkutan. *IMKU* 13, 33–40.

Abdullaev, K. 2001: Raskopki na Paenkurgane v Baysunskom rayone (Severnaya Baktriya). *Arkheologicheskie issledovaniya v Uzbekistane v 2000 g.* Samarkand, 25–30.

Abdullaev, K. 2006: Nakhodki hellenosticheskykh monet k severu ot Amudaryi – Oksa. *RA* 2006/3, 106–115.

Abdullaev, K. 2011a: Numismatic finds (2002–2006). In: Stančo, L. – Abdullaev, K. eds. 2011, 172–183.

Abdullaev, K. 2011b: General remarks and description of the landscape. In: Stančo, L. – Abdullaev, K. eds. 2011, 13–16.

Abdullaev, K. 2018: Layers of Early Iron Age in Dzhandavlattepa (Sherabad District, Surkhandarya Region of Uzbekistan). *AIT* 17, 123–142.

Abdullaev, K. – Stančo, L. 2003: Djandavlattepa: Preliminary report of the 2002 excavation season. *Studia Hercynia* VII, 165–168.

Abdullaev, K. – Stančo, L. 2004a: Jandavlattepa: Preliminary report of the 2003 excavation season. *Studia Hercynia* VIII, 156–160.

Abdullaev, K. – Stančo, L. 2004b: Arkheologicheskie raboty na Dzhandavlattepa. In: Shirinov, T. (ed.): *Arkheologicheskie issledovaniya v Uzbekistane* – 2003 god. (vyp. 4), 19–25.

Abdullaev, K. – Stančo, L. 2004c: Excavation of Jandavlattepa, Sherabad District, Northern Bactria. *Circle of Inner Asia Art* 19/2004, 3–10.

Abdullaev, K. – Stančo, L. 2005: Jandavlattepa: Preliminary report of the 2004 excavation season. *Studia Hercynia* IX, 273–275.

Abdullaev, K. – Stančo, L. 2006: Arkheologicheskie raboty na Dzhandavlattepa v 2004–2005 gg. Sherabadskiy rayon Surkhandarinskoy oblasti. In: Pidaev, Sh. (ed.): *Arkheologicheskie issledovaniya v Uzbekistane* – 2004–2005 gody (vyp. 5), 12–22.

Abdullaev, K. – Stančo, L. 2007: Jandavlattepa 2006. Preliminary excavation report. *Studia Hercynia* XI, 157–159.

Abdullaev, K. – Stančo, L. 2009: Arkheologicheskie raskopki Dzhandavlyattepa. Sezon 2006 goda, sentyabr-oktyabr. In: Berdimuradov, A. E. (ed.): *Arkheologicheskie issledovaniya v Uzbekistane, 2006–2007 goda (vyp. 6)*, 18–23.

Abdullaev, K. – Stančo, L. eds. 2011: *Jandavlattepa I. The Excavation Report for Seasons 2002–2006 vol. 1*. Prague.

Abdullaev et al. 2003 = Abdullaev, K. – Boháč, L. – Stančo, L.: Arkheologicheskie raboty na Dzhandavlyattepa Sherabadskogo rayona Surkhandarinskoy oblasti. Arkheologicheskie Issledovaniya v Uzbekistane 2002 god, 15–20.

Alcock et al. 1994 = Alcock, S. – Cherry, J. – Davis, J. L.: Intensive survey, agricultural practice and the Classical landscape of Greece. In: Morris, I. (ed.): *Classical Greece: Ancient Histories and Modern Archaeologies*. Cambridge, 137–170.

Aldrovandi, C. – Hirata, E. 2004: Buddhism, Pax Kushana and Greco-Roman motifs: pattern and purpose in Gandharan iconography. *Antiquity* 79, 306–315.

Annaev, T. 1988: *Rannesrednevekoviye poseleniya severnogo Tokharistana*. Tashkent.

Annaev, T. – Bobokhodzhaev, A. 1991: Khosiyattepa – gorod na perekrestke torgovoj trassy iz Termeza v Sogd. In: Askarov, A. A. (ed.): *Goroda i karavansarai na trassakh Velikogo Shelkovogo puti* (Tezisy dokladov Mezhdunarodnogo seminara JUNESKO), Urgench, 2–3 maja 1991 g. Urgench, 69–70.

Annaev, T. et al. 1988 = Annaev, T. – Bobokhodzhaev, A. – Rakhmanov, Sh. A.: Zamok Kuchuktepa. *IMKU* 22, 75–86.

Arshavskaya et al. 1982 = Arshavskaya, Z. A. – Rtveladze, E. V. – Khakimov, Z. A.: *Srednevekovye pamyatniki Surkhandar'i*. Tashkent.

Askarov, A. A. 1976: Raspisnaya keramika Dzharkutana. In: Masson, V. M. ed. 1976, 17–19.

Askarov, A. A. 1977: *Drevnezemledel'cheskaya kul'tura epokhi bronzy yuga Uzbekistana*. Tashkent.

Askarov, A. A. 1980: Khram pervobytnykh zemledel'tsev na yuge Uzbekistana. *ONU* 1980/7, 33–34.

Askarov, A. A. 1980: Raskopki poselenija Dzharkutan. *AO* 79, 444–445.

Askarov, A. 1996: The Beginning of the Iron Age in Transoxania. In: Dani, A. H. – Masson, V. M. (eds.): *History of Civilization of Central Asia, Vol. 1. The dawn of civilization: earliest time to 700 B. C.* Paris, 441–458.

Askarov, A. A. – Abdullaev, B. N. 1978: Raskopki mogil'nika Dzharkutan. (Rezul'taty rabot vesnoj 1975 g.). *IMKU* 14, 19–42.

Askarov, A. A. – Abdullaev, B. N. 1983: *Dzharkutan. K probleme protogoradskoy tsivilizatsii na yuge Uzbekistana*. Tashkent.

Askarov, A. A. – Al'baum, L. I. 1979: *Poselenie Kuchuktepa*. Tashkent.

Askarov, A. – Shirinov, T. 1989: Drevnebaktriyskiy khram ognia v yuzhnom Uzbekistane. In: Pugachenkova, G. A. (ed.): *Gradostraitelstvo i architektura*. Tashkent, 7–24.

Askarov, A. A. – Shirinov, T. Sh. 1991: O nekotorykh gruppakh kul'tovoj keramiki Dzharkutana. *IMKU* 25, 33–58.

Avanesova, N. A. 1995: Ogon' v pogrebal'noy praktike sapallinskoj kul'tury (po materialam mogil'nika Buston VI). In: *Markazij Osijoda urbanizatsija zharajonining pajdo bo'lishi va rivozhlanish bosqichlari*, 17–19.

Avanesova, N. A. 2000: Monofunktsional'nye sosudy dourbanisticheskoy Baktrii (po materialam issledovaniya mogil'nika Buston VI). In: *Srednyaya Aziya. Arkheologiya, istoriya, kul'tura*. Moskva, 119–127.

Avanesova, N. A. 2001: Rezultaty issledovaniy nekropolya Buston VI. *Arkheologicheskie issledovaniya v Uzbekistane* 2000, 31–37.

Avanesova, N. A. 2016: *Buston VI – the necropolis of fire worshipers of pre-urban Bactria*. Samarkand.

Avanesova, N. A. – Lyonnet, B. 1995: Bustan VI, une nécropole de l'âge du Bronze dans l'ancienne Bactriane (Ouzbékistan méridional): témoignages de cultes du feu. *Arts asiatiques* 50, 31–46.

Avanesova, N. A. – Tashpulatova, N. 1999: Simvolika ognya v pogrebal'noy praktike sapallinskoy kul'tury (po materialam issledovaniya mogil'nika Bustan VI). *IMKU* 30, 27–36.

Bakturskaya, N. N. 1979: Novie dannie o gorodishche Asanas. In: Vinogradov, A. B. – Vorobeva, M. G. – Itina, M. A. – Levina, L. M. – Nerazik, E. E. – Rapoport, Yu. A. (eds.): *Etnografiya i Arkheologiya sredney Asii*. Moskva, 127–133.

Bendezu-Sarmiento, J. – Mustafakulov, S. 2008: Arkheo-antropologicheskie issledovania na mogil'nike Dzharkutan. *IMKU* 36, 56–60.

Bendezu-Sarmiento, J. – Mustafakulov, S. 2013: Le site proto-urbain de Dzharkutan durant les âges du bronze et du fer. Recherches de la Mission archéologique franco-ouzbèke-Protohistoire. In: Bendezu-Sarmiento, J. (ed.): *L'archéologie française en Asie central. Cahiers d'Asie centrale* 21/22, 207–236.

Bevan, A. – Conolly, J. 2012: Intensive Survey Data from Antikythera, Greece. *Journal of Open Archaeology Data* 1(1), (DOI: http://dx.doi.org/10.5334/4f3bcb3f7f21d).

Bintliff, J. – Snodgrass, A. 1988: Off-Site Pottery Distributions: A Regional and Interregional Perspective. *Current Anthropology* 29/3, 506–513.

Bobokhadzhayev et al. 1990 = Bobokhadzhayev, A. – Annaev, T. – Rakhmanov, Sh. 1990: Nekatorye itogi izucheniya drvnikh I srednevekovykh pamyatnikov predgornoy i gornoy polosy Kugitang – Baysuntau, *IMKU* 23, 25–36.

Boroffka, N. 2009: Siedlungsgeschichte in Nordbaktrien – Bandichan zwischen Spätbronzezeit und Frühmittelalter. In: Hansen, S. – Wieczorek, A. – Tellenbach, M. (eds.): *Alexander der GroSSe und die Öffnung der Welt. Asiens Kulturen im Wandel*. Regensburg, 134–144.

Botirov, I. – Kholikov, Z. 2006: Mavzoley Kayragach-ata. *Moziyidan Sado (Ekho Istorii)* 29/1, 32–34.

Bousman, C. B. 2006: Satellite archaeology for everyone. *SAA archaeological record* 6(3), 32–34. Retrieved on March 21, 2009 from http://www.saa.org/Portals/0/SAA/Publications/thesaaarchrec/may06.pdf.

Casana, J. – Cothren, J. 2008: Stereo analysis, DEM extraction and orthorectification of CORONA satellite imagery: archaeological applications from the Near East. *Antiquity* 82, 732–749.

Danielisová et al. 2010 = Danielisová, A. – Stančo, L. – Shaydullaev, A.: Preliminary report of archaeological survey in Sherabad District, South Uzbekistan in 2009. *Studia Hercynia* XIV, 67–90, Pl. 28.

Doležálková, V. – Dorňáková, A. – Machačíková, T. 2012: Pottery finds from the Systamatical Field Survey in the Sherabad Distraict, South Uzbekistan – preliminary report. *Studia Hercynia* XVI, 22–33, pl. VIII.

Dvurechenskaya, N. D. 2015: Predvarite'nye materiály arkheologicheskikh rabot 2014 g. Na kreposti Uzundara. *PIFK* 1/47, 124–133.

Dvurechenskaya et al. 2014 = Dvurechenskaya, N. D. – Dvurechenskiy, O. V. – Mokroborodov, V. V. – Rukavishnikova, I. V. – Rukavishnikov, D. V. 2014: Marshrutnye issledovaniya na yuge Uzbekistana v 2013 godu. *KSIA* 236, 69–82.

Gardin, J.-C. 1957: *Céramiques de Bactries*. Mémoires de la délégation archéologique française en Afganistan XV. Paris.

Gardin, J.-C. 1998: *Prospection archéologiques en Bactriane orientale (1974–1978), vol. 3: Description des sites et notes de synthèse*. Paris.

Gentelle, P. 1989: *Prospection archéologiques en Bactriane orientale (1974–1978), vol. 1, Données paléogéographiques et fondamentes de l'irrigation*. Paris.

Gheyle et al. 2003 = Gheyle, W. – Trommelmans, R. – Bourgeois, J. – Goossens, R. – Bourgeois, I. – De Wulf, A. – Willems, T.: Evaluating CORONA: A case study in the Altai Republic (South Siberia). *Antiquity* 77, 391–403.

Goossens et al. 2006 = Goossens, R. – De Wulf, A. – Bourgeois, J. – Gheyle, W. – Willems, T.: Satellite imagery and archaeology: the example of CORONA in the Altai Mountains. *Journal of Archaeological Science* 33, 745–755.

Görsdorf, J. – Huff, D. 2001: C14- datierungen von materialien aus der Grabung Dzharkutan, Uzbekistan. *AMIT* 33, 75–87.

Grenet, F. 2002: Regional interaction in Central Asia and Northwest India in the Kidarite and Hephthalite periods. In: Sims-Williams, N. (ed.): *Indo-Iranian languages and peoples*. Proceedings of the British Academy 116, 203–224.

Grenet, F. 2005: Kidarites. *Encyclopedia Iranica*. Retrieved online from < http://www.iranicaonline.org/articles/kidarites >

Grenet, F. – Rapin, C. 2001: Alexander, Aï Khanum, Termez: Remarks on the Spring Campaign of 328. *BAI* 12, 79–89.

Harmatta, J. ed. 1994: *History of Civilization of Central Asia, Vol. 2. The development of sedentary and nomadic civilizations: 700 B.C. to A.D. 250*. Paris.

Huff, D. 1997: Deutsch-Uzbek Ausgrabungen auf dem Džandaulattepe und in Džarkutan, Süduzbekistan, 1993–1995. *Mitteilungen der Berliner Gesellschaft für Anthropologie, Ethnologie und Urgeschichte* 18, 83–95.

Huff et al. 2001 = Huff, D. – Pidaev, Ch. – Chaydoullaev, Ch.: Uzbek-German archaeological researches in the Surkhan Darya region. In: Leriche, P. – Pidaev, Ch. – Gelin, M. – Abdoullaev, K. (eds.): *La Bactriane au carrefour des routes et des civilisations de l'Asie centrale*. Actes du colloque de Termez, 1997. Paris, 219–233.

Huff, D. – Shaydullaev, Sh. 1999: Nekatoriye rezultaty rabot uzbecko-germanskoy ekspedicii na gorodishche Jarkutan. *IMKU* 30, 19–26.

Ionesov, V. 1996: K izucheniyu pogrebal'nykh kompleksov Dzharkutana. *IMKU* 27, 17–28.

Jalilov, A. H. 1996: The Arab Conquest of Transoxania. In: Litvinsky, B. A. (ed.): *History of Civilizations of Central Asia, vol. III: The Crossroads of civilizations: A.D. 250 to 750*. Paris, 452–460.

Kamaliddinov, Sh. S. 1993: O srednevekovykh gorodakh oblasti Termeza. *ONU* 1993/2, 37–43.

Kaniuth, K. 2007: Tilla Bulak 2007 – Vorbericht zur ersten Kampagne. *AMIT* 39, 31–59.

Kaniuth et al. 2009 = Kaniuth, K. – Herles, M. – Shejko, K.: Tilla Bulak 2008 – Vorbericht zur zweiten Kampagne. *AMIT* 41, 75–96.

Kaniuth, K. 2010: Tilla Bulak 2009. Vorbericht über die dritte Kampagne. *AMIT* 42, 129–163.

Karmysheva, B. Kh. 1976: *Ocherki etnicheskoy istorii yuzhnykh rayonov Tadzhikistana i Uzbekistana*. Moskva.

Khalilov, Kh. 1986: Novye kraniologicheskie materialy epokhi bronzy iz mogil'nikov Dzharkutan i Bustan. *IMKU* 20, 178–182.

Khamraev et al. 2011 = Khamraev, Sh. R. – Dukhovny, V. A. – Kadyrov, A. A. – Sokolov, V. I.: *Water resources management in Uzbekistan*. Tashkent.

Koshelenko, G. A. ed. 1985: *Drevneyshie gosudarstva Kavkaza i Sredney Azii*. Moskva.

Sarianidi, V. I. – Koshelenko, G. A. 1985: Srednyaya Aziya v rannem zheleznom veke. In: Koshelenko ed. 1985, 178–202.

Lhuillier et al. 2013 = Lhuillier, J. – Bendezu-Sarmiento, J. – Lecomte, O. – Rapin, C. 2013: Les cultures à céramique modelée peinte de l'âge du fer ancien: quelques pistes de réflexion d'après les exemples de Koktepe, Dzharkutan (Ouzbékistan) et Ulug dépé (Turkménistan). In: Bendezu-Sarmiento, J. (ed.): *L'archéologie française en Asie central. Cahiers d'Asie centrale* 21/22, 357–372.

Lhuillier et al. 2018 = Lhuillier, J. – Bendezu-Sarmiento, J. – Mustafakulov, S. 2018: The Early Iron Age occupation in southern Central Asia. Excavation at Dzharkutan in Uzbekistan. In: Lhuillier, J. – Boroffka, N. (eds.): *A Millennium of History. The Iron Age in southern Central Asia (2nd and 1st Millennia BC). Dedicated to the memory of Viktor Ivanovič Sarianidi. Proceedings of the conference held in Berlin (June 23–25, 2014).* AIT 17, 31–50.

Lipski, V. I. 1902: *Gornaya Bukhara. Rezul'taty trekhletnikh puteshestviy v'Srednyuyu Aziyu v'1896, 1897 I 1899 gody.* S. Petersburg.

Luneau, É. 2014: *La fin de la civilisation de l'Oxus. Transformations et recompositions des sociétés de l'âge du Bronze final en Asie centrale méridionale.* Paris.

Luneau et al. 2014 = Luneau, É. – Bendezu-Sarmiento J. – Mustafakulov, S. 2014: Ceramics and Chronology at Dzharkutan: A Revision of the Periodization of the Sapalli Culture (Uzbekistan, c. 2100–1500 BC). In: Bieliński, P. – Gawlikowski, M. – Koliński, R. – Ławecka, D. – Sołtysiak, A. – Wygnańska, Z. (eds.): Proceedings of the 8th International Congress on the Archaeology of the Ancient Near East 30 April–4 May 2012, University of Warsaw Volume 2 Excavation and Progress Reports Posters. Wiesbaden, 529–542.

Lyonnet, B. 1997: *Prospection archéologiques en Bactriane orientale (1974–1978), vol. 2, Céramique et peuplement du chalcolithique à la conquête arabe.* Paris.

Madry, S. 2006: An Evaluation of Google Earth for Archaeological Exploration and Survey. In: Clark, J. T. – Hagemeister, E. M. (eds.): *Digital Discovery Exploring New Frontiers in Human Heritage.* CAA 2006 – Computer Applications and Quantitative Methods in Archaeology. Proceedings of the 34th Conference. Fargo, United States, April 2006. Budapest, 329–337.

Mantellini et al. 2011 = Mantellini, S. – Rondelli, B. – Stride, S. 2011: Analytical Approach for Representing the Water Landscape Evolution in Samarkand Oasis (Uzbekistan). In: Redő, J. E. F. – Szeverényi, V. (eds.): *On the Road to Reconstructing the Past.* Computer Applications and Quantitative Methods in Archaeology (CAA). Proceedings of the 36th International Conference. Budapest, April 2–6, 2008. Budapest, 263–272.

Mantellini, S. 2014: Settlements dynamics, territory exploitation, and trade routes in the ancient Samarkand Oasis (Uzbekistan). In: Genito, B. – Caterina, L. (eds.): *Archeologia delle "Vie della Seta": Percorsi, Immagini e Cultura Materiale.* II Ciclo di Conferenze (6 Marzo–22 Maggio 2013), Centro Interdipartimentale di Servizi per l'Archeologia – CISA, 2014. Napoli, 37–59.

Mantellini, S. 2015: Irrigation Systems in Samarkand. *Encyclopaedia of the History of Science, Technology, and Medicine in Non-Western Cultures.* DOI 10.1007/978-94-007-3934-5 _9925-1.

Masson, V. M. ed. 1974: *Drevnyaya Baktriya. Predvaritel'nye soobscheniya ob arkheologicheskikh rabotekh na yuge Uzbekistana.* Leningrad.

Masson, V. M. 1974: Problema drevnego goroda i arkheologicheskiye pamyatniky severnoy Baktrii, in: Masson, V. M. ed. 1974, 3–13.

Masson, V. M. 1976: Kushanskie poseleniya i kushanskaya arkheologiya. In: Masson, V. M. ed. 1976, 3–17.

Masson, V. M. ed. 1976: *Baktriyskie drevnosti. Predvaritel'nye soobshcheniya ob arkheologicheskikh rabotakh na yuge Uzbekistana.* Leningrad.

Masson, V. M. 1979: Rannesrednavekovaya arkheologiya Sredney Azii i Kazakhstana. *Uspekhy sredneaziyatskoy arkheologii* 4, 3–7.

Masson, V. M. 1985: Severnaya Baktria. In: Koshelenko ed. 1985, 250–272.

Mokroborodov, V. V. 2007: Gishttepa v kishlake Pashkhurt. Predvaritel'nye itogi issledovaniy 2004–2006 gg. In: Rtveladze, E. V. (ed.): *Transoxiana – Mavarannahr.* A collection of articles. Tashkent, 148–155.

Mukhamedjanov, A. R. 1975: K istorii irigatsii v kushanskuyu epochu. In: *CAKE* II, 278–281.

Mukhamedjanov, A. R. 1994: Economy and Social Systems in Central Asia in the Kushan Age. In: Harmatta, J. ed. 1994, 256–282.

Mustafakulov, S. I. 1997: Analiz paleoantropologicheskikh materialov epokhi bronzy iz Bustana VII. *IMKU* 28, 28–33.

Nekrasova, E. G. 1976: Drevnjaja keramika Sherabadskogo oazisa (Po materialam shurfovok na melkikh poseleniyakh). In: Masson, V. M. ed. 1976, 76–83.

Nekrasova, E. G. – Pugachenkova, G. A. 1978: Keramika Dalverzintepe. In: Pugachenkova, G. A. – Rtveladze, E. V. (eds.): *Dalverzintepe, kushansky gorod na yuge Uzbekistana.* Tashkent, 143–160.

Nemtseva, N. B. 1989: Rannesrednevekovaya usad'ba i zamok u gorodishcha Babatepe na yuge Uzbekistana. In: Pugachenkova, G. A. (ed.): *Antichnye i rannesrednevekovie drevnosti yuzhnogo Uzbekistana. V svete novykh otkrytiy Uzbekistanskoy isskustvovedcheskoy ekspeditsii.* Tashkent, 132–162.

Nerazik, E. E. – Rapoport, Yu. A. 1981: *Gorodishche Toprak-kala (Raskopki 1965–1975 gg.).* Moskva.

Parfyonov, G. V. s.d.: Unpublished text. Manuscript deposited in Termez Archaeological Museum.

Parcak, S. H. 2009: *Satellite Remote Sensing for Archaeology.* New York.

Peel et al. 2007 = Peel, M. C. – Finlayson, B. L. – McMahon, T. A.: Updated world map of the Koppen-Geiger climate classification. *Hydrol. Earth Syst. Sci.*, 11, 1633–1644. www.hydrol-earth-syst-sci.net/11/1633/2007/; doi:10.5194/hess-11-1633-2007.

Pidaev, Sh. P. 1973: Otkrytiye novogo pamyatnika serediny I tysyacheletiya do nashey ery. *Obshchestvennyye nauki v Uzbekistane* 11/1973, 77–82.

Pidaev, Sh. R. 1974: Materialy k izucheniyu drevnikh pamyatnikov Severnoy Baktrii. In: Masson, V. M. ed. 1974, 32–42.

Pidaev, Sh. 1978: *Poseleniya kushanskogo vremeni severnoy Baktrii.* Tashkent.

Pidaev, Sh. R. – Rtveladze, E. V. 1978: Issledovanie Talashkan Tepe. *AO* 77, 533.

Plog et al. 1978 = Plog, S. – Plog, F. – Wait, W. 1978: Decision Making in Modern Surveys. *Advances in Archaeological Methods and Theory* 1, 383–421.

Pugachenkova, G. A. 1989: *Antichnye i rannesrednevekovye drevnosti iuzhnogo Uzbekistana.* Tashkent.

Pugachenkova, G. A. – Rtveladze, E. V. (eds.) 1978: *Dal'verzintepe. Kushanskiy gorod na yuge Uzbekistana.* Tashkent.

Pugachenkova et al. 1991 = Pugachenkova, G. A. – Rtveladze, E. V. – Kato, K. eds.: Drevnosti Yuzhnogo Uzbekistana/Antiquities of Southern Uzbekistan. Tokyo.

Rakhmanov, U. V. 1979: Raskopki keramicheskikh gornov kul'tury Sapallitepa na Bustane 4. *IMKU* 15, 35–43.

Rakhmanov, U. V. 1981: Zoomorfnye izobrazheniya na keramike pamyatnika epokhi bronzy Bustan 4. *IMKU* 16, 27–30.

Rakhmanov, U. V. – Baratov, S. R. 1995: Bustanskiy keramicheskiy kompleks kul'tury Sapalli. In: *O'rta Osiyo Tarikhi va Arkheologiyasining Dolzarb Muammolari*, 17–18.

Rapin, K. 2013: On the way to Roxane. The route of Alexander the Great in Bactria and Sogdiana (328–327 BC). In: Lindström, G. – Hansen, S. – Wieczorek, A. – Tellenbech, M. (eds.): *Zwischen Ost und West Neue Forschungen zum antiken Zentralasien. AIT* 14, 43–82.

Ross et al. 2010 = Ross, S. A. – Sobotková, A. – Connor, S. – Iliev, I.: An Interdisciplinary Pilot Project in the Environs of Kabyle, Bulgaria. *Archaeologica Bulgarica* 14, 69–85.

Ross, S. A. – Sobotková, A. 2010: High-resolution, multi-spectral satellite imagery and extensive archaeological prospection: Case studies from Apulia, Italy, and Kazanluk, Bulgaria. In: *Space, time, place*. Third international conference on remote sensing in archaeology, 17–21 August 2009: Tiruchirappalli, Tamil Nadu, India. Oxford, 25–28.

Rtveladze, E. V. 1974: Razvyedochnoe izuchenie Baktriyskikh pamyatnikov na yuge Uzbekistana. In: Masson, V. M. ed. 1974, 74–85.

Rtveladze, E. V. 1976: Novye drevnebaktriyskie pamyatniki na yuge Uzbekistana. In: Masson, V. M. ed. 1976, 93–103.

Rtveladze, E. V. 1980: Kala v Sherabade i Denau. *Stroitel'tsvo i architektura v Uzbekistane* 3, 31–33.

Rtveladze, E. V. 1982: Ob areale i chronologii sasanidskich zavoyevanii v severnoy Baktrii – Tokharistane (po dannym numismatiky). *Obshchestvennyye nauky v Uzbekistane* 1/1982, 47–54.

Rtveladze, E. V. 1987: Novye baktriyskie pamyatniki na yuge Uzbekistana. *IMKU* 21, 56–65.

Rtveladze, E. V. 1990: On the Historical Geography of Bactria-Tokharistan. *SRAA* 1, 1–33.

Rtveladze, E. V. 2002: *Aleksandr Makedonskiy v Baktrii I Sogdiane.* Tashkent.

Rtveladze, E. V. 2013: *Vydayushchiesya pamyatniki arkheologii Uzbekistana.* Tashkent.

Rtveladze, E. V. – Khakimov, Z. E. 1973: Marshrutnye issledovaniya pamyatnikov severnoy Baktrii. In: Pugachenkova, G. A. (ed.): *Iz istorii antichnoy kul'tury Uzbekistana.* Tashkent, 10–34.

Rtveladze, E. V. – Pidaev, Sh. R. 1993: Drevnebaktriyskaya krepost' Talashkan-tepe. *RA* 1993/2, 133–147.

Rtveladze, E. V. – Pidaev, S. R. 1981: *Katalog drevnikh monet juzhnogo Uzbekistana.* Tashkent.

Sagdullaev, A. S. – Rtveladze, E. V. 1983: *V strane zolotogo ognya.* Tashkent.

Sagdullaev, A. S. 1987: *Usad'by drevney Baktrii.* Tashkent.

Schachner, A. 1995: A Special Kind of Pattern Burnished Decoration on Late Kushan Pottery in Bactria and Afghanistan. *SRAA* 4, 151–159.

Schachner, A. 2004: Die Keramik der Grabungen 1993 am Džandavlattepe, Süd-Uzbekistan. *AMIT* 35–36, 335–372.

Sedov, A. V. 1987: *Kobadian na paroge rannego srednevekovya. Moskva.*

Shaydullaev, Sh. B. 1988: Talashkan I – krepost' rannego zheleznogo veka na territorii Severnoy Baktrii. In: Mukhamedzhanov, A. R. (ed.): *Ya. G. Gulyamov i razvitie istoricheskikh nauk v Uzbekistane.* Tashkent, 101–103.

Shaydullaev, Sh. B. 1990: Novye dannye o keramicheskikh kompleksakh perioda Kuchuk III i Kuchuk IV (Po materialam Talashkantepa I). *IMKU* 23, 42–46.

Shaydullaev, Sh. B. 2000: Severnaja Baktriya v epokhu rannego zheleznogo veka. Tashkent.

Shaydullaev, Sh. B. 2002: Untersuchungen zur frühen Eisenzeit in Nordbaktrien. *AMIT* 34, 243–339.

Shaydullaev, Sh. B. 2009: *Etapi vozniknoveniya i razvitiya gosudarstvennosti na territorii Uzbekistana (na primere Baktrii).* Avtoreferat dissertacii na soiskanie uchenoy stepeni doktor nauk. Samarkand.

Shaydullaev, Sh. B. 2011: Excavations in Sector 04 – the southern town gate. In: Abdullaev, K. – Stančo, L. (eds.): *Jandavlattepa. The Excavation Report for Seasons 2002–2006, vol. 1.* Prague, 94–98.

Shirinov, T. – Baratov, S. 1997: Bronzezeitliche Grabstätten aus der Nekropole Džarkutan 4 C (Süd-Uzbekistan), *AMIT* 29, 65–120.

Sims-Williams, N. 2015: A new Bactrian inscription from the time of Kanishka. In: Falk, H. (ed.), *Kushan Histories. Literary Sources and Selected Papers from a Symposium at Berlin, December 5th to 7th, 2013.* Berlin.

Sobotková, A. 2009: Remote Sensing and Extensive Archaeological Prospection Case Study from Kazanluk Region, Bulgaria. GeoEye Case studies. (http://geoeye.mediaroom.com/index.php?s=57&item=58)

Sobotková et al. 2010 = Sobotková, A. – Ross, S. – Nehrizov, G. – Weissová, B.: Tundzha Regional Archaeological Project Kazanluk Survey: Preliminary Report. Spring 2009 and 2010. *Studia Hercynia* XIV, 56–66.

Solov'ev, V. S. 2013: Raskopki na obekte V Dabilkurgana v 2010–2013 gg. *MTE* 9, 33–82.

Stančo, L. 2003: Džandavláttepa – Předběžná zpráva o archeologickém výzkumu v roce 2002. In: Pecha, L. (ed.): *Orientalia Antiqua Nova* III. Plzeň, 121–124.

Stančo, L. 2005: Současná archeologie severní Baktrie. *Auriga* 47, 54–64.

Stančo, L. et al. 2006 = Stančo, L. – Belaňová, P. – Grmela, L. – Halama, J. – Kysela, J. – Šmahelová, L. – Urbanová, K.: Jandavlattepa 2005. Preliminary excavation report. *Studia Hercynia* X, 167–172.

Stančo, L. 2009: The activities in Uzbekistan in the 2008 season: testing the Google Earth programme as a tool for archaeological prospecting. *Studia Hercynia* XIII, 115–122, Pls. 60–62.

Stančo, L. 2011a: General description of the site, history of research. In: Abdullaev, K. – Stančo, L. eds. 2011, 17–22.

Stančo, L. 2011b: Sector 20, the so-called "Citadel". In: Abdullaev, K. – Stančo, L. eds. 2011, 27–93.

Stančo, L. 2011c: Introduction. In: Abdullaev, K. – Stančo, L. eds. 2011, 9–12.

Stančo, L. 2015: An unusual Khotanese terracotta head from the Sherabad Oasis. *Studia Hercynia* XIX/1-2, 221–229.

Stančo, L. 2018a: New data on the Iron Age in the Šerabad district, South Uzbekistan. In: Lhuillier, J. – Boroffka, N. (eds.): *A Millennium of History. The Iron Age in southern Central Asia (2nd and 1st Millennia BC). Dedicated to the memory of Viktor Ivanovič Sarianidi.* Proceedings of the conference held in Berlin (June 23–25, 2014). *AIT* 17, 171–188.

Stančo, L. 2018b: Getting rotary: introduction of rotary quern stones in Ancient Bactria. In: Sagdullaev, A. S. (ed.), *The problems of history, archaeology and ethnology of Central Asia.* Tashkent, 118–128.

Stančo, L. 2018c: Kak dolgaya byla stopa Kanishki? Sistema edinits izmereniya v Kushanskoy imperii. Balakhvantsev, A. (ed.), *Epokha imperiy. Vostochnyy Ira not Akhemenidov do Sasanidov: istoriya, arkheologiya, kul'tura.* Institut vostokovedeniya RAN. Moskva. In print."

Stančo, L. SD: Sherabad Oasis: some notes on the settlement pattern in prehistoric and early historic periods. *ISIMU* 17, in print.

Stančo et al. 2015 = Stančo, L. – Shaydullaev, Sh. – Bendezu-Sarmiento, J. – Pažout, A. – Vondrová, H.: Kayrit burial site (south Uzbekistan): preliminary report for season 2014. *Studia Hercynia* XVIII/1-2, 31–41.

Staviskiy, B. Ya. 1977: *Kushanskaya Baktriya. Problemy Istorii I kul'tury.* Moskva.

Stride, S. 2004: *La Géographie Archéologique de la Province du Surkhan Darya (Bactriane du Nord, Ouzbékistan du Sud).* Unpublished dissertation at the Université Panthéon-Sorbonne (Paris), 5 vols.

Stride, S. 2007: Regions and Territories in Southern Central Asia: What the Surkhan Darya Province tells us about Bactria. In: Cribb, J. – Hermann, G. (eds.): *After Alexander. Central Asia before Islam.* London, 99–117.

Stride et al. 2009 = Stride, S. – Rondelli, B. – Mantellini, S.: Canals versus horses: political power in the oasis of Samarkand. *World Archaeology* 41(1), 73–87.

Suleymanov, R. Ch. 2000: *Drevniy Nakhshab, Problemy tsivilizacii Uzbekistana VII v. do n. e. – VII v. n. e.* Moskva.

Sverchkov, L. 2013: *Kurganzol. Krepost'Aleksandra na yuge Uzbekistana.* Tashkent.

Teufer, M. 2015: *Spätbronzezeitliche Grabfunde aus Nordbaktrien und benachbarten Regionen.* Berlin.

Tol'stov, S. P. – Vorobeva, M. G. eds. 1959: *Keramika Khorezma.* Moskva.

Tušlová, P. 2011a: Systematická povrchová prospekce v jižním Uzbekistánu. In: Pecha, L. (ed.): *Orientalia Antiqua Nova* XI. Plzeň, 174–185.

Tušlová, P. 2011b: Systematical Field Survey in Sherabad District, South Uzbekistan. *Studia Hercynia* XV/2, 17–25.

Tušlová, P. 2012a: Systematic Field Survey in the Sherabad District, Report of the 2011 Season. *Studia Hercynia* XVI, 12–21, pl. V–VII.

Tušlová, P. 2012b: *Systematic Field Survey in South Uzbekistan.* Unpublished MA-thesis, Charles University. Prague.

Ur, J. 2006: Google Earth and Archaeology. *SAA archaeological record* 6(3): 35–38. Retrieved online 21, 2009 from http://www.saa.org/Portals/0/SAA/Publications/thesaaarchrec/may06.pdf

Urbanová, K. 2011: Excavations in Sector 30: Preliminary research in the nearby environs of Jandavlattepa. In: Abdullaev, K. – Stančo, L. eds. 2011, 102–104.

Včelicová, T. 2015: *The Pottery of Sector 20 at Jandavlattepa.* Unpublished MA-thesis, Charles University. Prague.

Vakturskaya, N. N. 1959: Khronologicheskaya klassifikatsiya srednevekovoy keramiki Khorezma (IX-XVII bb.) In: Tol'stov, S. P. – Vorobeva, M. G. (eds.): *Keramika Khorezma.* Moskva, 262–342.

Yurkevich, E. A. 1965: Gorodishche kushanskogo vremeni na teritorii Severnoy Baktrii. *SA* 4/1965, 158–167.

Zapparov, Sh. Ch. – Retvaladze, E. V. 1976: Raskopki drevnebaktriyskogo poseleniya Talashkan-Tepa I. In: Masson, V. M. ed. 1976, 19–24.

Zeymal', E. V. 1983: *Drevnie monety Tajikistana.* Dushanbe.

Zeimal, E. V. 1996: The Kidarite Kingdom in Central Asia. In: Litvinsky, B. A. (ed.): *History of Civilizations of Central Asia, vol. III: The Crossroads of civilizations: A.D. 250 to 750.* Paris, 123–137.

Written sources

al-Baladhuri = Al-Imam abu-l Abbas Ahmad ibn-Jabir al-Baladhuri: *Kitab futuh al-Buldan.* Eng. transl. F. C. Murgotten. In: *The Origins of the Islamic State.* New York 1924.

Al-Balazuri = Akhmed Ibn Yakhya ibn Jabir al-Balazuri: *Zavoevaniya Khorasana (Izvlechenie iz sochineniya "Futukh al-Buldan").* Russ. transl. G. Gaibov. Душанбе 1987.

Curtius Rufus = Quintus Curtius Rufus: *Historiarum Alexandri Magni Macedonis.* Eng. transl. J. C. Rolfe. In: *Quintus Curtius* [*History of Alexander*]. Cambridge 1946.

Xuanzang = Xuanzang: *Record of the Western Regions.* Eng. transl. S. Beal. In: *Si-Yu-Ki. Buddhist Records of the Western World,* Vol. I. London 1884.

SHERABAD OASIS

Tracing Historical Landscape in Southern Uzbekistan

Editors
LADISLAV STANČO
PETRA TUŠLOVÁ

Published by Charles University
Karolinum Press
www.karolinum.cz
Prague 2019
Set by Karolinum Press
Printed by Karolinum Press
First edition

ISBN 978-80-246-3902-4
ISBN 978-80-246-3923-9 (pdf)